# Theoretical Lenses on Public Policy

## Series Editor, Paul A. Sabatier

*Policy Change and Learning: An Advocacy Coalition Approach,*
edited by Paul A. Sabatier and Hank C. Jenkins-Smith

*Institutional Incentives and Sustainable Development:*
*Infrastructure Policies in Perspective,*
Elinor Ostrom, Larry Schroeder, and Susan Wynne

FORTHCOMING

*Parties, Policies, and Democracy,*
Hans-Dieter Klingemann, Richard I. Hofferbert,
and Ian Budge

*Government, Business, and American Politics,*
Richard A. Harris and Jay A. Sigler

# Policy Change and Learning

## An Advocacy Coalition Approach

EDITED BY

# Paul A. Sabatier
*University of California–Davis*

AND

# Hank C. Jenkins-Smith
*University of New Mexico*

## Westview Press
BOULDER • SAN FRANCISCO • OXFORD

*Theoretical Lenses on Public Policy*

Table 7.2 is reprinted with permission of Warren Publishing, 2115 Ward Court N.W., Washington, D.C. 20037; (202) 872-9200.

Copyright © 1993 by Westview Press, Inc.

Published in 1993 in the United States of America by Westview Press, Inc., 5500 Central Avenue, Boulder, Colorado 80301-2877

Library of Congress Cataloging-in-Publication Data
Policy change and learning : an advocacy coalition approach / edited
   by Paul A. Sabatier and Hank C. Jenkins-Smith.
   p.   cm. — (Theoretical lenses on public policy)
   Includes bibliographical references and index.
   ISBN 0-8133-1648-0. — ISBN 0-8133-1649-9 (pbk.)
   1. Policy sciences.   2. Political planning.   I. Sabatier, Paul A.
II. Jenkins-Smith, Hank C.   III. Series.
H97.P642   1993
320'.6—dc20                                                         93-2987
                                                                        CIP

Printed and bound in the United States of America

The paper used in this publication meets the requirements
of the American National Standard for Permanence of Paper
for Printed Library Materials Z39.48-1984.

10   9   8   7   6   5   4

*To*

Liz and Susan

*for tolerating our foibles*
*and to*

Jenny

*who gets all too much pleasure from reminding*
*her dad of his proclivity for procrastination*

# Contents

# Preface

In this book we seek to present our theory of the policy process, which includes the manner in which problems such as crime, unemployment, and air pollution get defined as "political" problems, the remedies government devises for dealing with them, the implementation of those solutions, the impact of those supposed remedies on the problems, and the revision of the remedies in light of various groups' perceptions of their desirability. In pursuing our goal of understanding the policy process, we have started from at least two points of departure, one in the philosophy of science, the other in history.

Philosophically, we start from the premise that it is *logically impossible* to understand any reasonably complicated situation—including almost any policy process—without some theoretical lens ("theory," "paradigm," or "conceptual framework") distinguishing between the set of potentially important variables and causal relationships and those that can safely be ignored (Hanson, 1969; Kuhn, 1970; Lakatos, 1971). Given time and space constraints, even the most "atheoretical" case study author must decide what to include and what to leave out. In seeking to understand U.S. public policy, for example, scholars usually do not pay attention to the eye color, physical characteristics, or detailed genealogy of major actors because they *assume* these to be relatively trivial for the purpose at hand. Instead, researchers typically spend a lot of time describing the administrative agencies, legislators, interest groups, and chief executives who become involved—including their legal, financial, and technical resources—because the researchers assume these are important. In so doing, these scholars are adopting an institutional paradigm: Institutions and the resources they control are critical to understanding the policy process.

Given that conceptual lenses are inevitable, we believe they should be explicit rather than implicit. Implicit lenses are hidden from the author and from most readers. A fair amount of human experience suggests that ignorance has a remarkable tendency to produce error. In contrast, explicit lenses invite critical scrutiny of their key variables and causal relationships in terms of their logical properties—clarity, logical consistency, scope, fruitfulness—and in terms of the receptivity of their principal propositions to empirical verification (Lave and March, 1975). Such scrutiny produces revision, retesting, and at times, rejection. Some theories (or conceptual lenses) are better than others, and the process of winnowing the wheat from the chaff is facilitated if the theories are made as explicit as possible and then tested in a variety of empirical settings.

In the introductory chapter, we argue that the dominant contemporary theory of the policy process—the stages framework of Jones (1977), Anderson (1979), and many others—contains serious logical and empirical deficiencies. We then outline the advocacy coalition framework (ACF) as an alternative theory, and in subsequent chapters a number of scholars critically apply it to a variety of empirical settings. In light of their criticisms, the ACF is revised in the concluding chapter. Not surprisingly, we think that the ACF—particularly in its revised version—is superior to the stages heuristic. But that is for you, the reader, ultimately to decide. Our principal hope is that we have been clear enough to have been shown wrong and, in turn, to have made some sensible revisions to our original propositions. As Ted Lowi preached to his graduate students at the University of Chicago in the early 1970s, "Clarity begets clarity, mush begets mush."

Historically, this book had its origin in a job interview that Hank C. Jenkins-Smith gave at the University of California–Davis circa 1985. As a result of that visit, the two of us discovered that we had independently arrived at remarkably similar conceptions of the role of scientific information and policy analysis in the policy process and, moreover, that we shared the philosophical assumptions outlined above. Finally, but not trivially, we enjoyed each other's warped sense of humor. (Whose is more warped is a matter of some dispute, but we leave it to Ken Meier, the Christian Dior of Warped Humor, to resolve the question.)

The fruits of our collaboration have been delayed by the procrastination of the senior editor. This book is finally reaching the light of day because of the efforts of numerous people. They include Joseph Stewart and several other contributors who, with increasing frequency and exasperation, kept inquiring when their insights would be made available to the world; Jennifer Knerr of Westview Press and several reviewers, who suggested a number of important revisions in the organization of the manuscript; Dolores DuMont, who typed all the tables and figures in a standard format; and the excellent production crew at Westview, including Martha Robbins and Katherine Streckfus, who rendered our scholarese into typeset English. Finally, we would like to thank Ken Meier who, in gratitude for being named the Christian Dior of Warped Humor, has agreed to accept full responsibility for all errors of omission, commission, logic, and spelling in this book.

*Paul A. Sabatier*
*Hank C. Jenkins-Smith*

# The Study of
# Public Policy Processes

## HANK C. JENKINS-SMITH AND PAUL A. SABATIER

Many who study, teach, or practice policy analysis have experienced a growing dissatisfaction with the widely used concepts and metaphors of the policy process. Those concepts and metaphors—dubbed the "textbook approach" (Nakamura, 1987)—represent a broadly shared way of thinking about public policy. The shared language channels the way scholars frame research projects concerning the policy process and the way practitioners conceive the role of policy analysis. In our view, although the textbook approach has made important contributions and retains some heuristic value, it has outlived its usefulness as a guide to research and teaching.

In this chapter we will first discuss the historical contributions of the textbook approach to the study of public policy as well as why it has ceased to be a fruitful frame of reference for analyzing the policy process. Next, we shall present the rudiments of an alternative approach—the advocacy coalition framework of policy change—that holds greater promise. The final section will briefly outline the plan of the book.

## I. THE TEXTBOOK APPROACH AND ITS LIMITS

Policy researchers, practitioners, and teachers have broadly accepted a *stages heuristic* to public policy, derived from the work of Harold Lasswell, David Easton, and others.[1] Briefly put, the familiar stages model breaks the policy process into functionally and temporally distinct subprocesses. Easton (1965) elaborated a "systems model" of politics, which specified the functioning of input, throughput, output, and feedback mechanisms operating within broader "environments" (ecological, biological, social, personality, etc.). Lasswell (1951) developed a more policy-specific set of stages, including intelligence, recommendation, prescription, invocation, application, appraisal, and termination.

The functions and stages set out by Easton and Lasswell have been diffused throughout the literature of public policy, although the specification and content of the stages vary considerably. Among the most authoritative statements of the stages heuristic is Jones's *An Introduction to the Study of Public Policy* (1977) and Anderson's *Public Policy Making* (1979).[2] Both of these works, leaning heavily on Lasswell and Easton, make distinctions among the stages of problem identification, agenda setting, adoption, implementation, and policy evaluation. Both cast these stages within a broader environment characterized by federalism, political institutions, public opinion, political culture, and other constraints. Each of the stages in the process involves distinct periods of time, political institutions, and policy actors.

The widespread acceptance of the stages model results from important contributions made by that heuristic. As it evolved from the works of Easton (1965) and others, the concept of a *process* of policy making, operating across the various institutions of government, has provided an alternative to the institutional approach of traditional political science that emphasized analysis of specific institutions—such as the presidency, Congress, or the courts—or of public opinion. By shifting attention to the "process stream," the stages model has encouraged analysis of phenomena that transcend any given institution. Implementation of federal legislation, for example, typically involves one or more federal agencies, congressional policy and appropriations committees, federal court decisions, a multitude of state and local agencies, and the intervention of interest groups at multiple levels of government.

The reconceptualization accomplished by the stages heuristic has also permitted useful analysis of topics that were less readily perceived from within the institutionalist framework. Perhaps the most important of these has been its focus on policy impacts, that is, the ability of governmental institutions to accomplish policy objectives, such as improving air quality or assuring secure energy supplies, in the real world. Traditional institutional approaches tended to stop at the output of that particular institution—whether it be a law, a court decision, or an administrative agency rule—without specific attention to the ultimate outcome or impact of the policy.

Finally, the stages heuristic has provided a useful conceptual disaggregation of the complex and varied policy process into manageable segments. The result has been an array of very useful "stage focused" research, particularly regarding agenda setting (e.g., Cobb et al., 1972; Kingdon, 1984) and policy implementation (e.g., Pressman and Wildavsky, 1973; Bardach, 1977; Mazmanian and Sabatier, 1989).

In addition to the ready division of scholarly labor, scholars find the stages heuristic congenial because it fits the self-consciously rational method of the policy science disciplines. Bureaucrats find it attractive because it portrays a rational division of labor between the executive and legislative institutions of government, thereby legitimizing the role of the bureaucracy within representative systems. And for policy makers the stages model provides a view of the policy process that is in accord with democratic theory. According to the model, the decision maker draws on the inputs of the broader society to make policy, which is in turn handed over to other government players for implementation.

Despite its conceptual strengths and broad acceptance, we believe the stages heuristic has serious limitations as a basis for research and teaching:

1. First, and most important, the stages model is not really a *causal model* at all. It lacks identifiable forces to drive the policy process from one stage to another and generate activity within any given stage. Although it has heuristic value in dividing the policy process into manageable units for analysis, it does not specify the linkages, drives, and influences that form the essential core of theoretical models. This lack of a crucial component of causal models is why we prefer to refer to it as the "stages heuristic."

2. Because it lacks causal mechanisms, the stages model *does not provide a clear basis for empirical hypothesis testing*. Absent such a basis, the means for empirically based confirmation, alteration, or elaboration of the model are lacking. For example, even in the most recent edition of his text, Jones (1977) does not provide a coherent set of hypotheses about the conditions under which the policy process will move from one stage to the next.

3. The stages heuristic suffers from *descriptive inaccuracy* in its positing of a sequence of stages starting with agenda setting and passing through policy formulation, implementation, and evaluation. Although proponents often acknowledge deviations from the sequential stages in practice (see, e.g., Jones, 1977:28–29), a great deal of recent empirical study suggests that deviations may be quite frequent: Evaluations of existing programs often affect agenda setting, and policy making occurs as bureaucrats attempt to implement vague legislation (Lowi, 1969; Majone and Wildavsky, 1978; Nakamura and Smallwood, 1980; Barrett and Fudge, 1981; Hjern and Hull, 1982; Kingdon, 1984; but see Sabatier, 1986:31).

4. The stages metaphor suffers from a built-in *legalistic, top-down focus*. It draws attention to a specific cycle of problem identification, major policy decision, and implementation that focuses attention on the intentions of legislators and the fate of a particular policy initiative. Such a top-down view results in a tendency to neglect other important players (e.g., street-level bureaucrats), restricts the view of "policy" to a specific piece of legislation, and may be entirely inapplicable when "policy" stems from a multitude of overlapping directives and actors, none of them dominant (Sabatier, 1986).

5. The stages metaphor inappropriately *emphasizes the policy cycle as the temporal unit of analysis*. Examination of a range of policy areas demonstrates that policy evolution often involves multiple cycles. These are initiated by actors at different levels of government as various formulations of problems and solutions are conceived, partially tested, and reformulated by a range of competing policy elites against a background of change in exogenous events and related policy issue areas (Jones, 1975;

Heclo, 1974; Nelson, 1984; Sabatier and Pelkey, 1990). Thus, rather than focus on a single cycle intiated at a given (usually federal) governmental level, a more appropriate model would focus on *multiple, interacting cycles involving multiple levels of government*.

6. The stages metaphor fails to provide a good vehicle for integrating the roles of policy analysis and *policy-oriented learning throughout the public policy process*. The metaphor tends to confine analysis to the evaluation stage and to post-hoc assessments of the impacts of a given policy initiative. This approach is much too simple. Analysis clearly plays a large role in policy adoption (Jenkins-Smith and Weimer, 1985; Jenkins-Smith, 1990), agenda setting (Kingdon, 1984), and other stages. The practical result, in policy studies, has been to "ghettoize" the perceived role of analysis and learning, as evidenced by the development of two distinct literatures: one that focuses on the interplay of self-interested policy actors pursuing rational strategies in pursuit of predetermined goals (Riker, 1962; Niskanen, 1971, 1975) and another that elaborates the processes by which analysis and learning are integrated into policy making (Weiss, 1977a, 1977b; Caplan et al., 1975).

In general, then, while the stages metaphor served a useful purpose in the 1970s and early 1980s, it has outlived that usefulness and needs to be replaced or substantially revised. We believe that the most promising replacement will be one that attempts to integrate the literature on the politics of the policy process with that on the utilization of policy analysis.

## II. TOWARD AN ALTERNATIVE APPROACH TO THE POLICY PROCESS

Over the past two decades, a rather substantial literature has developed dealing with the utilization of policy analysis and other forms of relatively technical information by public-policy makers. Among its major findings have been the following:

1. Substantial cultural differences impede interaction between researchers and governmental officials (Dunn, 1980; Webber, 1983; but see Sabatier, 1984);
2. While policy analyses may seldom influence specific governmental decisions, they often serve an "enlightenment function" by gradually altering the concepts and assumptions of policy makers over time (Caplan et al., 1975; Weiss, 1977a, 1977b);
3. Policy analyses are often used for nonsubstantive reasons, such as to enhance organizational credibility, occupy "turf," and delay undesirable decisions (Rein and White, 1977; Jenkins-Smith and Weimer, 1985);
4. If researchers and policy analysts wish to have a significant impact on policy, they generally must abandon the role of "neutral technician" and instead adopt that of an "advocate" (Meltsner, 1976; Jenkins-Smith, 1982; Nelson, 1987).

While these contributions have been important, one of the most surprising—and distressing—aspects of the literature on knowledge utilization is that its development has been largely independent of the literature in political science on the factors affecting the policy process.[3]

In their efforts to understand public-policy making, political scientists have traditionally stressed such factors as:

1. Individual interests and values (Riker, 1962; Wilson, 1973);
2. Organizational rules and procedures (Kaufman, 1960; Fenno, 1973);
3. The broader socioeconomic environment in which political institutions operate (Easton, 1965; Hofferbert, 1974); and
4. The tendency for legislators, bureaucratic officials, and interest group leaders concerned with a specific policy area to form relatively autonomous policy subsystems (Fritschler, 1983; Hamm, 1983).

When they have dealt with the role of policy analysis—which has not been often—political scientists have generally argued that it is simply another resource used in an advocacy fashion to advance one's interests (Margolis, 1974; Wildavsky and Tenenbaum, 1981).

The focus of this book, the advocacy coalition framework (ACF) of the policy process, synthesizes many of the major findings of the knowledge utilization literature—particularly those concerning the enlightenment function and the advocacy use of analysis—into the broader literature on public-policy making (Sabatier and Jenkins-Smith, 1988). According to the ACF, policy change over time is a function of three sets of processes. The first concerns the interaction of competing *advocacy coalitions* within a policy subsystem. An advocacy coalition consists of actors from a variety of public and private institutions at all levels of government who share a set of basic beliefs (policy goals plus causal and other perceptions) and who seek to manipulate the rules, budgets, and personnel of governmental institutions in order to achieve these goals over time. The second set of processes concerns *changes external to the subsystem* in socioeconomic conditions, system-wide governing coalitions, and output from other subsystems that provide opportunities and obstacles to the competing coalitions. The third set involves the effects of *stable system parameters*—such as social structure and constitutional rules—on the constraints and resources of the various subsystem actors.

The ACF assumes that, with respect to both belief systems and public policies, one can distinguish "core" from "secondary" elements. Coalitions are organized around common beliefs in core elements; since these common beliefs are hypothesized to be relatively stable over periods of a decade or more, so is coalition composition. Coalitions seek to learn about how the world operates and the effects of various governmental interventions in order to realize their goals over time. Because of resistance to changing core beliefs, however, such "policy-oriented learning" is usually confined to the secondary aspects of belief systems. Changes in core elements of public policies require the replacement of one dominant coalition by another, and this transition is hypothesized to result primarily from changes external to the subsystem.

## III. THE PLAN OF THIS BOOK

The advocacy coalition framework is presented in Part I of this volume and then applied to six different policy areas in Parts II and III.

### Theoretical Chapters

In Chapter 2, Paul A. Sabatier outlines the major elements of the ACF, which deal with policy change over periods of a decade or more. He argues that policy change is best understood as the product of competition between several "advocacy coalitions." Although policy analysis can over time alter secondary aspects of a coalition's belief system, changes in the core aspects of a policy are usually the result of alterations in noncognitive factors external to the subsystem, such as macroeconomic conditions or the rise of a new systemic governing coalition.

In Chapter 3, we analyze the process of policy-oriented learning in greater detail but as applied to shorter time-frames. Although we assume that analysis will generally be used in an advocacy fashion to buttress and elaborate one's beliefs, we nevertheless propose a number of hypotheses concerning the conditions under which analysis produced by one coalition is most likely to alter the beliefs of opposing coalitions. We show how analytical debates are affected by the level of conflict (basically a function of whether core beliefs are being attacked), the analytical tractability of a problem, and the nature of the analytical forum.

### Case Studies

Parts II and III of the book critically apply the ACF to several histories of policy change. We used two criteria in selecting cases. First, we wanted cases involving a variety of substantive policy areas and governmental jurisdictions. The cases cover six different policy areas: secondary education, airline regulation, water supply, television regulation, energy production, and land use. They also cover several political systems: Three deal with the U.S. federal government, two with subnational systems in the United States, and one involves Canada. Second, we wanted the cases to be written by scholars with considerable expertise in the policy area. We each contributed a chapter from our own research programs. But, rather than pretend we could master a wide variety of policy areas ourselves, we chose other scholars to do four cases. In selecting other contributors, we specifically avoided recruiting scholars already sympathetic to the advocacy coalition approach; the criticisms of the ACF contained in these chapters attest to our success.

Richard P. Barke volunteered to apply the ACF to his ongoing research on the Federal Communications Commission because of the promise it offered for exploring policy-oriented learning in the development of television design standards. We asked Anthony E. Brown to do a chapter applying the ACF to airline deregulation because he had published a book on the topic (Brown, 1987). Moveover, that case offered an opportunity to explore the ability of policy-oriented learning (in this case, economists' critiques of the social costs of fare and entry regulation) to alter *core* aspects of a public policy, that is, to refute Hypothesis 5 (see Chapter 2). Brown subsequently asked Joseph Stewart, Jr., to join as coauthor. John F. Munro, who was writing a dissertation at the University of California at Los Angeles on California water politics, offered to apply the ACF to disputes over water allocation policy in California because he wanted to explore the differences between the ACF and his own "Kuhnian" approach. Finally, Hanne B. Mawhinney sent us a paper she had written applying the ACF in a very imaginative fashion to Canadian education; she readily agreed to do a revised version for this book.

In sum, although we make no claims that the set of cases depicts a representative sample of policy disputes, they do involve a wide variety of policy areas and political systems. The authors are all knowledgeable experts and have no particular personal interest in confirming the utility of the ACF.

Part II involves four case studies using primarily qualitative methods of data acquisition and analysis. In Chapter 4, Hanne Mawhinney (University of Ottawa) applies the ACF to efforts by the French-speaking minority in Ontario to gain their own secondary schools in that province. Her account, which focuses on the period from about 1970 to the approval of the Canadian Bill of Rights in 1983, offers some fascinating parallels to the struggles of southern blacks to abolish separate schools in the United States.

In Chapter 5, Anthony E. Brown (Oklahoma State University) and Joseph Stewart, Jr. (University of Texas at Dallas), analyze the deregulation of commercial airlines through the "lens" of the ACF. They review the rather stable coalitions within this subsystem over a very long period, with the late 1970s marking the transformation of a longtime minority coalition into majority status as the result of policy learning and external events.

In Chapter 6, John F. Munro (University of California at Los Angeles and BDM Consultants) examines California water supply policy over the past fifty years, with particular emphasis on the change from a clearly dominant water development coalition during the 1930–1969 period to a stalemate starting in the mid-1970s because of the growing strength of environmentalists (and, we would argue, efficiency-minded economists). Learning played an important role, as did external events—particularly drought, the energy crisis, and gubernatorial elections. The chapter also contains a fascinating case study about how extremists from both camps blocked an effort by former Governor Jerry Brown to broker a solution in the late 1970s.

In Chapter 7, Richard P. Barke (Georgia Tech) provides an imaginative analysis of how technical advisory committees of the Federal Communications Commission managed to develop a unified technology for the development of television in the 1940s. As predicted by the ACF, learning and eventual agreement was facilitated by the presence of a quasi-professional forum and tractable technical issues despite intense conflict involving enormous economic stakes.

Although the type of qualitative—and fairly subjective—methods of data acquisition and analysis used in Part II are extremely useful for obtaining a broad overview of changes in a policy area over several decades, the methods are not very replicable. In fact, the analysis of long-term policy change has been greatly hampered by the lack of data sets gathered in a careful, intersubjectively reliable manner. There have been some analyses of legislative roll calls (Poole and Daniels, 1985), court decisions (Wenner, 1982), and administrative agency decisions (Moe, 1985), but these studies focus on the decisions of a specific type of actor in a single institution or type of institution. They include only a small subset of the wide range of actors from administrative agencies, interest groups, legislative committees, and research institutions at multiple levels of government normally involved in any specific policy area. Nor do they get at the beliefs of various individuals and coalitions, an essential factor in advocacy coalition analysis. Some attitudinal data can be obtained from opinion surveys, but these seldom permit longitudinal analysis over several decades.

Fortunately, hearings before legislative committees and administrative agencies represent a virtually inexhaustible source of information on the expressed beliefs of a wide range of subsystem actors over decades. Although public testimony has some validity problems, these are no greater—and often less significant—than in alternative techniques such as mail questionnaires, personal interviews, perusal of documents, and participant observation. The Methodological Appendix discusses the strengths and limitations of various techniques and then proposes a method for analyzing the content of public hearings in an intersubjectively reliable manner.

Part III contains two chapters that present the results of such content analyses. They demonstrate that this technique, although time-consuming, provides some important advantages over a pure reliance on more traditional (and subjective) techniques. In Chapter 8, Jenkins-Smith and Gilbert K. St. Clair (University of New Mexico) examine twenty years of testimony before congressional committees dealing with petroleum exploration on the outer continental shelf (OCS). This is the same topic previously examined by Theodore Heintz, a senior policy analyst for the Department of Interior, using essentially the same sort of qualitative techniques employed in Part II (Heintz, 1988). Jenkins-Smith and St. Clair demonstrate how more systematic methods of data acquisition and analysis—when added to qualitative techniques—permit them to see the situation in much finer resolution, thereby allowing important distinctions to emerge.

In Chapter 9, Sabatier and Anne M. Brasher (University of California at Davis) analyze a variety of legislative and administrative hearings dealing with land use and water quality policy in the Lake Tahoe Basin between 1960 and 1984. They demonstrate how a rather fluid situation in the 1960s coalesced into two very distinct coalitions by the mid-1970s.

Part IV concludes the volume by assessing what we have learned about policy change and learning as a result of the cases and other information since the ACF was developed several years ago (Sabatier and Jenkins-Smith, 1988). We examine the strengths and limitations of the ACF, suggest a number of revisions, and discuss its implications for both scholars and practitioners.

This book seeks to accomplish a number of objectives. We present the ACF as an alternative to the stages heuristic, which has dominated the field for virtually twenty years as a conceptualization of the policy-making process (Part I). Second, a number of scholars apply the ACF to a number of policy areas in order to assess its strengths and weaknesses (Parts II and III). These applications lead to several significant revisions in the framework in the concluding chapter. Third, the last chapter also suggests some implications of the ACF for both scholars and policy practitioners. Finally, on the methodological side, we demonstrate the utility of the systematic analysis of testimony at public hearings as a means of examining the dynamics of policy change involving virtually the full range of actors found in most policy subsystems (Part III and Appendix A).

It is time to move beyond the stages heuristic to the development and testing of a variety of theories of the policy process that are more descriptively accurate, empirically testable, and willing to postulate a limited number of crucial causal forces. We hope this book will stimulate other scholars to apply the revised ACF to additional policy areas and to develop other frameworks of the policy process (see Sabatier 1991a for some suggestions).

## NOTES

1. *Webster's New Collegiate Dictionary* defines "heuristic" as "providing aid or direction in the solution of a problem but otherwise unjustified." As will be discussed in the following pages, the stages model is a useful heuristic because, by dividing the policy process into a set of stages, it provides aid in understanding that process. But it is not a causal theory at all because it contains no clear set of causal factors that drive the process from one stage to the next.

2. Jones's text was originally published in 1970 and Anderson's in 1975. Among the other public policy texts that rely heavily on the stages metaphor are Brewer and de Leon (1983), Peters (1986), Palumbo (1988), and Rushefsky (1990). Ripley (1985) combines the stages metaphor with Lowi's work on policy arenas.

3. There have been some exceptions, most notably dealing with the use of analysis in specific institutional settings, such as legislatures (Sabatier and Whiteman, 1985; Webber, 1986) and administrative agencies (Sabatier, 1978; Beyer and Trice, 1982).

# PART I

# *The Advocacy Coalition Framework*

# 2

# Policy Change over a Decade or More

**PAUL A. SABATIER**

In the mid-1950s, air pollution was scarcely a subject of public policy debate in the United States. Federal efforts were limited to a tiny program of technical assistance, and only a few states had more than paper programs. Governmental entities with active control programs were largely limited to a few cities—New York, Chicago, Pittsburgh, St. Louis, and Los Angeles—where the problem was perceived as one of dirty air arising primarily from coal combustion.

Ten years later, federal expenditures had risen more than twentyfold, the number of states with pollution control budgets of more than $100,000 had increased from three to twenty-two, California had instituted the first controls on automobile emissions, and the 1967 Federal Air Quality Amendments had attempted to provide some federal review of state programs (Davies, 1970:105, 129; Krier and Ursin, 1977). But increasing public concern about environmental degradation, criticism of state and federal programs, and partisan competition for the growing environmental constituency led to passage of the 1970 Federal Clean Air Amendments (Jones, 1975; Ingram, 1978). This landmark law transferred principal responsibility for pollution control from local and state governments to Washington and instituted a massive regulatory program designed to dramatically improve air quality by the mid-1970s. Passage of the 1970 Amendments was probably also assisted by the publication of federally sponsored research reports indicating that air quality posed significant health risks to many people in urban areas as well as increasing evidence that industry, utilities, and automobiles—rather than residential space heating—were the major sources of most pollutants (Sabatier, 1975).

The consensus in favor of stringent pollution control soon weakened, however, as new issues (e.g., energy prices) came to the fore and as people became aware of the technical and political difficulties of implementing such ambitious legislation. By the end of the 1970s, while emissions and air quality levels in many areas had improved, the implementation of increasingly stringent automotive emissions standards had been delayed several times. Public-policy makers and scholars increasingly became aware that much of the real authority lay with state and local governments (Ingram, 1977; Mazmanian and Sabatier, 1989:Chap. 4; Downing, 1984:Chaps. 11–13). During the 1980s, air pollution remained a controversial issue: The Reagan administration sought—with very mixed results—to substantially weaken the federal program (Vig and Kraft, 1984; Wood, 1988); economists argued for the replacement of uniform legal standards with more flexible economic incentives (White, 1982; Liroff, 1986); California continued to pioneer in a number of areas, such as alternative-fuel (nongasoline) vehicles; and repeated efforts were made to amend the federal law. These efforts finally bore fruit in the 1990 Clean Air Amendments, which strengthened the program in a number of areas, most notably by the adoption of an economic incentive approach to acid rain and the beginning of federal efforts to stimulate alternative-fuel vehicles (Cohen, 1992).

How is one to understand the incredibly complex process of policy change over a decade or more in air pollution control or any other policy area? On the one hand, the stages heuristic discussed in Chapter 1 provides some assistance. It draws attention to the iterative process of agenda setting, formulation, implementation, and reformulation—with major changes in federal law in 1967, 1970, 1977, and 1990. On the other hand, the stages heuristic would have difficulty explaining the continuing role of state and local governments—particularly California—in policy innovation. It also neglects the importance *throughout the policy process* of technical information concerning the effects of air pollutants on human health, the principal sources of various pollutants, the causes of acid rain, and the effectiveness of economic incentives as a policy instrument.

The traditional concerns of political scientists also provide some assistance. The dramatic increase in public support for environmental protection in the late 1960s was an important factor in the passage of the 1970 Amendments, and the public's equivocation over the tradeoff between energy security and environmental protection in the 1970s played some role in the 1974 and 1977 congressional approvals of delays in imposing more stringent automobile emissions standards. Likewise, the decentralization of power in Congress from party leaders to subcommittee chairs played a role in the passage of the 1970 Amendments and in the stalemate during the 1980s (Cohen, 1992). And political scientists' focus on "iron triangles"—in this case, the Senate Environment Committee, the House Commerce Committee, the Environmental Protection Agency, and concerned interest groups—certainly constitutes a necessary part of any explanation of federal air pollution policy implemented over the past thirty years. But the traditional preoccupations of political scientists also neglect the critical role of state and local implementing agencies, the continuing importance of California (and several other jurisdictions) as policy innovators, and the importance of technical information in framing the debate over such issues as acid rain, the validity of air quality standards (which substantially drive the entire policy process), and the debate over whether the dominant policy instrument should be uniform emissions regulations or more flexible economic incentives. In short, political scientists' traditional focus on specific governmental institutions (Congress, the presidency, interest groups) or specific types of political behavior (popular voting, legislative roll calls) encounters enormous difficulties when dealing with policy change over several decades. Policy evolution over that span of time usually goes way beyond a few critical institutions or types of political behavior to include hundreds of governmental institutions, dozens of important elections in various jurisdictions, and several dozen "iron triangles" at various levels of government. It also involves entire categories of behavior—particularly technical debates over critical policy issues—neglected by the vast majority of political scientists (Sabatier, 1991a, 1991b).

Both the stages heuristic and the traditional preoccupations of political scientists suffer from at least two major limitations in their ability to explain the evolution of air pollution policy in the United States over the past thirty years. First, they both suffer from severe cases of "Potomac fever," of assuming that almost everything of importance occurs in Washington, D.C. In the process, they dramatically underestimate the considerable discretion exercised by state and local agencies when implementing federal law as well as their ability to generate and implement innovative policies on their own.[1] Second, both neglect the role of ideas—particularly ideas involving the relatively technical aspects of policy debates—in policy evolution.

Fortunately, not everyone has been restricted by the blinders imposed by the stages heuristic or the concerns of most political scientists. A critical contribution to understanding policy change over time was made by Heclo's (1974) analysis of British and Swedish welfare policy during the initial decades of this century. On the one hand, Heclo agreed with political demographers who pointed to the role of changing social and economic conditions—such as population migrations, the emergence of new social movements, critical elections, and macroeconomic changes in inflation and unemployment—in providing the constituency base for major policy changes (Hofferbert, 1974; Hibbs and Fassbender, 1981; Burnham, 1970). Equally important in his view, however, was the interaction of specialists within a specific policy area as they gradually learned more about various aspects of the problem over time and experimented with a variety of means to achieve their policy objectives. In essence, Heclo saw policy change as a product of both (1) large-scale social, economic, and political changes and (2) the interaction of people within a policy community involving both competition for power and efforts to develop more knowledgeable means of addressing various aspects of the policy problem.

In many respects, Chapters 2 and 3 of this book represent an attempt to translate Heclo's basic insight into a reasonably clear conceptual framework of policy change over time. This chapter continues his focus on the interaction of political elites within a policy community or subsystem who attempt to respond to changing socioeconomic and political conditions. The first part presents an overview of the conceptual framework as it applies to policy change over periods of a decade or more. Subsequent sections deal with specific aspects, including external events affecting policy subsystems and the internal structure of subsystems. This chapter touches on—and Chapter 3 examines in some detail—the role of policy-oriented learning in policy change, particularly the conditions under which elites from different advocacy coalitions gradually alter their belief systems over time as a result of formal policy analyses and trial-and-error learning.[2]

## I. AN OVERVIEW OF THE FRAMEWORK

The advocacy coalition framework (ACF) has at least four basic premises: (1) that understanding the process of policy change—and the role of policy-oriented learning therein—requires a time perspective of a decade or more; (2) that the most useful way to think about policy change over such a time span is through a focus on "policy subsystems," that is, the interaction of actors from different institutions who follow and seek to influence governmental decisions in a policy area; (3) that those subsystems must include an intergovernmental dimension, that is, they must involve all levels of government (at least for domestic policy); and, (4) that public policies (or programs) can be conceptualized in the same manner as belief systems, that is, as sets of value priorities and causal assumptions about how to realize them.

The focus on time spans of a decade or more comes directly from findings concerning the importance of the "enlightenment function" of policy research. Weiss (1977a, 1977b) has argued persuasively that a focus on short-term decision making will underestimate the influence of policy analysis because such research is used primarily to alter the perceptions and conceptual apparatus of policy makers over time. A corollary of this view is that it is the *cumulative* effect of findings from different studies and from ordinary knowledge (Lindblom and Cohen, 1979) that has the greatest influence on policy. The literature on policy implementation also points to the need for utilizing time frames of a decade or more, both in order to complete at least one cycle of formulation, implementation, and reformulation and to obtain a reasonably accurate portrait of program success and failure (Mazmanian and Sabatier, 1989). Numerous studies have shown that ambitious programs that appeared after a few years to be abject failures received more favorable evaluations when seen in a longer time frame; conversely, initial successes may evaporate over time (Bernstein, 1955; Kirst and Jung, 1982; Hogwood and Peters, 1983).

The framework's second basic premise is that the most useful aggregate unit of analysis for understanding policy change in modern industrial societies is not any specific governmental institution but rather a policy subsystem, that is, those actors from a variety of public and private organizations who are actively concerned with a policy problem or issue such as air pollution control, mental health, or surface transportation. Following a number of recent authors, we argue that conceptions of policy subsystems should be broadened from traditional notions of "iron triangles"—limited to administrative agencies, legislative committees, and interest groups at a single level of government—to include actors at various levels of government active in policy formulation and implementation as well as journalists, researchers, and policy analysts who play important roles in the generation, dissemination, and evaluation of policy ideas (Heclo, 1978; Dunleavy, 1981; Milward and Wamsley, 1984; Scholz et al., 1991).

The third basic premise is that policy subsystems will normally involve actors from *all* levels of government. To examine policy change only at the national level will, in most instances, be seriously misleading. In the United States and many other countries, policy innovations normally occur first at a subnational level and then may get expanded into nationwide programs; even after national intervention, subnational initiatives normally continue. Air pollution is typical: Cities like Pittsburgh, St. Louis, Chicago, and New York had viable stationary source controls twenty years before any significant federal involvement occurred, and California has consistently been several years ahead of the feds on mobile source controls. Moreover, two decades of implementation research has conclusively demonstrated that state and local implementing officials have substantial discretion in deciding exactly how federal "policy" gets translated into thousands of concrete decisions in very diverse local situations.[3]

The fourth important premise is that public policies and programs incorporate implicit theories about how to achieve their objectives (Pressman and Wildavsky, 1973; Majone, 1980) and thus can be conceptualized in much the same way as belief systems. They involve value priorities, perceptions of important causal relationships, perceptions of world states (including the magnitude of the problem), perceptions of the efficacy of policy instruments, and so on. This ability to map beliefs and policies on the same "canvas" provides a vehicle for assessing the influence of various actors over time, particularly the role of technical information (beliefs) on policy change.

Figure 2.1 presents a general overview of the framework. On the left side are two sets of exogenous variables—the one fairly stable, the other more dynamic—that affect the constraints and opportunities of subsystem actors. Air pollution policy, for example, is strongly affected by the nature of air quality as a collective good, by the geographical contours of air basins, and by political boundaries, which are usually quite stable over time. But there are also more dynamic factors, including changes in socioeconomic conditions (e.g., public opinion and oil prices)

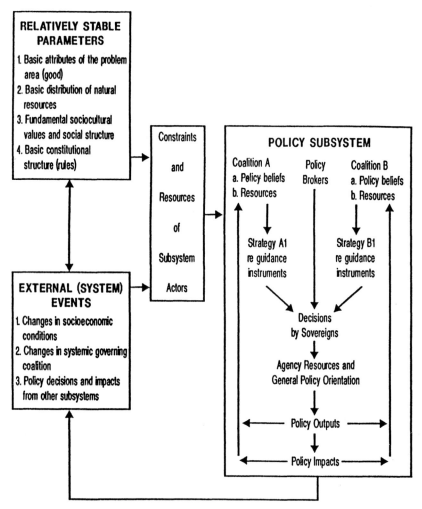

FIGURE 2.1   The advocacy coalition framework of policy change

and in the systemic governing coalition, which provide some of the principal sources of policy change.

Within the subsystem, it is assumed that actors can be aggregated into a number of advocacy coalitions composed of people from various governmental and private organizations who share a set of normative and causal beliefs and who often act in concert. At any particular point in time, each coalition adopts a strategy envisaging one or more institutional innovations that members feel will further policy objectives. Conflicting strategies from various coalitions are normally mediated by a third group of actors, here termed "policy brokers," whose principal concern is to find some reasonable compromise that will reduce intense conflict. The end result is one or more governmental programs, which in turn produce policy outputs at the operational level (e.g., agency permit decisions). These outputs—mediated by a number of other factors—result in a variety of impacts on targeted problem parameters (e.g., ambient air quality) as well as in various side effects.

On the basis of perceptions of the adequacy of governmental decisions and the resultant impacts as well as new information arising from search processes and external dynamics, each advocacy coalition may revise its beliefs or alter its strategy. The latter may involve the seeking of major institutional revisions at the collective choice level, more minor revisions at the operational level (Kiser and Ostrom, 1982), or even changes in the dominant electoral coalition at the systemic level, an arena outside of the subsystem itself.

Within the general process of policy change, this framework has a particular interest in policy-oriented learning. Following Heclo (1974:306), policy-oriented learning refers to relatively enduring alterations of thought or behavioral intentions that result from experience and are concerned with the attainment (or revision) of policy objectives. Policy-oriented learning involves the internal feedback loops depicted in Figure 2.1, perceptions concerning external dynamics, and increased knowledge of problem parameters and the factors affecting them. The framework assumes that such learning is instrumental, that is, that members of various coalitions seek to better understand the world in order to further their policy objectives. They will resist information suggesting that their basic beliefs may be invalid or unattainable, and they will use formal policy analyses primarily to buttress and elaborate those beliefs (or attack their opponents' views). Within this assumption of the prevalence of advocacy analysis, Chapter 3 identifies several factors that facilitate learning across advocacy coalitions.

Such learning comprises, however, only one of the forces affecting policy change over time. In addition to this cognitive activity, there is a real world that changes. This world, first of all, involves the realm of system dynamics depicted in Figure 2.1: Changes in relevant socioeconomic conditions and system-wide governing coalitions—such as the 1973 Arab oil embargo or the 1980 election of Ronald Reagan—can dramatically alter the composition and the resources of various coalitions and, in turn, public policy within the subsystem. Turnover in personnel—sometimes resulting from external conditions, sometimes merely from death or retirement—constitutes a second noncognitive source of change that can substantially alter the political resources of various advocacy coalitions and thus the policy decisions at the collective choice and operational levels.

The basic argument of this framework is that, although policy-oriented learning is an important aspect of policy change and can often alter secondary aspects of a coalition's belief system, changes in the core aspects of a policy are usually the results of perturbations in noncognitive factors external to the subsystem, such as macroeconomic conditions or the rise of a new systemic governing coalition. While the framework borrows a great deal from Heclo (1974, 1978), it differs in its emphasis on ideologically based coalitions and its conception of the dynamics of policy-oriented learning. It can also be clearly distinguished from analyses that view formal organizations as the basic actors (e.g., Krasnow et al., 1982) or that focus on individuals seeking to attain their self-interest through the formation of short-term "minimum winning coalitions" (Riker, 1962).

Although in presenting the ACF, we will illustrate relevant concepts and hypotheses with examples from U.S. air pollution policy, the ACF should be applicable to a variety of policy issues in most industrial societies.

## II. EXTERNAL FACTORS AFFECTING POLICY CHANGE WITHIN SUBSYSTEMS

Policy making in any political system or policy subsystem is constrained by a variety of social, legal, and resource features of the society of which it is a part (Heclo, 1974; Hofferbert, 1974; Kiser and Ostrom, 1982).

Our concern with the analysis of policy change means that stable external factors must be distinguished from more dynamic ones. In addition, the focus on policy subsystems means that a subsystem's relationship to other subsystems and to the broader political system must be taken into account. Thus, the framework distinguishes between (1) parameters that are relatively stable over several decades and (2) those aspects of the system that are susceptible to significant fluctuations over the course of a few years and thus serve as major stimuli to policy change.

### Relatively Stable Parameters

The following set of very stable factors may be either within or external to the policy subsystem. The difficulty of changing these factors discourages actors from making them the object of strategizing behavior. These factors can limit the range of feasible alternatives or otherwise affect the resources and beliefs of subsystem actors.

*Basic Attributes of the Problem Area (or "Good").* Public choice theorists have shown how various characteristics of goods, such as excludability, affect institutional (policy) options. For example, ocean fisheries and large underground aquifers give rise to common pool problems that markets cannot deal with efficiently and that make them candidates for governmental regulation (Ostrom, 1990).

Other aspects of the good or problem area (or issue area) affect the degree of policy-oriented learning likely to take place. For example, a problem's susceptibility to quantitative measurement affects the policy maker's ability to ascertain performance gaps. The extent of learning is likewise contingent upon the ease of developing good causal models of the factors affecting a problem. One would thus expect more learning on air pollution than on mental health (see Chapter 3).

Perceptions of various aspects of a good can change over time, often because of the activities of an advocacy coalition. Thirty years ago, cigarette smoking was widely regarded as a relatively harmless activity and there was virtually no concern with the effects of smoking on nonsmokers. The situation is quite different today, due in large part to a concerted campaign on the part of a public health coalition led by several surgeons general (Fritschler, 1983).

*Basic Distribution of Natural Resources.* The present (and past) distribution of natural resources strongly affects a society's overall wealth and the viability of different economic sectors, many aspects of its culture, and the feasibility of options in many policy areas. For example, the United States could encourage utilities to switch from oil to coal in the mid-1970s—with its potentially significant effects on sulfur emissions—while the French, lacking abundant coal reserves, turned to nuclear power as an alternative means of generating electricity.

*Fundamental Cultural Values and Social Structure.* Large-scale nationalization of the means of production is a viable policy option in many European countries, but not in the United States. Although such norms are not immutable, change usually requires decades.

Similarly, political power in most countries tends to be rather highly correlated with income, social class, and large organizations. Significant changes in the influence of various social groups—whether it be blacks and Chicanos or the auto companies—normally takes several decades. The political resources (or lack thereof) of many interest groups are slowly changing "facts of life" that actors within a subsystem must take into account in formulating their strategies in the short or medium term.

*Basic Legal Structure.* In most political systems, basic legal norms are quite resistant to change. The U.S. Constitution has not been significantly altered since the granting of women's suffrage in 1920. The institutions of the French Fifth Republic have remained virtually unchanged for thirty years, those of Great Britain for almost a century. Basic legal traditions—such as the role of the courts and the fundamental norms of administrative law—also tend to be rather stable over periods of several decades.

Constitutional and other fundamental legal norms can also affect the extent of policy-oriented learning. For example, Ashford (1981b:16–17) has argued that the concentration of policy-making authority in the British cabinet and higher civil service—coupled with the secrecy that permeates that system—inhibit outsiders from making intelligent evaluations of present policy. In a similar vein, public choice theorists have long argued that decentralized political systems with relatively autonomous local governments facilitate learning by providing arenas for policy experimentation and realistic points of comparison for evaluating different policy instruments (V. Ostrom, Tiebout, and Warren, 1961; E. Ostrom, 1982).

These relatively stable parameters—the nature of the good, the basic distribution of natural resources, fundamental cultural values and social structure, and basic legal structure—significantly constrain the options available to subsystem actors. Changing them is not impossible, but it is very difficult. Change at this level normally requires a concerted effort by an advocacy coalition for at least a decade—and often several decades. Major changes in public policy within a subsystem are more likely to come from the factors outside the subsystem discussed below.

### Dynamic System Events

Changes in the following factors external to a policy subsystem can be substantial over the course of a few years or a decade. Because such changes alter the constraints and opportunities confronting subsystem actors, they constitute the principal dynamic elements affecting policy change. They also present a continuous challenge to subsystem actors, who must learn how to anticipate them and respond to them in a manner consistent with their basic beliefs and interests. The process must be frustrating at times, as actors who have worked for years to gain an advantage over their competitors within a subsystem suddenly find their plans knocked awry by (external) events—such as the Arab oil embargo—over which they have little control.

*1. Socioeconomic Conditions and Technology.* Changes in these areas can substantially affect a subsystem, either by undermining the causal assumptions of present policies or by significantly altering the political support of various advocacy coalitions. For example, on the one hand, the dramatic rise in public concern with environmental degradation in the late 1960s played an important role in the passage of the 1970 Clean Air Amendments (Ingram, 1978). On the other hand, the Arab oil embargo of 1973–1974 contributed to such a depression in the domestic automobile industry that the United Auto Workers—previously a strong supporter of stringent air pollution programs—began echoing industry calls for a relaxation of costly and allegedly energy-inefficient automotive pollution controls (Mazmanian and Sabatier, 1989:104).

*2. Systemic Governing Coalitions.* Changes in the dominant coalition at a given level of government, that is, "critical elections" (Burnham, 1970), normally require that the same coalition control the chief executive's office and both houses of the legislature. Such changes in the system-wide governing coalition are quite rare.

More limited changes are more common but also have lesser effects. The 1980 national election, for example, resulted in both the presidency and the Senate changing from relatively liberal Democrats to relatively conservative Republicans. Although air pollution was only a minor issue in the election—a campaign dominated by the issues of stagflation and the Iranian hostage crisis—President Ronald Reagan attempted to fundamentally alter air pollution policy through appointing conservatives to key Environmental Protection Agency (EPA) positions, drastically cutting the EPA's budget, and proposing major amendments to the Clean Air Act (Vig and Kraft, 1984). In the final analysis, however, he failed. Most of his key appointees were forced to resign in scandal after a couple of years, the budget cuts were gradually restored, and his legislative proposals died in Senate committee. The reason is that members of the clean air coalition remained in control in the House, the Senate Environment Committee, and among EPA career officials (Wood, 1988; Cook and Wood, 1989; Waterman, 1989). Because there was no change in the system-wide governing coalition—but only in the presidency and a portion of the Senate—Reagan was unable to bring about a fundamental change within the air pollution subsystem at even the federal level, let alone in the states (Wood, 1991).

   3. *Policy Decisions and Impacts from Other Subsystems.* Subsystems are only partially autonomous. In fact, the decisions and impacts from other policy sectors are principal dynamic elements affecting specific subsystems.

   Examples are legion. The search for "energy independence" in the mid-1970s had significant repercussions on U.S. pollution control policy, as the Nixon and Ford administrations sought to require utilities to change from clean-burning natural gas to more abundant coal. Britain's entry into the Common Market (largely on foreign policy and economic grounds) has had repercussions on subsystems from taxation to pollution control because of the need to comply with European Economic Community (EEC) mandates. And there is evidence that drastic reductions in local tax revenues brought about by Proposition 13 have affected California land use policy by encouraging local governments to become more leery of the service costs of dispersed new housing developments (Inan, 1979).

## III. POLICY SUBSYSTEMS: INTERNAL STRUCTURE

   The complexity of modern society, the expansion of governmental functions, and the technical nature of most policy problems create enormous pressures for specialization. It is exceedingly difficult, except perhaps in small communities, to be knowledgeable about more than one or two policy sectors. When others specialize—as they do in any moderately large political system—generalists find it difficult to compete.

   Thus it has long been recognized that political elites concerned with a specific problem or policy area tend to form relatively autonomous subsystems (Griffith, 1961; Fritschler, 1983; Dodd and Schott, 1979; Hamm, 1983). But traditional notions of "whirlpools" and "iron triangles" suffer because they are generally limited to interest groups, administrative agencies, and legislative committees at a single level of government. They need to be expanded to include journalists, analysts, researchers, and others who play important roles in the generation, dissemination, and evaluation of policy ideas as well as actors at other levels of government who play important roles in policy formulation and implementation (Heclo, 1978; Wamsley, 1983; Kingdon, 1984; Sabatier and Pelkey, 1987).

Traditional notions of "iron triangles" also assume that conflict among participants is relatively restrained—which often is not the case. The ACF argues that the level of conflict will vary depending upon whether the relevant actors disagree on "secondary" versus "core" aspects of their belief systems.

### Delimiting Subsystem Boundaries

Let us define a policy subsystem as the set of actors who are involved in dealing with a policy problem such as air pollution control, mental health, or energy. Although it is often useful to begin with a networking approach to identify the actors involved at any particular point in time (Hjern and Porter, 1981), one must also be willing to identify potential ("latent") actors who would become active if they had the appropriate information (Balbus, 1971). In fact, activating latent constituencies is often one of the strategies of coalitions.

Latent constituencies are also an important factor in using technical information to affect policy change over time. For example, federal air pollution officials in the late 1960s identified a number of latent supporters of stricter pollution control programs and then developed several information and participation programs to encourage their involvement (Sabatier, 1975). This explicit effort to use information to expand the range of subsystem actors fundamentally altered air pollution politics in Chicago and several other cities.[4]

### Origins of Subsystems

The most likely reason for the emergence of new subsystems is that a group of actors become dissatisfied enough with the neglect of a particular problem by existing subsystems to form their own. For example, dissatisfaction with the laissez-faire approach to food safety (e.g., meat inspections) by the agriculture subsystem became so intense in the early 1900s that a new subsystem—centered around what was to become the Food and Drug Administration (FDA)—gradually separated from the agricultural subsystem over a period of several decades (Nadel, 1971: 7–17). Whereas this case involved a minority coalition breaking away to form its own subsystem, in other cases a new subsystem is essentially the product of a subset of a dominant coalition becoming large and specialized enough to form its own; an example would be the emergence of a housing subsystem out of the urban policy subsystem during the 1960s (Farkas, 1971).

### Subsystem Actors:
### Advocacy Coalitions and Policy Brokers

Whatever their origins, subsystems normally contain a large and diverse set of actors. For example, the U.S. air pollution control subsystem includes the following:

1. The Environmental Protection Agency;
2. Relevant congressional committees;
3. Portions of peer agencies, such as the Department of Energy, that are frequently involved in pollution control policy;
4. Polluting corporations, their trade associations, unions, and occasionally, consumer associations;
5. The manufacturers of pollution control equipment;
6. Environmental and public health groups at all levels of government;
7. State and local pollution control agencies;
8. Research institutes and consulting firms with a strong interest in air pollution;
9. Important journalists who frequently cover the issue;
10. On some issues, such as acid rain, actors in other countries.

Given the enormous number and range of actors involved, it becomes necessary to find ways of aggregating them into smaller and theoretically useful sets of categories.

After considering several alternatives, I have concluded that the most useful means of aggregating actors in order to understand policy change over fairly long periods of time is by "advocacy coalitions." These are people from a variety of positions (elected and agency officials, interest group leaders, researchers, etc.) who share a particular belief system—that is, a set of basic values, causal assumptions, and problem perceptions—and who show a nontrivial degree of coordinated activity over time.

I find this strategy for aggregating actors superior to the most likely alternative—that of viewing formal institutions as the dominant actors—because in most policy subsystems there are at least fifty to a hundred organizations at various levels of government that are active over time. Developing models involving changes in the positions and interaction patterns of that many units over a period of a decade or more would be an *exceedingly* complex task (Sabatier and Pelkey, 1987). Moreover, institutional models have difficulty accounting for the importance of specific individuals who move about from organization to organization within the same subsystem (Heclo, 1978). Finally, institutional models have difficulty accounting for the huge variation in behavior among individuals within the same institution, such as Congress, the federal district courts, the AFL-CIO, or even the same governmental agency (Mazmanian and Nienaber, 1979; Liroff, 1986). Thus I prefer to utilize advocacy coalitions as a more manageable focus of analysis, while certainly acknowledging that formal institutions have some capacity to constrain their members' behavior. Formal institutions also bring critical resources—such as the authority to make certain types of decisions—to the members of a coalition.

In most subsystems, the number of politically significant advocacy coalitions will be quite small. In quiescent subsystems there may only be a single coalition. In most cases, however, there will be two to four important coalitions—the number being limited by all the factors that push actors to coalesce if they are to form effective coalitions (Jenkins-Smith, personal communication; Kingdon, 1984). If one's opponents pool their resources under a common position, to remain without allies is to invite defeat; but allies create pressures for common positions, which tend to harden over time. This hardening of positions is strengthened by the importance of organizational actors (whose positions are usually slow to change) and by the tendency to perceive one's opponents as being more hostile and powerful than they probably are (Sabatier et al., 1987). This argument suggests, then, that there will be greater fragmentation of beliefs in recently formed subsystems than in more established ones (see Chapter 9 for a test of this hypothesis). Since most subsystems have existed for decades, however, one would expect the number of coalitions in each to be relatively small.

For example, the U.S. air pollution subsystem in the 1970s and 1980s was apparently divided into two rather distinct advocacy coalitions. One, which might be termed "the Clean Air Coalition," was dominated by environmental and public health groups, their allies in Congress (e.g., Senator Edmund Muskie, Congressman Henry Waxman), most pollution control officials in the EPA, a few labor unions, many state and local pollution control officials (particularly in large cities with serious problems), and some researchers. It had a belief system that stressed (1) the primacy of human health over economic development and efficiency; (2) a perception that air pollution was a serious health problem in many urban areas; (3) a focus on the inability of markets to deal with "negative externalities" such as air pollution; (4) a causal assumption that state and local governments' preoccupation with competitive advantage in attracting industry made them susceptible to industrial "blackmail" and thus required a strong federal presence; (5) a deep distrust of the motives of corporate officials and a consequent assumption of the necessity of forcing the pace of technological innovation; and (6) a strong preference for a legal command and control approach rather than reliance on economic incentives.

The competing coalition, which I'll call the Economic Feasibility Coalition, was dominated by industrial sources of air pollution, energy companies, their allies in Congress (e.g., Congressmen John Dingell and James Broyhill), several labor unions (particularly after the Arab oil embargo), some state and local pollution control officials, and several economists. Its belief system (1) stressed the need to balance human health against economic development and efficiency; (2) questioned the alleged seriousness of the health problem except in isolated instances; (3) believed that increasing social welfare generally required a deference to market arrangements; (4) generally disapproved of a strong federal role (largely on the assumption that their leverage was greater with local officials); (5) placed great emphasis on legally requiring only what was technologically feasible; and (6) expressed support (at least in principle) for the flexibility and cost-effectiveness of economic incentives rather than general legal commands (Downing, 1984).[5]

Not everyone active in a policy subsystem will "belong to" an advocacy coalition or share one of the major belief systems. Some researchers who are otherwise indifferent to the policy disputes may participate simply because they have certain skills to offer (Meltsner, 1976). The same would hold true for bureaucrats who actually adhere to the tradition of "neutral competence" (Knott and Miller, 1987). In addition, there will almost certainly be a category of actors—here termed "policy brokers"—whose dominant concerns are with keeping the level of political conflict within acceptable limits and reaching some "reasonable" solution to the problem. This is a traditional function of some elected officials (particularly chief executives) and, in some European countries like Britain and France, of high civil servants (Doggan, 1975). The courts, "blue ribbon commissions," and other actors may also play the role of policy broker. The distinction between "advocate" and "broker," however, rests on a continuum. Many brokers will have some policy bent, while advocates may show some serious concern with system maintenance. The framework merely insists that policy brokering is an empirical matter that may or may not correlate with institutional affiliation: While high civil servants may be brokers, they are also often policy advocates— particularly when their agency has a clearly defined mission.

The concept of an advocacy coalition assumes that shared beliefs provide the principal "glue" of politics. Moreover, as shall be discussed shortly, it assumes that people's core beliefs are quite resistant to change. These assumptions lead to one of the critical hypotheses of the entire framework:

*Hypothesis 1:* On major controversies within a policy subsystem when core beliefs are in dispute, the lineup of allies and opponents tends to be rather stable over periods of a decade or so.[6]

Thus the framework explicitly rejects the view that actors are primarily motivated by their short-term self-interest and thus that "coalitions of convenience" of highly varying composition will dominate policy making over time. This claim is consistent with the evidence from a number of studies, including (1) the history of U.S. energy policy by Wildavsky and Tenenbaum (1981), (2) Marmor's (1970) analysis of the politics of Medicare in the United States, and (3) numerous analyses of the composition of majority coalitions in multiparty European parliaments over the past several decades, which have found that—in contrast to Riker's (1962) "minimum winning coalition" model—coalition formation has been quite constrained by ideology.[7]

Of course, coalition stability could be the result not of stable beliefs but rather of stable economic and organizational interests. This objection raises very thorny methodological issues, in part because belief systems are normally highly correlated with self-interest and the causation is reciprocal.[8] For example, Sierra Club leaders and steel company executives typically have quite different views on air pollution control, but is this (1) because their organizations have quite different (economic) interests or (2) because people join organizations—and put in the effort to rise to prominence in them—out of affinity with the organization's stated goals? This framework uses belief systems, rather than "interests," as its focus because beliefs are more inclusive and more verifiable than interests. Interest models must still identify a set of means and performance indicators necessary for goal attainment; this set of interests and goals, perceived causal relationships, and perceived parameter states constitutes a "belief system." While belief system models can thus incorporate self-interest and organizational interests, they also allow actors to establish goals in quite different ways (e.g., as a result of socialization) and are therefore more inclusive. In addition, I personally have great difficulty in specifying a priori a clear and falsifiable set of interests for most actors in policy conflicts (see also Kingdon, 1988). Instead, it seems preferable to allow actors to indicate their belief systems (via questionnaires and content analyses of documents) and then empirically examine the extent to which these change over time.

### Advocacy Coalitions and Public Policy

Coalitions seek to translate their beliefs into public policies or programs (which usually consist of a set of goals and directions, or empowerments, to administrative agencies for implementing those goals). Although pressures for compromise generally result in governmental programs that incorporate elements advocated by different coalitions, the 1970 Federal Clean Air Amendments incorporated to an unusual degree most elements of the belief system of the Clean Air Coalition. The 1977 and 1990 Clean Air Amendments incorporated some compromises sought by the Economic Feasibility Coalition (such as the 1977 delays in imposing more stringent auto emissions standards and the 1990 Amendments' use of economic incentives in the acid rain program), but the overall philosophy of the federal Clean Air Act remains consistent with most beliefs of the Clean Air Coalition.

In any intergovernmental system, however, different coalitions may be in control of various governmental units. For example, the Economic Efficiency Coalition was apparently more powerful in Sun Belt states during most of the 1970s than at the national level. In fact, one of the basic strategies of any coalition is to manipulate the assignment of program responsibilities so that the governmental units that it controls have the most authority (Schattschneider, 1960).

While belief systems will determine the *direction* in which an advocacy coalition (or any other political actor) will seek to move governmental programs, *its ability to do so* will be critically dependent upon its resources. These include such things as money, expertise, number of supporters, and legal authority. With respect to the last, this framework acknowledges one of the central features of institutional models— namely, that rules create authorizations to act in certain ways (Kiser and Ostrom, 1982; Ostrom, 1990). The ACF differs from many institutional theories, however, in viewing these rules as the product of competition among advocacy coalitions and in viewing institutional members as providing resources to different coalitions.

The resources of various coalitions change, of course, over time. Some of this is intentional. In fact, most coalitions seek to augment their budgets, recruit new members (especially those with legal authority, expertise, or money), place their members in positions of authority, and employ the variety of other means long identified by interest group theorists (Truman, 1951; Berry, 1977). Some coalitions have a more difficult time than others in maintaining an effective presence and increasing their resources over time. This is particularly true in consumer and environmental protection, where the groups that originally championed regulation have had more difficulty than the regulated industries in finding sufficient organizational resources to monitor and to intervene in the extended process of policy implementation (Bernstein, 1955; Nadel, 1971; Quirk, 1981). Even more severe difficulties confront economically disadvantaged groups in their efforts to muster the resources necessary to remain active over any extended period of time (Goodwin and Moen, 1981).

Although coalitions will seek to increase their resources, the advocacy coalition framework argues that *major* shifts in the distribution of political resources will usually be the product of events *external* to the subsystem and largely external to activities of subsystem coalitions. For example, members of the Economic Feasibility Coalition attempted to utilize the 1973–1974 oil crisis and the 1980 election of President Reagan to increase their resources, but those changes were not sufficient to enable them to overcome the Clean Air Coalition on issues relating to the policy core incorporated into the 1970 Clean Air Amendments. In contrast, Chapters 4 and 5 of this book explore cases illustrating how subsystem coalitions successfully exploited and amplified opportunities arising from external events.

### Policy-Oriented Belief Systems

In its conception of the belief systems of individuals and coalitions, the framework has three basic points of departure. The first is Ajzen and Fishbein's (1980) "theory of reasoned action"—basically an expected utility model in which actors weigh alternative courses of action in terms of their contribution to a set of goals, but in which the preferences of reference groups (such as members of one's coalition) are accorded a more prominent role than in most utilitarian models. Second, rationality is limited rather than perfect. Thus the framework relies heavily upon the work of March and Simon (1958), Nisbett and Ross (1980), Kahneman et al. (1982), and many others in terms of satisficing, placing cognitive limits on rationality, carrying out limited search processes, etc. Third, because subsystems are composed of policy elites rather than members of the general public, there are strong grounds for assuming that most actors will have relatively complex and internally consistent belief systems in the policy area(s) of interest to them (Wilker and Milbrath, 1972; Cobb, 1973; Axelrod, 1976; Putnam, 1976:87–93; Buttel and Flinn, 1978).

These, however, are only starting points, for they tell us very little about what will happen when experience reveals anomalies—such as internal inconsistencies, inaccurate predictions, and invalid assertions—among the beliefs. Assuming some social and psychological pressures for belief consistency and validity, are conflicts resolved in an essentially random process—that is, with all beliefs accorded the same logical status—or are some beliefs more fundamental than others and thus more resistant to change? What, in short, is the *structure* of the belief systems of policy elites?

The literature on political belief systems is a mine field of conflicting theories and evidence.[9] But the most useful approach seems to be a synthesis of Putnam's (1976:81–89) review of the normative and cognitive orientations of political elites, Axelrod's (1976) work on the complexity of their causal assumptions, an adaptation of Lakatos's (1971) distinction between "core" and other elements of scientific belief systems, and Converse's (1964) contention that abstract political beliefs are more resistant to change than specific ones (also Peffley and Hurwitz, 1985; Hurwitz and Peffley, 1987).

Given that the basic strategy of the framework is to use the structure of belief systems to predict changes in beliefs and attempted changes in policy over time, that structure must be stipulated a priori if the argument to come in Hypotheses 2 and 3 is to be falsifiable. The unsettled nature of the field makes this a risky undertaking. Nevertheless, on the assumption that clarity—even if wrong—begets clarity and eventually improved understanding of a phenomenon, the framework proposes the structure of elite belief systems outlined in Table 2.1.

Table 2.1 outlines three structural categories: a deep core of fundamental normative and ontological axioms that define a person's underlying personal philosophy, a near (policy) core of basic strategies and policy positions for achieving deep core beliefs in the policy area or subsystem in question, and a set of secondary aspects comprising a multitude of instrumental decisions and information searches necessary to implement the policy core in the specific policy area. The three structural categories are arranged in order of decreasing resistance to

TABLE 2.1   Structure of Belief Systems of Policy Elites[*]

| | Deep (Normative) Core | Near (Policy) Core | Secondary Aspects |
|---|---|---|---|
| Defining characteristics | Fundamental normative and ontological axioms | Fundamental policy positions concerning the basic strategies for achieving normative axioms of deep core. | Instrumental decisions and information searches necessary to implement policy core. |
| Scope | Part of basic personal philosophy. Applies to all policy areas. | Applies to policy area of interest (and perhaps a few more). | Specific to policy area/subsystem of interest. |
| Susceptibility to change | Very difficult; akin to a religious conversion. | Difficult, but can occur if experience reveals serious anomalies. | Moderately easy; this is the topic of most administrative and even legislative policymaking. |
| Illustrative components | 1. The nature of man:<br>　i. Inherently evil vs. socially redeemable.<br>　ii. Part of nature vs. dominion over nature.<br>　iii. Narrow egoists vs contractarians.<br>2. Relative priority of various ultimate values: freedom, security, power, knowledge, health, love, beauty, etc.<br>3. Basic criteria of distributive justice: Whose welfare counts? Relative weights of self, primary groups, all people, future generations, nonhuman beings, etc. | 1. Proper scope of governmental vs. market activity.<br>2. Proper distribution of authority among various units (e.g., levels) of government.<br>3. Identification of social groups whose welfare is most critical.<br>4. Orientation on substantive policy conflicts, e.g., environmental protection vs. economic development.<br>5. Magnitude of perceived threat to those values.<br>6. Basic choices concerning policy instruments, e.g., coercion vs. inducements vs. persuasion.<br>7. Desirability of participation by various segments of society:<br>　i. Public vs. elite participation.<br>　ii. Experts vs. elected officials.<br>8. Ability of society to solve problems in this policy area:<br>　i. Zero-sum competition vs. potential for mutual accommodation.<br>　ii. Technological optimism vs. pessimism. | 1. Most decisions concerning administrative rules, budgetary allocations, disposition of cases, statutory interpretation, and even statutory revision.<br>2. Information concerning program performance, the seriousness of the problems, etc. |

[*]The Policy Core and Secondary Aspects also apply to governmental programs.

change, that is, the deep core is much more resistant than the secondary aspects.

U.S. air pollution policy once again serves as an example, in this case to illustrate the structure of belief systems. The Clean Air Coalition and the Economic Efficiency Coalition have been fundamentally divided over the extent to which the pursuit of individual freedom in a market economy should be constrained in order to protect the health of "susceptible populations" (e.g., those already suffering from respiratory diseases). Members of the Clean Air Coalition argue that the protection accorded susceptible populations should be virtually absolute, while members of the Economic Efficiency Coalition have been more willing to put these populations at some risk in the interests of individual liberty and increased production. This normative difference in the policy core of the two coalitions probably reflected a deep core difference in the relative priority accorded freedom (or efficiency) versus equality, a conflict underlying many policy disputes (Rokeach, 1973; Okun, 1975).

Differences on this issue and others helped members of the two coalitions to adopt quite different positions on such policy core issues as the proper scope of governmental (vs. market) activity, the proper role of the federal government, the advantages of using coercion vs. other policy instruments, the overall seriousness of the air pollution problem in the United States, and so on. These are the sorts of issues that were decided in the 1970 Clean Air Amendments and that, despite numerous attacks, have remained largely unchanged in law since then (Mazmanian and Sabatier, 1989:Chap. 4). While there have been some issues (most notably, nondegradation and acid rain) since 1970 that have involved core disputes, most policy making has focused on secondary aspects, such as determining which air quality standards are adequate to protect susceptible populations, which auto emissions standards would minimize emissions without wrecking the domestic auto industry, the feasibility of using parking surcharges as a tool for reducing vehicle miles traveled, and the technical validity of various techniques for monitoring atmospheric emissions.

It would be absurd to assume that all members of an advocacy coalition have precisely the same belief system. But, based upon the assumption that elite belief systems are hierarchical (i.e., that abstract beliefs are more salient and more resistant to change than more specific ones), the ACF hypothesizes that most members of a coalition will show substantial agreement on the policy core issues outlined in Table 2.1, which need to be addressed by any belief system. In addition, positions on these issues will be slower to change than those concerning the secondary (implementing) aspects of a belief system. In short:

*Hypothesis 2:* Actors within an advocacy coalition will show substantial consensus on issues pertaining to the policy core, although less so on secondary aspects.

*Hypothesis 3:* An actor (or coalition) will give up secondary aspects of a belief system before acknowledging weaknesses in the policy core.

While this argument leaves open the precise amount of consensus on the policy core necessary for an advocacy coalition to be said to "exist," its basic thrust should be quite clear. It is also far from self-evident, as it disagrees with those who proclaim the end of ideology (Bell, 1960), perceive the domination of short-term "coalitions of convenience" (Riker, 1962), view specific beliefs as more salient than abstract ones (Wilker and Milbrath, 1972), or see policy change as a muddled process in which policy technocrats play a major role (Heclo, 1978).

Methods for investigating the content of belief systems include elite surveys, panels of knowledgeable observers (Hart, 1976), and content analysis of relevant documents (Axelrod, 1976). Given the rather technical nature of many secondary aspects and the focus on changes in beliefs over a decade or more, content analyses of government documents (e.g., legislative and administrative hearings) and interest-group publications probably offer the best prospects for systematic empirical work on changes in elite beliefs (see the Methodological Appendix).

The entire notion of a belief system organized around a set of core values and policy strategies, plus implementing activities, assumes some psychological predilection for instrumental rationality and cognitive consistency on the part of policy elites. It does not, however, take issue with the implications of Simon's recent work suggesting that cognitive structures resemble semiautonomous filing cabinets into which one places new information (Newell and Simon, 1972; Simon, 1979). Instead, the framework supposes that policy elites seek to better understand the world within a particular policy area ("filing cabinet") in order to identify means to achieve their fundamental objectives. Such thought produces pressures for evaluative consistency (Tesser, 1978:295).

The framework also presumes some (modest) selection pressures in favor of policy elites with a capacity for reasoned discourse involving the major issues relevant to their policy subsystem (e.g., air pollution control). Insofar as policy discussions among insiders are based on reasoned argument, actors holding blatantly inconsistent or unsubstantiated positions will lose credibility. That loss may not be completely debilitating for their position, but it will force them to expend scarce political resources in its support and will eventually be to their competitive disadvantage (Brewer and de Leon, 1983).

Once something has been accepted as a policy core belief, however, powerful ego-defense, peer-group, and organizational forces create considerable resistance to change, even in the face of countervailing empirical evidence or internal inconsistencies (Festinger, 1957; Argyris and Schon, 1978; Janis, 1983). The literature on cognitive dissonance and selective perception is enormous and far from conclusive (Abelson et al., 1968; Wicklund and Brehm, 1976; Greenwald and Ronis, 1978; Innis, 1978). But, *when* salient beliefs and/or the egos of policy elites are at stake, the evidence of selective perception and partisan analysis is strong enough to warrant a prominent place in any model (Schiff, 1962; Smith, 1968; Steinbruner, 1974; Cameron, 1978; Innis, 1978; Nelkin, 1979; Mazur, 1981; Fiske and Taylor, 1984; Etheredge, 1985).

## IV. COALITION LEARNING AND EXTERNAL PERTURBATION

Policy change within a subsystem can be understood as the product of two processes. First, advocacy coalitions within the subsystem attempt to translate the policy cores and the secondary aspects of their belief systems into governmental programs. Although most programs will involve some compromise among coalitions, there will usually be a dominant coalition and one or more minority coalitions (Wamsley, 1983). Each will seek to realize its objectives over time through increasing its political resources and through policy-oriented learning (to be discussed in the following chapter). The second process is one of external perturbation, that is, the effects of *system-wide* events—changes in socioeconomic conditions, outputs from other subsystems, and changes in the system-wide governing coalition—on the resources and constraints of subsystem actors.

The framework argues, however, that the policy core of an advocacy coalition is quite resistant to change over time. This leads to the following hypothesis:

*Hypothesis 4:* The core (basic attributes) of a governmental program is unlikely to be significantly revised as long as the subsystem advocacy coalition that instituted the program remains in power.

This hypothesis assumes that a coalition seeks power to translate its core beliefs into policy. It will not abandon those core beliefs merely to stay in power, although it may well abandon secondary aspects and even try to incorporate some of the opponents' core as *secondary* aspects of the program.

Likewise, the relative strength of different advocacy coalitions within a subsystem will seldom be sufficiently altered by events *internal* to the subsystem (i.e., by efforts to increase resources or to "outlearn" opponents) to overthrow a dominant coalition. Hence:

*Hypothesis 5:* The core (basic attributes) of a governmental action program is unlikely to be changed in the absence of significant perturbations external to the subsystem, that is, changes in socioeconomic conditions, system-wide governing coalitions, or policy outputs from other subsystems.

These hypotheses suggest that, while minority coalitions can seek to improve their relative position through augmenting their resources and "outlearning" their adversaries, their basic hope of gaining power within the subsystem resides in waiting for some *external* event to significantly increase their political resources.

If Hypothesis 5 is correct, the type of policy-oriented learning discussed in the next chapter is unlikely by itself to significantly alter the *policy core* attributes of a governmental action program. But it can still lead to substantial changes in the secondary aspects. Learning by a minority coalition may demonstrate such major deficiencies in the core of a program that the majority will acknowledge these deficiencies or, more likely, a system-wide learning process will occur in which system-wide leaders eventually overturn the dominant coalition. A possible example would be the efforts of economists over the past twenty years to demonstrate the inefficiencies of governmental regulation of airline fares and entry—a campaign that eventually led to the abolition of the Civil Aeronautics Board (Derthick and Quirk, 1985; Brown, 1987; Nelson, 1987). The airline deregulation case is analyzed in detail in Chapter 5.[10]

## V. CONCLUSION

This chapter has presented the basic features of the advocacy coalition framework (ACF) of policy change over periods of a decade or more. The next chapter will discuss the dynamics of policy-oriented learning—one of the principal features of the ACF—in greater detail.

The ACF starts from three premises that, in my view, are prerequisites for any theory of policy change. First, it deals with periods of sufficient length to incorporate the enlightenment function of policy research and to give some attention to policy-oriented learning. Periods of a decade are also long enough to incorporate at least one policy cycle (consisting of formulation, implementation, and reformulation) at a specific level of government. Second, the ACF focuses on policy subsystems—rather than specific governmental institutions—as the principal unit for understanding policy change. This premise follows a long tradition in the policy literature, although the expansion of the list of subsystem actors beyond traditional iron triangles to include the generators and disseminators of ideas, as well as an intergovernmental dimension, is fairly recent. Third, the ACF emphasizes the intergovernmental nature of policy subsystems. Subsystems will usually include actors from all levels of government, and there is no a priori assumption that national actors are more important than subnational ones.

The ACF then incorporates four additional major building blocks. First, it follows Pressman and Wildavsky (1973) and Majone (1980) in assuming that public policies can be conceptualized in the same manner as political belief systems, that is, as sets of value priorities, perceptions of important causal relationships, perceptions of the seriousness of the problem, and perceptions of the efficacy of various sorts of institutional relationships as means of attaining those value priorities. Second, it builds upon aspects of Majone (1989) and the political belief system literature (Putnam, 1976) in assuming that both policies and belief systems have a structure composed of a very abstract deep core, a policy core relating to that specific subsystem, and a large number of secondary aspects. The abstract levels are hypothesized to be stable, in large part because they are largely normative issues inculturated in childhood and largely impervious to empirical evidence. Third, the ACF chooses advocacy coalitions—that is, sets of actors from both public and private institutions at various levels of government who share critical aspects of a belief system—as the principal vehicle for aggregating individuals into a manageable number of units. It perceives a coalition as seeking to manipulate institutional rules and actors in order to achieve its policy goals. The ACF thus represents a fundamental departure from most political science research, which tends to aggregate by type of institution (such as the Congress, presidency, and interest groups), usually at a single level of government. The choice of advocacy coalitions facilitates a focus on policy-oriented learning, as the actors within a coalition share basic values and search for means to accomplish them. It also facilitates an intergovernmental focus: A coalition doing poorly in Washington is not helpless but instead can focus its efforts at subnational levels where it is more powerful. Fourth, the ACF follows Heclo (1974) in distinguishing the internal dynamics within a subsystem from the perturbations in the broader political system and socioeconomic environment. It goes out on a limb by hypothesizing that the latter are necessary for changes in the core of governmental policy within a subsystem.

The ACF certainly represents a radical departure from the stages metaphor in its focus on belief systems, policy-oriented learning, subsystem vs. external system, and aggregation by advocacy coalitions and in its ability to deal with multiple, interacting sets of cycles, consisting of formulation, implementation, and reformulation, at different levels of government (or in different states or localities at the same level). It also differs from the stages metaphor in that it identifies two specific motors of change: (1) individuals' efforts to achieve their goals over time (with individuals aggregated into coalitions) and (2) the effects of perturbations exogenous to the subsystem (i.e., changes in system-wide governing coalitions, changes in socioeconomic conditions, or policy outputs from other subsystems) on the resources and beliefs of subsystem actors, and eventually on policy change.[11]

The ACF also differs from other major theories of the policy process:

*1. Lowi's Arenas of Power* (Lowi, 1964, 1972; Ripley and Franklin, 1982). The ACF ignores the fundamental tenet of this approach, namely, that the policy process differs substantially in distributive, regulatory, and redistributive arenas. Such differences may exist, but they are not deemed important enough to include in the ACF.

*2. Kingdon's Multiple Streams* (Kingdon, 1984). Kingdon is one of the few political scientists to deal seriously with the role of ideas and analysis in policy making. But the ACF views the "analytical" stream as much more integrated with the "political" stream than does Kingdon; it deals with the entire policy process, not just agenda setting and policy formulation; and it tries to relate Kingdon's "windows of opportunity" for major policy change to specific types of changes in events exogenous to the policy subsystem (see Sabatier, 1991a).

3. *Hofferbert's Funnel of Causality* (Hofferbert, 1974; Mazmanian and Sabatier, 1980). The ACF incorporates Hofferbert's emphasis on the importance of the socioeconomic environment but differs from him in distinguishing the policy subsystem from the broader political system, emphasizing policy-oriented learning, and stressing intergovernmental relations.

4. *Statist Theory* (Skocpol, 1979; Skowronek, 1982). The ACF completely rejects the fundamental tenet of this approach, that there exists a unified, relatively autonomous "state." In fact, this approach strikes me as highly dubious in countries like the United States, given federalism, the diversity of interests and values represented by various governmental institutions, and the permeability of most institutions to external influences. Statist theory is even misleading in supposedly centralized regimes like France (Ashford, 1981a).

5. *Institutional Rational Choice* (Kiser and Ostrom, 1982; Ostrom, 1990; Chubb and Moe, 1990). The ACF agrees with these scholars that institutional rules affect individual behavior. But it goes beyond them in viewing such rules as the product of strategies by advocacy coalitions over time. It also expands the range of guidance instruments from institutional rules to include changes in budgets and personnel (Sabatier and Pelkey, 1987). Finally, it gives socioeconomic conditions more importance than do most institutional rational choice scholars.

6. *Traditional Pluralist Theory* (Truman, 1951). On the one hand, the ACF accepts Truman's emphasis on the importance of interest-group competition in molding governmental institutions. On the other hand, advocacy coalitions are *not* simply constellations of interest groups; their "members" also include legislators, agency officials, researchers, and journalists. Second, the ACF completely rejects Truman's naive assumption that all latent interests will be effectively represented (Sabatier, 1992). Third, the ACF emphasizes policy-oriented learning and hierarchical belief systems, concepts completely neglected by Truman. Finally, unlike Truman, the ACF does not rely on cross-cutting cleavages to assure system stability; instead, the emphasis is on stable system parameters (e.g., social structure), policy brokers, and stable belief systems.

In short, the ACF differs significantly from not only the stages metaphor but other theories of the policy process as well. While it borrows elements from many of them—particularly Hofferbert, institutional rational choice, and pluralism—the basic insight was taken from Heclo's book on the evolution of welfare policy in Britain and Sweden. Moreover, several of the fundamental elements—including the importance of intergovernmental relations, the role of policy-oriented learning, and the ability to conceptualize public policy as a belief system—are derived primarily from the implementation literature (Pressman and Wildavsky, 1973; Mazmanian and Sabatier, 1981, 1989).

## NOTES

1. Fortunately, this situation is changing. A number of recent studies do an excellent job of exploring the intergovernmental dimension in several policy areas (Anton, 1989; Wood, 1991; Scholtz et al., 1991).

2. This chapter borrows heavily from Sabatier (1987, 1988).

3. The debate in the implementation literature between "top-downers" and "bottom-uppers" is *not* over whether "street level bureaucrats" exercise considerable discretion. Everyone agrees on that. Instead, the debate is over whether central decision makers have any real capacity to constrain that discretion or if they should basically accommodate themselves to whatever the street level bureaucrats wish to do (Sabatier, 1986; Palumbo, 1988).

4. On the one hand, the actual activation of latent interests depends upon the perceptions and strategies of actors within the subsystem. On the other hand, an analyst interested in predicting future events within a subsystem would do well to also identify latent constituencies and the circumstances under which they could be mobilized.

5. Beginning in the 1980s, one might consider adding a third, the Economic Efficiency Coalition. Its belief system relies very heavily on principles of welfare economics and includes both (1) critiques of EPA regulations and (2) a preference for substituting economic incentives for command and control regulation. Dominated by research economists such as Bob Hahn, Larry White, and Lester Lave, it would also include many officials in the EPA's Office of Policy Analysis, the Office of Management and Budget (OMB), the Environmental Defense Fund (EDF), and the California Legislative Analyst's Office, as well as a few legislators, notably former Senator Tim Wirth (Liroff, 1986; Cook, 1986; the 1988 symposium of the *Columbia Journal of Environmental Law;* Hahn and Hester, 1989). I have chosen not to add it as a third coalition, in part because most economists traditionally have mirrored the views of the Economic Feasibility Coalition (see, for example, White, 1982) and, in part, because it is not clear that the EDF and Wirth share the OMB's passion for critiquing EPA rules on welfare economics principles.

6. A weaker hypothesis would suggest that an advocacy coalition will consist of (1) a set of farily stable members with compatible policy cores and (2) temporary members who float in and out depending upon the particular policy dispute. For example, Ackerman and Hassler (1981) report that the ranks of the Clean Air Coalition were augmented during the mid-1970s by western coal companies, whose supply of low-sulfur coal led them to join environmentalists in seeking stringent emissions controls on utilities (which would give them a competitive advantage against high-sulfur midwestern coal). But this alliance was subsequently disrupted when Congressman Henry Waxman, one of the leaders of the Clean Air Coalition, suggested a uniform nationwide tax on utilities as a means of dealing with the acid rain problem and dealing equitably with the concerns of midwestern coal companies and utilities.

7. The literature on coalition formation in multiparty parliamentary regimes has found both minimum size and ideological constraints to be important factors, with their relative importance varying by country (Browne, 1970; de Swann,

1973; Taylor and Laver, 1973; Dodd, 1976; Warwick, 1979; Hinckley, 1981; Browne and Dreijamis, 1982; Franklin and Mackie, 1984; Zariski, 1984). Unfortunately, the literature on (interest-group) coalitions within subsystems over periods of at least a decade appears to be remarkably sparse and unsophisticated, with the study by Wildavsky and Tenenbaum (1981) among the more suggestive. The problem probably resides in methodological difficulties in determining what constitutes a coalition when using, for example, legislative and budgetary hearings as a data base.

8. In the case of air pollution control, the willingness of western coal companies to side with environmentalists against midwestern coal companies would be a case of self-interest (competitive market advantage) over laissez-faire ideology (Ackerman and Hassler, 1981). But the reluctance of manufacturers of pollution control equipment to openly ally themselves with environmentalists in most controversies over the past twenty years would suggest that ideology can likewise restrain the pursuit of self-interest.

9. Among the major strands in this literature are (1) the work of Converse (1964) and many others who view the Left-Right continuum as critical; (2) the "operational code" studies examining elite assumptions concerning the nature of political conflict (George, 1969; Putnam, 1973); (3) the work of Axelrod (1976) diagramming the causal assumptions of policy elites; and (4) the work of Conover and Feldman (1984) on "schema theory." For a summary of much of this literature, see Putnam (1976:Chap. 4). The distinction between "secondary aspects" and "core" is rather similar to Steinbruner's (1974) distinction between "cybernetic" and "cognitive" levels of thinking and to Argyris and Schon's (1978) analysis of "single" and "double loop" learning.

10. Brown and Stewart (Chapter 5) conclude that, while the economic critique played a critical role in deregulation, it was not sufficient to bring about a change in the policy core of federal airline policy. In short, their analysis basically supports Hypothesis 5, although they would argue that the distinction between internal and external events is not as clear as I have made it.

11. The basic forces producing change within a policy subsystem are thus similar to biological theories of change within an ecosystem: There are both individuals striving for specific goals and exogenous perturbations. This similarity is quite intentional. The major difference is that the ACF does not identify a single, dominant human goal analogous to biologists' assumption that individual organisms are "seeking" to maximize their reproductive success.

# 3

# The Dynamics of
# Policy-Oriented Learning

## HANK C. JENKINS-SMITH AND PAUL A. SABATIER

A central feature of the advocacy coalition framework (ACF) is its focus on the belief systems of advocacy coalitions. A belief system guides coalition members concerning the problems that should receive the highest priority, the causal factors that need to be examined most closely, and the governmental institutions most likely to be favorably disposed to the coalition's point of view. The coalition then seeks to alter the behavior of governmental institutions in order to achieve its policy goals over time.

Many aspects of a coalition's belief system are susceptible to change on the basis of scientific and technical analysis. In air pollution control, for example, the accumulation of scientific information over the past thirty years has greatly improved our knowledge of the concentrations of specific pollutants in different cities. It has altered the beliefs of many people in both the Clean Air Coalition and the Economic Efficiency Coalitions and changed their perceptions of the effects of several pollutants, notably ozone, on human health (Lave and Seskin, 1977). Science has dramatically increased our understanding of acid rain after two decades of debate between members of the two coalitions concerning the seriousness of the problem, the relative contributions of natural processes versus emissions from midwestern utilities as causal factors, and the appropriate policy instruments to be used in addressing the problem. The eventual policy compromise on acid rain incorporated into the 1990 Clean Air Amendments was the result of many factors, including the replacement of Ronald Reagan by George Bush in the White House. Nevertheless, the acid rain issue illustrates the potential importance of technical information in shaping the emergence of an issue as well as perceptions of its seriousness, its causes, and the likely consequences of various policy alternatives (National Acid Precipitation Assessment Program, 1990).

The ACF attempts to integrate the role of such technical analysis into the overall process of policy change. The previous chapter stressed that changing the really important components of a coalition's belief system—its policy core—is likely to require the gradual accumulation of evidence over a long period of time via "the enlightenment function" of policy and scientific research. It also hypothesized that the accumulation of such evidence is not, by itself, sufficient to alter core aspects of *public policy*; such alterations also require changes in the distribution of political resources of subsystem actors arising from shocks exogenous to the subsystem (Hypothesis 5).

Within these general principles, this chapter examines the role of technical analysis in greater detail. The first section provides an overview of the process of policy-oriented learning. The next lays out a basic scenario for that process. The bulk of the chapter examines the effects of a variety of factors—including the level of conflict, the analytical tractability of the issue, and the analytical forum utilized—in establishing conditions conducive to policy-oriented learning *between* coalitions with different belief systems.

## I. POLICY-ORIENTED LEARNING

Policy-oriented learning involves relatively enduring alterations of thought or behavioral intentions that result from experience and which are concerned with the attainment or revision of the precepts of the belief system of individuals or of collectivities (such as advocacy coalitions).

Given the ACF's focus on advocacy coalitions, policy-oriented learning is primarily concerned with changes over time in the distribution of beliefs of people within a coalition or within the broader policy subsystem. Such changes in the distribution of beliefs will be a function of several different processes, including: (1) individual learning and attitudinal change, (2) the diffusion of new beliefs and attitudes among individuals, (3) turnover in individuals within any collectivity, (4) group dynamics, such as the polarization of homogeneous groups or groups in conflict, and (5) rules for aggregating preferences and for promoting (or impeding) communication among individuals (Petty and Cacioppo, 1981; Rajecki, 1982; Kiser and Ostrom, 1982; Janis, 1983; Pierce and Rochon, 1984; Sabatier et al., 1987). Changes in the distribution of beliefs within a coalition generally will start with individual learning or turnover, be resisted by group dynamics, and then get diffused throughout the group. Diffusion depends upon the rate of turnover, the compatibility of the information with existing beliefs, the persuasiveness of the evidence, and the political pressures for change.

Policy-oriented learning can involve a variety of topics. The following are among the most important:

*Improving One's Understanding of the Status of Goals and Other Variables Identified as Important by One's Belief System.* Of particular importance is monitoring the status of critical goals to see if they fall below acceptable levels, thereby indicating a performance gap. For example, participants in the Clean Air Coalition have expended a great deal of effort monitoring air quality because that is a critical variable affecting one of their core values, the protection of public health. Conversely, members of the Economic Efficiency Coalition have concentrated on estimating the economic costs of pollution control programs because that deals with one of their critical variables, economic viability.

*Refining One's Understanding of Logical and Causal Relationships Internal to a Belief System.* This process typically focuses on the search for improved mechanisms to attain core values. For example, automotive emissions are a function of (1) emissions per vehicle mile and (2) vehicle miles traveled. Members of the Clean Air Coalition tried hard during the 1970s and 1980s to find effective means of reducing both. The former included R & D into low-emission propulsion systems and cleaner fuels. The latter involved a series of studies and experiments with carpooling, parking surcharges, and other "transportation controls."

Although proponents will be loathe to reexamine core beliefs, experience and opponents' activities may eventually force them to acknowledge erroneous assumptions or implicit goal contradictions. For example, the EPA's efforts during the 1970s to experiment with a variety of mechanisms to reduce vehicle miles traveled met with numerous local debacles, congressional rebuffs, and discouraging conclusions from contracted research. The agency was eventually forced by Congress in 1977 to give up its efforts to reduce vehicle miles traveled. While its reasons for persisting for so long were multiple, one of the more important ones was probably its (causal) assumption that such programs were *necessary* to achieve ambient air quality levels in many urban areas. Thus its inability to find effective and politically palatable policy instruments would entail a strategic retreat on its *core* value of protecting human health (Mazmanian and Sabatier, 1989:Chap. 4). For similar examples in other policy areas, see Cameron (1978) and Robinson (1982).

*Identifying and Responding to Challenges to One's Belief System.* Exogenous events, a loss of political resources, opponents' activities, or a variety of other factors, may force proponents to revise their belief systems by incorporating aspects of opponents' beliefs. But every effort will be made to restrict change to the secondary aspects and thus keep one's core beliefs intact.[1]

Since the early 1970s, for example, economists have criticized the inefficiency of the legal command and control approach of the 1970 Clean Air Amendments and have argued instead for a variety of economic incentives such as emission fees, transferable pollution credits, and so on (Kneese and Bower, 1968; Schultze, 1977; Friedlaender, 1978; White, 1982). The criticism eventually became too important to ignore. Rather than rethink the basic approach of the 1970 Clean Air Act, however, most EPA officials and their congressional supporters simply incorporated into the 1977 and 1990 Clean Air Amendments a few variants of economic incentives, such as offsets and bubbles, as optional instruments in their overall command and control strategy (Liroff, 1986; Cook, 1988). The lone exception was acid rain; the 1990 Amendments adopted a marketable permit system as the basic policy instrument. The reasons were multiple, but among the most important was the pivotal role of the Environmental Defense Fund (EDF), a national environmental group that has embraced economic incentives as the best means of achieving additional gains in environmental quality while also giving industry the flexibility to adopt least-cost solutions (Cohen, 1992).

Policy-oriented learning is an ongoing process of search and adaptation motivated by the desire to realize core policy beliefs. When confronted with constraints or opportunities, actors attempt to respond in a manner consistent with their policy core. Although exogenous events or opponents' activities may eventually force the reexamination of core beliefs, most learning manifests itself in the secondary aspects of a belief system or governmental program. There are two principal reasons why most belief change is concentrated in the secondary aspect. First, the policy core consists largely of items that are primarily normative—and thus largely beyond direct empirical challenge—while the secondary aspects consist of items more susceptible to change on the basis of empirical evidence. Second, the ACF assumes that beliefs are hierarchically organized, with the deep core and, to a lesser extent, the policy core consisting of rather abstract values learned in childhood that are tenaciously held (see, for example, Peffley and Hurwitz, 1985). Thus, changing an aspect of a coalition's policy core will almost always require the accumulation of considerable evidence from a variety of sources for over a decade or more—what Weiss (1977a) has termed "the enlightenment function of policy research"—and even revisions of its secondary aspects will usually take several years.

Policy-oriented learning normally entails experimenting with a variety of guidance instruments and other implementing mechanisms over time in an effort to achieve one's policy goals (Sabatier and Pelkey, 1987). Dissatisfaction with the performance of a specific mechanism—in terms of either its policy outputs at the operational level or its resultant inability to ameliorate the problem—will lead program proponents to reexamine their strategy (see the feedback loops in Figure 2.1, Chapter 2).

But learning from experience is very difficult in a world where performance gaps are difficult to measure, well-developed causal theories are often lacking, controlled experimentation is virtually impossible, opponents are doing everything possible to muddle the situation, and even allies' motives are often suspect because of personal and organizational rivalries. Little wonder that advocacy coalitions are constantly arguing about the advisability of different strategies or that many seek to explore simultaneously many strategies in the hope that a few will fall on fertile soil.

Nevertheless, policy-oriented learning does occur. In a world of scarce resources, those who do not learn are at a competitive disadvantage in realizing their goals. Raw political power may carry the day against superior evidence, but the costs to one's credibility in a democratic society can be considerable. Moreover, resources expended—

particularly in the form of favors called in—are not available for future use. Thus those who can most effectively marshal persuasive evidence, thereby conserving their political resources, are more likely to win in the long run than those who neglect technical arguments.

## II. THE ADVOCACY USE OF ANALYSIS AND POLICY-ORIENTED LEARNING: A SCENARIO

Policy-oriented learning occurs in the context of a *political* process where people compete over the authoritative allocation of values and over the ability to use the instruments of government—including coercion—in their behalf (Easton, 1965; Lowi, 1969). This process is not a disinterested search for "truth."

At least four principles govern the role of policy analysis (or technical information) in policy-oriented learning and eventually in policy change. First, analysis usually is stimulated by either threats to core values or perceived opportunities to realize core values (Jenkins-Smith and Weimer, 1985). Second, the crucial role of technical information is to alert people to the extent to which a given situation affects their interests and values. Third, once political actors have developed a position on a policy issue, analysis is used primarily in an "advocacy" fashion, that is, to justify and elaborate that position (Sabatier, 1978; Wildavsky, 1979; Mazur, 1981). Fourth, actors generally find it necessary to engage in an analytical debate—that is, to present technical substantiation for their positions—if they are to succeed in translating their beliefs into policy. In political systems with dispersed power, they can seldom develop a majority position through the raw exercise of power. Instead, they must seek to *convince* other actors of the soundness of their position concerning the problem and the consequences of one or more policy alternatives.

One scenario is depicted in Figure 3.1. A few people perceive a problem, such as air pollution, that affects their core values and then search for information concerning the seriousness of the problem and its causes. They identify one or more causes—such as emissions from a local steel mill—and based upon certain understandings of the institutional arrangements needed to correct emitters' behavior, they propose one or more policies (or governmental action programs) to accomplish their objectives. Those who feel themselves aggrieved by the proposed policy and have the resources to do something have a number of options. They can:

1. Challenge the validity of the data concerning the seriousness of the problem;
2. Challenge the causal assumptions concerning:
   a. The validity of technical aspects, such as the links between emissions, ambient air quality, and health effects;
   b. The efficacy of institutional arrangements that will provide the necessary changes in behavior;

46

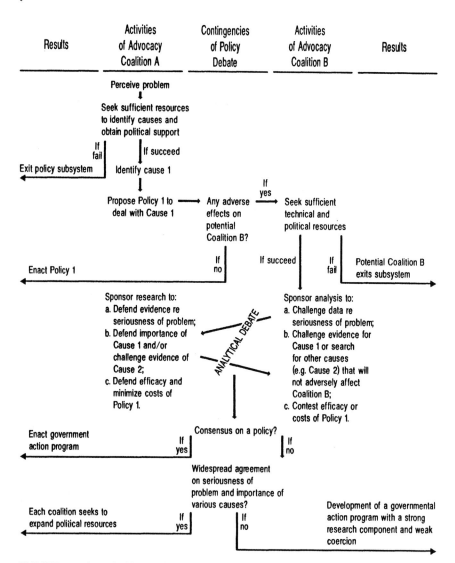

FIGURE 3.1   Analytical interactions between advocacy coalitions: initial stages

3. Attempt to mobilize political opposition to the proposal by pointing to costs to themselves and others, that is, by creating or enlarging their coalition.

The original group normally responds to these challenges, thus initiating a political and analytical debate. The process is usually mediated by policy brokers interested in keeping the conflict within acceptable limits, and the result is often some sort of governmental action program. In a new policy area, knowledge about the seriousness of the problem and the validity of various causal assumptions is normally sufficiently uncertain and the political resources of those challenging the status quo sufficiently modest that the initial governmental program involves a significant research component but little coercion.

If such research and policy analysis provides evidence of a reasonably serious problem, identifies one or more probable causes, and convinces people that a proposed set of institutional arrangements will address the problem without politically unacceptable costs, a more substantial governmental action program will result. Implementation will be assigned to one or more agencies and the problem will disappear into a relatively closed subsystem. Participants usually will seek to refine their understanding of the causal factors and the efficacy of various policy instruments over time. In order to keep potential losers from appealing to outsiders for assistance, efforts will be made to provide inclusive negotiated compromises within the parameters of the program core (Derthick, 1979; Wamsley, 1983). This strategy will normally continue until external (i.e., systemic) conditions change sufficiently to alter the balance of power within the subsystem.

In some cases, research can so substantially alter actors' perceptions of the problem that major changes result. For example, early pollution control efforts in Los Angeles were based on the assumption that household furnaces were the major source of emissions. But when Dr. A. J. Haagen-Smit of Cal Tech in the mid-1950s identified photochemical smog—not particulates—as the major pollutant and automobiles as one of its major sources, local control of the problem no longer made much sense and authority was gradually transferred to state and federal officials (Hagevik, 1970; Krier and Ursin, 1977). In a somewhat similar fashion, federally sponsored research into the health effects of various pollutants—combined with a very imaginative program for diffusing that information to interested citizens—led directly to the formation of clean air interest groups in many urban areas during the late 1960s. In the process the balance of power in several local and state air pollution subsystems was significantly altered (Sabatier, 1975).

But "knowledge" does not suddenly appear, become universally accepted, and suggest unequivocal changes in governmental action programs. Instead, findings challenging the accepted wisdom concerning the seriousness of a given problem and its principal causes tend to emerge gradually over time and to be challenged by those who perceive

their interests to be adversely affected; research findings thus give rise to
the sort of analytical debate depicted in Figure 3.1. In the case of Los
Angeles air pollution, for example, Haagen-Smit's findings implicating
automobiles and oil refineries first emerged in about 1950 and were
challenged by (1) the refineries, which hired the Stanford Research Institute to dispute them, (2) the automobile companies, which launched
their own research program, and (3) local citizens, who were outraged
that they—rather than nasty corporate interests—might be implicated.
It was not until six to eight years later, under the aegis of the independent Air Pollution Foundation (a professionalized forum), that
most parties to the dispute accepted Haagen-Smit's argument about the
nature and sources of the problem (Krier and Ursin, 1977:Chap. 6).
There then ensued an equally long debate about control measures, with
initial efforts focusing on relatively inexpensive technological fixes designed to get the pollutants out of the Los Angeles Basin. Only when
those were proven to be infeasible did primary attention shift to reducing automotive emissions, and thus to increasing state and federal
involvement (Krier and Ursin, 1977:Chaps. 7–10).


## III. CONDITIONS CONDUCIVE TO
## POLICY-ORIENTED LEARNING ACROSS
## BELIEF SYSTEMS OF DIFFERENT COALITIONS

Policy-oriented learning includes learning *within* a coalition's belief
system and learning *across* the belief systems of different coalitions. The
former is relatively unproblematic: Members of an advocacy coalition
are always seeking to improve their understanding of variable states and
causal relationships consistent with their policy core. Likewise, they find
it easy to convince each other that attacks on their core programs are
based on invalid understandings of the world. When two cores conflict,
however, the tendency is for each coalition to talk past the other and
thus for a "dialogue of the deaf" to persist until external conditions dramatically alter the power balance within the subsystem. An example is
the debate between proponents of "soft" versus "hard" energy paths in
the United States (Robinson, 1982; Wildavsky and Tenenbaum, 1981;
Greenberger et al., 1983).

The task, then, is to identify the conditions under which a productive
analytical debate between members of *different* advocacy coalitions is
likely to occur. The indicator of such a debate is that one or both coalitions are led to alter policy core aspects of their belief system—or at least
very important secondary aspects—as a result of an observed dialogue
rather than a change in external conditions. In our view, the probability
of such learning is a function of at least three variables: (1) the level of
conflict, (2) the analytical tractability of the issue, and (3) the presence of a
professionalized forum.

## Level of Conflict

Levels of conflict reflect the degree of incompatibility of basic beliefs of competing coalitions. Conflict arises over analytical claims that directly or indirectly threaten core values and precepts. The more directly the analytical issue supports or threatens such precepts and values, the higher the stakes and thus the higher the level of conflict attending that issue. In general, the level of conflict has two countervailing effects on the provision of, and receptivity to, policy analysis by subsystem participants. First, the higher the level of conflict (i.e., the more directly the core is threatened), the greater the incentives of both subsystem coalitions to commit resources to provide and use analysis to defend the core. Second, as conflict rises and both coalitions have more at stake, the receptivity of subsystem participants to analytical findings that *threaten* their existing belief systems declines. It is in cases of intense conflict—with core values and precepts at stake—that the use of analysis is most likely to be employed primarily as a political resource; in such cases, strident claims that the defended belief system is appropriate and that the opposing one is fundamentally flawed are the norm. All sides have great incentives to make their "best case" and to give as little ground as possible. Learning (belief system modification) by subsystem members is particularly difficult in this situation because the stakes are high and the core threatened. This principle is apparently what one congressman had in mind who, when asked whether he weighed scientific advice in arriving at policy positions, responded: "We don't. That's ridiculous. You have a general posture, you use the scientist's evidence as ammunition. The idea that a guy starts with a clean slate and weighs the evidence is absurd" (Kingdon, 1973:223).

It is important to note that the analytical issues that become the actual focus of intense conflict may only *reflect* deeper disputes over core values. An ostensibly secondary technical claim that supports the core can become the focus of intense conflict when the outcome of the analytical dispute over that claim is seen as crucial to attainment of a core value. This was the case, for example, in analytical disputes over the implications of alternative Alaskan oil export policies for federal tax revenues in 1981 and 1983 (Jenkins-Smith, 1990:Chap. 5). In that debate, core disputes centered on economic efficiency versus protection of the domestic tanker fleet, though much of the debate was cast in terms of budgetary effects of various export options. Thus, while intense conflict indicates struggle over core issues, the actual focus of the debate may be deceptively technical or secondary in nature.

When the cores of competing coalitions are less directly threatened by analytical issues, the level of conflict is moderated. When core values and precepts draw support from a large number of interrelated beliefs about the world, a successful assault on one of those beliefs may not seriously jeopardize the core itself. In such situations, neither coalition sees the outcome of the debate as *decisive* for the core, but a favorable outcome would provide marginal support for that core. Thus, while both coalitions are stimulated to provide information and analysis supporting their respective belief systems, neither has excessively high stakes in the outcome. In such situations of moderate conflict, subsystem members will show some (but not unlimited) flexibility in questioning and modifying their own belief systems.[2]

Finally, an element of the policy debate may be of little importance to any of the coalitions in the subsystem. In this case, neither side has much to gain by rigidly adhering to a set of beliefs on the matter, but—more important—neither side has much reason to introduce relevant information or analysis. The net effect is that the matter receives little attention, and perhaps (at best) superficial analysis, because the engines of interest in the policy debate are focused elsewhere.[3]

We thus come to the first hypothesized condition for facilitating policy-oriented learning across coalitions and belief systems:

*Hypothesis 6:* Policy-oriented learning across belief systems is most likely when there is an intermediate level of informed conflict between the two. In such a situation, it is likely that:

1. Each coalition has the technical resources to engage in such a debate; and
2. The conflict be between secondary aspects of one belief system and core elements of the other or, alternatively, between important secondary aspects of the two belief systems.

In addition to level of conflict, several other factors affect the manner in which analysts promote, refute, or adjust to potentially threatening analytical claims. These include (1) the analytical tractability of the issue under study and (2) the nature of the forum in which the debate is conducted. Both factors affect the latitude for analytically plausible responses and strategies by subsystem participants.

## Analytical Tractability

Policy analysis, like science, is a social activity. It is grounded in the process of finding agreement among practitioners regarding what count as valid bases for claims regarding policy-relevant facts and values (Brecht, 1959:114). Although the process in policy analysis is necessarily more tentative, less precise, and more eclectic than is true of the natural sciences (Landau, 1977; MacRae, 1975), policy analysts have nonetheless developed a substantial body of concepts, methods, and guidelines—many of them derived from welfare economics—that constitute broadly accepted means to analyze policy issues and provide advice (Weiss, 1972; Stokey and Zeckhauser, 1979; Nachmias, 1979; Jenkins-Smith, 1990). Within given policy subfields, analysts typically come to recognize and employ common sources of data, concepts, and theories regarding the subject at hand (Kingdon, 1984:84). These commonalities provide the epistemological basis for convincing subsystem participants of the veracity of policy-relevant assertions. When the techniques of analysis, theory, and data regarding an issue are well developed and widely agreed upon, the validity of such assertions can be assessed with respect to a common standard. Also of importance is the existence of an agreed-upon value or goal with which to compare options. Determining the least-cost route for a sanitation vehicle or the optimal location for a fire station within an urban area, for example, would readily permit such an assessment (Greenberger et al., 1983). On these issues, the range of professionally acceptable analytical disagreement is fairly narrow. Such issues are analytically tractable.

But some issues are less subject than others to commonly acceptable analytical theories, concepts, and sources of data. Difficulties are particularly likely when the focus of analysis is on complex phenomena, when causal relationships span several policy areas, and when the issue concerns conflicting policy objectives. On such issues, analysis is subject to a great deal of uncertainty, different analysts are prone to provide estimates and analytical conclusions quite at variance with one another, and sufficient uncertainty exists to permit wide substantive disagreement without placing any of the protagonists beyond the pale of analytical plausibility. In general, the less well developed an area of inquiry, the more elusive the necessary data, and (above all) the weaker the *agreement* on theory and data, the greater the analytical intractability. Such intractability, in turn, admits a greater degree of analytically plausible differences of opinion among analysts.

In the extreme, for some policy issues the complexity and uncertainty are sufficient to admit wholly divergent belief systems whose epistemological foundations are so dissimilar that common bases for evaluating the validity of policy-relevant assertions are lacking entirely. On issues characterized by such fundamental differences in basic beliefs, analysts cannot resolve competing analytical claims by recourse to a common body of analytic knowledge and technique.[4] In effect, there is no overlap—no common ground—across belief systems from which to develop consensual resolution of competing analytical claims. Resolution of the policy debate in such situations awaits change imposed on belief systems, typically from outside the subsystem, such as turnover in subsystem participants through large-scale electoral change.

In general, then, the greater the analytical tractability with respect to a policy issue, the wider the range of subsystem conflict that could accommodate the use of analysis to modify competing belief systems. Conversely, intractable issues permit a wide range of plausible analytical positions, allowing subsystem participants with conflicting belief systems to promote and defend their conflicting analytical claims with relative impunity. Thus intractability serves to *decrease* the range of conflict within which belief system adjustment and policy learning take place.

These considerations lead us to the following hypotheses:

*Hypothesis 7:* Problems for which accepted quantitative data and theory exist are more conducive to policy-oriented learning than those in which data and theory are generally qualitative, quite subjective, or altogether lacking.

*Hypothesis 8:* Problems involving natural systems are more conducive to policy-oriented learning than those involving purely social or political systems because in the former many of the critical variables are *not* themselves active strategists and controlled experimentation is more feasible.

Both of these reasons would lead us to expect more policy-oriented learning in air pollution control than in, for example, mental health.

Even meeting these two conditions, however, does not guarantee continually improved understanding. There will still be some issues, analogous to the effects of extremely small doses of pathogens on diseases with long latency periods, that are essentially "trans-scientific," that is, extraordinarily difficult for science to deal with (Weinberg, 1972).

The analytical tractability of a policy issue can change over time. All other things being equal, the greater the amount of time and analytical resources devoted to a particular policy question, the more analytically tractable the issue is likely to become. The natural gas deregulation debate of the 1970s and early 1980s provides some support for this argument (Weyant, 1988). In that dispute, tremendous differences among competing analyses regarding the effect of deregulation on gas prices in the 1977–1978 period were substantially reduced by 1983–1984. Much of this narrowing can be attributed to the emergence of new data involving the response of suppliers and consumers to changes in gas prices over a period of years. This narrowing occurred despite the fact that competing coalitions remained tenaciously and vociferously wedded to their opposing policy preferences. In short, the analytical tractability of the issue increased over time—thereby enhancing the prospects for learning and belief system adjustment—even in the presence of intense differences over the appropriate policy.

Sustained analytical attention may also *erode* the epistemological consensus within a subsystem necessary to resolve the competing analytical claims underlying (or justifying) policy differences. For example, Aaron (1978) concluded that the millions of dollars spent analyzing the causes of poverty and racism in the 1960s and early 1970s eroded away the "simple faiths" upon which the political movement of the Great Society was based (see also Banfield, 1980; Rein and White, 1977). In this case, though learning (as the refutation of "simple faiths") clearly took place, the range of plausible analytical claims probably has been *broadened*, thus permitting subsystem participants wider latitude than they had previously in employing analysis to support preferred positions.

### The Nature of the Analytical Forum

Because analysis is a social process in which subsystem participants discuss policy-relevant facts and values, the number and kinds of people involved in the discussion is important. The forum (locus of discussion) can range from one in which all interested parties can take part—an open forum—to one in which admission is strictly controlled through some kind of screening—a closed forum. The importance of the degree of openness of the forum is twofold: (1) Certain types of screening for admission to the debate may assure that those who do participate can speak a common analytic language and find common bases for verification of analytical claims and (2) screening may limit both the number of belief systems represented in the forum and the degree of conflict among them.

*Open fora* are those in which all mobilized participants within the subsystem are able to actively engage in the debate. The defining criteria are (1) the lack of shared norms of scientific investigation and resolution of competing empirical claims and (2) an open arena for expression of a wide range of differing points of view. A typical example is the legislature, in which floor debates and committee hearings provide ample opportunity for all sides to be heard. In open fora, because there is a very broad range of backgrounds and levels of technical sophistication among the participants, room exists for a very wide range of beliefs. Furthermore, the common training, experience, and professional peer-group pressure that might serve to constrain analytical claims are lacking. In such fora, analyses can be expected to back many sides of the debate and generally will not provide a basis for consensus in resolving competing analytical claims. As one observer remarked about the open congressional forum: "The dominant mode of analysis on Capitol Hill, the pressure-group model, is uncongenial to policy analysis based on other models. . . . Policy analysis is seen as merely the continuation of pressure politics by other means, another weapon to be used to support predetermined positions. What counts is . . . what side it supports" (Seidman, 1977).

Not all fora admit such a plurality and range of beliefs and assumptions, however. By design, some fora effectively screen participants in a manner designed to foster commonality of language, assumptions, and belief systems. These include *professionalized fora*, which admit participants on the basis of professional training and technical competence. Ideally, such a forum would be made up of analysts committed to scientific norms who shared common theoretical and empirical presuppositions and could thus resolve a wide range of analytical disputes. Examples include (1) the conferences and journals of professional groups, such as the Air Pollution Control Association and the Society of American Foresters, (2) advisory committees, such as those of the National Academy of Sciences, (3) some "blue ribbon" technical advisory committees (Bulmer, 1983), (4) certain temporary groupings, such as when there are periodic calls for a "science court" (Mazur, 1981), and (5) perhaps some interagency technical committees.

Although little empirical research has been done comparing the resolution of policy analytic conflict in open and professonalized fora, recent and ongoing work in this area suggests that within some professionalized fora, even highly contentious issues on which a great deal is at stake for competing parties can be resolved by consensus. See Chapter 7 for an example dealing with the regulation of television technologies. Whether consensus is made possible because verification of factual assertions is made easier or because certain claims are excluded by dint of professional blinders remains an open and important question.

Often the screening of participants in analytical fora takes place on bases other than technical and professional proficiency. With some frequency, admission is tightly controlled for one or more of the following reasons: (1) protection of national security; (2) the issue is politically sensitive and the involved decision makers wish to explore the issue without the glare of public scrutiny; and (3) to limit "spurious" conflict within the forum by excluding members of known (and disapproved) predispositions (Phillips, 1977). Screening for such reasons results in *closed fora.*

Occasionally the creation of a closed forum can result in seriously biased and misleading analysis. When decision makers are committed to a particular policy option and want analysis to serve mainly as justification for that course of action, compliant analysis can be obtained by screening participants according to the policy viewpoint. Such strategies were employed with some frequency within the EPA under Director Ann Gorsuch Burford. The EPA reportedly employed "secret science courts" that excluded participation by a large fraction of the policy subsystem—including "not only the traditional public interest groups, but the entire scientific and public health community as well" (Rushefsky 1984). The resulting analysis provided the desired conclusions, but only at the cost of alienation of much of the policy subsystem.

These considerations lead to the following proposition:

*Hypothesis 9:* Policy-oriented learning across belief systems is most likely when there exists a forum that is:

1. Prestigious enough to force professionals from different coalitions to participate; and
2. Dominated by professional norms.

In sum, the characteristics of the forum can materially affect the way analysis is used. In open fora, greater latitude exists for expression of conflicting analytical claims. In these cases, analysis is likely to be employed by all sides in the debate, and rarely will analytical conflict be resolved. Restricted fora may enhance prospects for consensus by ensuring that participants have shared bases for verifying analytical claims (professionalized fora) or by screening participants for policy viewpoint. In either case, restricted fora may bias the values and beliefs introduced into the analysis.

## IV. CONCLUSION

The advocacy coalition framework seeks to provide an understanding of policy changes over periods of a decade or more that integrates (1) political scientists' traditional preoccupation with elections, institutional rules, and socioeconomic conditions and (2) the concerns of Carol Weiss and other scholars with the role of scientific information and policy analysis in that process. The ACF attempts to achieve these goals by incorporating political scientists' traditional concern with policy subsystems, critical elections, major socioeconomic changes, and institutional rules. It uses the concept of a belief system as the template on which change is measured, both with respect to the beliefs of different coalitions and the actual content of public policy. Belief systems include basic values, perceptions of the status of critical variables, and perceived causal relationships.[5] Since the latter two are clearly susceptible to systematic empirical analysis, they offer the vehicle through which technical (scientific) information can be introduced into the study of belief change and, ultimately, of policy change.

Advocacy coalitions—particularly if they are not dominant—have substantial incentives to engage in policy-oriented learning in order to (1) document performance gaps in existing governmental programs and (2) improve their understanding of the causal reasons for such gaps. The dominant coalition has incentives to provide evidence that no such gaps exist. Unless the dominant coalition has overwhelming political resources, the result will be an analytical debate in which each side attempts to *persuade* the others—as well as neutral parties, particularly potential policy brokers—of the validity of its claims.

For the members of one advocacy coalition, such persuasion is relatively easy. Since they share, by definition, most of their core beliefs, their differences are largely limited to the secondary aspects of their belief system. The bulk of this chapter has focused instead on the difficulties of promoting learning *across* different coalitions, whose members, by definition, disagree on many core values and causal assumptions. We have argued that such learning across coalitions is facilitated by: (1) a moderate level of conflict, (2) an issue that is analytically tractable (i.e., has widely accepted theories and quantitative indicators), and (3) the presence of a professionalized forum in which experts from competing coalitions must justify their claims before their peers.

Absent these conditions, however, proponents of the different points of view are likely to engage in blatant advocacy analysis, to talk past each other, to view each other as unscrupulous rascals, and to build barricades around existing beliefs. Under such "a dialogue of the deaf," learning across coalitions is very unlikely.

NOTES

1. When change cannot be restricted to secondary aspects of a coalition's belief system or the official governmental policy, we would hypothesize that adherents would seek to modify their core in the following sequence: (1) Add a portion of the opposing coalition's core; (2) delete a portion of one's own core; (3) develop a synthesis of the two cores; and (4) acquiesce to a replacement of one's core by the challenger's, but try to get portions of it incorporated into new secondary aspects.

2. Note, however, that the less support for the core that is available from other indirect or direct sources, the more important the remaining support becomes. In that way, what was previously a matter of only moderate conflict can be escalated to intense conflict if other support has been successfully assaulted. The reverse is also true; what were highly tendentious issues in the past, permitting little learning among subsystem members, can become less crucial to the core through the cumulation of broader support from other sources. This process permits relaxation of the rigid defense of posture that accompanies the vital defense of the core.

3. It is interesting to note that economic efficiency, as a policy value, used to hold this status. Economists such as Charles Schultze and Alfred Kahn have attempted, with some success, to lift it from this status by the injection of "partisan efficiency advocates"—for whom economic efficiency is prominently a part of the core—throughout the policy subsystems of government (Schultze, 1968).

4. One example of such divergent analytical bases involved proposed federal legislation to protect U.S. oil refineries from foreign competition in 1980. Those who sought to protect the refiners argued that foreign owners would use political influence to subsidize their own refineries, thereby putting U.S. refiners at a disadvantage. Their case was based on a political judgment about the behavior of foreign oil-producing countries. Those who sought to block the refinery protections relied on an economic efficiency analysis to argue that the subsidies would be too expensive for the oil-producing countries. The differences in the two approaches were nicely summarized in 1979 testimony by Jack O'Leary, then deputy secretary of energy: "[Analysts who oppose refinery protections] tend to be educated in operations research and economics, not in politics, and what I am describing here [world refinery markets] is really the manifestation of political phenomena. None of the pure analysts predicted the success of OPEC. All of them . . . took the view that oil surpluses would result in ever stronger downward pressure on the price of crude oil over time, and they were caught aback by the politics, the political incursion that forged the world in which we live today. And it seems to me that if we let the same view dictate our refinery policy, if we take the view that this is a classical world that obeys the classical rules and the best thing to do is save money in the short run and let the refineries develop willy-nilly where they will . . . we may find ourselves in a tragic position a decade from now" (O'Leary, 1979).

In this case, the outcome was decided in large part by President Jimmy Carter's loss to Ronald Reagan and the subsequent turnover in the executive branch (Jenkins-Smith, 1990:Chap. 6).

5. The concept of a belief system is borrowed from Converse's (1964) pioneering essay. Unfortunately, most political scientists restrict the content of belief systems to essentially normative elements, usually on a Left-Right scale. We seek to expand the content to include causal perceptions (see Sabatier and Hunter, 1989, for a comparison of the two approaches).

# PART II

# *Qualitative Case Studies of Policy Change and Learning*

Part of the problem in evaluating the advocacy coalition framework—or any theory of policy change—stems from the immense difficulty involved in developing the necessary expertise and data over a sufficient range of cases to provide adequate tests for the theory's hypotheses. In developing this book, we quickly realized that rather than attempt to master a sufficient number of cases ourselves, the better part of valor would be to ask other scholars—particularly those with little investment in the ACF—to apply the theory to their own areas of policy expertise. The resulting case studies make up the chapters in Part II.

The chapters in this section involve traditional case studies of policy change—relying largely upon documentary records, interviews, and secondary analyses of others' research—that critically apply the ACF to the scholar's area of expertise. In Chapter 4, Hanne B. Mawhinney describes the policy debate regarding francophone education in predominantly English-speaking Ontario, Canada, over a twenty-year period and the resultant policy changes affecting education policy. In Chapter 5, Anthony E. Brown and Joseph Stewart, Jr., analyze the evolution of airline regulation at the federal level in the United States from 1940 to 1980. In Chapter 6, John F. Munro examines the politics of California water policy from the 1930s into the 1980s. And in Chapter 7, Richard P. Barke presents an analysis of the disputes over technical standard setting for television within quasi-public industry advisory boards attached to the Federal Communications Commission.

Of course, a complete test would call for more observations than variables—the classic degrees-of-freedom problem. We were unfortunately unable to amass such an abundance of cases. Nevertheless, these cases provide for impressive variation on a number of dimensions of importance to the ACF. The kinds of policy issues addressed include educational policy (Chapter 4), transportation policy (Chapter 5), natural resource policy (Chapter 6), and communications policy (Chapter 7).

The levels of government include the federal (Chapter 5) and state (Chapter 6) levels in the United States, as well as the Canadian provincial system (Chapter 4). Furthermore, Chapter 7 applies the ACF to a quasi-governmental forum—that of an industry advisory group. The levels of conflict associated with the policy disputes vary substantially both within and across cases, with most describing transitions from subsystems with a long-dominant coalition to intensive conflict by competing coalitions. Chapters 4, 5, and 6 describe cases in which significant exogenous events—both political and economic in origin—substantially affect the balance of resources and opportunities within subsystems. Finally, most of the cases—especially those dealing with airline deregulation and with television standard setting—give evidence regarding policy-oriented learning within the subsystem. Thus, despite the degrees-of-freedom problem, these cases do a good job of mobilizing evidence with which to provide at least a partial test of the ACF.

# 4

## An Advocacy Coalition Approach to Change in Canadian Education

### HANNE B. MAWHINNEY

Few policy fields have been as volatile as education in the second half of the twentieth century. Industrialized nations in North America and elsewhere have adopted an array of policies in response to shifting social values, political contexts, and changing educational ideologies. The province of Ontario has, for example, restructured educational governance by developing policies that recognize the collective educational rights of its French-speaking minority population (Jakes and Mawhinney, 1990). In the United States, the variety and extent of new education policy initiatives in many states during this time has been called "staggering" (Mitchell, 1988:459). Following the release of *A Nation at Risk* report in 1983 (National Commission on Excellence in Education, 1983), U.S. education has been buffeted by by "waves of reform" (Bacharach, 1990; Murphy, 1990).

The policy changes offered by education policy makers in response to these demands have, however, often proven ineffective. Critics argue that many of the new initiatives have not been consistent with research findings and are consequently ineffective and uninformed (Lynch, 1979; Chubb and Moe, 1990). Although a substantial body of research on education policy change has accumulated during the past decades, much of it has focused on specific issues and narrow time frames—and thus has failed to provide guidance for policy development and change beyond a rather narrow setting. Scholars need to examine the interaction of the variety of factors influencing policy change through the lenses of more general theoretical frameworks (McDonnell and Elmore, 1987).

Several lessons have emerged from research findings that are cited as critical. One of these focuses on the need for longer time frames to incorporate the knowledge that policy change is "steady work" occurring over time (Elmore and McLaughlin, 1988; Kirst and Jung, 1982). Another entails the recognition that policy change occurs within a policy subsystem comprised of multiple actors whose core values and beliefs are critical to the process (Marshall et al., 1989). Further, it is argued that the greatest need is for conceptual frameworks able to capture the dynamics of education policy change (Fullan and Stiegelbauer, 1991). The advocacy coalition framework (ACF) presented in Chapters 2 and 3 appears to fulfill these requirements.

Despite this apparent fit, the ACF has to date been assessed in only a few analyses of educational change (Mawhinney, 1991; Stewart, 1991). Stewart's analysis of U.S. policies supporting equal educational opportunity confirms the potential of the framework. But this potential needs to be explored outside the United States and outside the predominantly regulatory policy arenas in which the ACF was developed and has been most often applied (Heintz, 1988; Jenkins-Smith, 1988, 1990, 1991; Jenkins-Smith et al., 1990; Sabatier, 1988; Weyant, 1988).

This chapter provides such an assessment by applying the ACF to the process of education policy change for French-language minority education in one Canadian province. During the past two decades the province of Ontario has adopted and implemented a series of policy changes directed at Franco-Ontarian (the name given to the Ontarians who use French as their first language) education culminating in the recognition of the right of the francophone population to establish and govern their own school boards. Section I outlines the methodology employed in the analysis of the ACF undertaken in this article. Section II describes the relatively stable parameters of the Ontario education policy system that establish the constraints and resources of the subsystem actors involved in these changes. Section III relates the context of policy change for Franco-Ontarian education. Section IV analyzes key hypotheses proposed in Chapter 2, and the concluding section discusses several issues raised by the framework.

## I. METHODOLOGY

The cases of policy change analyzed in this chapter are derived from a larger investigation of the history of Franco-Ontarian educational governance from the 1700s until 1988 (Jakes and Mawhinney, 1990). This investigation reconstructed key events, the impetus for those events, their outcomes, and the core ideas involved using a combination of content analysis of government documents (e.g., legislative and administrative hearings), newspaper accounts, and interest-group publications (see, e.g., Krippendorff, 1980) as well as elite interviews and personal observation of public hearings. The qualitative research conducted involved an investigative process conducted progressively and iteratively (Douglas, 1976; Miles and Huberman, 1984).

This investigative method identified long-term trends as well as crises and key events in Ontario's policies for minority French-language education dating from the mid-nineteenth century. The following section begins this analysis by outlining the stable and changing parameters within which the education policy subsystem in Ontario has operated.

## II. THE STABLE PARAMETERS OF THE
## ONTARIO EDUCATION POLICY SUBSYSTEM

Education policy making in Ontario, as in any political system, is constrained by a unique set of "social, legal, and resource features." The ACF identifies four types of stable factors that establish the parameters within which policy subsystem actors operate: fundamental cultural values and social structure, basic legal structure, attributes of the "good," and distribution of natural resources.

### Fundamental Cultural Values and Social Structure

The ACF approach recognizes that the norms of a society guiding the choice of policy options change very slowly. Similarly, significant changes in the influence of various social groups in a country come gradually.

Canadian political culture has developed, in part, from the conflict between the contrasting ideologies of the two founding groups, the English and the French (Bell, 1984). It is this conflict that has produced a nation of "two solitudes": Although the French and English of Canada have shared a sense of historical continuity and a common fate, they "share no political myths" (Guidon, 1990:37). Originally part of New France, Upper Canada's early settlers and fur traders were French immigrants, most of whom were Catholic. The surrender of Québec to the English in 1760 marked the loss of French control over Canada. The intention of the British government was set out in the Royal Proclamation of 1763, which called for the assimilation of French Canadians into the anglophone culture. French Canadians, however, focused on preserving their language and laws and were finally granted religious and legal rights in the Québec Act of 1774. Although direct efforts at assimilation of francophones failed, the impact of the extensive influx of English-speaking immigrants into Canada during the next decades made the political framework that had defined the Québec colony unworkable. As a result, the British government divided Canada into two provinces, Upper Canada and Lower Canada. Although the provinces were ruled by a British governor, each had its own executive council and elected legislative assembly and its own policies regarding education. In Upper Canada, the region that became Ontario, the predominance of English-speaking immigrants ensured that the British assimilationist bias would, de facto, define the education policies for the French-language minority in the province.

A second force influencing education policies emerged from the impact of the American Revolution. Until 1776, the thirteen "American" colonies and the colonies in today's Canada shared similar liberal orientations that valued personal liberties. Beginning in 1784, as a result of the American War of Independence, thousands of United Empire Loyalists, who rejected republicanism in favor of the monarchy, emigrated to Upper Canada. The Loyalists suspected popular democracy and favored leadership of "elites chosen more by tradition and right than by popularity" (Lawton, 1989:30). They rejected rebellion in favor of law and order, separation in favor of unity with the British Empire, and republicanism in favor of the British Constitution (Berger, 1970). Related to these was a preference for the common good over individual liberty. The emerging ideology was reinforced after the War of 1812 when the influx of American immigrants was replaced by waves of British, Scottish, and Irish immigrants who shared a similar "loyalist" bias.

### Basic Legal Structure

A basic assumption of the ACF is that the legal traditions reflected in a political system's constitution tend to be stable over several decades. In Ontario, the British North America (BNA) Act of 1867 is the legal basis upon which education policy making is founded. Faced with the virtual impasse in governing the Canadian colony, representatives of both the British and the French sought a solution in the concept of a British North America made up of all the British colonies. The union was also seen as a solution to the threat of annexation by the United States in the face of the aggressive American approach to foreign policy that followed the American Civil War.

Unlike the situation in the United States eighty years earlier, when the Articles of Confederation were replaced by the U.S. Constitution without any reference to education, control of education was a major issue facing the drafters of the 1867 BNA Act. Negotiation of clauses assigning responsibility for education to the provinces and guaranteeing the continuation of existing privileges for Catholics in Upper Canada (Ontario) and Protestants in Lower Canada (Québec) were of central importance. It is likely that the provision of separate schools for Catholics in the largely Protestant Upper Canada would never have been recognized had it not been for the desire of the powerful Protestants in predominantly Catholic Québec to control their own schools and the willingness of Catholic legislators of both provinces to unite to assure similar guarantees for Ontario Catholics (Lawton, 1989).

With the signing of the BNA Act of 1867, education became a provincial matter subject to the generally accepted practices at that time. In Ontario, the School Acts of the 1840s and 1850s established those practices. The interaction of the educational goals of the loyalist refugees from the American Revolution and the waves of British, Irish, and Scottish settlers who followed ultimately produced the Common School Act of 1841, the first legislation providing for education in Upper Canada. The act contained the "separate school" clause to protect the rights of Catholic minorities. However, it is noteworthy that the legislation founding Ontario's educational system did not address the question of language. The BNA Act of 1867 provided constitutional guarantees on the basis of *religion* for Catholic and Protestant minorities in Ontario and Québec, but not directly for the linguistic minorities of the two provinces. It was the failure of the BNA Act to guarantee linguistic rights that was to confound the ability of Franco-Ontarians to establish publicly funded French-language schools for the next century.

A second difference in the founding legal documents of Canada and the United States concerns their fundamental political values. Whereas the Declaration of Independence promises "life, liberty, and the pursuit of happiness," the BNA Act promises "peace, order, and good government" (Lawton, 1989:31). The core ideology supporting individualism is inherent in the former. In contrast, the emphasis on the "common good" is evident in the BNA Act of 1867, which acted as the Canadian "Constitution" until it was amended in 1982.

For many Canadians, particularly Québécois, a third fundamental difference between the BNA Act and U.S. documents was the limitation stipulating that no provisions of the act could be amended by any Canadian legislature, but only by the British Parliament. This limitation meant that Canada was effectively an "appendage of the United Kingdom" and was delegated to a "quasi-colonial relationship" until the early twentieth century (Jackson et al., 1986:57). Although a series of statutes extended Canada's sovereignty during the twentieth century, the inability of the Canadian government to achieve constitutional reforms without appeal to the U.K. Parliament remained a limitation to the country's self-determination until 1982. At the request of the Liberal government of Prime Minister Pierre Trudeau, the British parliament voted to patriate (that is, to relinquish its residual decision-making powers to the Canadian government). Although patriation was largely symbolic, it did finally mark the full independence of Canada from Britain.[1]

### The Basic Attributes of the Problem Area (Good)

The ACF proposes that the characteristics of a problem or issue area affect policy options and the factors that influence policy change. The characteristics of minority French-language education in Ontario emerge from the constitutional provisions for education in Canada. The key provisions for education outlined in Section 93 of the BNA Act of 1867 established the basis for a collective rights emphasis to education in Ontario. The notable feature is that the right to particular schooling is granted to groups rather than to individuals, that is, "it is a collective right granted to the minority religious group, Protestant or Catholic, in a given community" (Lawton, 1991:2). Fundamental differences in the nature of the rights associated with education as a public good thus exist between the United States and Canada: the emphasis on collective (religious) rights in Canada in contrast to individual rights in the United States. Although these rights operate at the provincial level, it is the responsibility of the federal government to protect them. Moreover, they involve positive rights, that is, the right to receive a government service.

Between 1867 and 1968 the status of French-language education in Ontario changed very little. Although instruction in the elementary schools serving predominantly Franco-Ontarian communities was almost entirely in French, legally English was still the language of instruction and communication, particularly after the third grade. According to the federal government's Royal Commission on Bilingualism and Biculturalism (1968:51), this situation resulted in "a non-system of education for Franco-Ontarians. These schools operated in isolation: they were not part of the English-language system of education in the province, and they lacked the planning, the guidance, and the coordination essential to an adequate educational régime." Moreover, the schools Franco-Ontarians attended failed to provide an environment conducive to students continuing their studies in high school. Although student retention rates up to the eighth grade increased during the first half of the twentieth century, few francophone students completed the high school entrance examinations. The proportion of French-speaking students in each grade from ninth to thirteenth (the final year of high school in Ontario) did not change from 1938 to 1948.

One of the reasons for the low participation of Franco-Ontarians in secondary schooling was that most were Catholic, and therefore, supporters of separate schools. Franco-Ontarian support for separate schools meant that they were subject to the limitations imposed on Catholic secondary education in the province. In 1867, Catholic education in Ontario only extended to the elementary grades. Until the late 1960s access to Catholic French-language education for the high school years could only be obtained through a network of church-supported Catholic private secondary schools (Hope Commission, 1950). Although Ontario began to provide French-language secondary education within the public system after 1968, predominantly Catholic francophones were confronted with moving from Catholic schools to the public system. The provincial government did not extend full funding for Catholic secondary schools until 1986.

### Basic Distribution of Natural Resources

The influence of Ontario's wealth, derived from its geographical location and natural resources, on the provisions of public services such as education confirms the ACF's proposal that the distribution of such wealth influences the "feasibility of options in many policy areas." Ontario, it is argued, has been relatively easy to govern because "as the chief beneficiary of the Confederation arrangement, its industrial development has been secured by tariff protection and, during much of the twentieth century, by low-cost energy" (Morton, 1990:7). In the 1960s this prosperity was translated into major expansion of social services such as public housing, transit systems, and educational services.[2] From 1962 until 1971, education spending rose by 454%. During these boom years for education in Ontario, schools and universities were opened and a community college system was established.

Franco-Ontarians, like all students in Ontario, benefited from expanded programs. Beginning in 1962, schools were permitted to teach a number of subjects in French. In the late 1960s, further changes established complete secondary school programs in French, either in separate schools or in special classes. Ontario's wealth meant that such programs were not seriously constrained by lack of resources.

## III. POLICY CHANGE IN FRANCO-ONTARIAN EDUCATION SINCE 1867

Briefly summarized, the ACF adopts the policy subsystem as the most useful unit of analysis for understanding policy change over several decades. Policy change is viewed as the product of dynamic exogenous events confronting stable system parameters as well as the interaction of competing coalitions as they attempt to achieve goals derived from their core belief systems.

### The Development of a "Loyalist" Educational System

The Ontario education policy system is structured by the parliamentary tradition of government Canada has inherited from Britain. In the context of this parliamentary structure, the premier and cabinet have historically formed the "very heart of the government of Ontario" (Loreto and White, 1990:79). Because Ontario premiers have formed a homogeneous group of Protestant anglophones, often with strong British roots, the favored changes have reflected what has been called a "loyalist" bias favored by the province's dominant social groups (Wise, 1990:80; Loreto and White, 1990).

These groups have their roots in the Loyalist settlers and the masses of British, Irish, and Scottish settlers who flowed into the province during the 1820s and 1830s. The conservative value system associated with loyalty to Britain led to the use of the state to promote "peace, order, and good government" (Wise, 1990:47). During the latter part of the nineteenth century, these dominant values meant that the state was given an integrative role in the society. This role included the development of a highly centralized, universal, and tax-supported elementary school system. The role of the newly organized educational system was to assimilate newcomers into "Canadian" values and to "disseminate the conservative social and moral creed prized by the elite culture" (p. 47). The elite culture was anglophone and, for the most part, Protestant. It was this culture that the growing francophone population in the province confronted in attempting to establish French-language education in the early 1900s.

French-language education in predominantly Franco-Ontarian communities was tolerated during the formative years in which Ontario's educational system was first established.[3] At the time of Confederation in 1867, many predominantly Franco-Ontarian communities had French-language schools. The leniency toward French-language instruction

during this period may have been because the French-speaking population in Upper Canada was small. By the late 1800s, however, a number
of groups felt threatened by the increasing numbers of francophones
moving from Québec to Ontario who had not easily assimilated into the
anglophone culture. In 1885, for the first time, regulations were passed
requiring that candidates for a teacher's certificate be required to pass
English grammar examinations.

For Irish Catholics, the influx of French-speaking Catholics into
Ontario was of particular concern. Because the educational system was
established on the basis of religion, not language, Irish Catholics often
found themselves sharing educational services with francophones who
were becoming more militant in demanding French teachers and instruction. Irish Catholics supported English unilingualism because they
saw this francophone militancy as a threat to the existence of Catholic
separate schools with instruction in English.

In the early 1900s the Franco-Ontarians also faced the animosity of
the province's Orangemen. The Orange Order, founded in Ireland, was
dedicated to the preservation of Protestant supremacy and the British
imperial connection. Orangemen believed that the English language
was essential to the latter goal and were alarmed by the failure of
Franco-Ontarians to assimilate. The fact that francophones were, for the
most part, Catholic further upset members of the fiercely Protestant
Orange order. By 1910, members of the Order began pressuring the government to ensure that the children of the province be taught only in
English.

The government responded to the pressure from these groups by investigating the schools in the predominantly francophone communities
of the province. In his report, the chief inspector of public schools indicated that the "atmosphere of the schools is undoubtedly French. The
language of the teacher . . . is French" (Merchant, 1909:2). However, he
found that most children in these schools were proficient in neither
French nor English, a fact he attributed to the lack of training and experience of the teaching staff (pp. 3–5). Although the inspector's report was
generally supportive of francophones, he made a number of recommendations to ensure that French-speaking teachers were also able to
teach English.

### The Organization of a Franco-Ontarian Coalition

Fearing that French would be suppressed by government authorities,
Irish Catholics, and the Orange Order, Franco-Ontarians joined together
to defend their language and culture. In 1910, a congress was held to
"defend French schools" (Congrès d'éducation, 1910:60). Delegates
meeting to discuss their needs and difficulties heard reports that there
was in the province "not a trace of secondary bilingual education, with
the result that the mass of French-Canadian children are forced to limit
their studies to primary education" (Belcourt, 1910). In the early 1900s,

although instruction in public elementary schools in many francophone regions was conducted in French, there was no public support for French-language secondary education. It was not until the 1920s, after repeated failures to gain governmental support, that the Catholic church established a system of private secondary schools that also provided French-language instruction.

Nevertheless, two outcomes of the 1910 congress have had an enduring impact on French-language education in the province. First, the congress established a permanent organization to fight for Franco-Ontarian interests in the province. L'association canadienne-française d'éducation d'Ontario, later renamed l'association canadienne-française d'Ontario (ACFO), flourished and became the core of the Franco-Ontarian advocacy coalition that continues to operate in the province. A second enduring outcome arose as a backlash to demands for improved French-language education by delegates of the congress. Franco-Ontarian demands were attacked by members of the Orange Order who represented the powerful Protestant community and by Irish Catholics who were themselves attempting to gain greater government support for their separate (Catholic) schools. The government responded to these political pressures in 1910 by passing Regulation 17, which effectively limited French-language education in the schools of Ontario. The regulation meant that "government grants to schools would be contingent on the employment of teachers able to instruct in English; no textbooks other than those authorized by the Department of Education were to be used; and instruction in English was to begin as soon as a child entered any school" (Prang, 1969:91).

The regulation was revised, in 1913, in response to francophone criticisms. Although it was never fully implemented, it remained in force and became a rallying cry for francophones throughout the country until it was formally repealed in 1944. It is still cited by francophones as epitomizing their mistreatment by the dominant anglophone culture of Ontario. In Québec a massive campaign against English firms was staged and government grants were made to francophone schools in Ontario. This pattern was repeated throughout the century, and Québec's support of French-language education became a lever that Franco-Ontarians used in their confrontations with the government of Ontario.

The conflict surrounding the passage of Regulation 17 highlights the roots and underlying ideology of the dominant coalition that has governed Ontario during the twentieth century. The loyalist ideology expressed by the Orange Order has lost some of its strength as a result of the decline of British Protestants from 63% of the province's population in 1931 to 42% in 1971 (Dominion Bureau of Statistics, 1935:128–129; Statistics Canada, 1974:166–167). The conservative value system inherited from this loyalist tradition, however, has continued to manifest itself, particularly in the political parties who have governed the province. Although Ontario's three political parties—the Liberal, Conservative, and New Democratic parties—have shared power since 1980, during most of this century the Conservatives were clearly in control. The result has been a dominant political culture described as "ascriptive, hierarchical, stable, and restrained" (Wise, 1990:56).

In the case of demands for educational provisions by Franco-Ontarians, this conservative bias has been supported by politicians' fears of an anglophone backlash should they extend educational rights in Ontario. During the 1970s and early 1980s, provisions for French-language education emerged incrementally and grudgingly as the result of public pressure. According to one newspaper, during these years if francophones wanted their own schools, they practically had "to start one in a tent or disused post office" before the province stepped in to support education in French. "It's a nasty political procedure, but it works. In the long run, francophones get service in their own language but the government is able to convey the message that they have been forced to make another concession to a noisy and persistent minority" (*Globe and Mail*, June 1, 1982:7).

As is the case in the states, Canadian provinces adopted legislation providing for the creation of local school boards. Unlike the situation in the United States, where school boards have wide authority, Ontario school boards have largely been limited to matters such as setting teachers' salaries and providing buildings. The Ontario Ministry of Education retained responsibility for matters directly related to learning and instruction (Lawton, 1989:32). The result has been the development of a powerful Ministry of Education that has often confronted local school district resistance to its curricular and program directives. Much of this resistance stems from the fact that school districts, which depend upon local revenues, exhibit tremendous variation in financial resources. During the past decades some of these inequities have been addressed through consolidating small districts and adopting direct equalization payments to districts. Nevertheless, until recently, Franco-Ontarians demanding French-language classes or schools in many school districts in the province have confronted the resistance of local school trustees who must balance requirements for cost-efficient educational services with francophone demands for equity.

### Impacts from Other Subsystems

In some regions where the relations between anglophones and francophones grew strained during the 1970s, demands for French-language educational provisions were met with opposition similar to that expressed by the Orange Order in the early 1900s. That these tensions were a reflection of events occurring in Québec and at the national level confirms Sabatier's argument in Chapter 2 that subsystems are "only partially autonomous" and that "the decisions and impacts from other policy sectors are one of the principal dynamic elements affecting specific subsystems."

While Québec's resistance to assimilation by the English has been a persistent fact of Canadian political culture since the British victory in 1760, during the 1960s many people in Québec came to reject the basic assumptions of Canadian Confederation and sought instead increased provincial autonomy. Québec separatists argued that the BNA Act did not define a true federalism because it was not founded upon the principle of self-determination. Confederation, in the eyes of Québec nationalists, "was not established by the express will of the people affected, but imposed by statute by an imperialist mother country [Britain]" (Jackson et al., 1986:243).

As Québec nationalism grew during the 1960s and 1970s, Québécois intellectuals became divided. Some, such as Pierre Trudeau, who later became prime minister of Canada, proposed a bilingual and bicultural Canada in which Québec had no special status. In Québec, however, a growing number of francophones supported separation from Canada. René Lévesque formed the Parti Québécois (PQ), a provincial political party that adopted political independence from Canada as its goal. Another more extreme group of separatists, the Front de la Libération du Québec (FLQ), began a series of terrorist activities that culminated in the October Crisis of 1970. During the crisis, the FLQ's kidnap and murder of a Québec cabinet minister resulted in Prime Minister Trudeau proclaiming a state of "apprehended insurrection" and invoking the War Measures Act. In 1976, the PQ won the provincial election with the promise of holding a referendum on "sovereignty-association," that is, political sovereignty and economic association with Canada. The election of the PQ, and its introduction in 1977 of legislation designating Québec officially unilingual, increased the French/English tensions throughout the country. The months prior to the May 1980 referendum on sovereignty-association saw these tensions escalate further. As the following discussion illustrates, these events had a signficant impact on educational policy in Ontario.

## IV. AN ADVOCACY COALITION APPROACH TO POLICY CHANGE

Chapter 2 proposes several key hypotheses that define the ACF approach to policy change. In the following discussions, hypotheses related to coalition stability, the stability of belief systems, policy-oriented learning, and the impact of changes external to the subsystem are discussed in the context of the conflict over demands for a French-language high school in a small community in southern Ontario.

### Coalition Stability

One of the critical hypotheses of the ACF is the following:

*Hypothesis 1:* On major controversies within a policy subsystem when core beliefs are in dispute, the lineup of allies and opponents tends to be rather stable over periods of a decade or so.

Contained in this hypothesis are the key elements of the framework: the focus on a policy subsystem as the unit for analyzing policy change; the view that "shared beliefs" provide the principle "glue of politics"; and the assumption that core beliefs are resistant to change.

Each of these elements can be assessed in the context of the conflict over demands for a French-language high school by the francophones of Penetanguishene that erupted at the height of the turmoil created by the sovereignty-association referendum. This conflict confirms the hypothesis that when core beliefs are in dispute, advocacy coalitions remain relatively stable because it illustrates the durability of the Franco-Ontarian advocacy coalition and the persistence of the dominant loyalist ideology. In Penetanguishene, a small community in southern Ontario, the English- and French-speaking communities had cohabited in Simcoe County since the 1820s but grew uneasy with each other during the tensions created by Québec nationalism in the late 1970s. At that time, approximately half of Penetanguishene's total population of 8,500 was French-speaking.[4] The discord within the community grew increasingly intense as a debate emerged over whether the town needed a unilingual French school.

From 1966, French-language instruction had been available in all core high school programs at Penetanguishene Secondary School (PSS). The majority of students at the high school were English-speaking, although about 200 French-speaking students took some portion of their courses in French. The francophones of the community, however, had been pressuring the government for years to have a distinct and separate school with a completely French educational atmosphere. As was the case in many other francophone communities, their concern was that they would be assimilated into the increasingly dominant English culture. Francophone parents argued that "the quality of courses they had at PSS was good, but the environment was terrible" (*Globe and Mail*, February 15, 1979:19).

In February 1979, after two years of debate, the Simcoe County Board of Education decided not to build a separate French-language secondary school facility as had been proposed by a language commission established by the government of Ontario to settle French-language education disputes. The board indicated that the potential population of 200 students was insufficient to justify building another secondary school and instead proposed to build an annex to the existing high school. The francophone community rejected the offer to build an annex and, in September 1979, established a school on its own in a converted post office building using privately donated funds and with the assistance of the Franco-Ontarian Teachers' Association and ACFO. The Franco-Ontarian Teachers' Association recruited volunteer teachers and supplied furnishings and curriculum materials. The intent of the francophones in establishing the school was, according to one resident, "to put pressure on the Government" (p. 19).

The stability of advocacy coalitions in major controversies proposed by the ACF is confirmed in this case. The persistence of the Franco-

Ontarian coalition in the minority French-language education policy subsystem is evident in the involvement of ACFO, the Franco-Ontarian pressure group established during the Regulation 17 crisis in 1910. Other Franco-Ontarian education groups, such as the Teachers' Association, which had formed as educational provisions were extended during the 1960s and early 1970s, were also involved. Also included were local parents and the French Language Advisory Committee to the Simcoe County Board of Education. Their core beliefs in the collective rights of Franco-Ontarians were consistent with those expressed by Franco-Ontarians attending the organizing convention of ACFO fifty years earlier. The underlying belief system of this coalition supported the principle of separate educational institutions for Franco-Ontarians, and was translated into specific policy proposals for a French-language school in Penetanguishene.

Consistent with the ACF proposal that coalitions will include participation from all levels of government, in the Penetanguishene case the francophone coalition was indirectly supported by portions of the federal government and by the province of Québec. During the 1970s, representatives of ACFO were funded by the Canadian federal government to stimulate French-language cultural activities in communities such as Penetanguishene. Moreover, the federal government at the time actively promoted bilingualism as a national goal for Canada. Québec's involvement in the francophone coalition was also indirect, although some financial support from private groups was extended. Nevertheless, by drawing upon Penetanguishene as an example of English Canada's mistreatment of francophones, Québec politicians added legitimacy to the demands of Penetanguishene Franco-Ontarians.

The opposition to the policy position of the francophone coalition came initially from the school trustees, who represented the dominant anglophone culture rooted in a loyalist tradition. However, the clearly differentiated and opposing coalitions described by Sabatier in the air pollution control example did not emerge in the Franco-Ontarian education case. Although the school board opposed specific government proposals for French-language education during this time, no advocacy coalition emerged in which members shared a consistent core belief system. Rather, various groups opposed the proposals on the basis of differing near core beliefs. For example, opposition was expressed by the school trustees, who were concerned with the costs of providing French-language education. As the French/English tensions over the Québec referendum increased, the Penetanguishene conflict drew the attention of others whose opposition to French-language rights was more ideological. The opposition coalition was thus far less unified in its underlying beliefs than was the Franco-Ontarian coalition.[5]

### The Stability of Belief Systems

Belief systems are a central feature of the ACF. Although the framework recognizes that not all members of an advocacy coalition will share exactly the same belief system, it proposes that their policy core beliefs are substantially similar. Such abstract beliefs are more resistant to change than are more specific beliefs. Policy change in a subsystem emerges as advocacy coalitions within the policy subsystem "translate the policy cores and the secondary aspects of their belief systems into governmental programs" (Chapter 2). Because there will likely be one dominant coalition whose objectives influence the development of government programs, changes to these programs will be unlikely as long as the coalition continues to dominate the policy agenda. In the framework, therefore, core values remain relatively constant, although policy strategies and implementing activities can and do change. The following two hypotheses are derived from the assumption that coalitions seek to translate their beliefs into policies.

*Hypothesis 2:* Actors within an advocacy coalition will show substantial consensus on issues pertaining to the policy core, although less so on secondary aspects.

*Hypothesis 3:* An actor (or coalition) will give up secondary aspects of a belief system before acknowledging weaknesses in the policy core.

For francophones, a core belief in their collective right to maintain and develop their cultural heritage has been translated into a consistent strategy for achieving these normative goals. Their strategy has been to seek policy provisions for separate educational services, and it has remained fundamentally constant during the past decades. The need for separate French-language high schools has been seen by the coalition as particularly important because of the findings of studies indicating that Franco-Ontarians had about one-fourth the chance that English-speaking students had of entering the final year of high school (Royal Commission on Bilingualism and Biculturalism, 1968). Although the Franco-Ontarian coalition has maintained a consensus on their policy core demand for separate French-language educational services, during the 1970s there was less consensus on the secondary aspects, such as whether separate services required completely separate schools.

Although the government of Ontario developed a number of options for French-language education during these years, its policy core position resisting the creation of French-language schools and rejecting the extension of the right of francophones to the governance of those schools changed very slowly. Beginning in the 1960s, the government of Ontario gradually extended provisions for minority French-language education as a result of crises such as that in Penetanguishene and in response to the demands of the Franco-Ontarian coalition led by ACFO. These provisions were, however, generally granted grudgingly and as a result of substantial political pressure. The government of Ontario did not have a consistent policy on French-language services, with the result that decisions were generally left to the discretion of civil servants. The resulting implementation of imprecise policies led "to a general belief, in both the English- and French-language communities, that the francophone 'minority' should be granted only as much linguistic leeway as the majority determines to be good for it" (*Globe and Mail,* June 1, 1982:7).

This ideology was reflected in the government response to the demands for a French-language school in Penetanguishene. In October 1979, after weeks of discussion, the Ontario Cabinet rejected the demands for the high school, proposing instead financial help for boosting French culture and an enriched French program in the existing bilingual school. The Conservative government's minister of education at the time explained that, although a separate and distinct high school was preferable, in the case of Penetanguishene it would be financially impractical. She also argued that the right of Franco-Ontarians to a French-language education did not extend to having it in a separate building and proposed, instead, a separate French school within the existing Penetanguishene high school. This "homogeneous French-language school entity" would involve splitting the mixed secondary school into separate "entities" under their own principals, one English and one French; the two schools would share the same buildings and physical facilities but function separately. The "two schools in one building" approach contrasted with the mixed, bilingual schools that had commonly operated and that offered courses in both French and English.

Consistent with the hypothesis that members of an advocacy coalition will show less consensus on secondary aspects than on their policy core, Franco-Ontarians were split in their views of the "school-within-a-school" policy. At the time of the Penetanguishene crisis, francophone parents of students attending a French "school-within-a-school" in one community were calling for a completely separate school and said that "we feel that our kids are being assimilated completely" (*Globe and Mail,* October 9, 1979:5). Students in the school indicated they were speaking less French than when they came to the school, and they complained that they were "tired of being called 'frogs' and being afraid to speak French in the corridors" (*Globe and Mail,* April 10, 1981:6). Because students were scattered throughout the building, it was impossible to maintain a French ambiance. While some francophones thus favored completely separate schools, others objected that separate schools would create a wall between the two linguistic groups. In some predominantly francophone communities, parents worried that establishing a French school-within-a-school would mean that their children would not learn to speak English. Confirming the ACF's hypotheses, these examples suggest that although the Franco-Ontarians continued to support their policy core belief in their collective educational rights, they were far from unified on the secondary aspects of this core, such as the school-within-a-school option.

### Policy-Oriented Learning

A distinguishing feature of the ACF is its emphasis on policy-oriented learning within subsystems, the process of attempting to increase understanding in order to achieve policy core objectives (see Chapter 3). The following hypotheses suggest that the extent to which subsystem debate can result in significant policy-oriented learning depends upon the degree of conflict over a policy issue and the nature of the analytical forum in which the debate occurs.

*Hypothesis 6:* Policy-oriented learning across belief systems is most likely to occur when there is an intermediate level of informed conflict between the two. In such a situation, it is likely that:

1. Each coalition has the technical resources to engage in such a debate; and
2. The conflict be between secondary aspects of one belief system and core elements of the other or, alternatively, between important secondary aspects of the two belief systems.

*Hypothesis 9:* Policy-oriented learning across belief systems is most likely when there exists a forum that is:

1. Prestigious enough to force professionals from different coalitions to participate; and
2. Dominated by professional norms.

The extent to which policy-oriented learning is curtailed in situations of intense conflict and open policy fora is illustrated in the conflict that developed in Penetanguishene following the minister of education's rejection of demands for a separate French-language secondary school. By February 1980 the issue had made the town a cause célèbre for organizations promoting French-language rights across Canada. The conflict had escalated to the point where the Simcoe County Board of Education suspended negotiations with members of the French Language Advisory Committee (FLAC) after anonymous death threats were made to school board members. Members of the FLAC protested that the board was using the threats as an excuse to undermine the French school. Residents of the community were split. One commented that the issue of the French-language school was "turning French against French," with some supporting the demands for the French-language school and others supporting the existing bilingual school. The resident felt that the issue had been "stirred up by a bunch of outsiders" (*Globe and Mail,* Feb. 6, 1980:1).

One group of "outsiders" were the representatives of ACFO, who had launched a national campaign for funds to support the private school. ACFO had assisted local Penetanguishene residents in contacting major

Québec-based companies to ask for help in raising the $400,000 needed to keep the private French-language high school operating. Although these efforts were not completely successful, they did raise more than $90,000 from individuals, associations, and about a hundred corporations. In the context of the tensions created by the impending sovereignty-association referendum in Québec, the actions of ACFO were meant to embarrass the Ontario government into fulfilling the demands for the French-language high school in Penetanguishene.

ACFO succeeded. In March 1980, just two months before the referendum, the minister of education announced that "it is essential that this matter be resolved immediately" and offered to build a separate but temporary French high school in Penetanguishene. The school would be housed in portables attached to a French elementary school and, if the new secondary school had an enrollment of 350 in 1982, the ministry "would review the need for a separate French-language facility" (*Globe and Mail*, March 7, 1980:1). The plan was initially rejected by francophone parents, who complained that the inadequate facilities of the temporary school would never attract enough students to meet the minister's guidelines for a new school. The parents finally agreed to accept the temporary school if they had a say in its design and if it contained the appropriate back-up facilities. The issue was not settled until late April 1980 when, after months of delay and after the minister of education had threatened to use provincial legislation to force compliance, the Simcoe County Board of Education finally agreed to approve the construction of a new French school.

Not all anglophones supported the government's decision to build a high school in Penetanguishene. On May 20, 1980, while Québec residents voted on whether to secede from Canada, protesters, many from Tay Township (adjoining Simcoe) marched in front of the Ontario legislature to denounce the building of the school. The protesters carried signs saying French was being "shoved down their throats" (*Globe and Mail*, May 21, 1980). Protests against building the school continued in June, when representatives of Tay Township met with the premier, William Davis, to present a petition against the school's construction. The township official leading the protest indicated that he saw the Penetanguishene school dispute as an example of what would happen in the rest of the country: "There's no doubt in my mind that they (the French school supporters) are using Penetanguishene as an example. If they can get a French school built here, they'll be able to start pushing for French schools in 30 other areas. They're trying to rip the country apart" (*Globe and Mail*, July 4, 1980:2).

The spokesman for the Simcoe County FLAC declared that the views of the protesters were "pitiful." Even when a temporary French-language high school opened in September 1980, protests by anglophone community leaders continued. Members of Penetanguishene's planning committee indicated they would attempt to block the construction of the permanent French-language high school by vetoing the

necessary zoning changes. Despite this opposition, L'Ecole Secondarie
Le Caron, housing a maximum of 200 students, opened in April 1982.
After four years of conflict that deeply split the community and provided
a national example for supporters of separatism "to illustrate what was
wrong with English Canada and the Canadian confederation," Francophone groups were able to claim a victory (*Globe and Mail*, April 23,
1982:4).

The Penetanguishene conflict illustrates the ACF's proposal that
when core values are in question, conflict between advocacy coalitions
will ensure that policy-oriented learning will not be a primary force for
policy change. Some anglophones in the community viewed the proposal to build a French-language high school as a threat (French being
shoved down their throats) and as a possible loss (costs would increase).
Members of the francophone coalition believed that a French-language
high school was required to fulfill their right to cultural maintenance. In
the context of the publicity the issue received both in Québec and in the
national media, the policy debate was conducted in a very open forum.
Consistent with the logic of the ACF, neither coalition revised its policy
core beliefs. It was through the intervention of the minister of education,
under pressure from events occurring in Québec that were largely external to the Penetanguishene conflict, that the policy changes sought by
the francophone coalition were realized.

### The Impact of Changes External to the Subsystem

The ACF hypothesizes that the internal processes of a subsystem will
generally not be sufficient in themselves to substantially alter the policy
core aspects of government policy. As the following hypotheses suggest,
policy change generally requires significant disturbances external to the
subsystem:

> *Hypothesis 4:* The core (basic attributes) of a governmental program
> is unlikely to be significantly revised as long as the subsystem ad-
> vocacy coalition that instituted the program remains in power.

> *Hypothesis 5:* The core (basic attributes) of a governmental program
> is unlikely to be changed in the absence of significant perturba-
> tions external to the subsystem, that is, changes in socioeconomic
> conditions, system-wide governing coalitions, or policy outputs
> from other subsystems.

The decisions in the Penetanguishene case must be seen in the context of the broader political events of the time. The Québec government,
under the separatist Parti Québécois, had just announced that a referendum on sovereignty-association (political sovereignty with economic
association) would take place on May 20, 1980. Throughout Canada
both francophones and anglophones were polarized on the issue. As the

Penetanguishene conflict grew it became a national issue. The PQ used the case as an example of the poor treatment accorded Ontario francophones as opposed to the treatment of Québec anglophones, who at the time controlled the school boards. The PQ emphasized that minorities were better treated in "nationalist" Québec than in "federalist" Ontario (*Globe and Mail*, April 23, 1982:4).

The events in Québec forced Canadians to reconsider their vision for Canada. For many the renewed vision meant an affirmation of bilingualism. The federal Liberal party, led by Pierre Trudeau, shared the vision of a bilingual and bicultural country and, during the referendum campaign in Québec, pledged that if Québec rejected the referendum, Canada would begin a process of "renewal" and constitutional change to address the concerns of Québec citizens (Jackson et al., 1986:199). The Québécois did ultimately reject sovereignty association. Subsequently the federal government conducted a series of provincial conferences to discuss patriation, that is, a formal transfer of full decision-making power for the Constitution from the British Parliament and the entrenchment of the Charter of Rights and Freedoms in the amended Constitution.

The rise of Québec nationalism during the 1960s and 1970s made the need for a Bill of Rights more urgent in the eyes of politicians, such as Trudeau, who adopted a vision of Canada as a bilingual and bicultural nation in which Québec's status was like that of all other provinces. The PQ government, in contrast, viewed Québec as a separate and "distinct" nation and consequently passed Bill 101, which defined the province as distinctly and unilingually French. Bill 101 required all immigrants into the province to place their children in French schools, regardless of their first language. This policy represented a fundamental denial of Trudeau's vision of Canada as bilingual and bicultural. As a remedy, he proposed that the Charter of Rights include a minority-language educational rights section that would give parents the right to have their children educated in their own official language (French or English) wherever the number of students so warranted.

Québec's Premier Réné Lévesque, however, remained intransigent in rejecting the Charter of Rights provisions. The resulting failure of the provinces to reach agreement on these matters led to the federal government's threat to initiate the patriation process unilaterally. Ultimately agreement was reached between nine of the provinces, which resulted in the passage of the Constitution Act, including a Charter of Rights and Freedoms. This act was given Royal Assent on April 17, 1982, exactly 115 years after the BNA Act established the Canadian Confederation.

Québec's dissent caused grave concern during the next five years and ultimately led in 1987 to the Meech Lake Accord, an agreement between provincial premiers (requiring passage by all the provincial legislatures) that was intended to bring Québec into the Constitution. The failure of all the provincial legislatures to ratify the accord has left Canada in a constitutional crisis. The current revival of separatism in Québec, and the apparent disillusionment of Canadians with the bilingual and bicultural policies of the federal government, perpetuate the constitutional crisis.

Despite these tensions, the recognition of the right to be educated in English or French, now enshrined in the Canadian Constitution in Section 23 of the Charter of Rights and Freedoms, represents a major policy change. This affirmation of minority-language education rights signifies a belief system that supports the collective rights of French- and English-speaking minorities such as Franco-Ontarians. It rejects the dominant belief held by policy makers in the nineteenth and early twentieth centuries that promoted policies for the assimilation of francophones in Ontario.[6] As such, the charter represents a fundamental change in the policy core beliefs defining the Canadian federal government's basic position on French- and English-minority language education. Consistent with Hypothesis 5 of the ACF, the impetus for this major change in Ontario's educational policy came largely from national-level political tensions generated over Québec's relationship with the Canadian Confederation. As the ACF predicts, such exogenous events are often central forces driving change in a policy core. Yet, as the following discussion illustrates, in intergovernmental systems such as the Canadian Confederation, policy core changes at one level may influence other levels of government.

## Intergovernmental Relations After the Charter

The lack of recognition for French-language education rights prior to the adoption of the Charter of Rights meant that, in conflicts such as the one that occurred in Penetanguishene, francophones had to rely on public pressure tactics and the political will of the government to gain the policy changes they desired. Enshrining the Charter of Rights in the federal Constitution provided a new guidance instrument for Franco-Ontarians to use in seeking policy change. It also introduced the courts as an important policy broker in the education policy subsystem.

Section 23 of the charter contains two important rights for linguistic minorities: the right to minority-language instruction and the right to manage and control that education. The charter recognizes the right of citizens of Canada to have their children receive primary and secondary school instruction in either English or French, whichever is the minority language of the province in which they reside. The difficulty of this provision for francophones has been that the addition of the "where numbers warrant" clause restricts these rights. Implicit in the rights guaranteed in Section 23 is a right of francophone citizens to manage and control French-language education for francophone students.[7] The Franco-Ontarian coalition has, during the past few years, sought clarification of the meaning of these two important clauses.

One critical clarification resulted from a court action launched by

ACFO over the rights of francophones to manage their own affairs. In May 1983, ACFO and the Franco-Ontarian Teachers' Association launched a court action in the Ontario Supreme Court regarding their rights to self-governance. The court action was on behalf of parents from four Ontario communities with substantial francophone populations where the local school boards had refused requests to establish French-language facilities. The francophone groups maintained that provincial education legislation conflicted with their rights under the charter to manage and control French-language educational facilities. In response to the court action by francophones, and in order to speed up the judicial process, the Government of Ontario referred the case to the Ontario Court of Appeals. In 1984, the court gave Franco-Ontarians the right to manage and control their own institutions, thereby establishing a legal interpretation of French-language rights that applies to francophones in Ontario and all other English-speaking provinces.

The right to governance of French schools by francophones throughout the country received further affirmation in March 1990 when the Supreme Court ruled, in the case of *Mahe vs. R. in Right of Alberta*, that the Charter of Rights guarantees minority francophones the exclusive authority to make decisions related to the education of their children. The unanimous ruling by the Supreme Court of Canada decided that "such management and control is vital to ensure that the language and culture of francophone groups flourish" (1990 *Supreme Court Reports* 1:344). The ruling also stated that the right to manage and control may, depending on the numbers of students, require an independent minority-language school board.

The exclusivity of provincial control over education has thus been limited by the impact of judicial interpretations of educational rights in other provinces. The education policy subsystem has, in effect, been substantially "nationalized" by the Charter of Rights.

## V. CONCLUSION

The accumulated lessons of past educational policy research suggest that analysis of complex education policy changes requires the guidance of subtle yet powerful theoretical lenses (McLaughlin, 1990). The case of minority French-language educational provisions in Ontario described here provides an example of the complexities that arise because: (1) The policy changes have evolved from debates regarding some of the core values supporting public education dating from the province's early history; (2) the changes have directly involved two levels of government, the provincial government and local school boards, as well as the federal government, other provinces, and interest groups representing various linguistic and religious constituencies; (3) some of the debates have escalated from local-level arenas to the national-level public arena; (4) the policy changes reflect a fundamental shift in the dominant ideology forming the foundation of Ontario's education policies; and

(5) the policy changes described in this chapter have occurred prior to and following a significant restructuring of Canada's basic constitutional rules.

The advocacy coalition framework provides a useful conceptual lens to clarify the complexities of policy change for Franco-Ontarian education through its emphasis on several key elements influencing the process: (1) the interaction between opposing advocacy coalitions; (2) the analysis of external factors explaining policy change; and (3) the explication of belief systems of opposing coalitions. The framework focuses on policy subsystems composed of advocacy coalitions as the most useful unit of analysis of policy change. The identification of the advocacy coalition, defined on the basis of a shared belief system, as the aggregating unit within a subsystem is an important contribution of the ACF. The framework's specification of the three-level structure of belief systems based on scope and receptivity to change provides a conceptual schema with which to examine the persistence of core beliefs of key advocacy coalitions such as the Franco-Ontarian education coalition described in this case. Although the concept of a shared belief system underlying policy making has a long history in political science, it has only recently been the focus of some interest by those who study education policy.[8] Given the value-laden nature of education policy, this emphasis is critical.

The focus on the interaction of advocacy coalitions in education policy raises a number of conceptual issues. Stewart (1991) argued, for example, in the context of U.S. equal educational opportunity policy, that the ACF does not adequately account for the origins of advocacy coalitions. This analysis of French-language education policy change contradicts Stewart's argument. The ACF proposes that constitutional rules, fundamental cultural values, and social structure establish the constraints and opportunities for the emergence of advocacy coalitions. Although all of these elements were influential in the emergence of the francophone coalition, Ontario's political culture was particularly significant. In the policy change process described here, the impetus for the organization of Franco-Ontarians was their minority status within the dominant "loyalist" political culture. This analysis of French-language education policy change suggests that cultural biases may be central constraints on policy change and may provide an impetus for the emergence of minority advocacy coalitions that challenge majority positions.

Other conceptual issues arising from this application of the ACF concern the framework's hypothesis that the core of a "governmental program is unlikely to be significantly revised as long as the subsystem advocacy coalition that instituted the program remains in power" (Hypothesis 4). Stewart (1991) challenged this hypothesis by noting that in the case of equal educational opportunity policy change in the United States, the dominant prosegregation coalition was not replaced, even though there were changes in the policy core of government policy. He argued that, although the antisegregation coalition forced some key concessions from the prosegregation coalition, the latter group has maintained its dominance in many states.

A similar phenomenon is apparent in the case of policy changes for Franco-Ontarian education. In this case a number of influences converged to transform the "assimilationist" policy core of Regulation 17 into the collective rights policy core of current French-language education. The question of whether the changes in the policy core for French-language education reflected the replacement of a dominant coalition is a complex one. Although the British imperialist brand of loyalism has, for the most part, been replaced by a more tolerant view of minority-language rights, anglophones are still the dominant coalition within Ontario. The case, therefore, suggests that amendments to the ACF are required, particularly in relation to the framework's underlying assumption that the policy core within a subsystem will largely reflect the views of the dominant coalition.

These issues arise because of the complexity of policy change in intergovernmental systems. In the subsystem at the provincial level, the recently transformed policy core for Franco-Ontarian education does not necessarily reflect the views of the still-dominant anglophone coalition within the province. Rather, the policy core requiring separate French schools and school boards was imposed on Ontario's dominant coalition by the federal Charter of Rights as interpreted by the courts. This situation, where it is possible for the coalition dominant at the provincial or state level to disagree with a national law, occurs frequently in intergovernmental systems. Using the Charter of Rights as a lever, the minority francophone coalition has transferred fundamental authority for minority French-language education from the provincial to the federal level by seeking judicial interpretation of the charter. In so doing, the coalition has effectively shifted the "scope of the conflict" (Schattschneider, 1960) to the federal level, which has traditionally supported minority French-language rights as part of the policy core for a bilingual and bicultural Canada.

The ACF also needs to be modified in its assumption that events exogenous to a policy subsystem have a *direct, unmediated* impact on changes to a policy core. Rather, advocacy coalitions within a policy subsystem may manipulate, and even inflame, exogenous crises to their own purposes. The case of changes to the policy core for Franco-Ontarian education illustrates this process. The politics surrounding the significant changes in Canada's constitutional framework provided opportunities for the Penetanguishene francophone coalition to gain national attention for its policy goals. Actions such as appealing to Québec companies for funding a French-language school in the Ontario community during the height of the sovereignty-association controversy provoked and inflamed the national debate on French-language education rights. These actions provided a convenient lever for the Franco-Ontarian coalition to use in pressuring the Ontario government for their demands.

In summary, the advocacy coalition framework offers a new lens with which to examine the complex process of policy change over time. The assessment undertaken here confirms the utility of this lens in highlighting the significant factors that have influenced policy change directed at minority French-language educational governance in Ontario. This case also suggests several needed refinements to the ACF, particularly with respect to the relationship between dominant coalitions and public policy in intergovernmental systems and the process by which subsystem actors can *actively* exploit external events to augment their power within the subsystem.

## NOTES

1. Canada remains a member of the Commonwealth, the association of forty-five member states who share a common heritage derived from previously being a part of the British Empire.

2. During the 1960s, Ontario's population grew by over 20% and its gross provincial product by 122%. At the same time government spending rose by 296%, most of it in education.

3. Egerton Ryerson, the first superintendant of education (1841–1876), helped develop the universal, tax-supported common school system in the province and is generally credited with establishing the tolerant policies that allowed French to be taught if parents so desired.

4. For more information on the Penetanguishene case, see Jakes and Mawhinney (1990:91–96).

5. The lack of tight cohesion in the Loyalist Coalition may be attributable to the fact that it had been in power for so long that most of its leaders were government officials. During this period they also had to be concerned with (1) preserving Canadian unity against the seperatist challenge from Québec and (2) girding for the more important battle over state funding for Catholic schools. Hence their willingness to compromise on the issue of French-language schools.

6. The Regulation 17 controversy described in Jakes and Mawhinney (1990) outlines the nature of the belief system supporting assimilation of Franco-Ontarians into the dominant anglophone culture.

7. For a discussion of the state of minority rights in Canadian education as a result of Section 23, see Mandel (1989) and the Summer 1986 special issue of the *Canadian Journal of Education*.

8. See Marshall et al. (1989) for a "cultural theory" based on the notion of the assumptive world of educational policy making. Also see Townsend (1988) for an analysis of the belief systems of Canadian education politicians. Finally, Wildavsky (1982, 1987) would analyze the Canadian case as a conflict between "hierarchical" and "egalitarian" cultures.

# 5

## Competing Advocacy Coalitions, Policy Evolution, and Airline Deregulation

ANTHONY E. BROWN AND JOSEPH STEWART, JR.

For two decades now, deregulation has been a popular political rallying cry. By the 1980 presidential election, for example, the issue was not whether the winner should "get government off the backs of people," but whether incumbent president Jimmy Carter had been a "successful" deregulator or candidate Ronald Reagan should be elected to press the charge more vigorously. Among the achievements in this area to which Carter could point, perhaps foremost was airline deregulation. When Carter signed the Airline Deregulation Act of 1978 into law on October 24, 1978, he asserted, correctly, "for the first time in decades, we have actually deregulated a major industry" (*Weekly Compilation of Presidential Documents*, 1978:1837).

The adoption and implementation of economic deregulation in recent years has forced students of the regulatory process to reevaluate conventional assumptions about regulatory policy development. Conventional theories of regulation would have predicted deregulation only when conditions or interest groups' strategies resulted in displacement of key groups in the policy-making structure. Levine (1981:185) noted the disparity between theories of regulation and the trend toward deregulation and concluded that "the problem with these theories is that they cannot accommodate, or can accommodate only with extreme difficulty, moves by regulators or Congress away from regulation and toward efficiency and reduction in bureaucratic power." Concepts such as "capture," "iron triangles," and "the propensity to regulate" commonly found in interest-group and economic theories of regulatory policy development are not very useful in explaining the politics of deregulation (Wilson, 1980).

Traditional theories of regulation tend to ignore the possibility that, although the composition of interest groups in a policy area may be stable, the policy preferences of those groups may change. They assume that policy preferences are static and that interest-group displacement is the primary method of policy change. These theories cannot explain cases where dramatic policy change, such as deregulation, occurs without changes in the interest-group structure. Such cases suggest that attention needs to be paid not solely, nor perhaps even largely, to the replacement of significant policy makers but to ways in which the policy preferences of extant actors are transformed. If significant policy changes are the result of altered policy preferences, analysts of those changes must study the "preference formation process" and the tools—"arguments, persuasion, threats, bluffs, and education" (Wilson, 1980:372)—used in that process.

A focus on the preference formation process directs attention to the beliefs of policy actors and the conditions and strategies associated with altering or reinforcing those beliefs. These phenomena occupy a prominent place in the advocacy coalition framework (ACF) of policy development advanced in Chapters 2 and 3 of this book (see also Sabatier, 1987). Sabatier conceptualizes policy development in terms of alterations in the beliefs of policy actors and discusses the political process in terms of the conditions and behaviors that alter or reinforce beliefs that support policy preferences.

In this chapter, we evaluate the framework of policy development proposed by Sabatier and Jenkins-Smith by applying it to a case of significant policy reform—the deregulation of commercial aviation. We begins with a chronology of events leading to the passage of the Airline Deregulation Act of 1978. We then provide an analysis of the framework in terms of the airline case and evaluate its utility in understanding the politics of airline deregulation. We identify two advocacy coalitions and illustrate their historical impact on airline regulatory policy. One coalition, which has long been an advocate of more competition in the industry, formed an in alliance with academic economists who called for deregulation. In effect, the politics of deregulation in the 1970s were largely a continuation of the politics of regulation.

Next, we evaluate the concept of policy-oriented learning, the second major component of the framework. In this section, we argue that the analytical case for deregulation produced in the 1960s and 1970s and conditions promoting an active debate between the competing policy coalitions were critical in the adoption process. The overwhelming evidence in support of deregulation, however, was not sufficient to convince members of the opposing coalition of the merits of deregulation. Rather, crucial opponents of deregulation either acquiesced or reversed their position as a consequence of conditions and developments that afforded deregulation advocates a strategic advantage in the reform process. We describe these conditions and conclude the chapter with an overall assessment of the ACF.

## I. THE CHRONOLOGY OF AIRLINE DEREGULATION

Table 5.1 presents the chronology of events leading to passage of the Airline Deregulation Act of 1978.[1] The critical junctures in the reform pro-

TABLE 5.1   Chronology of Events Leading to Passage of the Airline Deregulation Act of 1978

---

**PHASE I (1967-1974):**
**CAB Implementation of Anticompetitive Policies Resulting in**
**Widespread Criticism of Airline Deregulation**

| | |
|---|---|
| 1967 | CAB under Chair Secor Browne begins reversing its competitive policy posture. |
| 1967-1969 | CAB grants two successive rate increases that are challenged in court by members of the House of Representatives. |
| 1970 | CAB orders Domestic Passenger Fare Investigation in response to criticisms of its rate policies. |
| 1973 | Robert Timm is appointed CAB chair by President Richard Nixon. |
| 1974 | Domestic Passenger Fare Investigation concludes and CAB begins acting on its proposals, including a rate increase, restrictions on discount fares, enforcement of restrictions on charter carriers, a proposal to regulate charter fares, and restrictions on service competition. CAB grants antitrust immunity to carriers, which allows them to negotiate reductions in scheduled flights. The Department of Justice challenges the policy. During Watergate hearings, it is revealed that two major airlines made illegal contributions to Nixon's reelection campaign committee. Chair Timm is accused of thwarting a CAB investigation into the matter. |
| June 1974 | Senator Edward Kennedy announces plans to hold oversight hearings on the CAB in early 1975. |
| Aug. 1974 | President Gerald Ford sworn into office. |
| Sep. 1974 | Economists advocate deregulation as an anti-inflation strategy at a conference on inflation sponsored by the White House. |
| Oct. 1974 | Ford links inflation to overregulation and asks Congress to create a National Commission on Regulatory Reform. Chair Timm is accused of accepting free travel from regulated carriers. |
| Dec. 1974 | President Ford refuses to reappoint Timm as CAB Chair. |

**PHASE II (1975-1977):**
**Statutory Versus Administrative Approaches to Reform Are Debated;**
**CAB Reverses Its Anticompetitive Policies**

| | |
|---|---|
| Feb. 1975 | Senator Kennedy's Subcommittee on Administrative Practice and Procedure begins oversight hearings on the CAB. CAB liberalizes its charter regulations. |
| April 1975 | Domestic Council Review Group for Regulatory Reform is organized in the White House and begins drafting regulatory reform bills. President Ford announces plans to submit a comprehensive regulatory reform package to Congress on transportation, including railroads, trucking, and airlines. |
| June 1975 | Ford meets with bipartisan group of twenty-four congressional leaders to promote regulatory reform. John Robson assumes CAB chair's position. |
| July 1975 | CAB terminates all remaining capacity reduction agreements. |
| Oct. 1975 | Ford proposes Aviation Reform Act of 1975. |
| Jan. 1976 | Senator Kennedy introduces an airline reform bill. |
| April 1976 | Senator Howard Cannon opens hearings on the Ford and Kennedy reform bills. During the hearings, CAB endorses a reduction in regulatory control of the industry. Senator Cannon announces he will introduce legislation to curtail airline regulation. |
| 1976 | Senators Cannon and Kennedy jointly introduce a compromise reform bill. A second reform bill is introduced by Senators James Pearson and Howard Baker. |
| Jan. 1977 | President Jimmy Carter endorses the Cannon-Kennedy bill and begins a White House initiative to organize interest groups to support it. |
| March 1977 | Senator Cannon conducts hearings on the Cannon-Kennedy and Pearson-Baker bills. During the hearings, United Airlines becomes the first major regulated carrier to endorse a statutory reduction CAB route and rate authority. |
| Spring 1977 | Senate Commerce Committee writes Air Transportation Regulatory Reform Act. |
| June 1977 | President Carter appoints Alfred Kahn as CAB chair. |

*(continues)*

(Table 5.1 *continued*)

**PHASE III (1978):**
**CAB Administratively Deregulates the Industry**
**and Opposition to Statutory Deregulation Dissipates**

| | |
|---|---|
| Spring 1978 | Kahn reorganizes CAB and places deregulation advocates in key staff positions. Restrictions on carrier pricing policies are lifted and route award policies liberalized through adoption of multiple permissive entry policy. |
| March 1978 | Two major carriers, Western and Braniff, join United in supporting CAB decontrol. House Public Works Subcommittee on Aviation begins markup of House version of the Senate's Air Transportation Regulatory Reform Act. Proposal to terminate the CAB is included in the bill for the first time. |
| April 1978 | United revises its earlier endorsement of reform to the more extreme position of total and immediate deregulation of the industry. Senate passes the Air Transportation Regulatory Reform Act. |
| May 1978 | House Public Works Subcommittee on Aviation agrees on a compromise bill that includes a CAB sunset provision. |
| June 1978 | Air Transport Association ends its opposition to statutory reform and calls for a reduction in CAB control of the industry. |
| Sep. 1978 | House passes the Air Service Improvement Act of 1978 that includes sunset of CAB. |
| Oct. 1978 | Conference committee strengthens House sunset proposal. House and Senate pass conference committee version of the reform bill. President Carter signs the Airline Deregulation Act of 1978. |

cess occurred in three phases. The first phase was characterized by widespread criticism of Civil Aeronautics Board (CAB) regulatory policies preceding deregulation. In the late 1960s, the airline industry began experiencing financial difficulties that were exacerbated in the early 1970s by double-digit inflation, a recession that depressed passenger demand, and rising fuel prices. The CAB responded by adopting an anticompetitive stance, discouraging rate and route competition, and using fare increases to offset declining carrier profits.

As industry conditions continued to deteriorate during the early 1970s, the CAB went to new extremes of anticompetitive regulation. It became more aggressive in restricting service competition and abandoned its traditional reluctance to intervene directly in this area. It also moved to severely restrict charter operations, going so far as to propose rate regulation for charter carriers. Finally, the CAB liberalized its use of the antitrust exemption by approving large numbers of anticompetitive route agreements among carriers. These actions were more extreme versions of CAB policies typically adopted during periods of industry financial stress.

The second phase of the reform process commenced in early 1975 when Senator Edward Kennedy's Subcommittee on Administrative Practice and Procedure began an oversight investigation of CAB regulation. The period was marked by debates over the relative merits of a statutory reduction in CAB regulatory intervention versus minor adjustments to the statutory framework that would leave the regulatory authority of the agency intact, that is, whether to diminish the existing regulatory framework or to refine it. The necessity of some degree of reform was clearly registered at the Kennedy hearings. The statutory reduction option gained support with the conversion of Senator Howard Cannon to the cause. Senator Cannon's conversion resulted in passage of a Senate reform bill in April 1978 that was based on the assumption that the problem with airline regulation was regulation itself. Working from this assumption, senators concluded that the solution was a reduction in regulatory intervention, not just tinkering with the framework.

The Senate's endorsement of reform set the stage for the third phase in the reform process. This phase was characterized by administrative deregulation as CAB Chair Alfred Kahn continued the liberalization trend initiated by his predecessor, John Robson, and took procompetitive policies to new extremes. Support for deregulation grew as the dire predictions about the supposed ill effects of nonintervention failed to be confirmed. Events in the few months preceding passage of the legislation dissipated opposition to deregulation, paving the way for a conference committee compromise that included a strong mandate for deregulation and termination of the CAB. It was that bill that President Carter signed into law.

## II. ADVOCACY COALITIONS, AIRLINE REGULATORY POLICY, AND DEREGULATION

The focus of analysis in Sabatier's model of policy change is on advocacy coalitions, a concept that is very useful in relating the airline deregulation movement to the dynamics of regulatory policy development under the CAB. The foundation for advocacy coalition development predated the airline regulation period. Coalitions formed around the fundamental issue of the propriety and efficacy of governmental regulation of the market. The Civil Aeronautics Act of 1938 gave the advantage to groups favoring economic regulation of the industry. But the fundamental conflict continued during the period of CAB regulation in the guise of competing prescriptions as to how the board should implement its mandate.

Table 5.2 presents the major advocacy coalitions in the field of airline regulatory policy for the period from 1938 through 1978. Each coalition is characterized in terms of its actors and dominant beliefs. Prior to the 1970s, the arena was dominated by factions that differed in their ideas about how CAB regulatory policy should be implemented, but neither coalition considered deregulation a viable policy alternative. In the 1970s, however, consideration of deregulation became the central issue. The traditional coalitions provided the foundation for the deregulation and antideregulation coalitions that developed in the 1970s.

### Advocacy Coalitions and CAB Regulatory Policy

By the late 1940s, two major, conflicting positions regarding the primary goal of regulatory intervention, each with its own distinct set of policy prescriptions, were apparent (Caves, 1962:280–282). The proin-

TABLE 5.2 Advocacy Coalitions in Airline Regulatory Policy: Actors and Beliefs

#### I. Procompetitive Coalition (1938-1970)

Actors: Smaller air carriers; consumer groups (freight shippers, business and recreation travelers, air travel clubs); large municipalities and airport operators.

Beliefs: Economic regulation of the industry is legitimate. The primary purpose of regulation is to ensure highly accessible, low-cost air service. This is best achieved with regulatory policies that promote rate and route competition among air carriers. Industry problems are the result of maladministration of the regulatory framework and not the result of economic regulation itself.

#### II. Anticompetitive Coalition (1938-1970)

Actors: Large scheduled passenger carriers; financial industry; employee unions; small municipalities and airport operators.

Beliefs: Economic regulation of the industry is legitimate. The primary purpose of regulation is to ensure the financial health and economic stability of the industry. Carrier rate and route competition is disruptive and should be discouraged by regulatory policy. Industry problems are the result of maladministration of the regulatory framework and not the result of economic regulation itself.

#### III. Deregulation Coalition (1970s)

Actors: Traditional procompetitive coalition; professional economists; Ford and Carter administrations.

Beliefs: Economic regulation of the industry is not appropriate because the industry's structure is inherently competitive. Regulation creates inflated fares, limits access to service, and damages the financial health and economic stability of the industry. Competition policed by antitrust laws will result in lower fares, greater access to a larger variety of air services, and a healthier industry. Termination of economic regulation, not reform of regulatory policies, is the solution to industry problems.

#### IV. Anti-deregulation Coalition (1970s)

Actors: Traditional anticompetitive coalition.

Beliefs: Economic regulation is necessary to ensure the financial health and economic stability of the industry. Deregulation will cause "cutthroat competition" resulting in carrier bankruptcies, service disruptions, and monopolization of the industry by larger carriers. Reform of regulatory policies, not termination of the regulatory framework, is the solution to industry problems.

dustry, producer faction advocated an anticompetitive approach to regulation. From the viewpoint of adherents of this school of thought, the primary purpose of regulation was to ensure the financial health and economic stability of the industry.

The large scheduled passenger carriers, the financial community, and others with a large stake in the fiscal well-being of the major airline firms formed the core of this anticompetitive coalition. Intercarrier price competition, competition for passengers, and CAB actions intended to curtail carrier profits were either discouraged or opposed by this group out of a desire to minimize the need for government subsidies. Competition as a regulatory tool was to be used cautiously because of its potential to destabilize carrier operations and profit levels. Service to unprofitable markets was to be curtailed to prevent carrier losses. When service suspension was not politically feasible, the carrier should be allowed higher profits on some routes to compensate for losses on unprofitable routes. Segregation of carrier classes should be maintained to protect a carrier's market from the encroachment of another carrier class.

Advocates of the contrasting school of thought argued that regulation should produce low-cost air service widely available to the public. Frequent supporters of this competitive approach to regulation included consumers of airline services, including freight shippers, business and recreation travelers, air travel clubs, and municipalities. They argued that the CAB should encourage price competition among carriers as a means of achieving the lowest possible fares. More efficient carriers, those able to underprice their competitors, should not be penalized by regulatory policy. Competition among carriers on the same route should be allowed and encouraged through liberal route entry policies. In regulatory actions, the public need for air service should take priority over the desire to minimize subsidies if subsidy reduction entailed restricting access to air service. Low-cost air service, such as that offered by charter carriers, should be promoted by the CAB, not restricted in an effort to bolster the profits of the larger scheduled carriers.

## Advocacy Coalitions and the Deregulation Debate of the 1970s

From this environment of dominant belief systems, the concept of deregulation arose. Deregulation was a more extreme version of the competitive approach to airline regulation. In many respects, the Airline Deregulation Act of 1978 represents the statutory endorsement of the procompetitive coalition's position on regulatory policy.

The traditional procompetitive coalition was the most likely ally of actors supporting deregulation. Nevertheless, many members of the coalition were initially skeptical of the likelihood or desirability of completely terminating economic regulation of the airline industry. During early congressional hearings on airline regulatory policy in the 1970s, the dominant position of the coalition was for statutory changes that limited the regulatory authority of the CAB, including codification of competitive policies but not total deregulation or CAB termination (Brown, 1987:95–127).

Early and leading proponents of deregulation were professional economists both in and outside of government (Derthick and Quirk, 1985:40–45). During the 1950s and 1960s, academic economists had developed an impressive body of literature critical of economic regulation (e.g., Keyes, 1951; Caves, 1962), and by the 1960s, a consensus began to emerge among economists favoring airline deregulation.

By the 1970s, members of the deregulation wing of the procompetitive coalition were well placed to have an impact. A variety of government agencies—the Antitrust Division of the Department of Justice, the Federal Trade Commission, the Department of Transportation, the Council on Wage and Price Stability, the Council of Economic Advisers, the Office of Management and Budget, and the CAB—had staff who supported deregulation (Derthick and Quirk, 1985:36).

Regulatory reform was a high priority for both the Ford and Carter administrations. During the Ford administration, a White House task force assisted in the organization of reform advocates and the drafting of

reform proposals. President Carter became personally involved in lobbying Congress for passage of the deregulation legislation and in supporting key legislative leaders such as Senators Edward Kennedy and
Howard Cannon.

The Carter White House was instrumental in organizing additional
members for the deregulation coalition. Joining in support of deregulation were Ralph Nader's Aviation Consumer Action Project, the
American Conservative Union, the National Association of Manufacturers, the American Farm Bureau Federation, and the National Federation of Independent Business, along with individual firms with large
shipping operations, such as Sears, Roebuck (Derthick and Quirk, 1985:
122). Generally, consumers of airline services joined the deregulation coalition in the belief that airline competition would yield better service and
lower rates.

A final part of the deregulation coalition included individual firms
and segments of the air carrier industry itself. Carriers that considered
themselves especially disadvantaged by regulation supported deregulation. For example, Pan American Airlines chafed at the CAB's refusal to
grant it authority to serve domestic routes. United Airlines had likewise
been prevented by the CAB from expanding its route system. Intrastate
carriers such as Pacific Southwest Airlines saw in deregulation the opportunity to expand their systems into an interstate network. Cargo carriers,
although deregulated in 1977, hoped passenger carrier deregulation
would bring them the opportunity to expand into the scheduled passenger market. Charter and commuter carriers desired freer access to the
denser and more lucrative routes served predominantly by the larger cer-
tificated carriers.

Not unexpectedly, the most vehement opposition to deregulation, or
for that matter to proposals for more modest changes in CAB authority,
came from the traditional anticompetitive coalition. Most members of the
coalition took the position that the problems with airline regulation were
the result of CAB abuse or misuse of regulatory authority, not a result of
statutory defects. They preferred an administrative, not statutory, redirection of CAB policy.

This antideregulation coalition included many of the larger scheduled
carriers (with the exceptions noted above) and their employees (Kahn,
1983:135–140). The national carriers were represented by their trade organization, the Air Transport Association; the Association of Local Transport Carriers spoke on behalf of the regional airlines. These carriers
feared that deregulation would lead to "cutthroat competition" among
carriers.

The scheduled carriers were joined in the coalition by several employee
unions that feared competition from nonunionized carriers, lower wages
and benefits, and threats to job security. These groups included the Airline Pilots Association, the International Brotherhood of Teamsters, the
Transport Workers Union of America, the Association of Machinists and
Aerospace Workers, the Brotherhood of Railway and Airline Clerks,
and the Flight Engineers International Association.

Two other components of the antideregulation coalition were organizations representing airport operators and ones representing small communities. While operators of regional airports saw the potential for new business and joined the proderegulation forces, operators of major hub airports feared loss of service to the smaller airports and joined the coalition opposing deregulation. Rural states and small communities opposed deregulation for fear that if the duty-to-serve obligation enforced by CAB regulation were ended, carriers would abandon the less heavily traveled routes serving rural areas for more profitable routes.

## III. POLICY-ORIENTED LEARNING, EXTERNAL CONDITIONS, AND AIRLINE DEREGULATION

A policy of deregulation was the logical extension of the core belief underlying the procompetitive coalition's position on government intervention in the marketplace. But since the advent of regulation in the 1930s this possibility had not been seriously considered. How then, in the 1970s, did deregulation emerge as an acceptable policy alternative?

First, the academic critique of regulation developed by economists made a significant contribution. Derthick and Quirk (1985:36) concluded that airline deregulation would never have occurred without this development. Keyes (1980:23) observed that "the framers of the reform legislation both in the administration and in Congress drew on the work of professional economists, and the Civil Aeronautics Board justified its reform program largely on the basis of academic economic analysis."

A central hypothesis in the advocacy coalition framework, however, is that the basic attributes of a governmental action program are unlikely to be changed in the absence of significant perturbations external to the subsystem. Such external events are classified as: (1) changes in socioeconomic conditions, (2) changes in systemic governing coalitions, and (3) policy decisions and impacts from other subsystems.

In terms of the airline case, the question is: Were the analyses of academic economists and studies conducted and publicized by the Kennedy investigation *sufficient* to ensure majority support for deregulation? Is "a revision of core aspects in the absence of perturbations from beyond the subsystem" possible? The events leading to deregulation suggest, however, that the airline case is *not* an example in which "learning by a minority coalition may demonstrate such major deficiencies in the core of a program that the majority acknowledges these deficiencies or, more likely, that a system-wide learning process occurs in which systemwide leaders eventually overturn the dominant coalition" (Sabatier, 1987:671). Other factors were necessary to ensure radical policy change.

### Policy-Oriented Learning and the Deregulation Movement

The ACF hypothesizes several conditions conducive to policy-oriented learning across belief systems. These conditions include an intermediate level of conflict among competing advocacy coalitions, a forum that facilitates debate, and the "analytical tractability" of the problem (see Chapter 3). Economists built the analytical case for deregulation during two decades of research and debate in the academic community over the impact of economic regulation. The Kennedy investigation provided the forum for the presentation of their findings.

Policy-oriented learning across belief systems is hypothesized to be most likely when there is an intermediate level of informed conflict between different advocacy coalitions. This condition was not met initially in the airline case because the analytical debate centered on the fundamental issue of the proper scope of government regulation. The policy core aspects of both belief systems were at stake. Under such circumstances, the framework suggests that the high level of conflict that results produces a "dialogue of the deaf" in that the coalitions do not engage in a productive debate until external conditions dramatically alter the power balance within the system. Such was the case in the 1960s. Widespread dissatisfaction with CAB regulation in the early 1970s, however, led to the Kennedy investigation of the CAB. This forum brought the two coalitions together and forced them to debate the merits of deregulation. Legislative initiatives subsequent to the Kennedy hearings incorporated compromises that moderated the level of conflict between the opposing coalitions.

Throughout the period culminating in adoption of the Airline Deregulation Act of 1978, policy evaluation was a significant feature of the deregulation process. The debate was marked by extensive analysis of CAB regulatory policies and proposed reforms. Senator Kennedy's staff director noted that by 1974 the airline industry was already a natural candidate for reform because of the large volume of academic studies critical of the anticompetitive effects of airline regulation (Breyer, 1979:604).

In one of the first academic studies to argue for deregulation, Keyes (1951) found CAB policies to be anticompetitive and protectionist of the revenues of the carriers holding route authority. She concluded that there was "no apparent reason" (342) for retaining either the specific rate powers of the CAB or the carrier certification requirements. In another influential study, Caves (1962) endorsed deregulation, arguing that CAB policies resulted in unnecessarily high air service costs. He concluded that "the air transport industry has characteristics of market structure that would bring market performance of reasonable quality without any economic regulation" (Caves, 1962:433, 447).

By the mid-1960s, economists were able to compare the operations of CAB-regulated interstate carriers to non-CAB-regulated carriers in the intrastate markets of California and Texas. These studies concluded that regulated carriers experienced higher operating costs and subsequently charged higher fares than a nonregulated carrier serving the same route (Levine, 1965; Jordan, 1970). The intrastate carrier experiences provided deregulation proponents concrete examples of their policy alternative at work, and apparently working well.

The Kennedy investigation in 1975 was significant for four reasons. First, it provided a public forum for the presentation of the deregulation alternative. Second, the hearings discredited the policies typically supported by the anticompetitive coalition. A variety of policy evaluations commissioned during and subsequent to the Kennedy hearings examined specific reform proposals, narrow aspects of airline regulation, or questions raised by deregulation opponents and contributed to the case for deregulation (Brown, 1987:135–136).

Third, the fact that the Kennedy subcommittee was an "outsider," that is, was investigating a program it did not also supervise, contributed to the credibility of its report. The subcommittee was not constrained nor tainted by direct political ties to the regulated industry, and the reports it spawned appeared to be objective.

Fourth, the hearings were broad in scope. They addressed most major objections to deregulation and, in the process, actively sought input from the various groups concerned. As a result, the recommendations of the Kennedy subcommittee were difficult to attack, and its report was praised for its thoroughness. President Ford wrote a personal letter to Senator Kennedy praising the subcommittee's work (*New York Times*, February 22, 1976:22).

The Kennedy subcommittee hearings were not, however, an apolitical forum for the analysis of policy alternatives. Kennedy's staff director, Stephen Breyer, in consultation with deregulation supporters, structured the hearings to favor the opponents of airline regulation. The critics of regulation were given the opportunity to offer their case first. And testimony was presented to discredit the major arguments for continued regulation of the industry. Furthermore, testimony by various agencies was coordinated to insure that it would be presented by deregulation advocates (Derthick and Quirk, 1985:40–45).

In addition to discrediting some of the strongest theoretical arguments against deregulation, the Kennedy investigation successfully attacked the CAB anticompetitive policies of the previous six years. The operative question was transformed from "Is there a need for reform?" to "What type of reform is needed?" Would a redirection of CAB discretionary authority and the reversal of specific, unpopular policies suffice? Would substantive reductions in CAB authority be required?

Any reform required the support of Senator Howard Cannon, chair of the Senate Commerce Subcommittee on Aviation and a strong supporter of regulation. Cannon's position was altered in 1976 by a unanimous CAB call for legislation to mandate competition and minimize government intervention in the industry. This endorsement of regulatory reduction by the regulators themselves provided the credibility for that position needed to ensure the support of this key legislative actor. Still, total deregulation and termination of the CAB were not generally accepted as viable policy alternatives. Even after subsequent hearings in 1977, chaired by Senator Cannon, when the Senate passed the Air Transportation Regulatory Reform Act in April 1978 there was inadequate political support for industry deregulation and termination of the CAB. The Senate bill simply restricted CAB regulation of airline rates and routes.

Events following passage of the Senate reform bill, however, strengthened the position of deregulation advocates. The House followed with its own bill in the summer of 1978, and for the first time actual deregulation of the industry was incorporated into proposed legislation. The term "deregulation" did not appear in the bill's title until the final version was reported out by the joint conference committee in September 1978, shortly before President Carter signed the bill into law.

### Conditions Supporting the Deregulation Advocates

A variety of conditions enhanced the credibility and political acceptability of the deregulation alternative. An environment receptive to deregulation efforts was created by a popular linkage between regulation and the evils of inflation and "big government," by events reinforcing the image of the CAB as an agency "captured" by the large regulated carriers, and by the cyclical dynamic of CAB regulatory policy. In addition, the deregulation proposal was advanced by strategic compromises that diminished concerns about the consequences of deregulation, by staffing decisions that placed deregulation advocates in strategic governmental positions, and by administrative deregulation by the CAB, which served to reduce fears about the consequences of deregulation and accelerate congressional action.

*Anti-Regulation Sentiment.* The proposal for curtailing airline regulation coincided with a general political reaction against regulation. In a discussion of the airline reform initiative, Kelleher (1978:274) noted, "there has been a growing public reaction against regulation of all kinds, manifested by sunset legislation, hostility against such agencies as the FDA [Food and Drug Administration] and OSHA [Occupational Safety and Health Administration] and disgust at the debacle which the [Interstate Commerce Commission] ICC has made of the railroads."

This antiregulation mood was attributable in part to the economic conditions of the 1970s. As one commentator observed:

> There is a growing political and popular disenchantment with many old government regulatory and promotional programs. There is a feeling that the programs have not ensured adequate supplies of goods and services at reasonable prices. The programs ... essentially grew out of New Deal times of oversupply and depression. That regulatory pattern does not necessarily fit the new economic order of shortages and inflation (Kohlmeier, 1974a).

*Inflation.* The deregulation proposal also coincided with a record peacetime inflation rate. The record-setting pace of inflation in the mid-1970s resulted in mounting public pressure to do something (Kohlmeier, 1974b). Academics and key political leaders in the Ford administration linked inflation and economic regulation.

The promise of lower prices and reductions in regulatory intervention made airline deregulation attractive to both consumer advocates and conservative groups. One informant attributed the proposal's success to its bipartisan appeal. In his words, "the most significant reason for passage of the act was its bipartisan support. Proconsumer Democrats joined with free-enterprise Republicans."[2]

In the fall of 1974, the Ford administration included regulatory reduction as a major component in the Whip Inflation Now (WIN) program—the centerpiece of the domestic program. In a series of inflation conferences held under the auspices of the White House, administration officials and academic economists argued that direct economic regulation was costly and anticompetitive. Economists' efficiency argument for deregulation fit well with the administration's goal of reducing costs and curbing inflationary pressures. Their position was also ideologically compatible with Ford's "small government" philosophy (Ralz, 1974).

Thus, when President Ford addressed Congress on the subject of the economy in early October of 1974, he endorsed regulatory reform. Echoing an earlier Nixon linkage between inflation and excessive regulation, Ford stated that "the Federal government imposes too many hidden and . . . inflationary costs on our economy." He asked Congress to establish a National Commission on Regulatory Reform to "identify and eliminate existing Federal rules and regulations that increase costs to the consumer" (Weekly Compilation, 1974:1241–1242).

*The Regulatory Policy Cycle.* A cyclical pattern in CAB policy behavior associated with competitive and anticompetitive approaches to regulation also strengthened the position of deregulation advocates. During the years of regulation, the CAB alternately shifted between procompetitive and anticompetitive policy stances (Brown, 1985). This regulatory policy cycle was due in part to the sensitivity of the airline industry to cyclical economic conditions and was in part a response to the two policy advocacy coalitions confronting the CAB. The CAB promoted carrier competition during periods of industry prosperity to placate the procompetitive coalition. However, when the economy worsened and passenger traffic declined, the CAB implemented anticompetitive policies in an attempt to bolster industry profits and placate the anticompetitive coalition. When the economy improved, the cycle was reversed.

As noted earlier, the CAB initiated a period of anticompetitive regulation in the late 1960s, precipitated by declining financial conditions in the industry. This policy stance, in combination with political scandal associated with the CAB in the early 1970s, contributed to reform agitation (Behrman, 1980). Both of these forces reinforced the prevailing wisdom of academic studies that "regulation by its very design protects only producers" (Anderson, 1981:7).

One informant contended that "deregulation would not have been well accepted if the CAB had not gone so far . . . in limiting competition" (Brown, 1987). In his view, "the horribles of the [CAB Chair] Timm administration preceded Ford, and the defenders of the status quo had no record on which to oppose change." According to another observer, CAB opposition to carrier requests to enter new routes and proposals for low fare operations "played into the hands of the deregulators. It proved the points made by the critics of regulation [i.e., that the CAB's top priority was to protect the large scheduled carriers from competition]." Timm's unabashed support for the large scheduled carriers, his close ties to the Nixon administration, and charges that he had accepted free travel from regulated carriers provided additional support for the protectionist thesis. In sum, CAB actions in the early 1970s lent credence to policy analyses critical of regulation, especially those that characterized CAB regulation as anticompetitive and controlled by the large scheduled carriers.

*CAB Appointments.* Support for deregulation was enhanced by the election of two successive presidents who supported deregulation and who staffed key agencies, particularly the CAB, with deregulation supporters. While Ford adopted deregulation as a major component of his anti-inflation program, neither he nor John Robson, his appointee as successor to Timm as chair of the CAB, used staffing to promote deregulation as consistently as did President Carter and his appointee, Alfred Kahn. Quirk (1981:74) argued that the appointment of Robson illustrated that Ford paid little attention to the policy attitudes of his appointees, even when they headed "agencies high on the list of those his administration was seeking to reform." Robson brought no clear position on deregulation to the CAB, and he appointed both supporters and opponents of deregulation while chair (Quirk, 1981:75). One informant, though, credited Robson with "creat[ing] the willingness to look at the problem of airline deregulation" and opined that "his instinct was to undo what Timm had done." Under Robson, the CAB hastened the swing back to the procompetitive posture that the CAB had held prior to the tenure of Secor Browne and Robert Timm. It should also be remembered that it was Robson's testimony in 1976 that helped convince Senator Cannon of the need for legislative reductions in CAB authority.

Alfred Kahn's tenure as CAB chair during the Carter administration reflected a more consistent use of staffing as a means of promoting regulatory reform than was seen during the Ford administration (Quirk, 1981:77–78). Carter, fulfilling campaign promises, appointed individuals known to support regulatory reform to positions in important regulatory agencies, including the CAB (Cohen, 1977a).

Kahn, the first economist to serve on the CAB, had indicated a preference for airline deregulation in testimony before the Kennedy subcommittee in 1975 and endorsed the Senate version of the deregulation bill during his confirmation hearings in 1977 (*Congressional Quarterly Weekly Report*, June 11, 1977:1156). Once at the CAB, Kahn implemented staffing and organizational changes that ensured organizational commitment to deregulation. To overcome staff dedication to traditional patterns of regulation, Kahn brought in new personnel and reorganized the agency to enable him to place proderegulation staff members in key positions. For example, a new Office of Economic Analysis, a new Bureau of Pricing and Domestic Aviation, and a new Bureau of Consumer Protection were created, each headed by someone from outside the CAB who was known to be an advocate of deregulation. In short, staffing and organizational changes in 1978—made before the House passage of the deregulation bill—were in accord with the CAB's officially stated intention to "produce an industry more promptly responsive to the workings of the marketplace, less tethered to regulations . . ." (U.S. Civil Aeronautics Board, 1977:1).

*Administrative Deregulation.* Administrative deregulation by the CAB in the months following passage of the Senate bill in April 1978 was crucial in securing passage of a strong final bill. Kahn led the CAB to abandon Robson's cautious approach to reform and to implement policies approximating rate and route deregulation (Bailey, 1979:19–40). The most significant procedural and policy changes that resulted violated regulatory precedents and were of questionable legality. As one informant remarked, "Robson was too much the lawyer and Kahn too little." Nevertheless, the Airline Deregulation Act passed before the administrative policies could be overruled by the courts. These policies also proved to be very popular, influencing two of the three CAB members to join in supporting Kahn's initiatives.

By the end of the summer of 1978, the CAB had on its own implemented most of the deregulation bill's provisions, even though the bill had not been passed. In fact, CAB policies in the months preceding House passage of the bill deregulated the industry even more than did the provisions of the final bill. Thus the opponents of the bill who predicted adverse consequences if it passed could be effectively refuted. Because implementation preceded adoption, legislators could accurately assess the short-term policy impact. Because airline profits rose significantly in 1977 and 1978, airline opposition to deregulation diminished. Although it was not clear whether improved financial conditions were due to the procompetitive policies of the CAB or simply the general upturn in the national economy in 1978, deregulation supporters attributed industry improvements to the deregulation thrust of CAB policies.

While some argued that the legislation was unnecessary because administrative discretion had been exercised to achieve the reforms deregulation proponents were seeking, legislation was finally adopted to stop further deregulation. As the CAB aggressively deregulated, traditional opponents of statutory reform became advocates out of fear that the CAB had gone too far.

As early as March 1978, two major carriers, Western and Braniff, joined United in supporting CAB decontrol. In April 1978, United revised its support for relaxing regulations to the more extreme position of total and immediate deregulation of the industry. Opposition by the Air Transport Association ended in June 1978, when its member firms in the scheduled passenger industry endorsed a policy statement calling for reductions in CAB control (Derthick and Quirk, 1985:147–164).

Major opposition from the airlines did not end just because of rising profits in the wake of administrative deregulation. The new CAB policies and the uncertain legislative future of the reform bill created an unstable regulatory environment that both the major airlines and other traditional opponents of statutory reform found disconcerting (Behrman, 1980: 118–119). Uncertainty about the industry's regulatory future adversely affected the carriers' ability to plan future marketing strategies and equipment purchases. Furthermore, lending institutions were hesitant to extend financial aid on favorable terms. Continuation of the new CAB policies was contingent on pending court decisions regarding their legality. However, litigation would take months, and legislative action presented the most expeditious route to stabilizing conditions in the industry.

The CAB had yet to totally deregulate routes and rates, but the fact that it had gone as far as it had and the possibility that it would go further without a legislative mandate aggravated some members of Congress and some airline companies. For these parties, the pending legislation was significant not because of the substantive reforms it proposed but because it provided the means for stopping "the madmen at the CAB." As one informant commented, "Kahn moved so fast he angered both the airlines and Congress. . . . Actually, the bill was passed in part to slow down the CAB." The intention of statutory reform to regain congressional control of the CAB was clearly stated in the conference report on the final bill (U.S. Congress, House, 1978:56): "In adopting this new, comprehensive legislation . . . Congress was mindful of recent activities of the CAB. This new charter is intended as a legislative mandate to the CAB both as to the direction . . . of aviation regulation and . . . , it should be noted, the limits of such a policy."

*Political Compromise.* Finally, political compromises played a key role in securing passage of a strong deregulation bill. The compromises incorporated into the final bill were of three types: (1) design compromises, (2) equity compromises, and (3) targeted benefit compromises. One commentator, reviewing the airline debate in 1977, observed that "where people part company is on how quickly the goal of greater competition can be attained and what protections the federal government should give during the transition period" (Cohen, 1977b).

Design compromises were those made in connection with the issues of timing and approach—when and how—in the implementation of airline deregulation. The central deregulation provision in the Airline Deregulation Act was a sunset proposal first added to the legislation during House markup of the Senate's bill. The House proposal represented the traditional "dropping the gauntlet" approach; it specified a future date for review and reauthorization of the entire spectrum of CAB operations. Design compromises agreed to during the House-Senate conference significantly strengthened the original sunset provision. Senate conferees proposed a phased sunset approach that created intermediate steps to CAB termination. Dates were specified for the elimination of individual blocks of CAB authority. Separating the CAB's key functions and assigning each a termination date was expected to facilitate abolition of the

CAB itself. This strategy, characterized by one architect of the proposal as "pulling the teeth of the tiger," was expected to present fewer political obstacles than comprehensive termination. If the CAB's major regulatory functions were successfully eliminated, there would be little justification for reauthorizing the agency.

Several equity compromises—provisions designed to prevent consequences unacceptable to opponents of deregulation—were included in the deregulation legislation. To placate members of the strong Airline Pilots Association, who feared loss of job security, Senator John Danforth added a provision that directed the secretary of labor to develop rules and regulations for the administration of monthly assistance payments to airline employees who were dismissed or forced to relocate because of reform-related disruptions in the industry. Furthermore, airline firms were required to give hiring preferences to dislocated or terminated airline employees.

Compromises included in the legislation that created benefits targeted at specific groups were crucial to the passage of the airline deregulation bill. Most targeted benefit compromises concerned specific classes of carriers, including several concerned with the commuter carrier industry. The final deregulation bill reversed CAB policies that had excluded commuter carriers from operating subsidies and from accepting federal loan guarantees for aircraft purchases and that restricted the size of aircraft that commuters could operate.

## IV. CONCLUSION

Vehement opposition to a significant change in airline regulatory policy was eventually modified as the result of several developments. Political compromises alleviated the fears of several strong opposition groups, including organized labor and residents of rural areas dependent on subsidized air service. CAB appointments, both coincidental and strategic, placed deregulation proponents in key legislative and executive branch agencies. This development nullified potentially effective opposition and placed proponents in a position to influence key policy brokers such as Senator Cannon. CAB initiatives under Kahn's leadership drove the remaining opponents of deregulation to support the legislation in order to prevent more radical deregulation by the agency.

The forum for debating deregulation was opened significantly in the 1970s. Prior to that time, airline deregulation debates largely took place in the relatively restricted forum of the academic community. The situation changed dramatically with the Kennedy hearings, where deregulation proponents presented their case effectively. Although organized to favor the deregulation coalition, the hearings were generally perceived as an open forum in which regulation advocates lost the debate. In the wake of the hearings, a large number of other committees and policy analysts examined and publicized the positions of both advocacy coalitions.

Over time the tractability of the policy problem improved. Accumulated analyses by academic economists provided extensive data challenging the appropriateness of economic regulation of the industry. Analytical tractability and the deregulation alternative were enhanced significantly by studies illustrating the higher operating costs of regulated carriers when compared to unregulated intrastate carriers in California and Texas. Prior to these studies, there had been little evidence to indicate the possible consequences of industry operations in a deregulated environment.

The airline case suggests that a productive policy debate among competing advocacy coalitions, although necessary for significant policy change, was not sufficient. The *stategic exploitation* of a variety of conditions—many of them external to the subsystem—by deregulation advocates was required to ensure passage of a strong deregulation bill. The relationship between a policy proposal and the context in which the proposal is developed and presented is critical in effecting significant policy change. Sabatier (1987) recognized this in his contention that established policies and the beliefs that undergird them are not likely to be altered without changes in other conditions or events that lend credibility to the policy alternative. External conditions, however, are not determinative; they simply present opportunities or constraints to advocacy coalitions. Policy actors themselves determine the impact of "external conditions" on policy change to the extent that they use them, or are able to use them, in promoting their policy preferences. Furthermore, conditions are not determinative because policy actors can alter conditions through their own decisions, a point illustrated by the CAB's administrative deregulation initiative.

Conditions provided the opportunity for policy advocates to strengthen their case for deregulation. Antiregulation and anti-inflation sentiment reinforced economic analyses that presented regulation as a political tool of the regulated carriers used to protect their economic position and a cause of industry inefficiency and inflationary price increases. In addition, the regulatory policy cycle contributed to the deregulation movement. The anticompetitive response of the CAB to declining economic conditions in the early 1970s, in conjunction with scandals associated with the Timm chairmanship, reinforced a capture interpretation of regulation. Improved economic conditions in the mid-1970s led to the CAB's traditional procompetitive response under Robson, with industry improvements attributed to airline competition.

The observation that conditions are not determinative but instead simply represent opportunities or constraints to policy advocates, points to the strategic dimension of the policy advocacy process. In Chapter 2, Sabatier argues that policy change is the result of two processes: (1) efforts of advocacy coalitions to translate their policy beliefs into governmental programs, and (2) the impact of exogenous factors or systemic events on the resources and opportunities available to subsystem actors. The airline case suggests that a key factor in understanding the policy change process—that is, the translation of beliefs into government action programs—is the *relating* of policy preferences to exogenous factors. The "efforts of advocacy coalitions" and the "impact of exogenous factors" are not independent of each other. Rather, they are highly interdependent, and the activity of relating them by policy actors constitutes an important dynamic in the policy change process. Despite conditions conducive to policy change, the deregulation thrust of the final bill would have been moderate, and inclusion of the CAB sunset provisions unlikely, absent the ability of deregulation advocates to exploit as well as create opportunities to promote their position. This point emphasizes the strategic and dynamic relationship between core belief systems and observable conditions.

From a strategic perspective, the analysis of policy change must move from the identification of conditions conducive to policy change to the analysis of tactics employed by policy advocates. Several tactics employed by deregulation advocates were effective in winning support for their government action program. They included:

1. The development of a clear alternative to the policy of economic regulation and a large number of policy evaluation studies supporting the alternative;
2. The ability to link the current policy to undesirable conditions (e.g., inflation) and to present the policy alternative as a remedy;
3. The presentation of the policy in a public forum sympathetic to their position (e.g., the academic economic community) or the manipulation of a public forum to ensure effective presentation of the position (e.g., the Kennedy hearings);
4. The staffing of key government positions with policy advocates (e.g., the appointment of Kahn and the resulting CAB reorganization);
5. The development of and willingness to accept political compromises that neutralized opposition or recruit coalition supporters without diluting the primary thrust of the proposed government action program (e.g., design, equity, and targeted benefit compromises);
6. The implementation of the alternative policy to the extent feasible within the current policy framework (administrative deregulation).

One important tactic was the interpretation of an event or exogenous condition to promote their policy preferences or discredit the policy agenda of the other coalition. For example, deregulation advocates blamed the economic hardships of the air carriers during the recession of the early 1970s on the anticompetitive nature of regulation itself. The presentation of deregulation as a means of reducing inflation also illustrates the point.

The effective presentation of a coalition's point of view is affected by the choice of fora. The airline case illustrates the importance of the nature of analytical fora and emphasizes that the distinction between open and closed fora (see Chapter 3) is along a continuum rather than discrete. The Kennedy hearings were technically an open forum, but they were stage-managed so effectively that they clearly served the interests of the deregulation advocacy coalition. This does not deny that learning may well occur under such conditions. But it does suggest that one should be wary of labeling a forum as "open" without due consideration of all of the nuances in the presentation of evidence.

Likewise, the airline case highlights the use of professional fora in mobilizing for policy change. Publications in academic journals and books read by Washington decision makers served both to disseminate the deregulation idea to important actors in the policy-making process and to lend credibility to the concept of deregulation. By the late 1960s, the problems of CAB regulation had become "common knowledge," which set the stage for the success of the deregulation advocacy coalition. The norms of the academic discipline provided at least a veneer of respectability and legitimacy for the positions taken by advocates of change.

Tactics used in the airline case also illustrate the point that the determinative character of exogenous conditions must also be qualified by the observation that policy actors themselves influence conditions. Strategic staffing and administrative deregulation were crucial to policy reform. Because "true believers" in airline deregulation had been placed in critical positions throughout the legislative and executive branches, that coalition had an advantage. Interestingly, these appointments led to the situation in which the antideregulation coalition was forced to take legislative action that certified the validity of the deregulation coalition's position (i.e., passing the deregulation bill) to prevent even further deregulatory actions. The implication is that strategically located policy advocates can create conditions conducive to adoption of their policy proposal.

Furthermore, strategically located coalition advocates were able to influence other strategically located actors. Senator Cannon, for example, was not persuaded by the Kennedy hearings. The position of economists was dismissed as academic theorizing, and the arguments of consumer advocacy groups were viewed as illegitimate and out of touch with the economic needs of the industry. When the CAB, however, took the position that anticompetitive regulation was detrimental to the economic health of the industry, Cannon adopted the position that competition was a viable remedy for industry ills.

A major implication of the advocacy coalition framework and the airline case is that the dichotomy drawn between political behavior and "external" conditions typical of more structured approaches to policy development should be replaced with a dynamic and strategic view of the actor-conditions relationship. Policy advocates must convince others of the soundness of their position. An analysis of *how* they convince is demanded by the advocacy coalition framework. Analysis must focus on the behavior of policy advocates that relate "exogenous conditions" to core beliefs.

Dissatisfaction with mechanistic explanations of policy change that ignore the cognitive function of information in policy making as well as theories of regulation built on tenuous assumptions about the "interests" of policy actors should stimulate the development of new approaches to policy development (see Needham, 1983:13, 19; Posner, 1974:340). The ACF fits into this category. In an effort to capture the dynamic character of policy making, such approaches will likely move analysis away from the "billiard ball theory of politics" (Bentley, 1908), with its emphasis upon interest-group structure and assumption of static policy preferences, and toward frameworks that focus on the *process* of policy development, including how policy preferences are changed over time.

## NOTES

1. The descriptive portions of this chapter draw heavily upon Brown (1987). Used by permission.

2. This and subsequent unattributed quotations are from personal interviews conducted by the senior author in June 1980.

# 6

## California Water Politics: Explaining Policy Change in a Cognitively Polarized Subsystem

JOHN F. MUNRO

As one flies from Sacramento south toward Los Angeles, the importance of water to California's economic and social well-being is dramatically apparent. The shimmer of irrigation ditches filled to the brim, the countless silver streaks interspersing millions of acres of productive cropland, the high-Sierra reservoirs holding millions of acre-feet of melted snowpack, the green lawns of desert towns and cities such as Fresno and Bakersfield, and the virtually limitless metropolitan expanse of Los Angeles—these scenes and images all communicate a sense of rationality, community, and cooperation to the high-flying traveler. However, any Lilliputian interpretation at 28,000 feet belies the truth. This vision of cooperation and community is largely a mirage. The physical reality of thousands of miles of concrete plumbing cloaks a long and intricate history of profound political and social conflict that at various times has involved miners, ranchers, urban dwellers, farmers (irrigationists versus dry-landers), northerners, southerners, environmentalists, governors, Mormons, Hispanics, legislators, industrialists, land developers, Native Americans, and the ordinary citizen. It is a conflict that continues today, splintering political coalitions and attenuating long-standing social, economic, and political relationships. However, under a north versus south regional overlay, this conflict is increasingly based on opposing beliefs and values.

Despite endemic water conflicts, California's political leaders have built one of the largest and most intricate water systems in all the world. Without it, California would not have grown into the Union's most populous state nor could it have fostered the world's sixth largest economy. California's water history, and particularly the development of the State Water Project (SWP), exemplifies the nature of institutional development and policy change within the context of profound social and political conflict. As the rest of the American West continues to grow, and as urban values increasingly collide with a political economy based on the development of natural resources and agriculture, many western states' water politics increasingly resemble California's. Consequently, exploring the nature of California water policy change through the advocacy coalition approach holds a key to understanding and predicting the course of water policy change for all states west of the ninety-eighth meridian, where average rainfall is less than twenty inches per year (Dunbar, 1983).

Policy change within the California water distribution system is conditioned and constrained by the fact that economic and population growth has centered in the south while about two-thirds of the average annual supply of water—70.8 million acre-feet—falls within northern California (Engelbert, 1982). California's post–World War II political leaders recognized the need for the SWP: an extensive system of state-administered storage and conveyance facilities that would facilitate the export of northern water supplies to urban areas in the southern half of the state. They also realized that such transfers would intensify political hostilities between northern and southern California. The 1950s included several tentative but ultimately unsuccessful attempts to enact legislation for statewide, comprehensive water resource development (Grody, 1971).

Ignoring the failures of his predecessors, Governor Edmund (Pat) G. Brown, Sr. (1958–1966) shepherded legislation creating the SWP through a regionally divided legislature in 1959. Like its federal predecessor—the Central Valley Project (CVP), enacted in the 1930s—the SWP would take water from the southern part of the Sacramento–San Joaquin Delta and export it several hundred miles via canals and pumping stations to southern California[1] (see Figure 6.1). Passage of legislation creating the SWP (the Burns-Porter Act) was attributable, in part, to Governor Brown's political acumen and, in part, to the existence of widely held prodevelopment core beliefs.

Evolving political conditions, however, were soon to shatter Governor Brown's hope for a cooperative future. During former President Ronald Reagan's tenure as governor of California (1967–1974), developmentalist beliefs came under attack and water policy–making process underwent destabilization. Environmental interests entering the political process argued that conventional rules and routines governing water policy making were inappropriate. From their perspective, rather than solving problems and contributing to a better world, water resource development was a fundamental threat to the quality of life to which future generations of Californians had an inherent birthright.

The growing involvement of environmental organizations and protectionist beliefs upset the policy-making applecart. Existing patterns of causal reasoning began to be openly questioned. State political actors committed to water resource development soon lost the ability to structure policy-making situations in a way that would bring about political compromise and policy accommodation.

From 1966 through 1982, conflict between environmentalists, devel-

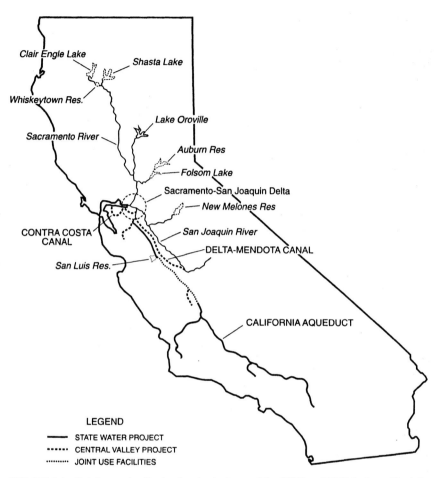

FIGURE 6.1   Existing and authorized major features of the SWP and CVP that provide delta supplies and divert from the delta
*Source:* California Department of Water Resources, *Key Elements—SB 346* (Sacramento: DWR, 1977)

opmentalists, and policy makers centered on the Peripheral Canal. The canal was intended to be an unlined ditch, 43 miles long, 400 feet wide, and 30 feet deep, that would carry water from the Sacramento River directly to the SWP and CVP pumps at the southern edge of the delta without traversing the main delta channels (Walker and Storper, 1982). Supporters hoped the canal would facilitate the transfer of high-quality water south, as it would no longer have to traverse the partially saline delta. The canal would also reduce the need for massive pumps to alter water circulation within the delta, thereby improving delta water quality and reducing the "entrainment" of fish in the pumps.² Opponents feared that it would simply facilitate a massive increase in the amount of water going south, thereby reducing the flow of fresh river water into the delta. With freshwater flows reduced, the delta would become more saline, a development that would harm fisheries as well as the farmers and urban populations of Contra Costa and San Joaquin counties who diverted water from the delta. Not surprisingly, the Peripheral Canal was embroiled in controversy virtually from its inception in 1966 as the official delta-transfer facility of the SWP (see Figure 6.2).

The conflict over California water policy making in general, and the Peripheral Canal in particular, provides an excellent case study of the determinants of long-term policy change. The case provides an opportunity to evaluate the advocacy coalition framework (ACF) of policy change and learning developed by Paul A. Sabatier and Hank C. Jenkins-Smith. The ACF, while not ignoring the role of political power, emphasizes cognitive processes (i.e., policy learning involving secondary beliefs) and major external events as primary causes of policy change.

This chapter applies the ACF to the California water policy–making process (1966–1984) to evaluate its usefulness in explaining long-term policy change. The following questions will be addressed:

1. What is the causal relationship between policy learning and long-term water policy change?
2. Was the nature and depth of policy learning within the California water policy–making system consistent with that posited by the model, that is, was it restricted to learning within belief systems or did it involve learning across belief systems? Did learning involve only secondary aspects or were fundamental policy beliefs involved?
3. Are mechanisms for promoting policy learning posited by the model supported by the facts of the California water policy–making case? Was the presence of a professionalized forum as important as external perturbations and political stalemate in promoting learning?
4. Generally, does the ACF provide useful explanations of long-term policy change? What are its limitations?

Section I compares Thomas Kuhn's (1970) model of scientific change to the ACF model of long-term policy change as described in Chapter 2 by Sabatier. Section II identifies the primary components of the California water policy–making system using the ACF. It also identifies the belief elements of both the developmentalist and protectionist policy-making coalitions. Section III reviews the recent (1969–1984) history of California water policy making and evaluates the extent to which the battle over the Peripheral Canal confirms or disconfirms the key features and tenants of the ACF. Section IV identifies examples of policy learning and change that have occurred despite core-to-core conflict over statewide water resource development. The concluding section addresses the key strengths and weaknesses of the ACF.

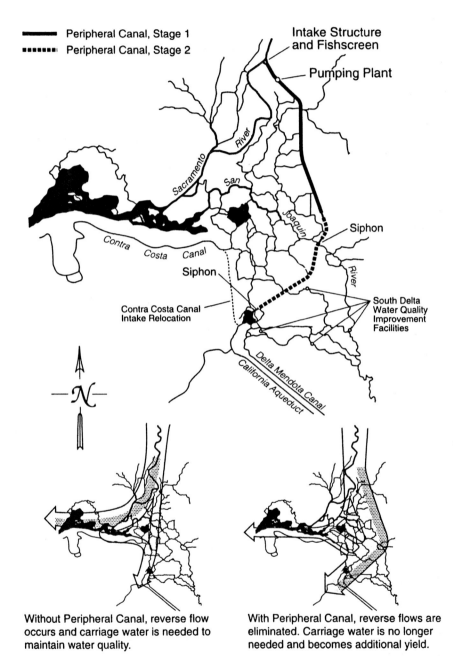

Without Peripheral Canal, reverse flow occurs and carriage water is needed to maintain water quality.

With Peripheral Canal, reverse flows are eliminated. Carriage water is no longer needed and becomes additional yield.

FIGURE 6.2   Proposed delta facilities in Proposition 9 (SB 200)
*Source:* California Department of Water Resources, *Department of Water Resources on Proposition 9* (Sacramento: DWR, 1982)

## I. THE NEXUS BETWEEN SCIENTIFIC CHANGE
## AND POLICY LEARNING: THE ACF AND
## KUHN COMPARED

Although Sabatier and Jenkins-Smith do not make the association, there are profound similarities between the ACF's model of long-term policy change and the way Thomas Kuhn evaluates the determinants and process of scientific change.

To Kuhn, science is a highly partisan and belief-driven activity; to Sabatier and Jenkins-Smith, long-term policy change is the product of advocacypolicy analysis leading to policy learning consistent with a particular advocacy coalition's core beliefs and values. Because both Kuhn and Sabatier and Jenkins-Smith fuse cognitive and political factors in order to better explain change, it is useful to compare the ACF to Thomas Kuhn's well-known treatise, *The Structure of Scientific Revolutions* (1970).

Both Kuhn and Sabatier posit the causal primacy of beliefs in determining the behavior of political and scientific decision makers. Kuhn's paradigm is simply a particular set of shared beliefs that guide the research efforts of scientific communities. To Kuhn, the paradigm sets limits on what explanations "make sense" and helps determine what phenomena are important and in need of future research (Jervis, 1976). It marks out areas to be ignored because they shed no light on problems defined as interesting. Accordingly, the bulk of science then consists of problem solving within the paradigm and "does not aim at novelties of fact or theory, and when successful, finds none" (Kuhn, 1970:52). Similarly, Sabatier argues that the common commitment to a set of "core" and "policy core" beliefs largely determine how members of particular advocacy coalitions view policy issues and search for new information to bolster their positions. Members of the Clean Air Coalition, for example, seek to improve knowledge of the effects of ambient air levels on human health because their belief system identifies that topic as critical (see Chapters 2 and 3).

The process of policy learning by the dominant coalition within a subsystem is equivalent to the conduct of normal science within a particular paradigm. Just as there are minor alterations or refinements in scientific theories to make them better fit the referent world, there are also incremental adjustments in the strategies pursued by different advocacy coalitions. As Sabatier argues, "the normal feedback loop of trial and error learning will thus encourage a revision in [secondary or tertiary] beliefs" (Chapter 2).

The ACF's distinction between learning within a belief system versus learning across belief systems is analogous to the difference between intraparadigm (normal science) and interparadigm conflict and change (revolutionary change). In the former case, scientists merely refine their theories to fit the empirical world; in the latter case, a fundamental transformation of beliefs and associated perceptions is required.

In response to anomalies and contradictory data, scientists and policy makers first alter their (re)search strategies (secondary aspects). If anomalies persist, scientists and policy participants may make alterations and adjustments to the paradigm (i.e., changes in policy core beliefs). Only when there has been a fundamental, unmistakable failure in the policy or scientific paradigm will scientists or policy makers consider altering normative and ontological axioms. Sabatier talks about this change as akin to religious conversion; Kuhn, in contrast, views changes of this magnitude as equivalent to political revolution.

Of course, learning across belief systems is always problematic. Many times, the definitive crisis never occurs and whether one's beliefs are consistent or in conflict with the realities of the situation remains ambiguous (Steinbruner, 1974). Kuhn would agree with Jenkins-Smith and Sabatier that "when two cores conflict . . . the tendency is for coalitions to talk past each other and thus for a dialogue of the deaf to persist until external conditions dramatically alter the power balance within the subsystem" (Chapter 3).

Policy learning in the ACF is equivalent to the conduct of normal science using the Kuhnian vernacular. Both are central to the process of change, but neither is the most important variable in moving scientific and policy communities into new realms of thought and action. According to Sabatier, external conditions (i.e., real world events like oil embargoes) are responsible for the most dramatic changes within policy communities. Specifically, significant perturbations external to the policy subsystem place the policy core of the dominant coalition under intense scrutiny. Under crisis conditions, the political resources of minority coalitions in the policy-making process (equivalent to scientific dissidents) may be markedly increased (e.g., system-wide leaders enter on the side of the minority policy coalition). Consequently, the governmental action program may undergo reformulation consistent with the beliefs of the minority coalition.

Kuhn argues that anomalies—which are nothing more than a fundamental disjuncture between the external empirical world and the belief-driven research of a particular scientific community—are the most important factors in causing scientific communities to adopt radically new conceptions of how the physical world operates. Like external perturbations in policy subsystems, anomalies may produce a crisis in a particular scientific community. In turn, efforts to resolve this crisis result in experimentation with novel and radically deviant procedures and theoretical interpretations. Ultimately, a new scientific paradigm is agreed upon. In such cases, minority or dissident scientists may rise out of obscurity to a position of prominence within the scientific community.

In contrast to the Kuhnian view of science, where one paradigm eventually replaces another through scientific revolution, Sabatier shows that competing belief structures often persist within the policy-making process. He argues that even in those cases when a fundamental transformation of the policy core is not feasible, incremental policy change may still occur as the result of policy learning. This process is aided, according to the ACF, "if authoritative and relatively 'depoliticized' communication fora exist that force competing professionals to address each other's findings" (Chapter 3).[3] By preventing the debate between opposing advocacy coalitions from gravitating toward "core" beliefs, fundamental scientific *norms* may facilitate productive exchange of views on secondary aspects.

Although the similarities between the ACF and the Kuhnian model are significant, there are also fundamental differences between the two approaches. The most significant is that the ACF views beliefs as held by individuals of advocacy coalitions. The Kuhnian model incorporates the premise that beliefs, under certain conditions, transcend advocacy coalitions to structure the behavior of entire scientific communities or political systems. [Editors' Note: The ACF provides for the latter as well under "fundamental sociocultural norms" within the Stable System Parameters, but apparently not as clearly as it should.]

An additional important difference between the ACF and the Kuhnian model is the emphasis Sabatier places on distinguishing cognitive from noncognitive factors, as well as the relative weight the framework assigns to external conditions in determining policy change. In the ACF, noncognitive factors, such as fundamental changes in socioeconomic conditions, have the potential of altering the basic political resources of advocacy coalitions and thus are primary determinants of fundamental policy change.

While Kuhn would agree that external perturbations (anomalies) are key to producing long-term change, he also underscores the point that the meaning of external events is often unclear. Events are generally interpreted through the "lens" provided by a particular paradigm. Rather than producing change in some predictable or predetermined way, external perturbations may actually lead to the unanticipated consequence of sustaining the dominant paradigm.

Differences between Kuhn and the ACF are significant in that they suggest possible refinements to the ACF. I will return to these differences in the final section of this chapter.

## II. THE CALIFORNIA WATER POLICY–MAKING SUBSYSTEM

This section describes the California water policy–making system through the lens of the ACF model of policy change. In particular, I discuss: (1) exogenous variables affecting the water policy–making subsystem; (2) the advocacy coalitions within the subsystem contesting for policy control; and (3) the core and policy core belief structures of the two major advocacy coalitions.

### *External Factors*

*Relatively Stable System Parameters.* The stable parameters that constrain and structure water policy making in California include:

(1) the complex body of water law, composed of riparian, appropriative, groundwater, pueblo, contractual, and federal reserved water rights; (2) the complex and cumbersome water management system involving at least six major federal agencies, two major state agencies, and nearly a thousand public and private entities (i.e., water districts, water agencies, and private water companies) at the regional and local levels (Engelbert, 1982:Chapter 9); (3) the unequal distribution of water within the state, where about two-thirds of the water supply originates in the North Coast and Sacramento river basins, while most of the agricultural expansion and population growth has centered in the central and southern parts of the state; and (4) the disproportionate use of water by the agricultural sector, which consumes approximately 83% of the 40.6 million acre-feet (MAF) utilized each year (California Department of Water Resources, 1987).

Other stable system parameters include the enduring regional conflict between northern and southern California. Northerners usually express a feeling of cultural separateness from the south. Over the past fifteen years, the antimaterialist values of the environmental movement have acted in concert with northern sectionalism to create an increasingly powerful and seemingly enduring counterforce to materialist values, which have tied economic growth to massive, large-scale water resource development. Northern fears that the more populous south will "steal" its water have been exacerbated by southern majorities in both houses of the legislature since the 1970 reapportionment as well as the fact that every governor since 1958 has come from the south.

Finally, widely held sociocultural beliefs embodied in institutions, policies, and routinized political behavior must also be viewed as a relatively stable system parameter. Governor Brown's success in securing passage of the SWP in 1959 was due in part to his ability to exploit developmentalist "core" and "policy core" beliefs. Brown was able to trade on the almost universal perspective that problems of insufficient water supply (e.g., slowed population growth rates and economic underdevelopment) could only be avoided through large-scale, state-directed water development and interbasin transfer projects.

In addition, Governor Brown used a traditional "pork barrel" strategy to help overcome regionally based opposition to the SWP by earmarking $130 million for local water construction projects in the north (Grody, 1971:406). By the early 1970s such distributive mechanisms could no longer constrain interregional battles over water. The failure of the pork barrel strategy was largely due to the onslaught of protectionist beliefs that undermined the long dominant prodevelopment water policy–making culture.

*External System Events.* Perturbations in social, economic, technological, and physical (climatic) conditions from outside the subsystem have dramatically influenced the evolution of California water policy making. Lagging growth rates in northern California during the nineteenth century set the stage for a general movement toward public policies that encouraged the expansion of irrigated agriculture. Droughts

during the 1920s contributed ultimately to the expansion of governmental authority in managing water resources, most notably the construction of the CVP by the U.S. Bureau of Reclamation in the 1930s
(Pisani, 1984). The 1976–1977 drought also forced a major rethinking of
the adequacy of the state's water system. In particular, it focused the
attention of the policy-making subsystem on sources of water in California and available means for conserving those sources; it also served
to highlight the principal strengths and weaknesses of the state's water
laws and management system.

Largely in response to the 1976–1977 drought, Governor Edmund
(Jerry) Brown, Jr. (Pat Brown's son) created the Governor's Commission
to Review Water Rights Law by Executive Order on May 11, 1977. This
commission attempted to take a nonpartisan and scientific approach
to California water problems. It roughly approximated the professionalized communication forum posited by the ACF as a key precursor to
policy learning across advocacy coalitions.

While the drought generated pressures for California to move away
from water resource development and adopt policies that encouraged
more efficient use of existing supplies and the protection of instream
values (e.g., fisheries), it also lent credence to the view of the state's
major water agencies and agricultural interests that additional water resource development—particularly the Peripheral Canal—was necessary
if California was to avoid serious water supply shortages in the future.
Countervailing interpretations of what were the correct lessons to draw
from the drought, however, undercut efforts to use this external event to
promote fundamental policy and institutional reforms.

Changes in portions of the systemic governing coalition during the
mid-1970s also affected the California water policy–making subsystem.
Specifically, in contrast to previous administrations, Governor Jerry
Brown (1975–1982) and Department of Water Resources (DWR) director
Ronald B. Robie openly questioned the validity of the developmentalist
perspective and initially refused to support the Peripheral Canal project.
They also attempted to change the basic policy and planning emphasis
of the state water bureaucracy.

Conflicts and events in other policy subsystems also affected California water policy making. In particular, the growing resistance of the
California public to increasing property taxes, which resulted in the passage of Proposition 13 in 1978, influenced the outcome of the Peripheral
Canal conflict. During the 1982 referendum campaign, environmentalists exploited the public's association between costly governmental
programs and higher taxes to heighten the level of opposition to the
Peripheral Canal, particularly in southern California. Consequently,
water development proponents in southern California were unable to
make optimum use of the south's higher voter population to counter
northern opposition (Munro, 1988:Chapter 7).

Another external condition affecting the behavior within the water
policy–making subsystem was increasing energy costs during the 1970s
and early 1980s. By 1984, farmers in the San Joaquin Valley were paying

the fixed costs of the SWP distribution system but were ordering less water due to increases in variable costs. These included the energy costs of pumping SWP water uphill at certain points during its 400-mile journey southward.

## The Internal Structure of the California Water Policy–Making Subsystem

The California water policy–making subsystem during the 1970s and 1980s can be segmented into two advocacy coalitions: the developmentalist coalition and the protectionist coalition. The former was composed of most personnel from the California DWR and the U.S. Bureau of Reclamation, agricultural interest groups and individual farmers (except in the delta), central and southern California water agency personnel, the California Chamber of Commerce, most central and southern California legislators, most members of the Senate Water and Agriculture Committee, the Association of California Water Agencies, and the California SWP contractors. During the Reagan (1967–1974) and Deukmejian (1983–1990) administrations, top political officials in the executive branch also were part of this coalition.

The protectionist water use coalition was composed of various environmental organizations including the Sierra Club, the Environmental Defense Fund, Friends of the Earth, and California Trout, many officials in the U.S. Fish and Wildlife Service and the California Department of Fish and Game, most northern urban legislators, top political officials within the administration of Governor Jerry Brown, and farmers in the Sacramento—San Joaquin Delta whose water quality was adversely affected by saltwater intrusion caused by diversions of fresh water to the south.

In the middle of these two advocacy coalitions were actors who at various times played the role of "policy broker." Legislators like Assemblyman Lawrence Kapiloff, a Democrat from San Diego, for example, vigorously attempted to keep the political conflict within reasonable bounds by proposing a constitutional amendment (ACA 90) that would provide additional legal guarantees for delta water quality protections included in Senate Bill 200 (i.e., the second Peripheral Canal bill). Governor Jerry Brown moved in and out of a brokering role. At some points during the legislative struggle over the Peripheral Canal (1977–1982), he attempted to mediate between the two advocacy coalitions. At other times, he was a card-carrying member of the protectionist advocacy coalition.

### Belief Structures

Belief systems are the central organizing principle for advocacy coalitions. Both the protectionist and developmentalist coalitions have distinctive and opposing belief structures. These beliefs can effectively be organized in accordance with the categories established by Sabatier. Specifically, each advocacy coalition has a deep (normative) core, a set of fundamental policy beliefs, and instrumental beliefs. Table 6.1 out-

TABLE 6.1  Coalition Belief Structures in California Water Policy

| Belief Category | Development Coalition | Protectionist Coalition |
|---|---|---|
| **I. Normative Core Beliefs** | | |
| Nature of man | Man has dominion over nature. | Man is part of nature, not superior to it. |
| Priority of values | Priority is placed on economic growth, economic security, material standards of living. | Aesthetic and ecological values should be on par with economic growth values. |
| Basic criteria for distributive justice | Human welfare needs to take precedence over nonhuman entities. | Individual actions must be constrained by public trust values and intergenerational equity considerations. |
| **II. Policy Core Beliefs** | | |
| Definition of problem | Water shortages occur because of the abandonment of large scale water resource development. | Wilderness and natural resources are being destroyed; existing water resources are used inefficiently. |
| Proper scope of government vs. private activity | Government's role should be limited to insuring that water is maximally developed for economic growth purposes. | Government intervention must be expanded to protect natural environments, but government should also encourage the development of water markets |
| Basic policy mechanisms | Large-scale government investments in water resource development. | Greater regulation combined with removing some institutional barriers to water markets |
| Proper distribution of authority among levels of government | Water development should be carried out by federal and state authorities; water consumption decisions should be centralized (i.e., in the hands of local water agencies and water districts). | While state regulatory power should be increased, individual ownership of water rights should be replaced local public control in cases where it will contribute to water use efficiency. |
| Desirability of participation | Decision making should be limited to traditional water development interests. | Public and environmental groups should have far greater role in water policy-making process. |

*(continues)*

lines the various beliefs of both the developmentalist and protectionist coalitions during the late 1970s and early 1980s.

During these two decades, the policy core and instrumental policy beliefs of some members of the protectionist advocacy coalition came to incorporate ideas and principles borrowed from economics—most notably, an emphasis on water transfers as an alternative to new water development projects. The incorporation of these economic ideas into the protectionist advocacy coalition's repertoire of beliefs is a concrete example of what Jenkins-Smith and Sabatier term "policy-oriented learning." But not all members of the protectionist coalition accepted these economic beliefs. Many environmentalists continued to emphasize that regulatory controls were the only legitimate approach to preserving natural water environments.

## III. THE CHANGING NATURE OF
## CALIFORNIA WATER POLITICS: 1966–1974

The central trend in California water politics from 1966 through 1984 was the movement away from conflict based largely on what group or

(Table 6.1 *continued*)

### III. Instrumental Policy Beliefs

| Cost/benefit ratio of new water development | The benefits from water development greatly outweigh specific environmental and financial costs. | Rarely are the benefits of new development greater than the costs. |
|---|---|---|
| Impact of stopping new water development | Disaster for farmers in the Central Valley; threat to southern California lifestyle and development. | Spare capacity in state and federal delivery systems makes new development unnecessary; with more efficient use of existing supplies, development can be indefinitely delayed. |
| Agriculture's use of water | Agriculture is a very efficient user of water. Further conservation efforts will not significantly increase efficiency but could result in lower yields. | Agriculture wastes water. By curtailing leakage, spillage, and seepage during storage and transport, as well as controlling deep percolation below the rootzone, significant supplies of water would become available. |
| The importance of water conservation | Water conservation/efficient water use can only make a limited contribution to California's growing water budget. Water conservation through regulation could also pose a threat to economic growth and quality of life. | Conservation/efficiency of water use will result in significant water savings. In turn, this water can be used to support new economic growth. |
| Necessity for institutional reforms | California's present water supply and distribution system is working well. Tampering with it will not result in additional water savings. However, it may jeopardize certain fundamental values such as local control. | California's present water laws and institutions are archaic. In order to signficantly increase water use efficiency, fundamental institutional reforms are necessary. |
| Adequacy of environmental protection | Existing protections of instream values are more than adequate. In fact, California's growing water needs will eventually require relaxing present standards of protection for both the Delta and North Coast rivers. | Instream values are not adequately protected. Many natural environments are in jeopardy of being destroyed. The Delta, North Coast rivers, San Francisco Bay, and Mono Lake all need additional protections. |

region materially gained or lost in the water development process. As the 1970s drew to a close, rather than concentrating upon the distributional consequences of particular pieces of legislation, groups and organizations that made up the two primary advocacy coalitions began to assess proposed policies according to how they impacted fundamental normative axioms and policy core beliefs. In other words, conflict became more ideological in character (Munro, 1988). Political leaders were also faced with the declining influence of development beliefs and the developmentalist coalition.

### *Defending the Core: The Reagan Administration's Response to Protectionist Water Use Beliefs*

Although the Reagan, Jerry Brown, and Deukmejian administrations were confronted with essentially the same phenomena of structural uncertainty and instability, their responses were quite different. For instance, William Gianelli, director of the Department of Water Resources during the Reagan governorship, defended the deep core and near (policy) core beliefs of the developmentalist paradigm. First, he attempted to maintain the causal assumption that continued economic growth was contingent upon further expansion of the state's water delivery system. Second, he attempted to refute the protectionist belief that new water resource development invariably led to population growth and ultimately to urban blight. Third, Gianelli attempted to demonstrate that development and protectionist objectives were not necessarily inconsistent. He emphasized in various public fora that it was not environmental protection per se that he was critical of, but the tactics of "self-serving" environmental groups.

Gianelli's efforts to defend the core beliefs of the developmentalist coalition were, however, unsuccessful. Not only was significant protectionist legislation passed during the 1972–1973 legislative session, but the Peripheral Canal, which both Reagan and Gianelli supported, was put on hold for the next administration to grapple with.

### Reconciling the Irreconcilable:
### The Brown Administration's Attempt to Balance
### Opposing Beliefs via the Peripheral Canal

The environmental movement matured into a potent political force in the period between the approval of the SWP in 1960 and the reelection of Governor Jerry Brown in 1978. Part of its influence resulted from the alliance struck between environmentalists and northern sectionalists who feared that the south would eventually rob the north of its water supply.

It also resulted from significant learning by environmentalists eager to reform the water policy–making process. As the decade of the 1970s grew to a close, a small but influential group of environmentalists—including Zack Willey of the Environmental Defense Fund (EDF) and Michael Storper of Friends of the Earth—began to use economic efficiency arguments to attain protectionist policy ends. Out of a pressing need to move beyond a strategy of obdurate obstructionism to water development projects, they began arguing for the more efficient use of available water supplies through better irrigation practices, water conservation in urban areas, and removal of legal barriers to the sale of agricultural water to urban users (who were usually willing to pay much higher prices than were agricultural users). In association with the protectionist belief that nonconsumptive uses (e.g., wilderness preservation, habitat protection) deserved priority within the policy-making process, more efficient water use became an alternative to the construction of new water projects in order to meet the needs of the state's increasing population.

Against the backdrop of an increasingly sophisticated environmental movement and escalating north/south conflict over water, Jerry Brown ran for governor in 1974. In contrast to other gubernatorial candidates, Brown openly questioned the validity of prodevelopment beliefs and policies. He refused to endorse the Peripheral Canal. He also chose to support an initiative (Proposition 17) that was aimed directly at halting work on the Corps of Engineers' New Melones Dam.

After winning the 1974 election, Governor Brown's allegiance to the environmental movement became even more striking. He appointed environmentalists to key positions within the state water bureaucracy, including Ronald B. Robie, a former Assembly Water Committee consultant and vice chairman of the State Water Resources Control Board (SWRCB), to lead the Department of Water Resources (the agency responsible for water planning and for operating the State Water Project).

In a 1975 speech before the prodevelopment Association of California Water Agencies, Robie articulated the primary tenets of the Brown administration's approach to water policy making:

> Water resources already developed shall be used to the maximum extent before new sources are developed.
>
> All alternative sources of supply, including water marketing, shall be considered.
>
> To maximize beneficial use, optimum application techniques and processes for water conservation shall be implemented and waste shall be avoided.
>
> Water shall be reused to the maximum extent feasible.
>
> Instream uses for recreation, fish, wildlife, and related purposes shall be balanced with other uses (Robie, 1975).

While Brown and Robie were committed to the beliefs and objectives of the protectionist coalition, they also recognized that contractual obligations, projections of water supply shortfalls, and political realities required a serious evaluation of various proposals to develop and transfer additional water supplies from northern to central and southern California. Consequently, in 1975 the Brown administration began a two-year review of the delta, the Peripheral Canal and its alternatives, and the future operation of the two major facilities for moving water from the Sacramento—San Joaquin Delta to the southern part of the state (the SWP and CVP).

Based on this review, on May 10, 1977, the Department of Water Resources and the Department of Fish and Game recommended that a staged Peripheral Canal be constructed. In June 1977, the Brown administration agreed to support Senate Bill 346—the Peripheral Canal Bill—after a coalition of water, environmental, labor, farming, and other groups agreed to a number of amendments. The governor claimed that he had secured "the most significant water compromise in a decade" (*Los Angeles Times*, June 24, 1977).

The compromise had something for everyone. The Peripheral Canal would provide additional high-quality water supplies to southern California farmers and urban areas. It would provide additional high-quality water supplies to those portions of the delta (especially Contra Costa County) experiencing saltwater intrusion from the operation of the SWP and CVP. It committed the state to restoring delta fisheries to their historic levels by removing pumping plants responsible for reverse water flows within the delta and by putting in place fully tested "bypass" fish screens at all projected water project diversion points. It included significant efficiency-of-use provisions, including funds for agricultural water conservation and the official planning assumption that 700,000 acre-feet of the total additional water supplied by the SWP in the year 2000 would be provided by water conservation and waste water reclamation programs.

Governor Brown's attempts to broker a compromise between opposing advocacy coalitions initially appeared to work. Senate Bill 346 moved through the Senate. However, by the time it reached the Assembly, the coalition of protectionist and development interests supporting the Peripheral Canal was breaking apart. Repeated efforts to secure final approval of Senate Bill 346 failed; Governor Brown and Ronald Robie finally threw in the political towel in August 1978 (Munro, 1988: Chapter 7).

Three causally important factors combined to undermine the brokering strategy pursued by the Brown administration. First, development interests and farmers from southern California believed that if they held out long enough, the legislature would eventually come around and support legislation with fewer guarantees for the delta. Specifically, the 65,000-acre Salyer Land Company and the 155,000-acre J. G. Boswell Company worked with water development purists within the California Farm Bureau to caution fellow water and agricultural interests that they would be worse off with the passage of the Brown water package than without it. From their point of view, Senate Bill 346 was nothing more than a "Trojan horse" that would provide an incremental increase in water supplies in return for the destruction of the developmentalist water policy regime (Munro, 1988:Chapter 7).

A second factor working against the delicate compromise sought by the Brown administration was the increasing strength of "sectarian" (Douglas and Wildavsky, 1982:114–115) elements within the environmental movement.[4] Compromise and incremental change, the hallmark of a pluralistic political process, were not included in the vernacular of these environmentalists who believed that if new development was brought to a standstill, natural events (e.g., higher energy-based water prices) would eventually force society to embrace a new policy-making regime. This regime would be founded, of course, on the normative axioms of the protectionist coalition.

The third and related factor working against Brown's delicate compromise was that the common cognitive and normative commitment to water resource development, which historically had mitigated and constrained sectional conflict, was now absent. By the late 1970s, certain northern legislators and their constituents had adopted the language and beliefs of environmental sectarians. The perception that the south was both indifferent to the 1976–1977 drought and stealing the north's water supplies, of course, underlay the receptivity of northerners to the sectarianism of certain environmental organizations like Friends of the Earth.

During the 1979–1980 legislative session, the Brown administration renewed its efforts to enact Peripheral Canal legislation. With the assistance of the Metropolitan Water District of Southern California (the largest water wholesaler in the region), the Brown administration shored up support for its new legislative water package, Senate Bill 200. The governor also supported the passage of Assembly Constitutional Amendment 90 (ACA 90), which was intended to provide additional legal guarantees for the protectionist sections of Senate Bill 200 while making it far more difficult for development interests to overturn existing legal protections for North Coast wild rivers.

Northerners in general and environmentalists in particular were not persuaded. They worked to derail Senate Bill 200 by adding amendments consistent with the core beliefs of the protectionist coalition but completely unpalatable to even moderate prodevelopment interests. Not only did they attempt to attach mandatory groundwater management provisions to Senate Bill 200 and more stringent delta water-quality guarantees, but they also attempted to tie implementation of the Peripheral Canal legislation to voter approval of ACA 90.

Governor Brown refused to link approval of SB 200 to either voter approval of ACA 90 or additional water policy reform amendments. He thus avoided giving hardline development interests like Salyer Land Company and J. G. Boswell Company sufficient ammunition to defeat the canal in the legislature. On July 18, 1980, Governor Brown signed SB 200 into law.

Ultimately, however, protectionist and developmentalist sectarians would have the final say. Given political energy by northern and southern California environmentalists and consumer activists, and financed by Boswell and Salyer, the Coalition Against the Peripheral Canal managed to place an anti–Peripheral Canal proposition on the June 1982 ballot.[5] The projected cost of the Peripheral Canal quickly became the mechanism by which the hardline protectionists and developmentalists turned public opinion against the Brown water package. While both Governor Brown and Ronald Robie mounted a last-ditch effort to sway public opinion, on June 6, 1982, almost 60% of the electorate voted to reject the Peripheral Canal (Munro, 1988:Chapter 7).

*The Peripheral Canal Referendum: The Triumph of Sectarianism over a Policy Broker*

Although Governor Brown could have been more active in the referendum battle, ultimately the defeat of Peripheral Canal legislation cannot be laid at his feet nor those of Ronald Robie. Both men judiciously and cleverly applied the political resources at their disposal in an attempt to broker a policy compromise. They used classic rational-analytic procedures to identify a water package that optimized on several value dimensions. They were sensitive to the beliefs and interests of opposing advocacy coalitions and from the outset attempted to bring both protectionist and development interests into the policy-making process as full participants.

Despite the political and analytical rationality of Brown administration officials, time after time their efforts were frustrated by sectarian interests and organizations committed to opposing core beliefs. To development sectarians, even incremental movements toward protectionist and efficiency-of-use policies constituted a fundamental threat. To environmental sectarians, policies that attempted to strike a balance between developmentalist and protectionist values and beliefs were politically and ethically insufficient. Policy extremists in both the developmentalist and protectionist advocacy coalitions made it virtually impossible for the Brown administration and middle-of-the-road legislators to broker a policy compromise.

Ultimately the efforts of developmentalist and protectionist sectarians were aided by a political institution (i.e., the referendum) that facilitated intervention by the electorate within the water policy–making process. Specifically, by taking the battle outside the relatively insulated walls of the state legislature, sectarians effectively neutralized Governor Brown. He simply could not afford to vigorously fight for a water plan that was opposed by many northerners and most environmentalists and still expect to harbor any hopes of winning a U.S. Senate seat in 1982.

## IV. POLICY LEARNING IN AN ERA OF INSTITUTIONAL STALEMATE

The Brown administration was not able to set in place a comprehensive water package that actually balanced protectionist and developmentalist beliefs. Instead, its accomplishment was that it set in place an enduring set of stimuli for long-range cognitive and behavioral change.

When Governor George Deukmejian (1983–1990) attempted to secure legislative approval of his own water transfer program during the 1983–1984 legislative session, he found that the Brown administration had established a *policy floor* that he simply could not circumvent or undermine. The original Deukmejian water plan ignored most of the protectionist and efficiency-of-use components included in the Brown administration's Peripheral Canal legislative package. After finding out that its through-delta water conveyance system faced almost certain defeat within the legislature, the Deukmejian administration subsequently sent to the Senate a set of proposals that included a plan to "save one-million acre-feet of water by the end of the century through conservation and water reclamation." Other provisions of this revised water plan included a commitment to clean up the polluted San Joaquin River and to establish additional protections for fish affected by cross-delta water shipments. Despite these modifications, his plan was defeated and the

1983–1984 legislative session ended with the state's water development future in limbo (Munro, 1988:Chapter 7).

In addition to a policy floor, the Brown administration established a wide variety of demonstration projects and research programs geared to protection and efficiency-of-use objectives. Among the most important was the California Irrigation Management System (CIMIS). CIMIS promoted improved irrigation management by providing weather information to growers through a small computer with a telephone modem, thereby maximizing crop production while reducing the amount of water applied. Although these projects have not resulted in farmers abandoning new development as the policy option of choice, demonstration projects like CIMIS continue to grow in popularity (Munro, 1988:Chapter 6).

The Brown administration's protectionist-efficient water use legacy is evident in a third way. By incorporating protection and efficient water use as primary policy objectives into Department of Water Resources planning documents (California Department of Water Resources, 1976, 1978, 1982b), Brown and Robie established an administrative and planning structure that future administrations would find difficult to ignore (Munro, 1988:Chapter 6).

Despite attempts by certain hardliners within the DWR to "gut" water conservation programs and policies during the transition period between the Brown and Deukmejian administrations, funding for water conservation has remained stable. Robie's persistent efforts to imbue the public and policy-making elites with a protectionist-efficiency-of-use ethic—aided by the 1976–1977 and 1984–1991 droughts—continues to influence the course and character of California water policy making.

The Governor's Commission to Review Water Rights Law (1977)—which represented an effort by Brown administration officials to establish a "professionalized communication forum" (ACF, Chapter 3)—failed to produce dramatic changes relating to the policy core beliefs of either coalition. It did, however, facilitate some changes in secondary aspects, including the passage of various pieces of legislation during the late 1970s and early 1980s that attempted to protect water rights during periods of nonuse and voluntary water transfers (Engelbert, 1982: Chapters 8 and 9). The enactment of statutes encouraging water transfers and marketing continued during the 1980s, until very few legal impediments remained by the end of the decade (Grey, 1989).

The approval of legislation supporting voluntary, limited water transfers reflects learning on the part of water and agricultural interests who historically viewed water markets and transfers as threats to local control. It also reflects learning on the part of the environmental community, which until the mid-1970s ignored the potential contribution of markets to meeting California's water needs. Policy learning on the part of the environmental community was facilitated by recognition that government-established water markets could work hand-in-hand with traditional regulatory controls to forestall development and protect natural water environments.

This learning process was aided by generational change within the environmental movement. By the late 1970s, the California environmental movement included a small but politically aggressive contingent of young "econocrats." Included in this group were Zach Willey, a senior economist for the Environmental Defense Fund, and Michael Storper, a Berkeley-trained Ph.D geographer who also had some training in economics, who represented Friends of the Earth in Sacramento (Munro, 1988:Chapter 4).

The establishment of water markets in California was furthered by the regulatory actions of the Brown administration. Responding to a complaint that attributed the rise in the Salton Sea (east of San Diego) and the corresponding inundation of adjacent fields to wasteful water use practices by the Imperial Irrigation District (IID), the Department of Water Resources conducted a study of IID's water use practices under Section 175 of the Water Code. Based on this study, the State Water Resources Control Board (SWRCB) ruled in 1984 that IID was wasting water, which, under California law, meant that it could lose rights to that water. Already confronted with a 55% reduction in its historic supply from the Colorado River, the IID began negotiations with the Metropolitan Water District whereby MWD would pay for improving irrigation canals, and then much of the "conserved" water would then be sold to MWD. This proposal was strongly supported by the Environmental Defense Fund.

As a direct consequence of both forced and unforced learning, water markets are evolving into policy options that lie within the "acceptable [policy] space" of both developmentalist and protectionist advocacy coalitions (see Chapter 2).

## V. CONCLUSION

From the vantage point of the 1990s, the example of California water policy making in the late 1970s and early 1980s underscores the explanatory utility and predictive power of the advocacy coalition framework.

Core-to-core conflict continues to prevent the passage of legislation that would allow increases in the amount of water exported from north to south, including the construction of the Peripheral Canal. Although the water industry continues to enjoy political clout (particularly in the Deukmejian administration), it is blocked by legislative leadership that is pro-north and sympathetic to environmental concerns and beliefs.

The post-1984 record validates the ACF thesis that "self-interested" policy learning is an important force in promoting long-term, albeit incremental, change. The most dramatic example is the recent agreement between the MWD and the IID. This agreement demonstrates the combined importance of intervention by state actors and external events and pressures in facilitating policy learning and change. Without the specter of MWD losing a significant portion of its Colorado River entitlement,[6] the agency would never have entered into negotiations with IID. Likewise, early intervention by Ronald Robie and the State Water Resources Board was necessary for IID to recognize the advantages that would result from MWD's overhaul of its water distribution infrastructure.

The MWD-IID agreement also underscores the limitations of policy learning. Without a doubt, the new-found emphasis by MWD on market arrangements demonstrates that the organization has adopted specific secondary beliefs of the protectionist advocacy coalition. As of 1989, however, MWD had not backed away from the core belief that the development of new water supplies is crucial to the well being of southern California (MWD, 1989).

After years of conflict and institutional stalemate, the core beliefs of the developmentalist coalition remain unaltered. While traditional development interests such as the MWD are willing to accept market arrangements as interim solutions, ultimately their hearts and minds still focus on the development of new water supplies. The continuance of these beliefs and the fusion of protectionist and efficient water use beliefs in the minds of certain influential environmentalists supports the ACF's argument that policy learning is usually restricted to secondary aspects of belief systems.

Despite its overall explanatory utility, several criticisms of the ACF emerge from its application to the California water policy–making process. First, current applications of the model tend to underestimate the importance of systemic beliefs (similar to the relatively stable parameter Sabatier calls "fundamental sociocultural values") in affecting the rate and nature of long-term change within water policy–making systems. Belief structures, at least those that reach the political and social status of a stable system parameter, work their effects through a socialization process that limits and molds behavior across the entire subsystem by determining the universe of legitimate policy opportunities and constraints. By exploring the process by which beliefs are diffused from specific advocacy coalitions into the wider cultural and social context in which a particular policy-making subsystem operates, one can better understand why certain policy battles between advocacy coalitions center on secondary policy aspects and others center on the triumph or displacement of core beliefs.

During the 1950s, for instance, water policy conflicts centered on secondary aspects (i.e., who would economically win and who would lose if the State Water Project were built). By the early 1970s, however, conflicts centered on which core beliefs and values would provide the cognitive "structure" in which water politics was played out. The decline in the efficacy of development beliefs and the concomitant increase in the importance of protectionist and efficiency-of-use beliefs fundamentally changed the character of political conflict in California. Indeed, the pre-1970 consensus on water resource development has been replaced by conflict between two opposing visions of California's water future.

Second, the ACF is limited by its lack of attention to the role of extremists (sectarians) within advocacy coalitions. In the case of California water policy making, for example, the electorate's defeat of the Brown administration's "balancing" approach to water policy in the 1982 Peripheral Canal referendum resulted from the domination of both advocacy coalitions by *sectarian* interests (Douglas and Wildavsky, 1982) that worked to protect the core beliefs of their respective belief structures. Sectarians rejected out-of-hand the balancing of developmentalist, protectionist, and efficient water use objectives within one legislative package.

In the absence of hardliners on both sides, the political debate probably would have centered on secondary policy aspects, thereby making compromise between northern and southern California more likely. Ironically, and in apparent refutation of Hypothesis 1, which states that "on major controversies within a policy subsystem when core beliefs are in dispute, the lineup of allies and opponents tends to be rather stable over periods of a decade or so" (Chapter 2), it was sectarians in both advocacy coalitions who united in the prototypical short-term "coalition of convenience" to defeat the Peripheral Canal. By bringing back the status quo ante, developmentalists and protectionist sectarians believed their respective belief cores would *ultimately* triumph.

While the ACF has broken new ground in moving from individual interest groups to advocacy coalitions, it is important not to allow the framework to lead students of long-term change to view advocacy coalitions as unitary actors. Coalitional behavior appears distinctly more fluid than the ACF would suggest. Particular attention need to be accorded differences between "extremists/sectarians" and "pragmatists" within any coalition.

The third and final limitation of the ACF is the importance Sabatier and Jenkins-Smith assign to the "professionalized communication fora" and the "analytical tractability" of a policy problem in explaining when and where policy learning across belief systems will occur. While these factors can promote policy learning, their causal importance will differ significantly from case to case.

The California experience suggests that policy learning over the long term is the child of political stalemate. Indeed, the *political intractability* of the Peripheral Canal issue has forced traditional development interests to compromise their principles and look to greater efficiency of use as a viable policy option. Political intractability in association with activist state-level political actors, external perturbations like drought, and long-term socioeconomic changes (rising energy costs, lack of accessible dam sites) are responsible for the gradual ascendence of protectionist and efficient water use beliefs. No longer is water resource development automatically the policy solution of choice.

Despite these criticisms, Sabatier and Jenkins-Smith have outlined an important and empirically useful approach to studying the motor forces of long-term policy change. The framework should, however, (1) place greater emphasis on the process by which beliefs can come to act as relatively stable parameters for the entire policy-making community, (2) give a more prominent role to differences between sectarians and pragmatists in many coalitions, and (3) focus on political crisis and stalemate as a primary cause of policy learning and change. As anomalies beget scientific transformations, political crises can beget policy learning and change. One could also reasonably expect that the framework's current normative commitment to "professionalized fora" as significant promoters of policy learning and change would be reconsidered.

## NOTES

1. The CVP primarily benefits farmers in the southern San Joaquin Valley (e.g., Fresno County), while SWP water primarily goes to urban areas in Orange, Los Angeles, and San Diego counties.

2. The pumps are so powerful that they actually make water flow *upstream* in the San Joaquin River. These "reverse flows" draw additional salt water from San Francisco Bay into the delta, which threatens water quality for both agricultural and urban users who divert from the delta.

3. There is some similarity between Popper's and Lakatos's view of science as determined by "rules of reason" and the Sabatier and Jenkins-Smith commitment to "professionalized fora," where informed analytical debate can lead coalitions to revise their belief systems. This overly rational concept of policy learning conflicts with Kuhn's approach to scientific change. For an excellent analysis of Kuhn and his critics, see Barnes (1982).

4. "Sectarianism" is an approach to politics characterized by a dichotomized worldview in which policies that are consistent with one's core values are always good, those that aren't are evil, and compromise is unacceptable. While Douglas and Wildavsky (1982) focus on secretarian environmental organizations, this review of California water politics indicates that development organizations can be equally sectarian.

5. Under California law, citizens had three to six months after passage of SB 200 in June 1980 to obtain the signatures to put the issue to a referendum. They did so, but not in time for the November 1980 general election. The vote was then postponed to the next statewide general election, in June 1982. The implementation of SB 200 was put into abeyance pending the results of that election.

6. MWD's annual entitlement to Colorado River water has recently been about 1.2 million acre-feet. Settlement of various Indian rights claims and prior perfected rights, plus evaporation and seepage losses, could mean that MWD's effective future allotment might be reduced to as little as 400,000 acre-feet annually.

# 7

# Managing Technological Change in Federal Communications Policy: The Role of Industry Advisory Groups

RICHARD P. BARKE

Throughout its history the Federal Communications Commission (FCC) has been faced with the emergence of new technologies that have challenged existing regulatory practices and precedents. The FCC's adaptation to many of these innovations (such as microwave telephony and cable television) was slow and fitful, as would be explained by theories of regulatory behavior that focus on political and economic conflicts (e.g., Peltzman, 1976). Yet other innovations have been handled by the FCC with much less conflict. In the commission's decisions regarding technical standards for broadcast television, for example, the economic stakes were enormous but there often was cooperation between the FCC and the affected firms as well as among the firms. These actions are the subject of this chapter, which explores the FCC's ability to learn from the successes and failures of its attempts to set technical standards.

I will examine FCC behavior in several cases over a span of several decades involving a particular type of technological change. After a general discussion of policy change and a more specific examination of the effects of technological change in public-policy making, I will turn to an analysis of FCC standard setting for broadcast television technologies. Finally, I will offer conclusions about the possibilities for policy learning when conflict is weak and when technological and market constraints on policy alternatives are strong. In cases where disputes involve highly tractable issues, policy formation and adoption have been successfully delegated to professional fora that produced consensual recommendations to public officials.

## I. POLICY CHANGE AND POLICY LEARNING

In Chapters 2 and 3 of this volume, Sabatier and Jenkins-Smith developed the advocacy coalition framework (ACF) for understanding policy

change and policy learning. Like all models, theirs is not intended to capture all the complexities of the real world but rather to explain some of
what we observe. Before applying that framework to FCC technical standard setting, I shall first briefly discuss the most relevant components of
that model and summarize the substance of the particular policy to be
examined.

### Policy Subsystems and Advocacy Coalitions

Even in the most pluralist political system, no policy issue is salient to
all individuals or groups. Each issue involves a group of public and private actors who are affected by the policy in question and who therefore
provide the demands, political support, economic incentives, and procedural constraints that shape the policy process. These subsystems are divided into coalitions that advocate policies based on their basic values,
causal assumptions, and problem perceptions—or belief systems—and
on the resources available to them. Their actions are constrained by relatively stable factors, such as the Constitution, cultural values, and social
and economic structures. In addition, the laws of nature and the requirements of technology often impose limits on the choices available to coalitions, as illustrated by the cases to be described here.

In applying the concept of advocacy coalitions, it may be tempting to
implicitly treat them as more narrow, stable, or influential than they actually are. The limits imposed upon policy actors can explain more than
their basic values, and although these limits may be stable, they may also
be far more specific than constitutions or cultural values. For example, in
response to innovations in microwave technology during the 1940s and
1950s, the FCC was petitioned to allow firms to compete with AT&T's
long-distance telephone microwave hegemony. The FCC's inability to
challenge AT&T was caused in large part by legal constraints that were
beyond the agency's control—such as permissible delays by AT&T
and the FCC's lack of power to discover the relevant cost and technical
data. Such constraints operate regardless of the belief systems of the
participants.

Although conflicts over belief systems are usually the instigators of
policy disputes, they must be fought in an arena shaped by both general
and specific institutional constraints. The judicial and statutory mandates
that limit an agency's choices are often based on precedents and doc-
trines that have nothing to do with economic markets, political coalitions,
or even current conflicts over belief systems. When an appeals court told
the FCC in 1956 to consider whether the Hush-a-Phone device (a rubber
cup that attached to a telephone mouthpiece for private conversations)
physically impaired AT&T's facilities, it did not consider (as had the
FCC) whether a significant economic or political demand for the product
existed. The end of the era of foreign attachment prohibitions had begun
because of an exogenous event—which the Hush-a-Phone company had
anticipated and used strategically. Thus, it should be remembered that
the interaction among advocacy coalitions that is so central to Sabatier's

framework may itself interact with external constraints to produce policy changes.

## Policy Change

The relevant question for most studies of policy change is not "Did policy change?" but "What type of change occurred, and why?" At the narrowest scale, a policy program changes frequently in at least some aspects in order to track the changing real world (by which I mean those conditions that are beyond the immediate control of the policy maker and must be taken as given). If policy consists of the goals, principles, and general strategies of government, then here, too, change will be the norm. General strategies, like particular programs, must be flexible enough to respond to changes in real-world conditions and to evaluations of previous strategies. Majone and Wildavsky have argued that "[p]olicies are continuously transformed by implementing actions that simultaneously alter resources and objectives" (1978:109). However, we must assume that changes in broad goals are usually incremental and that they occur slowly enough to provide the continuity that makes policy evaluations possible (Mazmanian and Sabatier, 1989:8).

Two methodological problems in explaining policy change should be emphasized. First, any study of change requires a constant frame of reference which is often lacking in public policy (as, for example, when we see simultaneous change in legislative mandates, political coalitions, "real world" conditions, and public policy). Second, as the case of the telephone mouthpiece attachment illustrates, policy change can result from exogenous events to which the policy process may respond, but not necessarily adapt, or from turnover in personnel. It may also occur because of a shift in the decision-making arena from federal to state government, from public to private actors, or from one federal agency to another. Policy change can occur without policy learning.

## Policy Learning

In Chapter 3, Jenkins-Smith and Sabatier define "policy-oriented learning" as "relatively enduring alterations of thought or behavioral intentions that result from experience and that are concerned with the attainment (or revision) of public policy." Specifically, they draw attention to learning with regard to: (1) deep core beliefs (fundamental normative axioms), (2) policy core beliefs (basic strategies for achieving those fundamental goals in a specific policy area), and (3) secondary aspects (new information relevant to policy strategies). Operationally, we can look for policy learning in explicit or consistent changes in behavior that make outcomes more congruent with stated or inferred goals. The relevant learning may be about procedures that make goal attainment more likely, or it can be about the substance of policies, such as empirical facts, causal relationships, political necessities, and so on.

Policy learning may be very difficult to detect. There is an important difference between "Type I" learning (not changing that which seems to work well) and "Type II" learning (becoming better at avoiding mistakes). Thus, sometimes policy learning is revealed by an absence of policy or procedural change. In addition, policy learning may take the form of procedural changes that are manifested in substantive change only after a long time. And what is labeled policy learning may actually be familiar policies dressed in new clothing. For example, the FCC of the 1980s proclaimed that it had learned from the deregulatory movement to rely on the marketplace, but there are many decisions predating the commission's self-proclaimed learning experience that suggest a previous alteration of decision criteria.

### Professional Fora

The framework proposed by Sabatier and Jenkins-Smith relates policy change and learning to the location of conflict resolution. In Chapter 3, for example, they discuss the open forum, in which all subsystem members may participate, as an extension of the pluralist political system, and the professional forum, which admits only those participants who possess the particular skills needed to analyze technically complex issues. The type of forum is hypothesized to have a significant effect on policy learning and the resolution of conflict among advocacy coalitions.

Technical standard setting is a topic beyond the expertise or interest of most people and groups. In the conclusion to this chapter, I will explore the implications of the substantive policy problem for the development of coalitions, the formation of industry advisory groups, and the interaction of the public and private spheres in policy learning. Broadcast television standard setting illustrates the mutual and often simultaneous dependence of coalition behavior, forum formation, and policy learning.

### II. CONSTRAINTS ON AGENCY DISCRETION

The Communications Act of 1934 directed the FCC to regulate broadcasting apparatus "with respect to its external effects and the purity and sharpness of the emissions," to "study new uses for radio, provide for experimental uses of frequencies, and generally encourage the larger and more effective use of radio in the public interest," and to require that television receivers "be capable of adequately receiving all frequencies allocated by the Commission to television broadcasting." Congress did not forget its mandate to the FCC. The FCC Authorization Act of 1983 included a statutory presumption that "any new technology or service is in the public interest" and "required the FCC to make a public interest determination as to any new technology or service within one year after a petition of application is filed" (Shooshan and Krasnow, 1985). Similarly, the courts continued to remind the FCC of its responsibility for the development and promulgation of new technologies. In 1978 the U.S. Supreme Court stated that "although a statutory void cannot itself create jurisdiction in an agency, and although neither agencies nor courts receive legislative powers not exercised by Congress, the rapid growth of communications technology requires a unified system of regulation, and enough flexibility and breadth of mandate to permit the FCC, confronted with new technology not governed by statute but having serious impact on technology that is, to adopt such regulations as will enable it to protect the public interest" (*Midwest Video v. FCC*, 439 US 816), Thus, technological change has been a basic condition for the FCC's work.

Institutional constraints such as legislative oversight and judicial review can overshadow and overwhelm battles among ideologically based coalitions. Intervention from the courts or Congress may be unexpected and unsolicited, but it also may be the result of attempts by advocacy coalitions to engage their opponents in additional arenas.

## III. TECHNICAL STANDARDS AND PUBLIC POLICY

Technical standards serve several purposes, of which only one (compatibility) is explicitly mentioned in the 1934 Communications Act. Standards fit Paul Samuelson's definition of a public good because they are available for use by all, their use by one does not reduce the amount available for others, and they have strong economies of scale, that is, the more standards are used, the more all gain in comparability and interchangeability (Samuelson, 1954; Artle and Averous, 1975; Kindleberger, 1983). Standards benefit consumers (owing to mass production, price competition resulting from standardized product features, a reduction in information costs, and protection against rapid obsolescence) and regulators (who may be able to use standards to reduce future decision costs). Standards also reduce uncertainty for firms, not only because risk-averse consumers are calmed into making purchases but also because the future market is bounded by product features. When a regulatory agency withholds technical standards, firms are reluctant to invest in R&D that may become worthless if standards are eventually imposed.

Technical standards also have vices. They may lock current technology in place because of sunk costs to firms and because regulators may see no short-term benefits to overturning established standards. Furthermore, standards—whether regulatory or imposed de facto by a dominant firm—can radically shape competition among firms (Adams and Brock, 1982). In his decision regarding the breakup of AT&T, Judge Harold Greene of D.C. district court found that because of the need for compatibility in telecommunications, competitors' "inability to obtain Bell technical information/compatibility standards constitute(d) an insuperable barrier to entry" (U.S. v. ATT, 524 F. Supp. 1336). In fact, sometimes no standard is actually a double standard: By refusing to issue a standard for AM stereo radio in the early 1980s, the FCC increased the uncertainty about which of four competing systems would prevail, thereby delaying the introduction of a competitive threat to FM stereo radio. In addition, the choice of single technical standard must be based on assumptions about future technological changes and the potential reaction of consumers to a market with multiple standards or no standards at all. Multiple or voluntary standards leave both choice and risk with consumers, who may benefit from the rapid availability of innovations but who may also later suffer the costs of obsolescence as a single industry standard evolves. These are the issues that not only defined the choices that the FCC made regarding broadcast television standards but also shaped the coalitions within the policy subsystem. Technical standards have the potential of arousing intense conflict because of enormous potential economic consequences. At the same time, standards in developed technologies may involve very tractable questions about engineering capabilities or network compatibility. As we shall see, these two features were critical in the FCC's attempts to make broadcast television policy.

### The Broadcast Standard Setting Subsystem

The policy subsystem for broadcast standard setting consists primarily of the FCC, broadcasters, receiver and transmitter manufacturers, Congress, and the courts. Consumer (viewer) groups and advocates have been noticeably absent as participants because of the technical nature of the subject. The prevailing stances (or belief systems) of Congress and the courts have been discussed already; they were only occasionally directly involved with technical standard setting. The belief systems of FCC commissioners and staff on this topic have been relatively consistent across the years regardless of systemic governing coalitions or political trends. Perhaps the only relevant deep core belief of the FCC was its perception of the public as those present and future television viewers whose welfare would be affected by the commission's decisions.[1] Its significant policy core beliefs were technological optimism, insistence that the welfare of the industry was dependent upon the satisfaction of viewers, and a desire to avoid decisions when the marketplace or industry actions might suffice (again, these policy beliefs were generally held regardless of who occupied the White House). At the secondary level, the FCC appears to have taken seriously its mandate to maximize the size of the viewing public and their choices, and it usually recognized the inadequacy of available information relevant to standard setting.

One of the most important characteristics of this policy issue has been the apparent similarity between the core belief systems of the FCC and the private firms with an interest in technical standards. For example, broadcasters have a strong interest in maximizing the number of viewers (and thereby maximizing their advertising revenues). In a dynamic technological product market, broadcasters are subject to short-run benefits and long-run costs similar to those of consumers; they will benefit from quick, stable, and adequate single standards. In contrast, manufacturers have a strong interest in obsolescence after the market is saturated,[2] so they might be expected to have an interest in multiple standards based on short-run costs (due to slow consumer acceptance) and long-term benefits (when replacement occurs). Thus, the cases to be discussed share two peculiar common features. First, the parties involved generally showed little conflict over core beliefs such as the desirability of standards, but because of the different economic incentives for the exact nature of those standards, there remained intense conflict over other issues. Second, these secondary conflicts were bounded by the network of standards that evolved from a starting point in which, during the formative years of television, the dominant manufacturing firm was also the dominant broadcasting firm: the Radio Corporation of America (RCA). This phenomenon of overlapping interests and belief systems shaped the FCC's responses to subsequent technical innovations.

### Consensus and Policy Negotiation

The FCC needed to promulgate policies that would be supported by all relevant interests; while compromises are acceptable in some realms, electronic components are not very flexible (see Hypothesis 3 of the ACF). In addition, a firm that was excluded from considerations on technical standards might convince Congress or the courts that it had been denied competitive entry into a market. Therefore, technical standard setting became an exercise in the development of consensus not only between the FCC and the firms but also among firms.

It is difficult to precisely define consensus. "Does it mean unanimity; no 'reasonable' dissent; concurrent majorities, in which a majority of each interest agrees; a substantial majority of those present; a simple majority; or some other calculation?" (Harter, 1982:92). For television standards there was agreement on what was to be maximized (the "satisfaction" of the viewing public), but there were intense disputes about how that goal was to be achieved. The analytical tractability of the issue, derived from the issue itself rather than the sophistication of the analysts, made learning and adjustment possible but did not resolve the disputes. In each standards case there remained a crucial intractable issue: how to balance today's interests of consumers against their interests after technology has advanced.

Philip Harter's discussion of the conditions that facilitate regulatory negotiations and the development of a consensus can be adapted to the Sabatier and Jenkins-Smith framework: (1) Each coalition can impose costs on the others, creating an incentive to bargain; (2) the number of coalitions is small enough that bargaining is feasible; (3) the coalitions have agreed to limit the range of options under discussion; (4) no disturbing breakthrough or new information is expected that could alter core belief systems; (5) another party will make a decision if no agreement is reached; (6) several different (non–deep core) issues are under consideration, allowing compromises across issues; and (7) a regulatory agency will consider and perhaps implement the agreement (Harter, 1982:45–51). Points (2), (3), and (4) relate to the professional fora discussed in Chapter 3. As the cases below illustrate, when all of these conditions were present, successful policy changes were adopted by the FCC (as hypothesized by the ACF).

## IV. BROADCAST TELEVISION STANDARD SETTING

I will illustrate the characteristics of policy learning in the broadcast television arena by examining three cases. The first stems from the period 1939–1941, when the FCC was pressed by pioneering firms to adopt technical standards for black-and-white (or monochrome) television. In the second, from the years following World War II, the FCC faced a similar set of problems with regard to color television standards. Third, in the early 1980s the FCC was asked to issue standards for direct broadcast satellites.

### Monochrome Television

From the earliest days of television development in the 1920s, it was recognized that large-scale commercialization of television would require agreements on equipment compatibility and frequencies. In 1928 the Radio Manufacturers Association (RMA) formed a Television Standardization Committee, which recommended standards that were obsolete on the day they were issued. Although the Federal Radio Commission rejected the recommendation, the precedent had been set for intra-industry planning (Udelson, 1982:45).

The regulators' task was difficult and closely watched. Patent disputes were raging between the systems of television pioneer Philo T. Farnsworth and RCA's Vladimir Zworykin; meanwhile, television was being hailed as "a new 'frontier' industry which can be developed to break the back of the depression" (*Telecommunications Reports,* June 6, 1935:1). In its first year of existence the FCC took a step toward commercial television by requesting that the members of the RMA cooperate in devising standards that would be agreeable to all manufacturers. When offered, those standards were rejected by the FCC because the industry was still too "unstable," and in spite of persistent appeals from manufacturers for standards, the FCC insisted that it would not allow the public to be misled into buying expensive receivers before the industry had stabilized.[3]

Under great pressure from Congress, the FCC adopted rules in early 1940 to allow "limited commercial service" in order for experimental work to continue and to allow the industry to defray some of its growing research expenses. RCA responded by running full-page newspaper ads proclaiming that television was ready for the home and that the price of RCA receivers had just been greatly reduced. Three days later the FCC suspended limited commercialization and ordered RCA to explain why its advertisements failed to warn the public about the possible obsolescence of their new receivers. The FCC suspected RCA of trying to establish a de facto technical standard and thereby gain a virtual monopoly over receiver production.[4] Newspaper editorials attacked the FCC's "usurpation of power," and a Senate investigation was launched. President Franklin D. Roosevelt was forced to announce that the FCC had his complete backing as it protected the public against monopolization and the freezing of standards. The conflict had moved into the realm of near core beliefs.

The industry was now divided into those firms (RCA, General Electric, and Farnsworth Television and Radio) that supported standards immediatley and those (Philco, Zenith Radio, DuMont Laboratories, and CBS) that argued that standards were still premature. The conflict took on several dimensions. First, there were genuine questions about the technical superiority of various systems, the acceptability of the television image to viewers, and the adaptability of each system to further improvements. Second, some firms continued to insist that no standards should be imposed. Third, and most important, the leading firm, RCA, aroused intense suspicion because of its control of vital television patents and its eagerness to recoup its R&D expenses by beginning commercial broadcasts. The FCC even subpoenaed RMA files to determine the extent to which it was controlled by RCA.

To break this deadlock by isolating the analytically tractable issues from broader questions, a General Electric engineer proposed an industry advisory group that would recommend a consensus television standard. Formed by the RMA on July 17, 1940, the National Television Systems Committee (NTSC) included representatives of all major (and most minor) broadcasting and manufacturing firms as well as several small firms (see Table 7.1). All dimensions of conflict were represented; moreover, the seven conditions for successful negotiation discussed by Harter were fulfilled by the NTSC, which served as a professional forum to resolve secondary aspects of the policy dispute. The incentive to participate and cooperate was clear: Without an agreement, the television industry would go nowhere.[5]

Following nine months of testimony, experimentation, and discussion, the NTSC produced its recommendations after a compromise (suggested by GE's Donald Fink) on the most contentious technical question was

TABLE 7.1 Members of First NTSC, 1941

|  | Broadcaster | Manufacturer | Trade Association |
|---|---|---|---|
| Bell Telephone Laboratories |  | x |  |
| Columbia Broadcasting System | x |  |  |
| Don Lee Broadcasting | x |  |  |
| DuMont Laboratories |  | x |  |
| Farnsworth Television and Radio | x | x |  |
| General Electric |  | x |  |
| Hazeltine Electronics |  | x |  |
| Institute of Radio Engineers |  |  | x |
| National Association of Broadcasters |  |  | x |
| Philco |  | x |  |
| Radio Corporation of America | x | x |  |
| Stromberg-Carlson |  | x |  |
| Television Productions | x |  |  |
| Zenith Radio |  | x |  |

accepted on an 11-2 vote. "[E]ngineers from RCA and Philco complained good-naturedly to Fink that he had chosen the wrong value, too high and too low, respectively; the fact that both seemed equally unhappy was perhaps evidence that the compromise was a proper one" (Fink, 1976:1327). The next month, the FCC formally approved the monochrome NTSC standards, which, for the most part, remain in effect today. Finding that the standards represented "with but few exceptions, the undivided engineering opinion of the industry," the FCC lauded the NTSC for compiling eleven volumes of evidence to support its recommendations.[6] The NTSC had served as an effective professional forum for the formation of a near-consensus on engineering matters.

## Color Television

Research on color television began in the 1920s. By 1940 it was sufficiently developed that, in its order adopting the NTSC monochrome standards, the FCC encouraged "immediate experimental color program transmissions." The key actors in color television R&D were two firms with deep pockets: After World War II CBS and RCA pursued very different color television technologies. CBS was committed to a system that used a spinning wheel to pass red, blue, and green filters in front of the receiving tube as it displayed corresponding images; existing monochrome sets would not be able to receive any picture unless converted. Not only was such a system unwieldy, but it also required extra frequency bandwidth, so when CBS filed a petition in 1946 for adoption of its system as the industry standard it also asked the FCC to allocate two adjacent UHF channels for each station. At the same time RCA promised that within five years it would have perfected an all-electronic system using existing bandwidths that would be fully compatible with monochrome sets. In 1947 the FCC rejected the CBS petition as premature.

Soon afterward (in September 1948), the FCC froze the licensing of additional television stations because VHF slots were filled in many cities and UHF broadcasting had not begun, even experimentally. Intended to last only about six months, the freeze granted breathing room for the FCC and for television manufacturers, who were anticipating a resolution to the dispute over color standards. Since no one had demonstrated that color television could fit into the bandwidth allocated to monochrome, large pieces of the UHF spectrum could be reserved for wide color channels if necessary. UHF broadcasts could not begin without color standards because (1) bandwidth requirements had to be determined before UHF allocations were made, and (2) the end of the freeze would cause a rapid increase in the sales of television sets that could become obsolete if color standards were not adopted first (Table 7.2). In May 1949 the FCC consolidated its proceedings on UHF and color standards.

Although many were suspicious of RCA (which received more than 75% of all television industry patent royalty payments), most manufacturers realized that its fully compatible all-electronic system had much greater potential than CBS's spinning wheels. On its side, CBS had Edwin

TABLE 7.2 Percentage of Households with a Television Set, 1946-1975

| Year | Black and White Only | Color | TOTAL |
|------|---------------------|-------|-------|
| 1946 | 0.02 | -- | 0.02 |
| 1947 | 0.04 | -- | 0.04 |
| 1948 | 0.4 | -- | 0.4 |
| 1949 | 2.3 | -- | 2.3 |
| 1950 | 9.0 | -- | 9.0 |
| 1951 | 23.5 | -- | 23.5 |
| 1952 | 34.2 | -- | 34.2 |
| 1953 | 44.7 | -- | 44.7 |
| 1954 | 55.7 | -- | 55.7 |
| 1955 | 64.5 | -- | 64.5 |
| 1956 | 71.8 | -- | 71.8 |
| 1957 | 78.4 | 0.2 | 78.6 |
| 1958 | 82.9 | 0.3 | 83.2 |
| 1959 | 85.4 | 0.5 | 85.9 |
| 1960 | 86.5 | 0.6 | 87.1 |
| 1961 | 88.0 | 0.8 | 88.8 |
| 1962 | 88.9 | 1.1 | 90.0 |
| 1963 | 89.6 | 1.7 | 91.3 |
| 1964 | 89.4 | 2.9 | 92.3 |
| 1965 | 87.7 | 4.9 | 92.6 |
| 1966 | 84.0 | 9.0 | 93.0 |
| 1967 | 78.3 | 15.3 | 93.6 |
| 1968 | 71.7 | 22.9 | 94.6 |
| 1969 | 64.6 | 30.4 | 95.0 |
| 1970 | 57.9 | 37.3 | 95.9 |
| 1971 | 52.4 | 43.1 | 95.5 |
| 1972 | 45.3 | 50.5 | 95.8 |
| 1973 | 38.3 | 57.7 | 96.0 |
| 1974 | 31.4 | 64.7 | 96.1 |
| 1975 | 28.3 | 68.8 | 97.1 |

*Source:* Television Digest, *Television Factbook*, (Washington, D.C.: Television Digest, Inc., 1977), p. 66-a. Households with color sets may also have black-and-white sets.

Johnson, chairman of the Senate Interstate and Foreign Commerce Committee, who had been prodding the FCC to resolve the entire television issue; he wrote to the FCC chairman that "compatibility, while desirable, certainly should not be a primary basis for a decision" (*Telecommunications Reports*, Nov. 21, 1949:23). The report of the Senate Select Committee on Color Television Standards revealed the dilemma facing the FCC; refusing to make a recommendation, the committee noted that "the CBS system has progressed furthest toward full realization of its potentialities," while the RCA system "can be expected to improve substantially" (*Telecommunications Reports*, July 17, 1950:21). Many interpreted this as a finding that the RCA system would soon surpass the CBS system.

After five months and more than 11,000 pages of testimony, the FCC's hearings on color television ended in October 1950 with a 5-2 ruling that found the RCA system to be inferior to the CBS system, which was now authorized for public commercial broadcasting in spite of its incompatibility with existing receivers. However, the FCC left a crack in the door: "The Commission is of the opinion that if a satisfactory compatible system were available, it would certainly be desirable to adopt such a system."

There was little chance at this stage for a compromise. Both companies had invested millions of dollars in completely different approaches to color television, and their suspicions of each other had been publicly announced. Thus, RCA was infuriated by an FCC request that it make available to CBS the latest developments in RCA's tricolor tubes and, after refusing the request, filed for an injunction against regular operation of the CBS system. The district court granted RCA's request, but on May 28, 1951, the U.S. Supreme Court ruled 8-0 that it would defer to the FCC's "special familiarity with the problems involved in adopting standards for color television." CBS claimed exoneration and victory, RCA vowed to continue fighting, and many manufacturers announced that they would refuse to produce CBS-system receivers—which led CBS to buy a television manufacturing plant.

Ironically, the issue was about to become moot. In November 1951 the manufacture of color television sets was banned because of materials shortages caused by the Korean War—a development that the ACF would term a prototypical "exogenous event." By the time the war production ban was lifted in the spring of 1953, the superiority of the now-perfected RCA system had become indisputable and CBS had dropped all plans to broadcast color programs or to manufacture receivers using its system. In December 1953 the FCC formally adopted standards based on a refined version of the RCA system (which was not fully compatible with existing monochrome sets), and color broadcasting was authorized in 1954. What caused such a dramatic change in policy?

Because of the intense conflict over the CBS and RCA systems, the FCC had not been able to forge a compromise. Yet because the conflict was primarily over vital technical aspects and not near or deep core beliefs, a professional forum was appropriate. In 1949 the RMA formed a Joint Technical Advisory Committee (JTAC), but the FCC rejected its recommendation of the RCA system on the basis of the commission's in-house technical studies (which many industry engineers claimed were faulty). After all, the cutting edge of technology was in industry, so FCC staff were likely to be underinformed.

In April 1951 a second NTSC (see Table 7.3) was organized in an effort to convince the FCC that compatible color was feasible. Its task was much more difficult than that of the first NTSC. The new committee included twice as many members and accumulated an estimated 1 million work-hours—compared to 8,000 work-hours for the first NTSC (Fortune, November 1955:163). Not only did it face a technical challenge that was enormously complex, but it also faced economic stakes that were much higher than in 1941. CBS alone had invested at least $5 million in research and development, and at the time that the CBS standards were endorsed

TABLE 7.3 Members of Second NTSC, 1951-1954

| | |
|---|---|
| ABC | Hazeltine Electronics |
| Admiral | Hogan Laboratories |
| Baltimore Sun | Magnavox |
| Bendix Radio Division | McGraw-Hill Publishing |
| CBS-Columbia | Motorola |
| Chromatic Television Labs | Philco |
| Color Television | Radio Corporation of America |
| Crosley Div., AVCO | Raytheon Television Radio |
| DuMont Laboratories | Sentinel Radio |
| Emerson Radio & Phonograph | Sylvania |
| Federal Telecommunications Labs | Tele-King |
| General Electric | Tele-Tech, Caldwell-Clements |
| General Teleradio | Tele-Tone Radio |
| Dr. Alfred N. Goldsmith | Westinghouse Electric |
| Hallicrafters | Zenith Radio |

by the FCC, more than 7 million television sets were in danger of becoming obsolete. In other words, the technical dispute was being overshadowed by its economic implications, and the conflict moved from Sabatier's secondary aspects to policy core aspects of belief systems.

Largely because RCA was active in the second NTSC, the FCC greeted the committee with open suspicion and hostility, and one FCC commissioner hinted of possible antitrust actions against "advisory committees which frequently remind me of the interlocking directorates the public utilities used" (*Telecommunications Reports,* January 23, 1950:34). Not until 1952 did FCC engineers begin regularly attending NTSC field tests, and by then the technical merits of the RCA system had become convincing even to CBS. The dispute once again was about secondary aspects that were reduced to tractable engineering questions; as in the monochrome standards case, the professional forum proved extremely useful to the FCC in spite of its suspicions.

### Direct Broadcast Satellites

As communications satellites began to reshape the communications industry during the 1960s and 1970s, the FCC needed to formulate new policies regarding spectrum allocation, technical standards, and other issues. By 1971 some were proposing Direct Broadcast Satellite (DBS) systems, which would transmit to earth with enough power for television signals to be received by small rooftop antenna dishes. As late as 1979, the FCC opposed DBS at the World Administrative Radio Conference on grounds of economic and technological infeasibility, but by early 1981 Japan and Canada had demonstrated DBS systems and U.S. firms were professing a willingness to invest huge sums in DBS ventures (Rice, 1980). In April 1981, the FCC began proceedings to establish rules for DBS and accepted the applications of a Comsat subsidiary to establish a three-channel experimental DBS service for home viewers; thirteen additional firms and individuals soon filed DBS applications. By the end of

1982 the FCC had approved eight construction permits for DBS, but it had imposed no ownership rules or technical standards beyond those required by international agreements.

It was not until June 1983 that the FCC created a professional forum as a method of gaining industry consensus. The Advisory Committee on Technical Standards for the DBS Service (ACTS) was split into three subcommittees to study signal format, receivers, and signal scrambling. Soon afterward, the Direct Broadcast Satellite Association (DBSA) was organized by industry in part to establish voluntary technical standards that would permit compatibility with existing home receivers.

In June 1984 the ACTS delivered its report, stating that it had begun with "widely divergent viewpoints," had made "significant progress," but had failed to reach a "total consensus" (*Federal Register*, February 19, 1985:6972). The subcommittees on transmission standards and encryption produced only a few voluntary standards, thereby obstructing the receiver standards group, which was divided on the crucial question of whether receivers should be required to be "universal," that is, capable of receiving all DBS signals (but very expensive). In February 1985 the FCC proposed to adopt most of the standards recommended by the ACTS and announced that its goal was "to adopt only those standards which are required to limit interference among DBS systems and to assure a reasonable degree of interoperability of systems and receivers in the hands of the public" (*Federal Register*, February 19, 1985:6972). Although the stakes were enormous—the Comsat subsidiary alone had invested $140 million in DBS before withdrawing—the FCC's decision was not strongly criticized by any participating interest.

Why did the FCC wait to form an industry advisory group, and why were its recommendations of so little use? The delay was partly due to the development of international technical guidelines at a conference in July 1983; the United States adopted most of its recommendations as a starting point for national standards. At the same time, there was absolutely no consensus on either the size or the characteristics of the market for DBS; one market analyst referred to DBS as "a solution to a problem that nobody has" (*Broadcasting*, July 2, 1984:38)—which hardly had been the case with either monochrome or color television. In other words, the DBS problem was intractable: unbounded, undefined, and unripe. With such uncertainty any mandatory technical standard was in great danger of becoming obsolete or even obstructive within a short time, so a professional forum would be of little help. Only three firms were still pursuing DBS by March 1985, and there was little demand for technical standards.

## V. CONCLUSION

Other related technological changes in television could be discussed here. The progress of FCC policies affecting high-definition television, stereophonic television sound, AM stereo radio, cellular radio, FM subcarrier authorizations, and other innovations could be encompassed in this survey. Nevertheless, the cases discused here suffice to suggest some general conclusions.

## The Policy Subsystem

The episodes described above show that the following major actors participated in setting policies on technical standards at the FCC at various times:

Broadcasters
Manufacturers
The Federal Communications Commission
Congressmen (individually and in committees)
Federal courts
The White House
The Department of Justice
International organizations

Consumer interests were served in this policy-making process—indirectly by the tension between the interests of broadcasters and manufacturers, and, presumably, directly by the FCC. Only the first three types of actors on this list were directly involved in all cases, however. The first two—broadcasters and manufacturers—had their most significant impacts through industry advisory groups (IAGs).

## Industry Advisory Groups

Professional advisory panels such as those formed by broadcasters and manufacturers have come under increasing scrutiny in recent years (e.g., Petracca, 1983; Cardozo, 1981). The Supreme Court has referred to such a group as "in reality an extra-governmental agency, which prescribes rules for the regulation and restraint of interstate commerce" and ruled that they therefore must adhere to careful procedural safeguards [*Fashion Originator's Guild v. FTC*, 312 U.S. 457, 465 (1941)]. In recognition of their increasing importance, in 1976 Congress imposed controls on the procedures of many advisory groups under the Federal Advisory Committee Act (FACA). Significantly, advisory groups in which governmental agencies are not formally involved (but which they may have funded) are not subject to the open meeting requirement of FACA; this provision would have applied to nearly all of the groups discussed here.

Like policy entrepreneurs, IAGs help to "make the government's job easier and less costly and help to assure that programs will be carried out by persons well acquainted with the specialized matters involved"; an advisory group may serve as "a ready-made organization for the implementation of specialized policies, technical or generally useful information enhancing effective administration, advice reflecting a genuine understanding of the sector, and the cooperation of group members" (Moe, 1980:60). These functions are illustrated by the Advisory Committee on

Reactor Safeguards (a nongovernmental group of technical experts to whom the Nuclear Regulatory Commission refers nuclear power plant construction applications) and the Consensus Development Program of the Office for Medical Applications of Research of the National Institutes of Health (Larsen and Rogers, 1984). The range of questions to be addressed by such groups usually is closed at the outset; they often take a proposal, a research paper, or a specific request from an agency as a starting point in their deliberations. Thus, a partial explicit screening of admissible conflicts is common. In fact, the phenomenon of screening is probably universal if for no reason other than the tendency of decision makers to latch on to the first "solution" that appears; this tendency would render formal screening less useful as a predictor of forum behavior and policy learning.

Cooperation among the members of advisory groups does not result from total agreement on all dimensions of potential conflict. In the cases of broadcast standards, tradeoffs and uncertainty characterized all of the advisory groups' decisions. But core beliefs were never at issue and the policy space under the groups' jurisdiction was tightly bounded, if not single-dimensional. The cases discussed here provide a useful test of many of the ACF's hypotheses regarding policy learning and change.

The prediction (Hypothesis 5) that the basic attributes of a government program will remain stable unless perturbed by forces from outside the policy subsystem is supported by the stability of broadcast technical standards in the absence of related technological innovation. Jenkins-Smith and Sabatier also suggest that policy learning is more likely when conflict is at an intermediate level, which requires that each side have adequate technical resources and that neither is risking core beliefs (Hypothesis 6). These conditions clearly are met in the case of broadcast standards.

Similarly, the ACF's arguments about professional fora are supported by these cases. Policy learning appears to be more likely when the conflict is conducted in a professional forum that includes members from different coalitions (Hypothesis 9) who can rely on quantitative indicators (Hypothesis 7) focusing on natural systems (Hypothesis 8). Because of their analytical sophistication and the cohesiveness imposed by technological and market constraints, these groups were able to inform and simplify the FCC's responses to technological changes.

However, two critical questions about professional fora and policy learning remain: What type of policy learning occurred, and by whom? I suggested above a distinction between Type I and Type II learning. There also is a difference between substantive and procedural learning. The FCC delegated the task of substantive learning (that is, learning about the substance of a policy issue) to industry advisory groups, but the most important type of learning that occurred at the FCC itself related to procedure: how to decide, not what to decide.

### The FCC

The FCC has responded to its complex environment by trying to avoid speculation, by excluding some relevent variables from its agenda, and by simplifying its decision-making structure (Mosco, 1976:6–7). It has, however, been susceptible to changes in the broader political system beyond the broadcast subsystem. For example, at the end of 1984 the FCC adopted a Final Rule arguing that "marketplace forces are sufficient to ensure that broadcasters will continue to meet high quality standards without Commission regulation." This rule allowed the FCC to eliminate many technical requirements (such as those relating to "interoperability") (*Federal Register,* December 12, 1984:48309). Thus, technical standards could be changed or relaxed not because the commission had learned more about the technical substance of broadcasting, but because of a partial change in the systemic governing coalition (that is, the Reagan administration).

The strongest failures of policy learning occurred when the FCC staff attempted to substitute their analyses and judgment for those of broadcasters and manufacturers (in color television and AM stereo, for example).[7] In its more successful decisions, the Commission has avoided unnecessary speculation about technical and market developments by delegating the task of substantive learning to IAGs. Policy learning was most likely when the distinction between the public and private arenas of decision making was obscured. This situation occurred when the three policy "process streams"—problem recognition, the formation and refining of proposals, and politics—were combined within the advisory groups and outside the FCC (Kingdon, 1984).

## Policy Change and Learning

Television regulation is not a typical policy subsystem, largely because of its unusual structural characteristics. It is very difficult in this realm of public policy to designate the client and the agent. Was the FCC serving the industry by providing stability through technical standards, or was the industry serving the FCC by providing it with ready-made analysis and consensus? In addition, the cohesiveness of this subsystem was mandated by the technological phenomena of complexity, arcane engineering, and networking. The "multiple dimensions of value" and manipulation of policy (Jenkins-Smith, 1988) were not important factors here because adversarial conflict was isolated into a tight forum that eliminated spurious analytical issues. Learning occurred, but at the level of the FCC it was primarily procedural learning, in contrast with the substantive learning that took place in the advisory groups.

Finally, the cases of broadcast television standard setting involved no conflicts over deep normative values held by competing coalitions. There have been changes in policy core beliefs, however. The evolution toward marketplace standards in the 1980s has been reflected in FCC restraint in setting new standards and in its efforts to remove old ones. Similarly, there have also been changes in attitudes toward the proper instruments by which policy should be carried out, that is, whether mandatory, voluntary, or de facto marketplace standards should be set. Yet because these changes have been gradually implemented by the FCC advisory group subsystem of professional and constrained consensus, the transitions have been relatively peaceful.

The advocacy coalition framework developed by Sabatier and Jenkins-Smith is useful in understanding why the advisory group forum for policy analysis and decision has generally worked well—especially if we define success in terms of congruence with political forces, stability over time, and lack of legal challenge. Whether the decisions on technical standards were correct in the sense of engineering optimality is difficult to assess; there have been arguments over whether the monochrome and color standards were indeed the best possible (the NTSC color system has been called the "Never Twice the Same Color" system). Nevertheless, our understanding of policy making and policy change is aided by the concepts developed here.

## NOTES

Portions of this work appeared in an earlier form in Richard P. Barke, "Regulation and Cooperation Among Firms in Technical Standard-Setting," *Journal of Behavioral Economics* 14 (Winter): 141–154. Used by permission.

1. In its motion to the U.S. Supreme Court to dismiss the case of color standards, the FCC referred to "its sole aim of making available to the people of the U.S. at the earliest practical time a satisfactory system of color television" (*Broadcasting*, February 12, 1951:63).

2. During the 1940 television dispute, CBS claimed that because it was only a broadcaster, it represented the interests of viewers, while RCA (as both a manufacturer and a broadcaster) had more complex motives (Statement of CBS to FEE, FCC Docket 5806, January 15, 1940:2). David Sarnoff, chairman of RCA, added to this perception at an industry association meeting when he admitted, "We live on obsolescence in this industry" (Minutes of the RMA Board of Directors Meeting, February 8, 1940, in FCC Docket 5806).

3. There was no dispute over the FCC's jurisdiction to investigate or establish standards. See the statement of RCA's general counsel in the FCC Report, "Order No. 65 Setting Television Rules and Regulations for Further Hearing," May 28, 1940, 2.

4. The FCC's suspicions were discussed openly at the RMA Directors meeting in February 1940 (see note 2).

5. Sarnoff warned the RMA Directors that the association stood "lower than a snake's belly in Washington" and that a *unanimous* recommendation to the FCC was necessary to restore confidence (see note 2).

6. FCC Report on March 20, 1941, Television Hearing, Docket 5806, 2.

7. Two FCC engineers found one of the AM stereo systems to be technically "clearly superior" to the others but explained that the commissioners' decision was based not only on technical analyses but also on economic and legal factors (*Broadcasting*, April 5, 1982:7).

# PART III

# Quantitative Analyses of Policy Change

One of the great strengths of the traditional case study is the breadth of evidence that can be brought to bear, including such sources as interviews, legislative and administrative documents, election results, media reports, secondary sources, and direct observation. The cases included in Part II of this book are rich in detail, and a glance at their references shows that they draw upon a wide range of sources of data for their analyses. The Achilles' heel of such case studies, however, stems from the difficulty in replicating their results: Different scholars examining the same topic and utilizing the same types of sources can arrive at quite different conclusions.

The limitations of case studies are a particularly serious problem for theories of policy change precisely because such theories have traditionally drawn almost entirely upon such studies. Data for systematic testing of hypotheses involving the dynamics of subsystem coalitions over time have been notably lacking (see the Methodological Appendix). The chapters in Part III present analyses of policy change that are self-consciously systematic and replicable. Using the technique for coding and analyzing public documents developed in the Methodological Appendix, the authors present two detailed analyses of policy change. In Chapter 8, Hank C. Jenkins-Smith and Gilbert K. St. Clair use content analysis of nearly 400 testimonies before the U.S. Congress spanning two decades to create a dataset reflecting the expressed (or officially sanctioned) beliefs of an array of regularly participating groups in the energy policy subsystem dealing with petroleum leasing on the outer continental shelf of the United States. Using these data, tests of hypotheses concerning coalition stability, hierarchically structured belief systems, and the effects of exogenous events are conducted. Next, in Chapter 9, Paul A. Sabatier and Anne M. Brasher develop a dataset using the same content analysis technique for a large number of groups and individuals involved in the policy disputes surrounding environmental preservation and development at Lake Tahoe over the past thirty years. Among other things, these data permit tests of the evolution of advocacy coalitions as the policy debate progressed over a span of several decades. Note that this technique of data acquisition and analysis can be used wherever governments publish the testimony presented at public hearings.

In both cases, the methods utilized in Part III permit a more systematic and detailed analysis than is typically possible using the traditional case study approach. The ability to distinguish clearly among coalitions, to observe the degree of coalescence into competing coalitions over time, and to systematically analyze the exogenous and endogenous bases for changes in policy beliefs and preferences are all facilitated by this approach. The general strategy is to use traditional methods to establish the overall policy context, and then to use these systematic methods of data acquisition and quantitative analysis to examine specific topics in greater detail. This type of analysis is replicable and can be extended to a wide variety of cases to permit wider and more systematic tests of competing theories of policy change.

# 8

## The Politics of Offshore Energy: Empirically Testing the Advocacy Coalition Framework

HANK C. JENKINS-SMITH AND GILBERT K. ST. CLAIR

Much of the emphasis of the advocacy coalition framework (ACF) is on the structure of beliefs of competing advocacy coalitions and the patterns of change in these beliefs. This chapter systematically examines the changes in expressed beliefs regarding both policy core and secondary issues by the coalitions involved in the ongoing dispute over oil and gas exploration and development on the U.S. outer continental shelf (OCS).[1] Following a brief description of the OCS policy dispute, we test a subset of the hypotheses developed in Chapter 2 by using data obtained from coding the expressed beliefs of OCS policy elites over a twenty-year period (see the Methodological Appendix for a full discussion of the coding technique). In addition, we examine several rival hypotheses drawn from the principal-agent literature and raise questions about the scope of validity for several of the key premises of the ACF. The intent is to provide a reasonably exacting test for the ACF and to indicate where the framework might be usefully modified to incorporate insights drawn from principal-agent theory.

## I. THE OCS POLICY SUBSYSTEM

The OCS oil and gas leasing policy debate is of particular value to students of long-term policy change for several reasons. First, the debate has been in progress for over two decades (1969 to the present), during which time a relatively consistent set of organizational elites has remained active within the subsystem. Second, since 1969 the subsystem has been subject to a number of well-defined exogenous events: major energy crises, oil spills, changes in presidential administrations, and congressional elections. Third, the debate has been subject to intense political conflict in which the fundamental values and policy positions of opposing advocacy coalitions have been at stake (Heintz, 1988; Jones, 1987).

Thus the OCS policy debate provides an opportunity to test for change, and for the causes of change, in the positions of policy elites and in the composition of advocacy coalitions within a highly conflictual policy subsystem.

Using a traditional case-study method, Heintz (1988) has provided one of the best studies of the OCS policy debate. Based on his knowledge of the written record and his extensive experience in the OCS debate as a senior policy analyst in the Department of Interior, Heintz argued that in the 1970s and early 1980s, the subsystem was characterized by two very stable and deeply opposed coalitions: the prodevelopment coalition, intent on oil and gas exploration on the OCS, and the conservation coalition, equally intent on limiting or stopping OCS exploration and development. The prodevelopment coalition was made up chiefly of oil and gas companies, associated service companies, and government agencies (the Departments of Interior and Energy) charged with management of the OCS. The conservation coalition was primarily made up of environmental groups. The members of the opposing coalitions were found to have deeply held policy core beliefs (akin to religious convictions) and associated policy and secondary beliefs. But the debate and conflict hinged on policy core disputes, precluding any significant cross-coalition learning or change (Heintz, 1988).

In this chapter we examine the OCS policy dispute with greater rigor by employing longitudinal data derived from expressed policy beliefs and policy preferences of organizational elites involved in the dispute. The data were coded from transcripts of congressional hearings held by a range of committees and subcommittees and include both formal and informal testimony. Using these data we test hypotheses concerning differences in the relative constraint on (1) changes in policy positions taken by different kinds of policy elites, (2) the overall stability of subsystem coalitions, (3) the change over time in *levels* of opposition between coalitions, as evidenced by divergence or convergence of stated beliefs and policy positions, and (4) the impetus for defections to and from subsystem coalitions.

## II. ADVOCACY COALITIONS AND AGENT BEHAVIOR

Following Heclo (1978), Kingdon (1984), Sabatier (1987), and Salisbury et al. (1987), we conceive the policy process as operative within partially segmented "policy subsystems" made up of those institutions and actors that are directly involved in the policy-making process in a specialized policy area. Members of subsystems include representatives of businesses, interest groups, trade associations, executive agencies, and relevant legislative committees as well as the elected officials, scholars, and members of the press that regularly track and seek to influence the course of public policy in the issue area.

The ACF holds that, within policy subsystems, coalition members will tend to cluster into competing coalitions that advocate distinct policy viewpoints (Hypothesis 1). The prospects for significant change in the beliefs and policy positions of these elites are hypothesized to depend in large part on the intensity of conflict within the subsystem. The more direct and serious the threat to core or near core beliefs, the more intense the subsystem conflict. The more intense the conflict, the less the willingness of organizational elites to alter the affected policy positions and beliefs. Thus, under extreme conflict we would expect to see very stable coalitions, over extended periods of time (Hypothesis 1), with change in the policy positions of coalition members resulting almost exclusively from political or socioeconomic events exogenous to the subsystem (Hypothesis 5).

The ACF also holds that members of advocacy coalitions will adhere to hierarchically structured belief systems in which the most basic beliefs—e.g., fundamental ontological and normative axioms—constrain specific or operational beliefs and policy positions (Hypotheses 2 and 3). An alternative hypothesis, taken from more traditional explanations of coalition formation (e.g., Riker, 1962), holds that coalition members may rally around a "bottom-line" policy position; in other words, they are primarily concerned with the matter of who gets (or loses) what, when, and how. In this view, the bottom-line action may be a matter of profit: who pays, how much, and how is it allocated? In regulatory policy issues, the bottom-line action is likely to concern the perceived adequacy (or severity) of restrictions, enforcements, and sanctions regarding the activity in question.

Theories of group representation (Wilson, 1973; Moe, 1980, 1981) have suggested that distinct kinds of subsystem elites will behave in quite different ways. In line with principal-agent theories, Wilson and Moe argued that elites from purposive and material organizations face differing degrees of constraint on their expression of their respective organizations' officially sanctioned positions and beliefs. Representatives of purposive organizations, which primarily attract members (principals) on the basis of ideological or policy orientations intended to benefit "some larger public or society as a whole" (Wilson, 1973:46), must maintain a relatively strict adherence to the set of beliefs and policy positions espoused by the organization; to deviate is to risk loss of membership.[2] Material organizations, by contrast, pursue more narrowly the interests of their members—typically profits—and principals (or stockholders) may give the agent relatively broad latitude to pursue that objective.[3] Applied to the pattern of expressed elite beliefs in subsystems, these arguments suggest that agents for purposive organizations may take positions and express beliefs in a manner consistent with Hypotheses 2 and 3, while the behavior of agents for material organizations may be better represented by an alternative bottom-line hypothesis.

In addition to political or organizational principals, subsystem elites may respond to events and circumstances exogenous to the policy process, such as national security crises, changes in economic conditions, or environmental disasters (Hypothesis 5). Exogenous events present subsystem participants with opportunities or obstacles for translation of their policy beliefs and preferences into public policy. For example, Moe (1985) pointed to the effects of the rates of employment and inflation (along with electoral results) on the proportion of prolabor decisions by the National Labor Relations Board (NLRB). Kingdon (1984) noted that exogenous events may open "windows of opportunity" that permit advocates of policy initiatives to push them onto the agenda.[4]

In the following sections we test an array of hypotheses drawn from Chapters 2 and 3 as well as an important rival hypothesis. First, we test a new hypothesis regarding the relative stability of the stated beliefs of purposive versus material group representatives:

> *Hypothesis 10:* Elites of purposive groups are more constrained in their expression of beliefs and policy positions than elites from material groups.

In addition, we test Hypotheses 2 and 3, from Chapter 2, regarding the structure of coalition member beliefs. Specifically, we will test for similarities and differences in expressed beliefs within and across the coalitions identified by Heintz (1988). In addition, we test for the stability of those patterns of beliefs: Do the patterns of similarity of beliefs across subsystem elites change significantly over time?

Next, for those organizations that *do* switch coalitions, what is the impetus for the defection? Following Chapter 2, we hypothesize that in an intense policy dispute of this kind, the primary impetus for change in policy core beliefs and policy positions by coalitions will be events exogenous to the subsystem, including electoral changes as well as oil crises, oil spills, or changes in energy prices (Hypothesis 5).

In Section III, we present an overview of the data and methodology employed in this analysis. In Section IV, we examine the characteristics of the OCS policy subsystem, first by comparing the relative stability of the expressed beliefs of the representatives of the different kinds of organizations, and second by employing a cluster analysis method to assess the membership and stability of the OCS advocacy coalitions over time. In Section V, we examine in greater detail the impetus for change in the positions taken by representatives of the U.S. Department of Interior, a central player in the OCS policy subsystem. Using linear regression corrected for autoregression, we conduct tests for a range of hypotheses about the sources of changes in policy positions. We conclude by assessing the characteristics of change in subsystem coalitions in highly charged policy debates.

## III. METHODS AND DATA

### Methods

*Data Collection.* The method of data collection used here employs content analysis of public documents. Public documents in which policy elites express policy positions, values, and beliefs can provide an alternative to surveys and scorecards as a source of data (see, e.g., Holsti, 1969; Krippendorff, 1980). More readily than surveys, public documents permit retrospective analysis and—where the same individual or representative repeats expression of policy beliefs over time—analysis of change in expressed beliefs. A particularly fruitful source is congressional hearings, the transcripts of which contain formal, informal, and interrogatory expression by those individuals most extensively involved in attempts to shape the policy debate.[5]

The method involved the development of a coding frame to capture expressed beliefs, which range from statements of fundamental values and ontological beliefs to narrow causal assumptions and policy preferences specific to the policy issue. The items in the frame were selected by: (1) identification, from the existing literature (e.g., Heintz, 1988) of the beliefs, values, and policy positions that were matters of dispute over the course of the debate, and (2) corroboration and extension of those items through content analysis of a sample of testimonies that spanned the time period under study.

Because the items represent values, policy positions, and beliefs that were *matters of dispute*, it was possible to frame each one on a five-point Likert scale, with endpoints representing the extreme positions taken in the dispute. The result was a code form containing 113 items.[6] The coding frame was applied to all congressional hearings listed in the Congressional Information Service index that focused on OCS energy-leasing policy from 1969 to 1986.[7]

*Target Population.* The target population for coding has been variously defined as an "issue network" (Heclo, 1978), a "policy subcommunity" (Kingdon, 1984), and a "policy subsystem" (Chapter 2). These are sets of policy elites—interest group representatives, government officials, experts, and members of the press—who regularly follow and seek to influence the course of the policy debate. For this study, the selection of public hearing participants for coding was based upon a sampling of OCS hearing participants taken from indices of hearing documents that spanned the period of analysis. Organizations and individuals that appeared regularly over significant periods of time were included in the study. The most persistent actors included representatives of the following groups: the National Ocean Industry Association (NOIA), an OCS support industry trade group; the American Petroleum Institute (API), representing primarily the integrated oil producers; the American Gas Association (AGA), representing producers of natural gas; Exxon and ARCO, oil companies; the U.S. Department of Interior (DOI) and the U.S. Department of Energy (DOE); the Environmental Protection Agency (EPA); the National Oceanic and Atmospheric Administration (NOAA); and several environmental groups, including the Environmental Policy Center (EPC), the Sierra Club, the Natural Resources Defense Council (NRDC), and the Audubon Society. A listing of the years in which each of these groups provided codable testimony on OCS issues is presented in Table 8.1.

TABLE 8.1  Regular Participants in the OCS Policy Subsystem, 1969-1987

| Year | NOIA | API | AGA | Exxon | ARCO | DOI | DOE | NOAA | EPA | Sierra | EPC | NRDC | Audubon |
|---|---|---|---|---|---|---|---|---|---|---|---|---|---|
| | Energy Companies & Trade Associations | | | | | Government Agencies | | | | Environmental Groups | | | |
| 1969 | | | | | | x | | | | x | | | |
| 1970 | | x | | x | | x | x | | | x | | | x |
| 1971 | x | | | | | x | | | | | | | |
| 1972 | x | x | | | | x | | | | | | | |
| 1973 | | | | | | x | | | | x | | | x |
| 1974 | x | x | x | x | | x | x | x | x | x | x | x | |
| 1975 | x | x | x | x | x | x | x | x | x | x | x | x | x |
| 1976 | | | | | | x | | | | | | | |
| 1977 | x | x | x | x | x | x | x | x | x | x | x | | x |
| 1978 | x | x | x | | | x | x | x | | x | x | x | |
| 1979 | x | x | x | x | x | x | x | x | x | x | x | | |
| 1980 | | x | | x | x | x | x | x | x | x | x | x | x |
| 1981 | x | x | | x | | x | x | x | x | x | x | x | |
| 1982 | x | | | x | | x | | | | x | x | x | x |
| 1983 | x | x | | x | x | x | | x | | x | x | x | x |
| 1984 | x | x | x | x | x | x | | | x | x | x | x | x |
| 1985 | x | x | | x | | x | x | x | x | x | x | x | x |
| 1986 | | x | | | | x | | | | x | x | x | |
| 1987 | x | x | | | | x | | x | x | x | x | x | |

*Data Validity.* The validity of the coded data depends in part on what one has attempted to measure. Because the context of the hearing is often one in which the testifier attempts to *persuade* policy makers, it is probably not reasonable to assume that the coded data unfailingly represent an unbiased expression of the speakers' "true beliefs." Furthermore, variations in the committee or subcommittee membership or control (e.g., shifts from Republican to Democratic majorities) may alter the context in ways that affect which beliefs the testifier chooses to express and emphasize (Goggin, 1984; King, 1989). In fact, it is likely that sophisticated testifiers pitch their presentations in a manner that will appeal to the prominent members of the committee.[8] For these reasons, we will refer to "expressed" beliefs and policy positions rather than beliefs per se.

Despite these caveats, there are factors in the policy subsystem and hearing setting that serve to restrain outright distortion or misrepresentation of beliefs for strategic purposes. First, as described above, most regular hearing participants are *representatives* (or agents) of interest groups, trade organizations, private firms, or government agencies and therefore are probably constrained to some degree to express the "officially sanctioned beliefs" of their organization. Second, speakers who are regular actors in the subsystem stand to lose credibility—and diminish persuasiveness—should their formally expressed beliefs prove to be (gratuitously) inconsistent over time.[9] Thus, there are reasons for hearing participants to weigh carefully the strategic use of formal expression.

While the data employed here must be used with a degree of caution, it is important to remember that more traditional data sources also have limitations for the analysis of long-term policy change. Scorecard data, which rely on composite roll call votes, are limited to legislators and thus omit the bulk of subsystem players. Panel survey data that track elite policy beliefs for sufficient periods of time are very scarce. The point is that the data used here are not alone in raising validity (and other) concerns and should be seen as one among several data sources in the study of long-term policy change.

*Data Reliability.* The coding process has been extensively tested for intercoder reliability and has performed reasonably well. The test consisted of a comparison of the results of two coders who coded 339 codable elements (three hearings). Each item could be coded "0" (a missing value) or 1 through 5. To facilitate evaluation of the results, we have compared them with the results to be expected from a random assignment of code values. In thematic content analysis of this kind, reliability must be assessed regarding two distinct coder decisions: (1) the decision to code a particular piece of the testimony, and (2) the decision to impute a particular code value. The majority of the coder errors stemmed from "splits," wherein one coder provided a positive code and the other provided a "missing" code on the same item. Of the 339 codable pairs, 51 (15%) were splits, whereas a random assignment of codes would have resulted in 94 splits (28%). Once both coders decided to code, the results proved quite reliable: In 98% of such cases, the coders applied code values no more than a point apart. The expected result by chance would be only 52%. Overall "error," including splits and dissimilar values, was 16%. These results are shown in Table 8.2. To ensure that the coding process remained as reliable as possible, intercoder reliability tests were conducted approximately every twentieth hearing. This procedure permitted the containment of coder "drift" and allowed for frequent "recalibration" of the coding decision-rules.

Owing to the scope of the coding frame, many items were subject to extensive missing data. This is to be expected because the salience of the various aspects of the policy issue are likely to rise and fall over the course of a nineteen-year policy debate. When salience is low, that aspect of the issue is less likely to be mentioned (and, therefore, coded). In general, the broader the scope of the coding frame—that is, the greater the number and range of subissues included—the greater the percentage of missing data one should expect. On average, individual items in the OCS coding frame were coded as "missing" 83% of the time.

Needless to say, the frequency of missing data creates problems for analysis: Many potentially useful statistical procedures cannot be applied to the raw data. When necessary, our approach has been to collapse the raw data over time (e.g., find the average value for an organization representative for a given six-month period) or over very similar items (as described below).[10] To date, approximately 350 testimonies have been coded spanning the years 1969 to 1987. These testimonies provide the data employed in the following sections.

TABLE 8.2  Results of Intercoder Reliability Tests:  Actual Versus Expected Random Results

|  | Actual | Random |
|---|---|---|
| Only one coder codes ("splits") | 51  (15%) | 94  (28%) |
| Both coders agree to code | 85  (25%) | 235  (69%) |
|    2 codes similar (within 1 point) | 83  (24%) | 122  (36%) |
|    2 codes differ | 2  (1%) | 113  (33%) |
| Both coders agree not to code | 203  (60%) | 10  (3%) |
| Total codable elements | 339 (100%) | 339 (100%) |

## Variables

In coding the expressed beliefs, we sorted statements into deep core, policy core, and secondary statements. As noted earlier, the data were subject to a high rate of missing values. Unfortunately, the rate of missing values was highest among the deep core beliefs. Nevertheless, a sufficient number of closely related and highly correlated expressed beliefs were codable to allow time series analysis.

This analysis relies on three composite variables designed to capture policy beliefs and positions on three critical OCS policy issues over time. In each case, the composite variable was derived from conceptually similar variables that are also highly correlated ($r \geq 0.7$). For each composite variable, the five-point ordinal scale was retained by calculating an unweighted average of each of the sets of variables for each of the subsystem participants. The variables and their component parts are as follows:

*Lease,* which concerns the appropriate speed and breadth of OCS lease sales, combines three variables: (1) an evaluation of the existing frequency of OCS lease sales, (2) an evaluation of the breadth of existing sales, and (3) preferences for changing (increasing or decreasing) the pace of leasing. The values for *lease* include:[11]

1. Increase speed and breadth of leasing substantially—too many precautions are currently taken;
3. Speed and breadth of leasing are about right now—current precautions are reasonable;
5. Decrease speed and breadth of leasing substantially—too few precautions are currently taken.

This variable clearly falls into the domain of secondary beliefs, though it is also the "bottom-line" issue in the dispute because it concerns the ability of energy companies to explore for and develop oil and gas on the OCS.

*Regulation* concerns the adequacy of OCS environmental regulation

and planning and is comprised of four raw variables: (1) an evaluation of
the adequacy of existing environmental restrictions on OCS activity, (2)
preference for more (or less) formal planning of OCS development, (3)
preference for more (or less) regulatory restriction to protect the environment, and (4) preference for more (or less) regulatory restriction to protect the onshore environment from OCS development activities. The
range of values for *regulation* include:

1. Regulation and planning should be kept at a minimum and should
   be decreased from current levels;
3. The level of regulation and planning is about right now and should
   not be increased or decreased;
5. The level of regulation and planning is insufficient and should be
   increased.

The constituent parts of this variable all fall in the secondary domain,
though in aggregate they come close to a policy core position regarding
the appropriate level of governmental interference and appropriate types
of policy instruments for environmental protection.

*Federalism* concerns evaluations of, and prescriptions for, the role of
the coastal state governments in the OCS leasing process. Included are
variables representing: (1) the appropriate relative powers of the states
and federal government in establishing OCS policy, (2) the perceived
need for consistency of OCS development with the states' coastal zone
development plans, (3) prescriptions for more (or less) state and local
government roles in OCS policy making, (4) evaluation of the willingness
of federal agencies to share policy-making decisions with state and
local governments, and (5) evaluation of the responsiveness of federal
agencies to the concerns of state and local governments. The values for
*federalism* include:

1. The federal government should have an exclusive role in setting
   OCS policy; state and local concerns can be adequately handled by
   federal agencies;
3. States should have a formal advisory role in setting OCS policy and
   should be able to delay leasing to assure that state concerns are
   addressed by federal agencies;
5. States should have a strong role in establishing OCS leasing policy
   and should be able to veto leasing decisions that fail to adequately
   address state concerns.

This variable falls closest to the policy core, representing beliefs about
the proper relationship among the federal, state, and local levels of
government.

The composite variables, aggregated for each subsystem participant,
provide the basis for the analyses performed in the following sections.
Note that, for consistency in presentation, the composite variables have

been coded in such a manner that a high score indicates the presumed position of the environmental coalition, while a low score is consistent with the presumed views of the development coalition.

## IV. CHARACTERIZING THE OCS POLICY SUBSYSTEM

### *Constraints on Organizational Representation*

Heintz (1988) has argued that the OCS policy debate is best characterized as one of intense political conflict over issues of central importance to competing advocacy coalitions. On one side are oil companies and energy industry trade associations, which are usually aligned with federal agencies, while on the other are environmental groups. Repeated policy conflict regarding the pace and breadth of OCS leasing and regulation to protect onshore and offshore environments has resulted in entrenched policy positions from which change would (according to Heintz) be "akin to religious conversion." But have there been systematic variations in the willingness of the agents of different kinds of organizations to modify policy positions?

Following Wilson (1973) and Moe (1980, 1981), we hypothesized that agents of purposive groups, who primarily attract and retain members on the basis of the organization's official ideology and policy positions, will evidence greater constraint—or consistency—in expression of policy positions than will agents of more bottom-line-oriented material groups. Our dependent variable is thus the variance in expressed beliefs by purposive and material group elites, and if our hypothesis is correct we should expect to see smaller variance in the expressed policy positions of agents of purposive groups than in those of material groups.[12] We used the chi-square distribution to test for differences in the observed sample variances for the variables *lease, regulation* and *federalism*. The results are shown in Tables 8.3, 8.4 and 8.5, respectively.

The variable *lease,* which concerns the speed and breadth of energy leasing on the OCS, shows only modest variance by agents of both purposive and material organizations. The average sample variance for agents of the purposive organizations is 0.28; for the material organizations it is 0.20. Comparing individual groups, we find statistically significant differences between sample variances in five (of twenty) pair-wise comparisons; in all of those five, expression by agents of the material organizations evidenced *less* variance than it did for those of the purposive organizations. Only one of the material groups—ARCO—demonstrated consistently larger variance in expression, and none of these differences were statistically significant. Thus, with respect to this bottom-line policy position, the material groups tend to be characterized by *less* variation in expressed beliefs than are purposive groups, though the sample variances across most groups are statistically indistinguishable.

On the variables *regulation* and *federalism,* however, the pattern is substantially reversed. As shown in Table 8.4, expression on *regulation* by

TABLE 8.3 Comparing Variance in Expressed Policy Positions Across Group Representatives: Lease Variable

F-values Comparison of Sample Variance Where $F = \dfrac{s^2 \text{Purposive}}{s^2 \text{Material}}$

| Material Groups | Purposive Groups | | | |
|---|---|---|---|---|
| | Sierra (n = 25) ($s^2$ = .20) | EPC (n = 14) ($s^2$ = .26) | NRDC (n = 23) ($s^2$ = .47) | Audubon (n = 7) ($s^2$ = .17) |
| NOIA (n = 21) ($s^2$ = .16) | 1.25 | 1.62 | 2.94* | 1.06 |
| API (n = 29) ($s^2$ = .11) | 1.82 | 2.36* | 4.27** | 1.55 |
| AGA (n = 8) ($s^2$ = .08) | 2.50 | 3.25 | 5.87* | 2.12 |
| Exxon (n = 17) ($s^2$ = .17) | 1.18 | 1.53 | 2.76* | 1.00 |
| ARCO (n = 10) ($s^2$ = .50) | 0.40 | 0.52 | 0.94 | 0.34 |

*Note*: * denotes statistical significance at the 0.05 level; ** at the 0.01 level. In computing the F = value, the greater variance goes in the numerator. In this table, purposive groups show more internal variance; in the next two tables, material groups do so.

purposive group agents varied minimally, with an average sample variance of only 0.14. Agents of material groups, in contrast, had an average sample variance of 0.69. In a comparison of the variance across specific groups, we find a statistically significant difference in more than half of the sample variances, in all cases with the greatest variance in expression by agents of material groups. For *federalism*, as shown in Table 8.5, material groups[13] again showed greater willingness to alter expressed policy positions, with an average sample variance at 0.63 compared to 0.39 for the purposive groups. With the notable exception of the Audubon Society,[14] purposive group agents' variance was uniformly lower, usually to a statistically significant degree, than that of their material group counterparts.

These results provide substantial support for the hypothesis that agents of purposive and material groups face systematically different levels of constraint on expression of group positions. But the difference is not merely one of greater or lesser constraint; it concerns the locus of constraint. Material groups in the OCS subsystem seem to have behaved consistently with the bottom-line hypothesis; expression by group agents was highly constrained on the most basic policy issue—leasing OCS acreage for oil and gas exploration and development. Yet on the issues of regulation of OCS activity and the role of the coastal states in OCS policy making, these agents appear to have been more willing to deviate, with average variance in expression significantly larger than that of their purposive adversaries. The agents of purposive groups, however,

TABLE 8.4 Comparing Variance in Expressed Policy Positions Across Group Representatives: Regulation Variable

F-values Comparison of Sample Variance Where $F = \dfrac{s^2 \text{Material}}{s^2 \text{Purposive}}$

| Material Groups | Purposive Groups | | | |
| --- | --- | --- | --- | --- |
| | Sierra (n = 26) ($s^2$ = .09) | EPC (n = 12) ($s^2$ = .33) | NRDC (n = 25) ($s^2$ = .15) | Audubon (n = 9) ($s^2$ = 0.00) |
| NOIA (n = 17) ($s^2$ = .81) | 9.00** | 2.45* | 5.40** | ∞** |
| API (n = 28) ($s^2$ = .85) | 9.44** | 2.58* | 5.67** | ∞** |
| AGA(n = 5) ($s^2$ = .59) | 6.56* | 1.79 | 3.93 | ∞** |
| Exxon (n = 18) ($s^2$ = .65) | 7.22** | 1.97 | 4.33** | ∞** |
| ARCO (n = 10) ($s^2$ = .53) | 5.89** | 1.61 | 3.53* | ∞** |

*Note:* * denotes statistical significance at the 0.05 level; ** at the 0.01 level.

showed significant constraint in expression in all three policy areas. Their behavior appears to have been more consistent with Hypotheses 2 and 3, as stated in Chapter 2.[15] These results lend support to the arguments of Wilson (1973) and Moe (1980, 1981) that constraints on representation vary systematically across types of groups. They also suggest that research should examine the locus, as well as the relative degree, of variance in representation of policy positions across types of groups. Thus, this analysis suggests that the ACF should be modified to incorporate different kinds of constraints on the beliefs of purposive and material coalition members.

Regarding differences in variation of beliefs across levels of belief systems, these data do not provide much support for the ACF Hypotheses 3 and 4. As noted above, the *lease* variable most clearly represented a secondary belief because it involves a specific and fairly narrow policy position. Yet, as shown in Table 8.3, it was on this belief that material groups, on average, showed *least* variance (an average $s^2$ of 0.204). These groups showed much greater variance regarding their expressed beliefs for *regulation* and *federalism*, which should fall much closer to the policy core of the belief system (average $s^2$ of 0.686 and 0.633, respectively). The pattern of variance among the purposive groups also fails to confirm Hypotheses 3 and 4; *federalism*, which is most clearly in the policy core, has the highest average variance for this group (an average $s^2$ of 0.358), while *regulation* has the lowest (an average $s^2$ of 0.143). While these results may reflect, in part, the difficulty in obtaining codable expression of unalloyed deep and policy core beliefs, they also suggest that the pattern

TABLE 8.5  Comparing Variance in Expressed Policy Positions Across Group Representatives: Federalism Variable

F-values Comparison of Sample Variance Where $F = \dfrac{s^2 \text{Material}}{s^2 \text{Purposive}}$

| Material Groups | Purposive Groups | | | |
|---|---|---|---|---|
| | Sierra (n = 26)<br>$(s^2 = .19)$ | EPC (n = 18)<br>$(s^2 = .05)$ | NRDC (n = 25)<br>$(s^2 = .20)$ | Audubon (n = 9)<br>$(s^2 = .99)$ |
| NOIA (n = 16)<br>$(s^2 = .36)$ | 1.85 | 7.35** | 1.78 | 0.36* |
| API (n = 17)<br>$(s^2 = .61)$ | 3.12** | 12.41** | 3.01* | 0.62 |
| Exxon (n = 6)<br>$(s^2 = .58)$ | 2.95 | 11.73** | 2.85 | 0.59 |
| ARCO (n = 7)<br>$(s^2 = .98)$ | 5.04* | 20.04** | 4.86* | 1.00 |

*Note*: * denotes statistical significance at the 0.05 level; ** at the 0.01 level.

of constraints across beliefs may be more variegated across groups, and generally more complex, than is indicated by the ACF.

### Coalition Stability

Heintz (1988) has argued that the OCS policy debate has been characterized by intense conflict, with stable coalitions advocating and opposing OCS energy leasing. Following Heintz, and Hypothesis 1 from Chapter 2, we hypothesized that stable advocacy coalitions, based on common policy beliefs, will be evident in the OCS policy subsystem over the 1969–1987 period.

This hypothesis can be tested by using cluster analysis, which employs a euclidean spatial distance measure between all pairs of observations (Romesburg, 1984). For this study, the proximity of groups refers to the similarity of policy positions taken. Since the combination of values on the three variables for a given group can be thought of as coordinates in a three-dimensional space, the euclidean distance is essentially the linear distance between points in a 4×4×4 cube. The cluster procedure calculates the linear distance between closest pairs in the cube then "agglomerates" by finding the next closest point and successively adding more distant points. At each addition, the procedure calculates the average euclidean distance between the new point and the existing "cluster" of points (Romesburg, 1984; SPSSX, Inc., 1986:Chapter 40). We present the pairing and euclidean distances between points in an intuitively useful manner in dendrograms (Figures 8.1 and 8.2a through 8.2d) that represent proximities via the horizontal distance from the vertical axis. Clusters—or coalitions—are evident when there is close proximity within subsets of representative positions, while the subsets themselves are spaced at considerable distance. A persistent pattern of distinct clusters across time would support the hypothesis that stable and opposing coalitions populate the OCS policy subsystem.

Using *regulation, lease* and *federalism,* we performed cluster analyses for the average of the agents' expressed policy positions for the entire 1969–1987 interval and for four subsegments of that interval. The first subsegment, from 1969 through 1976, spans the period from the Santa Barbara oil spill, through the 1973–1974 "oil crisis," to the end of the Ford administration. This period is intended to capture the rise of the opposition between conservation and prodevelopment groups under successive Republican administrations. The second time period, from 1977 through 1978, covers the early ("precrisis") Carter years, a period during which many conservation advocates (notably Secretary of Interior Cecil Andrus) were placed in important administrative posts. The third time period, 1979–1980, was a period of extensive energy crisis, including domestic natural gas shortages, insecure oil supplies, and skyrocketing oil prices resulting from the Iranian revolution and the onset of the Iran-Iraq war. The fourth period, from 1981 through 1987, covers most of the Reagan years, the gradual, then precipitous decline in oil prices, and the aggressive OCS leasing policy pursued by Interior Secretary James Watt and his successors. The results of the cluster analyses are shown in Figures 8.1 and 8.2a through 8.2d.

Generalizing across the entire 1969–1987 period, we find that distinct coalitions are apparent. However, as shown in Figure 8.1, there appear to be three (rather than two) clusters of organizations. The first, as Heintz (1988) predicted, is a tight coalition of conservation groups including the Sierra Club, NRDC, EPC, and the Audubon Society. The second, also predicted by Heintz, is made up of prodevelopment oil companies and trade

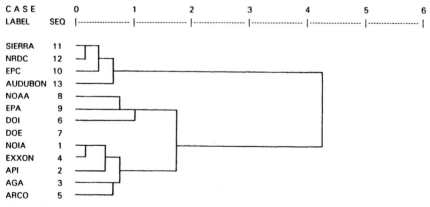

FIGURE 8.1    Cluster analysis (dendrogram) for 1969–1987

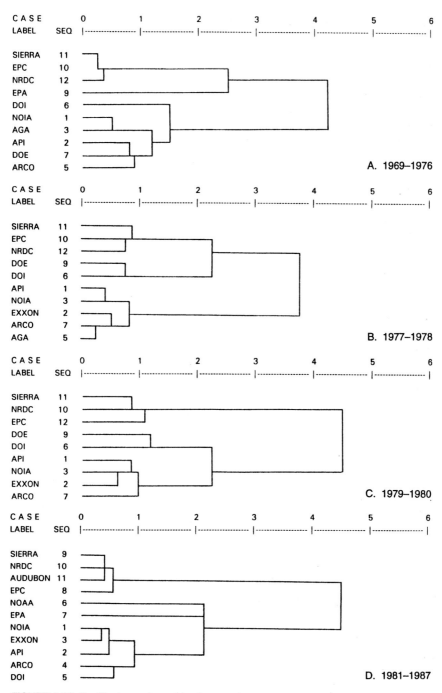

FIGURE 8.2A–D  Cluster analyses (dendrograms)

associations (NOIA, Exxon, API, AGA, and ARCO). The third cluster, consisting of the government agencies (DOI, DOE, EPA, and NOAA), is spatially sandwiched between the conservation and prodevelopment coalitions. Note that DOI and DOE are quite closely aligned and are joined at some distance by NOAA and EPA. Also, as indicated in Figure 8.1, the government agencies fall closest to the prodevelopment side. Finally, note that the average distance between groups in the prodevelopment and conservation coalitions (as shown in the dendrogram in Figure 8.1) is 4.23 units, out of a maximum possible distance of 6.93 units.[16]

Disaggregation over the four time periods, however, shows significant variance in coalition membership over time. In the 1969–1976 period (Figure 8.2a), a fairly tight prodevelopment coalition, including DOE (then called the Federal Energy Administration, or FEA), ARCO API, AGA, and NOIA, was joined at modest distance (1.53) by DOI. Three environmental groups—EPC, Sierra, and NRDC—formed a tight conservation coalition, which was joined at greater distance (2.50) by the EPA. The average euclidean distance between groups in the opposing coalitions in the three-dimensional space for this period was 4.16.

The 1977–1978 period (Figure 8.2b) shows a substantial realignment: Under President Carter DOI and DOE shifted positions such that, while still sandwiched between coalitions, they became more closely aligned with the conservation coalition.[17] Also of note, the euclidean distance between coalitions decreased modestly (from 4.16 to 3.80), which indicates a slight moderation in the level of opposition between subsystem coalitions in the precrisis Carter years.

The 1979–1980 period (Figure 8.2c) shows an equally marked shift: With the onset of the energy crisis, DOI and DOE shifted back to closer proximity to the prodevelopment coalition on all three variables. DOI and DOE are lumped at some distance—2.09—from the more tightly clumped API, NOIA, Exxon, and ARCO. The primary basis for this intra-coalition distance is that API, Exxon, and NOIA took more extreme pro-leasing and antiregulatory positions than did the government agencies. In addition, some of the conservation groups, most notably the EPC and the Sierra Club, moderated their positions on *lease* and *regulation*. In general, while members *within* coalitions tended to be more loosely aligned than had been true in prior periods, the average distance *between* coalitions jumped markedly to 4.59 (an increase of over 20%).

By the 1981–1987 period (Figure 8.2d), the subsystem had become increasingly polarized: Distance between nongovernment members *within* coalitions declined significantly—by an average of almost 50%—while the distance *between* coalitions remained nearly unchanged at 4.57. Among the government agencies, DOI was in tight alliance with the regular prodevelopment members.[18] Other federal agencies remained aloof: Under the Reagan administration, EPA and NOAA had been drawn somewhat closer to the prodevelopment side but remained at arm's length from the other coalition members (a distance of 2.01).

The pattern revealed by the cluster analysis thus partially supports Heintz's (1988) contention that the OCS subsystem is inhabited by two stable advocacy coalitions. A prodevelopment coalition made up of NOIA, API, AGA, Exxon, and ARCO is consistently juxtaposed to a conservation coalition made up of the EPC, Sierra Club, NRDC, and the Audubon Society. Also of importance is the evidence that these coalitions have become increasingly polarized since the late 1970s. To this extent, the results also support the ACF hypothesis that subsystems with sustained conflict will be inhabited by stable and competing advocacy coalitions.

The government agencies, in contrast, proved to be more mercurial. In the 1969–1976 period, government agencies (with the exception of the EPA) were loosely aligned with the prodevelopment groups. By the 1977–1978 period—the precrisis Carter years—DOI (under the guidance of Interior Secretary Cecil Andrus) and DOE had shifted in the direction of the conservation coalition. Late in the Carter administration, apparently in response to the 1979–1980 energy crisis, DOI and DOE moved back toward the prodevelopment coalition while NOAA and the EPA became relatively silent about the issue of OCS leasing. Remarkably, the presidential shift from Carter to Reagan appears to have had little, if any, effect on the agencies' positions; the shift toward the prodevelopment coalition had already been accomplished under Carter. Finally, in the 1981–1987 period under the Reagan administration, DOI and DOE became very tightly aligned with the prodevelopment groups while the subsystem coalitions generally became more polarized. These results indicate that, in the generally stable OCS subsystem, government agencies (and DOI in particular) were uniquely prone to change alliances. To what can their defections be attributed?

## V. BASES OF PUBLIC AGENCY DEFECTION WITHIN THE OCS SUBSYSTEM

As discussed above, analysis of the OCS subsystem over time showed that defections to and from coalitions were restricted to federal agencies. Why did those defections occur? The ACF suggests that, given the intensity of conflict in the subsystem, the predominance of change in coalition member behavior will result from events exogenous to the subsystem—including both presidential or congressional elections and energy or environmental crises. Similarly, when viewed through the lens of principal-agent theory, federal agencies have multiple principals who can employ a number of institutional mechanisms to constrain the agents' behavior. The principals, primarily the president and the Congress, can exercise appointment, confirmation, budgetary, and oversight powers to control and channel the behavior of their agents (Weingast and Moran, 1983; Beck, 1982; Moe, 1985). Drawing on this literature, we will focus on two primary hypotheses: Can the shifts in expressed policy positions by federal agencies be explained by events exogenous to the policy subsystem (Hypothesis 5)? If so, what exogenous events (or combinations of events) can explain these shifts?

We limit the focus of the analysis to change in the expressed policy positions of DOI. Only DOI provided sufficient testimony to enable us to track its positions on *lease* and *regulation* over equal (biannual) time intervals for the full 1969 to 1987 period.[19] Because DOI is the agency primarily responsible for implementation of OCS leasing policy, it (along with other subsystem participants) was frequently called upon to testify about OCS legislation and also provided frequent OCS testimony associated with budgetary and oversight hearings. DOI policy expressions taken from those testimonies were averaged for the biannual time periods from 1969 to 1987. Thus, our data on DOI policy positions are relatively complete.[20]

Because the observations of DOI's expressed policy positions over time may be autocorrelated, a modification of ordinary least squares (OLS) regression techniques is necessary. We employed the Cochrane-Orcutt (1949) method to estimate the value of the beta coefficients and serial correlation coefficient $r$.[21] The resulting estimates are equivalent to those provided by OLS, with the exception that the serial correlation is estimated and controlled for in the estimation of the beta coefficients for the independent variables.[22] Because we presumed that the series would be autocorrelated, we utilized the Cochrane-Orcutt procedure even when the estimated $r$ was statistically insignificant.[23]

Using the multiple interrupted time-series approach (Lewis-Beck, 1986), we were able to test for both changes in the intercept (a dummy variable representing an immediate change associated with an event) and the slope (a slope dummy to capture changes in the trend associated with an event) of the dependent variable. Thus, an energy crisis may stimulate a large displacement in favor of increased OCS leasing, followed by a shift in the trend that corrects for the jump by turning back toward moderated OCS leasing. We also controlled for overall trend in policy positions, using a trend dummy variable for the full series.

Following the analysis of coalitions provided in Section IV, we hypothesize that expressed DOI policy preferences responded to (1) the 1973–1974 energy crisis and Arab oil embargo; (2) the administration of President Carter in 1977–1980; and (3) the second energy crisis in 1979–1980. We anticipated that DOI would shift in a proleasing direction (negative coefficients) for the two crises and in an antileasing (positive) direction under Carter. We also tested for change due to (4) the administration of President Reagan (1981–1987), (5) the congressional elections of 1982, and (6) the congressional election of 1984. For the Reagan era, we expected DOI to shift in the proleasing direction and hypothesized an antileasing shift following the two congressional elections.[24] Both trend and intercept dummies were included for the energy crises, the presidential administrations, and the 1982 and 1984 congressional elections. We also included a variable to represent (7) changes in oil prices (price in period $t$ divided

TABLE 8.6 Modeling Change in Expressed Policy Preferences Regarding Adequacy of Speed and Breadth of OCS Leasing Activity

| Model Component | Estimated Effect on *Lease* Expression | *t* Statistic |
|---|---|---|
| Overall slope | -0.21 | -3.22 |
| Slope change for 1973-1974 oil crisis | 0.27 | 2.63 |
| Intercept change for Carter presidency | 0.89 | 2.11 |
| Slope change for 1979-1980 energy crisis | -0.56 | -5.32 |
| Slope change for Reagan presidency | 0.59 | 5.15 |
| Intercept change for 1984 congressional elections | 0.86 | 2.73 |
| Slope change for 1984 congressional elections | -0.30 | -2.69 |
| | | |
| First-order autoregressive term | -0.03 | 0.15 |
| Constant term | 3.38 | 7.68 |

| | |
|---|---|
| $R^2$ | 0.70 |
| Adjusted $R^2$ | 0.61 |
| Durbin-Watson | 2.05 |

by price in period $t-1$) to capture the potential response to price changes.[25] This variable permitted us to assess whether DOI responded primarily to the rapidly rising oil prices or to the more generalized atmosphere of crisis over the 1973–1974 and 1979–1980 periods. We expected that rising prices would be associated with a shift toward a proleasing position.

Results of the model run for DOI's stated leasing-policy positions (*lease*) and model diagnostics are shown in Table 8.6. The observed values and model estimates for *lease*, are shown in Figure 8.3. The adjusted $R^2$ is 0.61, which demonstrates that independent variables can explain a good portion of the change in policy positions by DOI over the 1969–1987 period. And, as shown in Figure 8.3, the model does a reasonable job of replicating the observed expression of leasing policy positions by DOI. Examining components of change in DOI's stated preference for OCS leasing policy, we detected a statistically significant trend in the direction of increased leasing over the full time period (with a coefficient of −0.21). In addition, five of the seven hypothesized independent variables proved to be statistically significant.[26] Surprisingly, the intercept dummy for the 1973–1974 energy crisis had no statistically discernible effect on DOI's leasing policy positions, but the slope dummy for the crisis indicates a statistically significant shift toward *moderated* leasing (+0.27). Thus, having started from a very proleasing position in 1973, DOI's response following the 1973–1974 energy crisis was to incrementally moderate its calls for expanded and accelerated leasing. With the advent of the Carter administration, DOI shifted markedly toward the position of the conservation coalition (an intercept change of +0.89). Following the 1979–1980 energy crisis, DOI dramatically altered the trend in policy positions toward the prodevelopment side (−0.56). No shift in the intercept for the 1979–1980 crisis was detectable. The effect of the Reagan administration

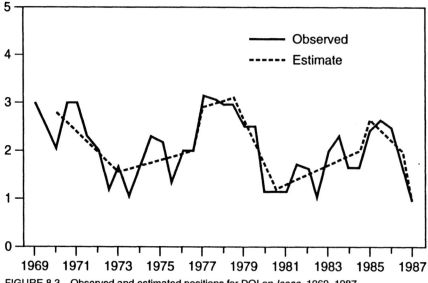

FIGURE 8.3   Observed and estimated positions for DOI on *lease*, 1969–1987

was again a change in slope rather than intercept: Having inherited the very proleasing position following the 1979–1980 energy crisis, DOI moderated its proleasing position over subsequent years (with a coefficient of +0.59). Finally, the 1984 congressional elections altered *both* intercept and slope. DOI's leasing policy position shifted considerably toward the conservation position (+0.86), then progressively shifted back toward the position of the prodevelopment coalition (−0.30).

The model for analyzing change in *regulation*, DOI's expressed positions regarding regulation of OCS activity, included the same slope and intercept dummy variables as did the model for *lease*. This time, however, the dependent variable was logged to adjust for variance nonstationarity. The model results and diagnostic statistics are shown in Table 8.7. The observed log of the *regulation* time series, and the predicted values for the log of *regulation*, are shown in Figure 8.4.

The model resulted in an adjusted $R^2$ of 0.60, indicating that DOI's position on OCS regulation was considerably influenced by the hypothesized exogenous variables. Furthermore, as shown in Figure 8.4, the model again did a reasonable job of predicting DOI's stated position on OCS regulatory policy. Analyzing the components of change in DOI's expressed positions, we find that five of the hypothesized variables proved to have a statistically significant effect. First, DOI's position on *regulation* shifted toward a proregulation (positive) direction as oil prices rose, which indicates that higher oil prices—controlling for the effects of crises—led DOI to call for more stringent OCS regulations. DOI opted for markedly *reduced* regulation at the onset of the the 1973–1974 oil crisis but

TABLE 8.7 Modeling Change in Policy Expression Regarding Adequacy of Regulation of OCS Leasing Activity

| Model Component | Estimated Effect on Logged *Regulation* Expression | *t* Statistic |
|---|---|---|
| Oil price change | 0.05 | 1.67 |
| Intercept change for 1973-1974 oil crisis | -0.26 | -5.72 |
| Slope change for 1973-1974 oil crisis | 0.04 | 4.44 |
| Intercept change for Carter presidency | 0.14 | 2.83 |
| Slope change for Carter presidency | -0.10 | -6.82 |
| Slope change for 1979-1980 energy crisis | 0.07 | 5.19 |
| First-order autoregressive term | -0.31 | -1.48 |
| Constant term | 0.51 | 16.90 |
| $R^2$ | 0.68 | |
| Adjusted $R^2$ | 0.60 | |
| Durbin-Watson | 2.05 | |

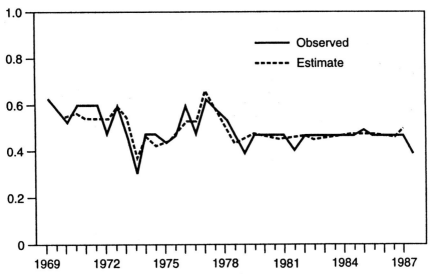

FIGURE 8.4   Observed and estimated positions for DOI on *regulation*, 1969–1987

altered the trend in the direction of *increased* regulation following the crisis. Following the election of President Carter, DOI quickly opted for increased regulation (positive intercept dummy) but dramatically altered the slope toward less regulation (negative slope change dummy). Surprisingly, there was no statistically significant change in the intercept associated with the 1979–1980 energy crisis. The slope changed in a positive (proregulation) direction, offsetting the deregulatory trend associated with Carter's election. Neither Reagan's presidency nor the congressional election showed any statistically discernible effects on either the slope or the intercept dummies.

These changes, along with those identified for *lease*, explain the defection of DOI, and quite probably other federal agencies as well, from (and back to) the prodevelopment coalition. In particular, the large shifts in the intercept terms toward slower leasing and more stringent regulation associated with Carter's presidency, followed by a shift in slope toward faster leasing (following Carter's election) and relaxed regulation (following the onset of the 1979–1980 oil crisis) can explain the variations in DOI's defection from and return to the proleasing coalition. What makes these defections particularly interesting is that they *are not* associated with the change from Carter to Reagan. Rather, this analysis indicates that the shifts in coalitions by DOI preceded Reagan and were merely maintained—or even moderated—under the Reagan presidency.

The results provide substantial support for the hypothesis that exogenous events drive much of the change observed among actors within polarized policy subsystems. In particular, the analysis higlights the importance of *nonelectoral* exogenous events—in this case, energy crises—as drivers of bureaucratic behavior. In fact, with respect to positions on OCS regulation, the separate and statistically significant effects of changes in the price of oil *and* the dummy variables for the two oil crises suggest that DOI was responding both to the direct effects of the crises on the economy (price changes) and to the more diffuse atmosphere of crisis. Furthermore, regarding DOI's leasing-policy positions, the magnitude of the change in slope associated with the 1979–1980 energy crisis—even controlling for presidential and oil price change effects—had a larger *cumulative* effect than did the Carter administration (see Table 8.6). The substantial effects of the energy crises on DOI's regulatory posture were also clearly demonstrated (see Table 8.7). These findings reveal a remarkable level of bureaucratic responsiveness to large-scale economic events exogenous to the policy subsystem.

These results also provide support for recent empirical findings that bureaucracies can and do respond to multiple principals wielding a range of mechanisms of control (Moe, 1985; Wood, 1988). The Carter administration, in particular, had significant effects on DOI's policy positions. Carter's influence seems to have been strongly proconservationist early in his term, but it seems that this influence reversed (as suggested by the negative slope change variable) even before the onset of the 1979–1980 energy crisis. The effects of the 1982 and 1984 changes in Congress were nil with respect to DOI's regulatory policy positions, but the 1984 elections seem to have had an incremental effect on DOI's leasing positions. These effects seem to have been in line with the increasing use of congressional budgetary moratoria to restrict leasing acreage over that period (particularly for offshore California) and with DOI's attempts to resist the restrictions on leasing imposed by the moratoria.[27]

## VI. CONCLUSION

We have employed data derived from content analysis of congressional hearings to analyze the dynamics of coalition behavior within subsystems over time. Focusing on the highly charged policy debate waged over OCS energy leasing from 1969–1987, we have used stated policy positions of agents of organizations that are regular participants in the subsystem to analyze characteristics of group representation as well as the content and stability of advocacy coalitions. Further, we have used regression analysis, corrected for autocorrelation where necessary, to explain defection from and to advocacy coalitions by federal agencies. Overall, we have sought to depict the internal workings of subsystems—and their responsiveness to exogenous events—in a highly polarized policy dispute and to thereby systematically test some of the primary hypotheses posed by the ACF.

One set of tests concerned the premise that advocacy coalition members will be constrained by hierarchical systems of belief (Hypotheses 2 and 3). Our test was indirect. We questioned whether advocacy coalition members would show consistent patterns of constraint across types of beliefs bearing on the policy conflict, or, as the principal-agent literature would suggest, if agents of purposive organizations would evidence a broader scope of constraint than representatives of material groups (Hypothesis 10). Examination of the degree of constraint on expressed beliefs by representatives of organizations active in the subsystem revealed that variance in expression regarding the primary bottom-line issue (the pace and breadth of OCS lease sales) was roughly equivalent for material and purposive groups. However, expression by agents of material groups on the somewhat less central (to bottom-line profits) issues of regulation of OCS activities and the role of the states in OCS policy making showed a pattern of significantly more variance than was true of their purposive adversaries. Thus, our analysis suggests that, over the array of issues under dispute in the OCS policy subsystem, agents of purposive groups tend to be more tightly constrained to express the officially sanctioned beliefs of their members than are the agents of material groups. Even more, it suggests that the *breadth* of that constraint varies across types of groups: For material groups, the degree of constraint on expression may be every bit as great (or even greater) as that on purposive group expression, but over a far narrower range of issues. That is, material group agents are particularly attentive to their groups' bottom-line positions, but allow greater latitude than purposive group agents in strategic alteration of expression (or even learning) on other, less central, issues. In contrast, expression of policy positions by agents of purposive groups showed relatively greater constraint over a wider range of issues.

The implication of these findings are that an important element of the ACF should be revised; at least as indicated by expressed beliefs, material group representatives *do not* appear to be constrained by an hierarchical system of beliefs, as was proposed by the framework. For these groups, the orientation of beliefs—and willingness to change policy positions—appears to be anchored on a bottom line representing the critical interests of the represented groups. Outside that concern, considerable flexibility is evident in positions taken. Representatives of purposive groups, in contrast, appear to be more tightly constrained in the expression of beliefs. Expression of beliefs and policy positions by these agents thus seems to conform to the more structured belief system hypothesized by the ACF. Thus, the ACF should be modified to allow for different structures of beliefs for different kinds of subsystem actors. These different kinds of belief structures, in turn, would impose different patterns of constraint on subsystem actors as they adjust to changes in exogenous events and to learning within the subsystem.

A second hypothesis test (Hypothesis 1) concerned the relative stability of the coalitions within the OCS subsystem. Through the use of cluster analysis, we identified two advocacy coalitions that remained quite stable over the 1969–1987 period. One coalition favored increased pace and breadth of leasing, generally less regulation of OCS activity, and a dominant federal role in establishing OCS policy. The other advocated slower and more circumscribed leasing, far greater regulation of OCS activity, and an enhanced state and local government role in OCS policy making. The coalitions persisted over the entire 1969–1987 period and appeared to become increasingly polarized by the mid-1980s. Thus, our data support the ACF's Hypothesis 1, which suggests that stable advocacy coalitions will be evident in the highly conflictual OCS subsystem.

But the pattern of change within the OCS subsystem was complex. Sandwiched between the two coalitions were the involved government agencies. However, these agencies—particularly DOI and DOE—shuttled from one coalition to the other and back again over the period of the analysis. Furthermore, the fact that defection to and from coalitions was limited to federal agencies demonstrates that even in highly polarized and stable subsystems, public agencies—which are by definition important players in nearly all policy subsystems—may be quite mercurial as they respond to their various principals and to exogenous events. Thus, even in highly conflictual subsystems, considerable change in the make-up of advocacy coalitions can occur.

Our third hypothesis (drawn from Hypotheses 4 and 5 in Chapter 2)— that exogenous events such as electoral change, crises, and socioeconomic change would explain coalition defections—is strongly supported by analysis of DOI's expressed OCS leasing and regulatory policy positions. On the most fundamental variable (leasing), DOI responded significantly to the 1973–1974 energy crisis, Carter's presidency, the 1979–1980 energy crisis, Reagan's presidency, and the 1984 congressional elections. Regarding OCS regulation, DOI responded to changes in oil prices, both energy crises, and the administration of President Carter. These factors explain DOI's shifts from one advocacy coalition to the other. Thus, as the

ACF predicts, changes in policy positions within polarized subsystems can be attributed largely to economic and political events exogenous to the subsystem.

A final point to be made from this analysis concerns the contributions of systematic empirical analysis of subsystem change over time. While traditional case studies of the kind presented in Part II of this book provide an essential mode of analysis of policy change, the level of resolution provided by such studies tends to be somewhat limited. The excellent case study of the OCS policy subsystem provided by Heintz (1988) is a case in point. That study indicated that the subsystem was inhabited by two highly polarized and stable advocacy coalitions in which federal agencies (DOI and DOE) were firmly on the prodevelopment side. But the more precise level of data acquisition and analysis provided in this chapter shows that the involved government agencies must be seen as distinct from the two primary opposing coalitions; indeed, the government agencies are shown to have defected to and from coalitions over the course of the 1969–1986 period. Given the resources of the agencies in subsystem politics, this distinction and the revisions of the ACF that it suggests are important. Thus, while qualitative case studies will remain indispensable, we believe it is equally indispensable that policy scholars develop and employ systematic quantitative analytical techniques as a means of putting their theories to harder tests. One such approach, using quantitative analysis of public documents, is detailed in the Methodological Appendix.

## NOTES

1. This chapter borrows from the work presented in Jenkins-Smith et al. (1991).

2. Sometimes the loss of membership can occur because the organizational leaders adhere *too strictly* to the officially espoused position of the organization. The American Civil Liberties Union's defense of the Nazis' march through Skokie, for example, cost it numerous members (Mann, 1978).

3. Salisbury (1984) argued that the key distinction for interest representation involves membership organizations versus institutions (such as businesses). The former will be more attentive to member interests and put more constraints on members to express the officially sanctioned positions of the organization.

4. Obvious examples relative to OCS leasing would be the 1969 Santa Barbara oil spill as well as the spills involving the *Exxon Valdez* in 1989 and the *American Trader* in 1990.

5. For an alternative use of the content analysis of congressional testimony, see King (1989).

6. The development of the coding frame was an iterative process. When the initial frame was applied to the testimonies, it was apparent that some items needed to be added and others modified. Once modifications were made, all previously coded testimonies had to be recoded. This process was repeated several times over many months before we were satisfied with the frame.

7. The specific topic of a hearing was sometimes an issue only indirectly linked to OCS leasing, such as coastal zone management.

8. In a future project, we plan to code each hearing by environmental score-card rating of the committee chair and membership to ascertain the degree to which committee ideology may affect the expression of policy beliefs in hearings.

9. Representing one's organization and remaining personally consistent over time can create cross-pressures on hearing participants. Over the span of this analysis, for example, Barbara Heller initially represented EPC, then DOI under the Carter administration, and then returned to EPC in 1981. Her expressed beliefs were moderated on key items—especially regarding the risks of OCS oil spills—while at DOI and only partially readjusted back to her pre-DOI beliefs upon her return to EPC.

10. The frequency of mention of an issue can itself be used to analyze "issue attention cycles" (Downs, 1972; Hason and Simmons, 1989) and the strategic provision of information, that is, what is said and what is left out (Goggin, 1984).

11. On each of the scales, values 1, 3, and 5 have been demarcated. A value of 4 would be equidistant between 3 and 5; for *Lease,* it would be "decrease speed and breadth of leasing *somewhat.*

12. This hypothesis is appropriate unless the basic policy positions of the organizations (the principals) also changed over time. In the case of the OCS subsystem, however, our analysis and that of Heintz (1988) give us reasonable confidence that the basic policy positions of subsystem participants have remained quite stable since the early 1970s.

13. The AGA is not listed in Table 85 due to insufficient data on the *federalism* variable.

14. In 1980, an Audubon representative urged a Senate subcommittee to limit the states' role in coastal zone planning because states and localities were too prone to local development pressures. By 1981, under the less environmentally concerned Reagan administration, Audubon reversed its position and (together with the Sierra Club, EPA, and NRDC) urged Congress to give the states a greater role in coastal zone planning. This example indicates that, for Audubon at least, the role of the states was an *instrumental* (i.e., secondary rather than core) concern. If the issues represented by *federalism* held this status for the environmental groups in general, their relative stability on this variable is all the more indicative of the relative constraint under which purposive groups operate.

15. Testing the hypothesis concerning hierarchical constraint in elite belief systems would require tests of relative constraint across levels. Our data do not yet contain sufficient instances of expressions of deep core and policy core beliefs to conduct such tests.

16. The spatial characteristics of the three-dimensional issue space should be thought of as a cube, with dimensions of 4 units by 4 units by 4 units. Thus, using the Pythagorean theorem, it can be seen that the coordinates $(0, 0, 0)$ and $(4, 4, 4)$ are 6.93 units apart. Recall that 6.93 is the Euclidean distance rather than the squared Euclidean distance (the latter is used in Chapter 9).

17. Because of missing data, EPA and NOAA had to be excluded from the cluster analysis for this period. Inspection of the mean values for regulation and federalism in the second period showed that EPA and NOAA remained positioned between coalitions.

18. Because of missing data, DOE had to be excluded from the *federalism* variable for this time period. Based on mean values for the *regulation* and *lease* variables, however, DOE appears to be tightly clustered with the proleasing coalition.

19. The *federalism* variable was excluded from the analysis because of insufficient observations. The *regulation* and *lease* variables produced thirty-seven biannual time periods for this analysis.

20. Although the time series had a few missing observations, fortunately none of these fell in a period for which we were testing the effect of a specific event. Nevertheless, interpolated data may skew the variance, thus biasing the estimated effects of the interventions. For each missing data gap then, we ran the models with three types of "plugs": interpolated average of $t - 1$ and $t + 1$; equal to $t - 1$; and equal to $t + 1$. In no case did the "plug" significantly affect the results.

21. The Cochrane-Orcutt method successively estimates new values for the serial correlation coefficient (Cochrane and Orcutt, 1949; Hanushek and Jackson, 1977).

22. Although other techniques (including the Box-Jenkins approach) are available, the Cochrane-Orcutt approach has the advantages of (1) permitting both discrete and continuous variables and (2) performing well with small samples (Hanushek and Jackson, 1977:173; Lewis-Beck, 1986).

23. Even with small and statistically insignificant $p$'s, the Cochrane-Orcutt procedure should not bias the estimated slope and intercept coefficients. This lack of bias was reaffirmed by running OLS regressions for all models with statistically insignificant $p$'s to ensure that the estimate coefficients did not diverge. In all such cases, the Cochrane-Orcutt and OLS models produced very similar results.

24. The Republicans lost twenty-six seats in the House and had no net change in the Senate in 1982. In 1984, they gained four House seats but lost two in the Senate. Given Reagan's impressive victory in 1984, these modest results in congressional elections may well have undermined support for the proleasing coalition on Capitol Hill.

25. We assumed that expressed DOI policy positions would respond rapidly to changing oil prices because such changes can be readily monitored and because responses to prices concern changes in expressed policy positions—rather than changes in policies per se. Thus we used the rate of change in oil prices.

26. Following the procedure specified in Lewis-Beck (1986), we dropped the variables with statistically insignificant effects from the model to reduce specification error.

27. More than 40 million acres of the OCS were placed under leasing moratoria by Congress in the mid-1980s (Heintz, 1988).

# 9

## From Vague Consensus to Clearly Differentiated Coalitions: Environmental Policy at Lake Tahoe, 1964–1985

PAUL A. SABATIER AND ANNE M. BRASHER

The advocacy coalition framework (ACF) is designed to help explain policy change over periods of a decade or more in relatively complex situations. Typically these involve policy subsystems incorporating large numbers of actors from a variety of institutions at multiple levels of government as well as interest groups, researchers, and journalists. The long-standing controversy over land-use and water-quality planning in the Lake Tahoe Basin represents such a case.

This chapter uses data from a content analysis of testimony at public hearings over a twenty-year period to examine several critical hypotheses of the ACF. As will be recalled from Chapter 2, coalitions are assumed to coalesce around rather abstract (policy core) beliefs rather than calculations of short-term self-interest. Given the former's resistance to change, one would expect substantial coalition stability over time:

*Hypothesis 1:* On major controversies within a policy subsystem when core beliefs are in dispute, the lineup of allies and opponents tends to be rather stable over periods of a decade or so.

In addition, the ACF shares the assumptions that political belief systems are hierarchically structured (Converse, 1964; Peffley and Hurwitz, 1985) and thus that abstract beliefs are more resistant to change than more specific ones:

*Hypothesis 3:* An actor (or coalition) will give up secondary aspects of a belief system before acknowledging weaknesses in the policy core.

. Note that this chapter deals only with a portion of the ACF. We do not attempt to seriously examine the factors affecting policy change over time (Hypotheses 4 and 5) nor the factors conducive to policy-oriented learning across coalitions (Hypotheses 6 through 9).

The first section of the chapter provides an introduction to environmental politics in the Lake Tahoe Basin since the early 1960s, including a preliminary application of many of the key features of the ACF. The next section discusses the principal database, involving the coding of 190 testimonies presented at eleven hearings before a variety of legislative and administrative institutions between 1964 and 1985. The third section presents our results. While the data generally support the two hypotheses, the most interesting findings concern the evolution of subsystem dynamics over time. At Tahoe, a new subsystem went from a vague consensus in the early 1960s that something needed to be done about urbanization and its effects on environmental quality to an increasingly bifurcated set of coalitions with well-integrated belief systems containing markedly different positions on a wide range of issues. Throughout, our methods and findings will be compared with those in the previous chapter dealing with petroleum development on the outer continental shelf (OCS).

## I. ENVIRONMENTAL POLITICS AT LAKE TAHOE

### Historical Background

Lake Tahoe is a large (190 sq. mi.), extraordinarily clear alpine lake located in the Sierra Nevada Mountains on the California-Nevada border about 200 miles east of San Francisco. For decades its inaccessibility in winter meant that Tahoe was primarily used as a summer resort by families from the San Francisco Bay Area and northern California. The opening of a major interstate highway, the 1960 Winter Olympics at nearby Squaw Valley, the expansion of ski areas and Nevada gaming casinos, and the general prosperity of the 1960s fueled a boom in tourism and second-home construction around the lake during the 1960s and much of the 1970s. As a result, the permanent population of the Tahoe Basin went from 12,200 in 1960 to 45,000 in 1980 and the number of visitors on a peak summer weekend increased from 30,000 in 1956 to 150,000 in 1978 (Ingram and Sabatier, 1987).

While these trends were viewed with favor by most local government officials and business owners, others involved in the basin pointed to the negative consequences of this growth: the urbanization of a beautiful mountain setting as well as increases in the pollution of a lake whose renowned clarity is matched only by Crater Lake in Oregon and Lake Baikal in the Soviet Union (Goldman, 1981).

In the early 1960s, inadequate septic systems were regarded as the major threat to water quality. Following the 1963 recommendations of a prestigious team of engineers and scientists, in 1965–1966 the two states and the federal government agreed to ban all septic tanks in the basin, to replace them with sewers, and to export all sewage from the basin by 1970 (Strong, 1984).

That agreement did not, however, lead to any discernible improvement in water quality. Moreover, sewering allowed additional development in some areas and thus contributed to further urbanization (Sabatier and Pelkey, 1990). Because land development was increasingly perceived by many people as contributing to both aesthetic and environmental degradation of the area, attention shifted in the late 1960s and early 1970s to land-use practices. Scientists began to argue that development contributed to soil erosion, which caused the release of nutrients and sediment into the lake, which in turn increased the production of algae and degraded water clarity (U.S. Soil Conservation Service, 1971; Goldman, 1973, 1974). The past twenty years has witnessed periodic, often very intense, controversies between environmentalists and development interests over the desirability of various land-use controls and their effects on environmental quality, the viability of the basin's economy, and property rights.

Starting in the mid-1960s, many people began to argue that any sort of long-term solution to urban and environmental problems at Tahoe would require some form of institutionalized cooperation among the two states, five counties, and one incorporated city in the basin. In 1967, a study committee appointed by the two state legislatures recommended the creation of a bistate regional planning agency with authority to regulate development in the basin (Costantini and Hanf, 1973; Strong, 1984). After several years of conflict between environmental groups and state resource agencies, on the one hand, and most local businesses and government officials, on the other, in 1969 the legislatures of the two states and the U.S. Congress approved an interstate compact creating the Tahoe Regional Planning Agency (TRPA).

The TRPA Compact (PL 91-148) reflected its compromise origins. The agency's governing board consisted of five officials from each of the two states, a majority of whom were to be representatives of local government. The agency was required to develop a regional plan within eighteen months that would balance resource conservation and orderly development. Its authority to control development was hindered by convoluted voting procedures and by restrictions on its authority over public works projects and casinos approved prior to 1970.[1]

During its initial years, the TRPA was fairly successful in steering a middle ground between environmentalists, who wanted to severely restrict development, and most local business and governmental officials, who wished to see more deference to market forces. Its 1971–1972 General Plan and Land Use Ordinance used an imaginative technique for mapping erodible lands to downzone large portions of the basin while also allowing sufficient expansion of existing urbanized areas to satisfy most local government officials. The middle soon crumbled, however, under protests and lawsuits from downzoned property owners, on the one hand, and environmental groups and many California state officials, on the other. The latter were enraged by the way in which the TRPA's voting procedures resulted in the approval of a new shopping center and several new casinos in the summer of 1973 (see note 1).

The League to Save Lake Tahoe, the principal environmental group, essentially gave up on the TRPA in the summer of 1973 and began to seek assistance from its allies in Sacramento. These efforts were greatly strengthened by the election of Jerry Brown as governor of Calfornia in December 1974. Throughout the remainder of the 1970s, the league and its allies pursued a strategy of seeking assistance from a variety of other institutions—including the California Tahoe Regional Planning Agency (CTRPA), the California regional and state water-quality boards, California air pollution agencies, the EPA, the U.S. Forest Service, and several members of Congress—in their efforts to restrict land development in the basin and perhaps to transform the basin into a national scenic area (Ingram and Sabatier, 1987; Sabatier and Pelkey, 1990).

Although these efforts angered basin business and governmental officials and property rights groups, they eventually led to several major institutional innovations in 1980. First, after several years of often bitter negotiations, the two states and the Congress agreed to revise the TRPA Compact to provide for a majority of state officials on the governing board, to alter decision rules to make project denials much easier, and to require the agency to develop a new regional plan that would meet various environmental quality standards ("thresholds"). Second, in the spring of 1980 the California State Water Resources Control Board (SWRCB) approved regulations that essentially prohibited development of about 12,000 parcels on relatively steep slopes or near streams, even though most of them were in subdivisions that had previously been approved by local governments and sometimes even by the TRPA. Third, recognizing that the SWRCB regulations and the new TRPA Plan would adversely affect many property owners, both the federal and California state governments approved legislation to purchase a substantial amount of undeveloped property in the Tahoe Basin.

Conflict continued over the development of the thresholds and the TRPA Plan, with the balance of power on the TRPA Governing Board fluctuating with gubernatorial elections in the two states. In fact, after the League to Save Lake Tahoe and the California attorney general were successful in obtaining a court injunction in June 1984 prohibiting virtually all development in the basin pending revisions in the TRPA's proposed plan, the State of Nevada came very close to withdrawing from the TRPA Compact in 1985. Finally, under the leadership of a new TRPA executive director, the agency was able to forge a compromise plan in 1986–1987 that led to a settlement of the lawsuits and the renewal of building at levels below those of the 1970s (Sabatier and Pelkey, 1990).

This is a capsule summary of an enormously complicated case. For more complete, but still essentially atheoretical descriptions, see Strong (1984), Ingram and Sabatier (1987), and Sabatier and Pelkey (1990:Chapter 2). We shall now briefly apply aspects of the Advocacy

Coalition Framework of policy change outlined in Chapter 2 to the Tahoe case.

## Factors External to the Tahoe Land-Use/Water-Quality Subsystem

The first task in applying the ACF is to designate the policy subsystem of interest. In this case, it is those actors and institutions active in land-use and water-quality issues in the Lake Tahoe Basin. Although subsystem actors operate with a fair degree of autonomy, their resources and beliefs are affected by aspects of the larger political system, some of which remain stable over many decades, while others may fluctuate substantially and thus serve as major stimuli to policy change within the subsystem.

*Stable External Factors.* These include such things as the basic attributes of the problem area (good) and fundamental social and legal norms. At Tahoe, for example, the very fact that the lake's water quality is a common pool resource creates an argument for governmental intervention because of the inability of pure markets to deal efficiently with such resources.

Basic legal structure is also important. The lake's location astride two semi-sovereign states and five counties means that enormously complicated efforts are required to deal with the basin's problems because dissenting actors have numerous routes of appeal, including three court systems, two legislatures, and two governors. The constitutional protection of private property rights has constrained regulatory agency behavior. Also of importance has been the legalization of casino gaming in Nevada since the 1930s and the critical role of that industry in the state's economic and fiscal structure (Nevada Gaming Commission, 1970).

*External Events.* Other factors external to the policy subsystem can vary significantly over the course of a few years, thus affecting the constraints and opportunities facing subsystem actors. The ACF identifies the following categories:

*1. Changes in Socioeconomic Conditions.* The nationwide emergence of the environmental movement in the late 1960s and early 1970s played an important part in strengthening the environmental coalition at Tahoe. Likewise, macroeconomic changes in disposable income and interest rates within California have significantly affected demand for housing in the Tahoe Basin over the past twenty-five years (Sabatier and Pelkey, 1990).

*2. Changes in System-wide Governing Coalitions.* Although there probably have not been any realigning elections in either California or Nevada during the period under review, gubernatorial elections in the two states have certainly had major impacts on land-use and water-quality policy in the basin via gubernatorial appointments to the TRPA Board and various state agencies. While Jerry Brown was governor of California (1975–1982), for example, the Tahoe environmental coalition witnessed an enormous increase in its political resources via Brown's appointments to the TRPA Board, his support of the CTRPA, and the aggressive policies pursued in the basin by his appointees to the State Water Resources Control Board (SWRCB) and the Air Resources Board (ARB). Brown's replacement by George Deukmejian, a conservative Republican, in 1983 resulted in a significant change in California's appointees to the TRPA Board, but this shift was partially offset by a change in the Nevada Governor's Office from a conservative Republican (Robert List) to a moderate Democrat (Richard Bryan) in 1983 (Ingram and Sabatier, 1987).

   *3. Policy Decisions from Other Subsystems.* The second-home boom of the 1960s at Tahoe was fueled by such exogenous events as the opening of an interstate highway between San Francisco and Reno and the decision to hold the 1960 Winter Olympics at Squaw Valley, about ten miles outside the basin. Similarly, national decisions concerning interest rates, FHA loans, and taxation (e.g., the deductibility of interest charges on second homes) have significantly affected housing demand in the basin (Sabatier and Pelkey, 1990).

   Keeping the importance of these external factors in mind, we can now turn to a brief analysis of politics within the Tahoe land-use subsystem since 1960.

### Subsystem Structure: A Preliminary View

   Reviews of various Tahoe histories (Costantini and Hanf, 1973; Strong, 1984; Ingram and Sabatier, 1987) suggest that the Tahoe land-use subsystem during the 1960–1985 period contained a diverse set of actors, including:

1. Six local governments within the basin, including three Nevada counties (Washoe, Ormsby, Douglas), two California counties (Placer, El Dorado), and the city of South Lake Tahoe;
2. Seven special districts providing sewer, water, road, and/or recreation services within the basin;
3. The Tahoe Regional Planning Agency;
4. The California and Nevada Tahoe Regional Planning Agencies;
5. Water-quality control agencies in California and Nevada;
6. Highway and air pollution agencies in the two states;
7. The Nevada Department of Conservation and Natural Resources and the California Resources Agency;
8. The U.S. Environmental Protection Agency (and its predecessors);
9. The U.S. Forest Service (which owns about 70% of the land in the basin);
10. U.S. representatives and senators from the basin and/or interested in the basin;
11. California and Nevada legislators from the basin and/or interested in the basin;
12. The governors of California and Nevada;

13. The attorney general of California;
14. Basin businesses, particularly the casinos and businesses related to tourism or construction;
15. Realtors and other property rights groups in the basin, including the Tahoe-Sierra Preservation Council;
16. The League to Save Lake Tahoe and other environmental groups;
17. Several newspapers and other mass media in the basin, northern California, and northern Nevada;
18. Researchers at the University of California at Davis, the University of California at Berkeley, the University of Nevada at Reno, the U.S. Geological Survey, the U.S. Soil Conservation Service (SCS) and several consulting firms interested in the basin.

Note that the subsystem has included agencies and elected officials from all three levels of government as well as a diverse set of interest groups and people interested in generating and transmitting policy information.

General histories of the basin and analyses of elite surveys done in 1972 and 1984 (Sabatier et al., 1987, 1990) suggest that these actors can probably be aggregated into two rather distinct advocacy coalitions during much of the 1960–1985 period.

The Environmental Coalition was dominated by environmental groups and their allies in Congress and in the two state legislatures; most officials from state and federal pollution control agencies, the U.S. Forest Service, the CTRPA, and the TRPA staff; several out-of-basin newspapers (e.g., the *San Francisco Chronicle* and *Sacramento Bee*); several researchers (most notably limnologist Charles Goldman of UC Davis); and, at times, the California attorney general. The Environmental Coalition apparently had a belief system that stressed: (1) the primacy of environmental protection over economic development and property rights; (2) a perception that environmental values (e.g., water quality) were being seriously threatened by housing and commercial development; (3) a preference for government regulation rather than private markets for dealing with those problems; (4) a causal assumption that local governments were too dependent upon development for fiscal and economic reasons to seriously restrict it; and (5) a perception that a regional regulatory agency was needed to deal with the basin's problems.

The competing Economic Growth/Property Rights Coalition was dominated by local businesspeople in construction and tourism, property rights advocates, most local governments and special districts, most basin representatives to Congress and the two state legislatures, and most of the mass media in the Tahoe Basin. It seemed to have a belief system that stressed: (1) economic growth and the protection of property rights over environmental quality; (2) skepticism that environmental quality was declining; (3) a perception that erosion from housing construction could be handled through remedial measures; (4) substantial skepticism concerning the efficiency and rationality of governmental regulation; (5) a preference for local control of land-use decisions, as locals are more democratically accountable and more interested in problem solving than outsiders; (6) a perception that environmental controls were having serious adverse consequences on the local economy; and (7) an insistence that any diminution of property values by governmental regulation be compensated at full market value.

In addition to advocacy coalitions, the ACF refers to "policy brokers," that is, actors preoccupied with keeping the level of political conflict within acceptable limits and with reaching compromise solutions. At Tahoe, this is a very difficult role because of the level of conflict and the necessity of combining technical expertise with substantial political skill. There have been at least two successful instances; both involved the TRPA executive director's ability to forge compromise solutions in developing regional plans in 1971–1972 (Dick Heikka) and in 1986–1987 (Bill Morgan).[2]

Having provided this preliminary overview, we can now turn to the detailed analysis of testimony at public hearings over the past twenty-five years to see if these general impressions are confirmed by more systematic analysis.

## II. METHODS AND DATA BASE

The data base consists of a total of 190 testimonies by 141 different people presented at eleven sets of hearings regarding land use and water quality in the Tahoe Basin between 1964 and 1985. These data represent virtually the complete set of legislative and administrative hearings with verbatim transcripts that we could locate (see Appendix A at the end of this chapter for details). They include hearings before federal regulatory agencies, congressional committees, legislative committees of the two states, and the California State Water Resources Control Board. We coded virtually all testimonies except for those given by individuals unaffiliated with governmental or private organizations.

Table 9.1 lists the hearings used in our analysis as well as the frequency of testimony from representatives of important organizations. Note that representatives of Nevada local governments were the most frequent testifiers, with twenty-one appearances, but numerous other categories— including California administrative agencies, California local governments, Nevada administrative agencies, Nevada legislators, business organizations, property rights groups, the League to Save Lake Tahoe, and regional planning organizations—each testified at least fourteen times. No category had representatives testifying at all eleven hearings, although representatives of California local governments, California administrative agencies, Nevada administrative agencies, the League to Save, and regional planning organizations appeared at least eight times. Although governmental officials tended to testify primarily within their own state, at most hearings there was some representation from the other state.

The data base used in this chapter differs from the one utilized in

TABLE 9.1 Testimony by Various Interests at Legislative and Administrative Hearings Concerning Land-Use and Water-Quality Policy at Lake Tahoe, 1964-1985 (number of testimonies by an interest at a hearing, N = 190)

| Hearing | Federal Agency | Calif. Exec. Agency | Calif. Leg. | Calif. Local Govt. | Nevada Exec. Agency | Nevada Leg. | Nevada Local Govt.[a] | Public Utility Dist. | Business Group[b] | Property Rights Group | League to Save Tahoe | Other Envir. Group[c] | Researchers | Regional Planning Agency/Groups[d] | TOTAL |
|---|---|---|---|---|---|---|---|---|---|---|---|---|---|---|---|
| 1964 Calif. Legislature on Regional Planning | 1 | 2 | | 3 | 1 | | 1 | 3 | 1 | | | 3 | | 1 | 16 |
| 1966 Fed. Water Quality Admin. on Tahoe | 4 | 5 | 1 | 2 | 3 | | 1 | 3 | | | 1 | | | 3 | 23 |
| 1968 Nevada Legislature on TRPA Compact | | | 1 | | 3 | 4 | 8 | | 2 | | 2 | | | 2 | 22 |
| Dec. 1972 Calif. Legislature on TRPA | | 4 | 1 | 1 | 1 | 1 | | 1 | 4 | | 2 | 2 | 1 | | 18 |
| Sept. 1973 U.S. EPA on Fed. Involvement | 2 | | 3 | | | | | | | 1 | 2 | 2 | | 2 | 12 |
| 1977 Nevada Legislature on TRPA Compact | | | | 1 | 1 | | 4 | | 4 | 2 | 1 | 1 | 1 | 1 | 16 |
| 1977 Nevada Legislature on Gaming | | | | | | 3 | 3 | | | 1 | | 1 | | 1 | 9 |
| 1980 Nevada Legislature on TRPA Compact | 1 | | | 1 | 2 | 6 | 1 | | 1 | 2 | | | | | 14 |
| 1980 Calif. SWRCB on 208 Plan | 1 | 4 | | 8 | | | | | | 8 | 5 | 2 | | 2 | 30 |
| 1984 Calif. Legislature on Land Acquisition | | 3 | 1 | 1 | | | | | | 1 | 2 | | 1 | 2 | 11 |
| 1985 Nevada Legislature on TRPA Withdrawal | | | | | 3 | 5 | 3 | | 2 | 2 | 1 | | 2 | | 18 |
| TOTAL | 9 | 18 | 7 | 17 | 14 | 19 | 21 | 7 | 14 | 17 | 16 | 11 | 5 | 14 | 189 |

[a]Many of these were from Douglas County (15 of 19 local government spokesmen and 8 of 19 legislators).
[b]Includes Chambers of Commerce, casinos, and prominent developers.
[c]Includes the Sierra Club and the League of Women Voters.
[d]Includes the TRPA, CTRPA, NTRPA, and LTAC.

Chapter 8 on OCS petroleum leasing. Whereas Jenkins-Smith and St. Clair dealt exclusively with testimony before congressional committees, the set of hearings used in this chapter were held by a variety of federal and state legislative committees and administrative agencies. The OCS study was fortunate in finding hearings for every year between 1969 and 1987, whereas our hearings occurred at irregular intervals. Finally, the testimonies used in the OCS study came from a rather narrow set of national organizations that testified repeatedly over that period, including three business trade organizations, two integrated petroleum companies, four environmental groups, and four federal agencies. In contrast, the testimonies in our data set came from fourteen *categories* of organizations representing all three levels of government, both legislators and administrative agencies, several categories of interest groups, and even a few researchers.

Each approach has its strengths and weaknesses. On the one hand, by focusing on the testimony of a few specific organizations that testified virtually every year, Jenkins-Smith and St. Clair were able to measure change in specific organizations (critical for their interest in principal-agent models) and to do the sort of time-series analysis of the Department of Interior that requires data points for every variable for every time period (e.g., year).[3] On the other hand, the Tahoe data set probably better illustrates the variety of governmental and private actors who populate most policy subsystems. Our challenge will be to see whether the ACF enables us to make sense out of a less systematic set of hearings and testimonies.

The coding frame used in the Tahoe project was very similar in development and organization to that used in the OCS study.[4] The set of items were developed in an iterative process starting from the belief system components identified by the ACF (see Figure 2.1) and our general knowledge of Tahoe events and then expanding through a preliminary scan of the hearings to obtain a list of the topics discussed. The final coding frame consisted of 235 variables with responses on five-point interval or ordinal scales. Items not addressed in a particular hearing testimony were coded as "missing/not mentioned." Because of the length of the coding frame and the necessity of including the entire set of possible items raised over two decades, the average testimony contained codable responses on only twenty-one items. In order to reduce the missing data problem to manageable levels, we decided to use only the subset of forty-six items with at least twenty valid responses over the 190 testimonies.

Consistent with the presumed structure of elite belief systems posited in Table 2.1 of Chapter 2, the coding frame was divided into three main parts. Section A dealt with a few deep core items designed to tap people's fundamental normative and ontological orientations concerning the proper relationship between humans and nature, general value priorities, and general criteria of distributive justice. Perhaps because the deep core concerns very general attitudes—that is, ones *not* specifically related to the policy area of interest—the testimonies contained so few codable responses that analysis of this section proved infeasible. Section B of the coding frame contained twenty-seven policy core items relating to fundamental normative orientations and perceptions regarding land use and water quality in the Tahoe Basin, of which fourteen had sufficient testimonies to be utilized in this analysis. These included items dealing with the proper division of authority among various levels of government for resolving Tahoe issues, the value of Lake Tahoe as a natural resource, the salience and magnitude of threats posed to three core values (property rights, environmental quality, and economic viability) in the basin, and desired tradeoffs among these critical values on Tahoe land-use issues. Finally, about 200 items in the coding frame dealt with so-called secondary aspects of the belief systems of Tahoe elites. Of these, thirty-two had sufficient testimonies to be included in the amended data set for this Chapter. These involved: (1) a multitude of causal perceptions (e.g., the relative importance of various sources affecting the lake's water quality, as well as the impacts of land-use regulation in the basin), (2) the importance of various problems at Tahoe, (3) the desirability of alternative strategies for reducing siltation, (4) perceptions of the factors affecting the behavior of local, state, and regional officals, (5) evaluations of the performance of subsystem actors, and (6) preferences concerning a variety of enduring TRPA issues. A copy of the full Tahoe coding frame is found in the Methodological Appendix.

Given the length and complexity of the coding frame, reliability tests between the three coders were conducted at regular intervals. Standard reliability tests (Holsti, 1969; Tinsley and Weiss, 1975; Mitchell, 1979) are inappropriate for data sets such as this that include a large number of "missing/not mentioned" value codes because to include them inflates reliability. If we were to omit "missing values" from the reliability test, however, we would fail to recognize that agreeing not to code an item is critical. Consequently, in conjunction with Jenkins-Smith, we devised a two-part reliability test specifically for this type of data (see the Methodological Appendix for details). The overall intercoder reliability levels were measured as the percentage of agreement both on decisions to code an item as having been mentioned (versus missing) and on the numeric code given. On the decision to code or not to code, all three coders agreed 89% of the time and two of three coders agreed 91% of the time. On the total set of items coded affirmatively by at least two coders, an analysis of pairs of coders showed that 91% of the time the codes were within one value of each other and 54% of the time they were identical. Thus we are reasonably confident of the intersubjective reliability of our results.

## III. DATA ANALYSIS AND RESULTS

Given our focus on changes in coalition composition and elite beliefs over time, the selection of time periods for comparing results is critical. The brief history of Tahoe events presented earlier suggests four eras:
   *1. The Sewering Era (1960–1966).* Inadequate septic tanks and sewage

treatment facilities were perceived as the main threat to water quality, and the collection of all human wastes in sewers and their export from the basin was the solution decided upon by government officials in 1965–1966.

2. *The Formative Years of Regional Planning (1967–May 1973).* During this period, the TRPA Compact was being negotiated by the two states and the TRPA developed its 1971–1972 regional plan.

3. *Disillusionment with the TRPA (June 1973–October 1980).* When the TRPA's "dual majority" voting procedures led to a major shopping center and several new casinos being "deemed approved" in the summer of 1973, environmental groups, many legislators in both states, and even the TRPA Board concluded that the 1969 Compact was fundamentally flawed. This era witnessed repeated efforts to amend the compact, as well as intervention of the other California agencies, most notably the CTRPA and the SWRCB.

4. *Environmental Supremacy (1981–1987).* After revisions to the TRPA Compact and the SWRCB erosion control regulations in late 1980, the law favored the environmental coalition. This period witnessed continued struggles over the implementation of those changes, including the successful litigation by the League to Save Lake Tahoe and the California attorney general over the 1984 TRPA Plan, the subsequent building moratorium, a major effort by property rights groups to convince Nevada to withdraw from the compact in 1985, and the final drafting of a compromise TRPA Plan in 1986–1987.

As will be recalled from Table 9.1, our data set includes at least two sets of hearings and a minimum of twenty-nine testimonies for each of the four eras.

In addition to designating the time periods, the other essential preliminary step in our data analysis was the development of a number of multi-item scales. These are superior to the use of single items for two reasons. First, such scales minimize the effects of measurement error by using several indicators of the same basic concept (Leege and Francis, 1974). Second, they provide a means of dealing with our missing data problem by permitting a testifier to have a scale score even if he or she addressed only one of the items on the scale. Like Jenkins-Smith and St. Clair, we used correlation analysis to identify items that dealt with the same basic concept and that correlated rather highly (in most cases, $r > .50$). We then created a simple additive scale for each set of items. A person-testimony's score on the scale was the mean of the valid (nonmissing) scores of the items comprising that scale.

We obtained seven scales: two at the policy core level, one that is a mixture of policy-core and secondary aspects, and four dealing with secondary aspects. For more details, see Appendix B.

A. Policy Core Scales
   1. Nonlocal Scale (n = 107 valid testimonies). A score of 5 indicates a strong preference for nonlocal control, while 1 indicates a strong preference for local government control.

2. Environmental Priority Scale (n = 144). A score of 5 indicates a strong preference for environmental quality and the perception that it is threatened, while a 1 indicates a strong preference for economic development and/or property rights and the perception that they are threatened.

B. Mixed Policy Core and Secondary Aspects
   3. Environmental Regulation as a Policy Instrument (n = 148). A high score suggests a preference for stringent environmental regulation (including reducing the rate of development) over less burdensome regulations and purchase of property as a general strategy or policy instrument.

C. Secondary Aspects of Belief Systems
   4. Water-Quality Problems and Regulation Scale (n = 105). A score of 5 indicates that water quality at Tahoe is perceived as a serious problem and that stringent measures to regulate housing development are appropriate; a score of 1 indicates that water quality is not perceived as a problem and that development controls are undesirable. Sewage as a source of water quality problems did *not* load highly on this scale and thus was excluded.
   5. Urbanization Problems Scale (n = 82). A score of 5 indicates that urbanization and air quality are perceived as serious problems and that stringent controls on casino expansion are needed to address them; a score of 1 indicates the reverse.
   6. Proregional Planning Scale (n = 143). A score of 5 indicates a perception that regional agencies can effectively deal with the basin's problems and ought to be strengthened; a score of 1 indicates the reverse.
   7. Local Government Deficiences Scale (n = 139). A score of 1 indicates great faith in local government while a score of 5 indicates a preference for the intervention of nonlocal (primarily state of California) authorities.

These seven scales incorporate a total of thirty-seven items out of the forty-six mentioned in at least twenty testimonies.

The actual data analysis proceeds in two parts. The first involves an overview of the relationship among the seven scales and provides an initial indication of changes in those relationships over time. The second section focuses on changes over time in both coalition stability (Hypothesis 1) and different belief levels (Hypothesis 3). Throughout, the unit of analysis is a "person-testimony," that is, the testimony of an individual at a hearing.

*General Relationship Among Belief Scales*

Figure 9.1 provides the correlation coefficients (Pearson r) among the seven scales. The scales are organized into two levels, policy core and secondary aspects, and are also divided into two topics, one dealing with intergovernmental relations, the other with substantive value priorities and perceived problems.

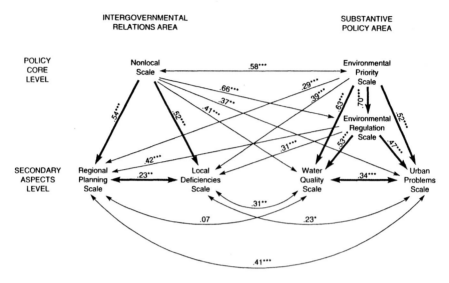

FIGURE 9.1   Correlations among elements of belief systems at Lake Tahoe, 1964–1985

The results suggest that this method is a reasonable way of portraying belief system structure among Tahoe policy elites. First, relationships *within* the two topical areas—intergovernmental relations and substantive values—were stronger than *between* them. Second, *within* each topical area, the correlations were stronger between the policy core and secondary aspects than they were between different scales in the secondary aspects. This finding provides some preliminary support for the assumption that belief systems are hierarchically organized, that is, that more abstract beliefs in the policy core constrain more specific ones in the secondary aspects within the same topical area.[5] Third, the strongest correlations *between* topical areas occurred at the most abstract level—that is, among the nonlocal scale, the environmental priority scale, and the environmental regulation scale. This finding would also seem to be consistent with the ACF's general assumption that abstract beliefs across topical areas are more integrated than are secondary ones. Finally, since all the correlation coefficients except one are statistically significant and generally quite strong ($r > .40$), the professed beliefs of Tahoe policy elites actually do seem to form a "belief system." Beliefs on quite different topics, ranging from value priorities to intergovernmental relations to water quality to urban problems, seem to be integrated in a sensible fashion.

Did this structure emerge in the early 1960s, at the start of Tahoe environmental conflict, or did it develop over time? Figure 9.2 compares belief system structure in two periods: 1964–May 1973 (the sewering era and the formative years of regional planning) and June 1973–1984 (disillusionment with the TRPA and environmental supremacy).

## PERIOD I: 1964-1972

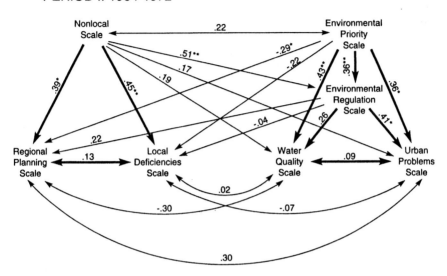

## PERIOD II: 1973-1984

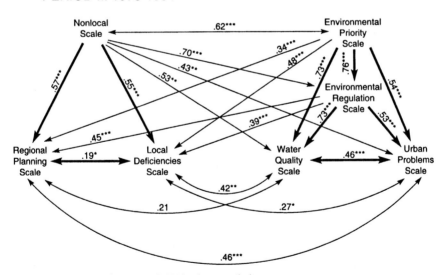

*,**,*** = significant at .05, .01 and .001 levels, respectively

FIGURE 9.2   Development of much more integrated belief system between 1964–1972 and 1973–1984

Figure 9.2 provides striking evidence that the belief systems of Tahoe elites—as expressed in their testimony at public hearings—became better integrated after 1973. Whereas only eight of the twenty coefficients were statistically significant (p<.05) in the earlier period, all except one were significant in the later period. Many of the correlation coefficients doubled or tripled in magnitude; the number in which r>.50 went from one in the earlier period to ten after 1973. In addition, a few even changed direction: Whereas the relationship between environmental priorities and regional planning was negative (and significant) in the earlier period, it switched to positive (and significant) after 1973. This finding suggests that as Tahoe elites gained experience with regional planning and environmental policy, they increasingly realized that intergovernmental relations and substantive value priorities were related, that protecting environmental values required dealing with both water quality and urbanization, and that doing so required stringent environmental controls. By the same token, people valuing economic development and property rights became increasingly aware of the costs of environmental controls on those values.

### From Vague Initial Consensus to
### Distinct Coalitions

The data in Figures 9.1 and 9.2 describe the aggregate patterns among all members of the Tahoe environmental policy subsystem. But if one is to understand belief change over time, policy actors have to be disaggregated into meaningful groups to see whose beliefs change first and in what manner.

Table 9.2 divides the Tahoe policy elite into eleven categories of group affiliation based upon the general history presented earlier as well as analyses of cross-sectional opinion surveys done in 1972 and 1984 (Sabatier et al., 1987, 1990). It then presents the mean score for each group on three *substantive policy scales*—environmental priorities, environmental regulation, and water-quality regulation—for each of the four time periods.[6] Recall that all of these scales range from 1 to 5, with 5 indicating that environmental problems are serious and that stringent controls on development are needed. The far right-hand columns indicate the overall mean for that scale during that time period, as well as whether a one-way analysis of variance (ANOVA) indicated statistically significant differences *across groups*. We also did a one-way ANOVA to see if there were significant differences in group means *across the four time periods*.

The results clearly show that, on these substantive policy issues, Tahoe went from a mushy consensus in the 1964–1967 period to substantial polarization after 1973. On none of the three scales were there significant differences across groups during the 1964–1967 period. On environmental priorities, for example, the group means ranged from 3.0 to 3.9, indicating fairly strong support for environmental protection measures. That rough consensus lasted through the 1968–1972 period for environ-

TABLE 9.2 Changes in Various Groups' Mean Scores on Substantive Policy Scales Over Time, 1964-1984 [Mean (number of testimonies)]

| Scale & Period | Local Govt. | Business/ Property Group | Nevada Leg. Basin | Nevada Leg. Nonbasin | Nevada Exec. Agency | Regional Agency or Group | Federal Agency | Researcher | Calif. Exec. Agency | Calif. Leg. Basin | Calif. Leg. NonBasin | Envir. Group | Overall Mean[a] | ANOVA Across Groups[b] |
|---|---|---|---|---|---|---|---|---|---|---|---|---|---|---|
| **POLICY CORE LEVEL** | | | | | | | | | | | | | | |
| **1. Environmental Priority Scale** | | | | | | | | | | | | | | |
| 1964-1967 | 3.4 (5) | 3.0 (1) | -- | -- | 3.0 (1) | 3.3 (4) | 3.9 (5) | -- | 3.2 (6) | -- | 3.0 (1) | 3.6 (4) | 3.4 | NS |
| 1968-1972 | 3.2 (5) | -- | 3.0 (1) | 3.6 (2) | 3.5 (2) | 3.2 (2) | 3.4 (2) | 4.0 (1) | 3.5 (2) | -- | -- | 3.9 (6) | 3.5 | NS |
| 1973-1980 | 3.0 (13) | 2.5 (17) | 1.9 (3) | 3.0 (2) | 3.9 (3) | 3.8 (3) | 3.2 (2) | 3.5 (2) | 4.0 (6) | 3.5 (1) | 3.9 (11) | | 3.2 | *** |
| 1981-1984 | 2.3 (3) | 2.0 (4) | 2.5 (4) | 2.5 (1) | 3.5 (3) | 3.9 (1) | -- | 4.5 (1) | 3.5 (4) | -- | 4.2 (1) | 4.1 (4) | 3.1 | ** |
| **2. Environmental Regulation Scale** | | | | | | | | | | | | | | |
| 1964-1967 | 3.9 (7) | 3.5 (1) | -- | 3.0 (1) | 3.3 (3) | 3.8 (5) | 3.7 (3) | -- | 3.8 (6) | -- | -- | 3.5 (2) | 3.7** | NS |
| 1968-1972 | 2.9 (8) | 3.0 (1) | 2.0 (1) | 4.0 (2) | 4.0 (3) | 3.2 (2) | 3.6 (2) | 5.0 (1) | 3.6 (3) | -- | -- | 4.2 (7) | 3.6 | # |
| 1973-1980 | 2.8 (13) | 2.0 (16) | 2.3 (3) | 3.4 (4) | 3.2 (3) | 4.2 (3) | 3.2 (2) | 4.2 (2) | 3.8 (6) | 3.7 (1) | 4.0 (3) | 3.9 (11) | 3.1 | *** |
| 1981-1984 | 2.5 (2) | 1.8 (4) | 2.2 (3) | 2.0 (1) | 3.3 (3) | 4.0 (1) | -- | 4.0 (1) | 3.8 (4) | -- | 4.0 (1) | 3.9 (3) | 3.0 | ** |
| **SECONDARY ASPECTS** | | | | | | | | | | | | | | |
| **3. Water Quality Regulation Scale[c]** | | | | | | | | | | | | | | |
| 1964-1967 | 2.9 (6) | -- | -- | -- | 2.3 (4) | 3.2 (4) | 3.2 (3) | -- | 2.7 (7) | -- | -- | 4.3 (1) | 2.9* | NS |
| 1968-1972 | 3.2 (6) | -- | -- | 4.0 (1) | 4.0 (2) | 3.0 (1) | 4.0 (2) | 4.4 (1) | 3.6 (3) | -- | -- | 3.7 (3) | 3.6 | NS |
| 1973-1980 | 3.3 (6) | 2.2 (13) | 3.0 (1) | 3.0 (1) | 3.0 (1) | 3.7 (2) | 4.0 (1) | 3.8 (1) | 3.8 (6) | -- | 4.0 (1) | 4.0 (8) | 3.2 | *** |
| 1981-1984 | 2.6 (3) | 2.4 (3) | -- | 3.2 (2) | 3.7 (1) | 4.2 (1) | -- | 4.0 (2) | 3.6 (4) | -- | 4.4 (1) | 3.9 (3) | 3.4 | # |

[a]This is the overall mean across all groups for that period. #, *, **, *** = overall means differ *across time periods* at .10, .05, .01, and .001 levels, respectively.
[b]For that time period, means *differ across groups* at .10, .05, .01 and .001 levels, respectively; NS = no statistically significant difference.
[c]Remember this scale does not deal with sewage issues.

mental priorities and for water-quality regulation.[7] On the environmental regulation scale, however, the consensus began to break up during the late 1960s. Note particularly that the mean scores for local government officials went from 3.9 (for seven testimonies) in 1964–1967 to 2.9 (for eight testimonies) in 1968–1972. At the other end of the spectrum, environmental groups became more supportive of stringent regulation (mean increased from 3.5 to 4.2).

The divergence of opinions expressed and the development of clear-cut coalitions became manifest after 1973. In the latter two periods, significant differences across groups emerged for all three scales.[8] At one end of the spectrum (with mean scores around 2.2), business and property rights groups—joined by Nevada legislators from within the Tahoe Basin—became more vocal and hostile to environmental controls. Local government officials also joined this camp in the 1980s. At the other end, with mean scores above 3.5, were representatives from environmental groups, California executive agencies, and, much of the time, Nevada executive agencies; they were joined by one or two spokespersons from regional agencies (usually the TRPA), the research community (usually the Tahoe Research Group headed by Charles Goldman), and California legislators from outside the basin. There were, however, some differences across scales. On environmental priorities (measuring environmental quality versus economic development and property rights), the overall mean did not change appreciably but there was a break-up into distinct coalitions. On environmental regulation, the overall mean decreased significantly because of the emergence of vocal opposition from businesspeople, property rights groups, Nevada legislators from the basin, and local government officials. In contrast, support for water-quality regulation (chiefly regarding housing construction) increased overall because of growing support after 1966 from regional agency officials, Nevada and California agency offcials, and researchers.

Changes in various groups' scores on the Water-Quality Regulation Scale provides an excellent example of policy-oriented learning in the secondary aspects of belief systems. As evidence started accumulating in the late 1960s and early 1970s that water quality was declining and that runoff from land disturbance was partially responsible (Goldman and Armstrong, 1969; U.S. Soil Conservation Service, 1971; Goldman, 1973, 1974, 1981; Western Federal Regional Council, 1979), officials in environmental groups and state natural resources agencies readily broadened their perceptions of the factors affecting water quality to include erosion as well as sewage. Local businesspeople never accepted these findings because their implications for development controls were too discordant with their policy core values of economic development and property rights. Local government officials were also reluctant to accept them. The latter had been in favor of environmental regulation when it meant sewering the basin—much of which was paid for by state and federal agencies and which would facilitate additional development as well as improve water quality. But when attention shifted to regulating development, local government officials were reluctant to go along because of the adverse implications for their (and their constituents') fundamental beliefs in property rights and economic growth (Sabatier and Pelkey, 1990; Sabatier et al., 1990). This result is generally consistent with the assumption of Hypothesis 3 that elites will alter secondary aspects of their belief systems more readily than their policy core values and perceptions.

When one turns to changes in group testimony over time regarding topics in *intergovernmental relations*, the results are very similar. As indicated in Table 9.3, during the 1964–1966 period there were no significant differences across groups and, in fact, a fairly general consensus in favor of some form of supralocal intervention, including a regional planning agency. Starting in 1968, however, significant differences across groups became manifest in each time period. By 1968–1972, local government officials, local businessmen, and Nevada legislators were opposed to granting (additional) authority to nonlocal officials (the nonlocal scale). Although they had ambivalent attitudes concerning regional planning during the formative years of the TRPA, by 1973 these groups were generally opposed to it. In contrast, environmental groups, California state officials, and a few nonbasin legislators were generally skeptical of local officials and supportive of state and federal intervention. With respect to regional planning, environmental groups became disenchanted—particularly after 1973—while Nevada and California state officials remained supportive.

Thus far we have looked at differences across institutional affiliations. But the ACF clearly acknowledges the potential for people in the same organization—including government agencies—to belong to different coalitions. To examine the structure of coalitions in different time periods using individuals (rather than group affiliations) as the unit of analysis, Figures 9.3 through 9.6 present dendrograms reporting the results of a series of cluster analyses. Cluster analysis refers to a set of techniques that first determines the distance between two cases (testimonies) across a set of variables and then agglomerates the cases into clusters. We used a combination of squared euclidean distance and Ward's method of hierarchical agglomeration (Aldenderfer and Blashfield, 1984).[9] The intent was to use all four scales with the greatest number of testimonies—environmental priorities, environmental regulation, regional planning, and local deficiencies—as the empirical basis for estimating clusters, but in three of the time periods one of the scales had to be deleted in order to significantly increase the number of cases.[10]

The cluster results confirm the absence of any coherent coalitions at Tahoe in the 1964–1966 period, their gradual emergence in 1968–1972, and then the development of full-blown advocacy coalitions during the 1973–1980 period.

Figure 9.3 deals with the 1964–1966 period. On the left is the year of testimony and the testifier's identification number and institutional affiliation. The scale at the top gives the relative distance between an existing cluster and another case/cluster. An examination of Figure 9.3 does not

196

TABLE 9.3 Changes in Various Groups' Mean Scores on Intergovernmental Relations Scales Over Time, 1964-1984
[Mean (number of testimonies)]

| Scale & Period | Local Govt. | Business/ Property Group | Nevada Leg. Basin | Nevada Leg. Nonbasin | Nevada Exec. Agency | Regional Agency or Group | Federal Agency | Researcher | Calif. Exec. Agency | Calif. Leg. Basin | Calif. Leg. Nonbasin | Envir. Group | Overall Mean[a] | ANOVA Across Groups[b] |
|---|---|---|---|---|---|---|---|---|---|---|---|---|---|---|
| **POLICY CORE LEVEL** | | | | | | | | | | | | | | |
| **1. Non-Local Scale** | | | | | | | | | | | | | | |
| 1964-67 | 3.0 (5) | 4.0 (1) | 3.0 (1) | -- | 3.0 (1) | 3.4 (3) | 4.0 (2) | -- | 3.5 (4) | -- | -- | 3.2 (2) | 3.4[*] | NS |
| 1968-72 | 2.2 (9) | 2.0 (1) | 1.7 (1) | 4.0 (1) | 4.2 (3) | 3.0 (1) | -- | -- | -- | -- | -- | 4.1 (4) | 3.0 | ** |
| 1973-80 | 2.4 (13) | 2.8 (9) | 1.4 (3) | 3.1 (4) | 3.2 (4) | 4.0 (3) | 4.0 (1) | -- | 3.5 (2) | 3.2 (2) | 3.6 (2) | 4.3 (6) | 3.0 | * |
| 1981-84 | 1.3 (3) | 1.1 (3) | 1.2 (4) | -- | 3.7 (1) | 4.0 (1) | -- | -- | 3.7 (1) | -- | 4.0 (1) | 3.7 (3) | 2.4 | *** |
| **SECONDARY ASPECTS** | | | | | | | | | | | | | | |
| **2. Regional Planning Scale** | | | | | | | | | | | | | | |
| 1964-1967 | 3.4 (4) | 3.5 (1) | 3.0 (1) | -- | 3.5 (3) | 3.5 (4) | 4.0 (1) | -- | 3.6 (5) | -- | -- | 3.7 (1) | 3.5[***] | NS |
| 1968-1972 | 2.9 (9) | 3.0 (2) | 2.3 (2) | 3.0 (2) | 3.5 (3) | 3.3 (2) | 3.4 (2) | -- | 3.5 (2) | -- | -- | 3.1 (6) | 3.1 | NS |
| 1973-1980 | 2.7 (13) | 2.3 (14) | 2.2 (4) | 3.4 (3) | 3.6 (3) | 3.3 (3) | 2.0 (1) | 3.3 (2) | 3.6 (6) | 4.0 (2) | 3.0 (3) | 2.6 (11) | 2.8 | * |
| 1981-1984 | 2.0 (4) | 1.9 (5) | 1.4 (4) | 2.5 (1) | 4.1 (3) | 2.8 (1) | -- | 3.0 (1) | 3.2 (4) | -- | 2.0 (1) | 2.9 (4) | 2.5 | ** |
| **3. Local Deficiencies Scale** | | | | | | | | | | | | | | |
| 1964-1967 | 3.0 (9) | -- | 4.0 (1) | -- | 3.7 (1) | 3.3 (3) | 3.1 (3) | -- | 3.4 (5) | -- | 4.0 (1) | 3.6 (4) | 3.3[*] | NS |
| 1968-1972 | 3.0 (10) | 3.3 (1) | 2.0 (1) | 4.0 (2) | 2.8 (3) | 2.7 (1) | 3.4 (2) | 2.0 (1) | 4.1 (3) | -- | -- | 3.6 (6) | 3.2 | ** |
| 1973-1980 | 2.1 (12) | 2.6 (17) | 2.3 (4) | 2.5 (5) | 3.7 (3) | 4.1 (3) | -- | 3.5 (2) | 3.3 (3) | 3.2 (2) | 3.5 (1) | 3.7 (12) | 2.9 | ** |
| 1981-1984 | 2.0 (2) | 2.3 (3) | 1.9 (2) | 2.0 (1) | 1.0 (1) | 2.5 (1) | -- | -- | 3.7 (3) | -- | 3.8 (1) | 3.4 (4) | 2.7 | * |

[a]This is the overall mean across all groups for that period. #, *, **, *** = overall means differ across time periods at .10, .05, .01, and .001 levels, respectively.

[b]For that time period, means differ across groups at .10, .05, .01, and .001 levels, respectively; NS = no statistically significant difference.

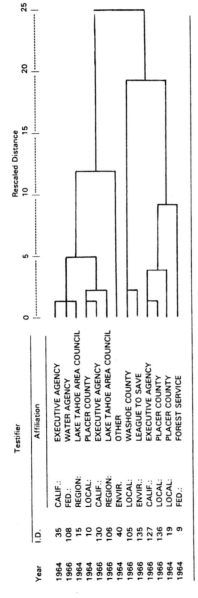

| Year | I.D. | | Affiliation |
|------|------|------|-------------|
| 1964 | 35 | CALIF.: | EXECUTIVE AGENCY |
| 1966 | 108 | FED.: | WATER AGENCY |
| 1964 | 15 | REGION: | LAKE TAHOE AREA COUNCIL |
| 1964 | 10 | LOCAL: | PLACER COUNTY |
| 1966 | 130 | CALIF.: | EXECUTIVE AGENCY |
| 1966 | 106 | REGION: | LAKE TAHOE AREA COUNCIL |
| 1964 | 40 | ENVIR. | OTHER |
| 1966 | 105 | LOCAL: | WASHOE COUNTY |
| 1966 | 135 | ENVIR.: | LEAGUE TO SAVE |
| 1966 | 127 | CALIF.: | EXECUTIVE AGENCY |
| 1966 | 136 | LOCAL: | PLACER COUNTY |
| 1964 | 19 | LOCAL: | PLACER COUNTY |
| 1964 | 9 | FED.: | FOREST SERVICE |

FIGURE 9.3   Cluster analysis (dendrogram) for 1964–1966

suggest any coherent clusters during this period. The top six cases are reasonably close and include several California agencies, the Federal Water Quality Control Administration (FWQCA, the precursor to the EPA), a regional interest group (Lake Tahoe Area Council, or LTAC), and a representative from Placer County (the most progressive local government in the basin). But Placer representatives are also found in another cluser of four testimonies at the bottom (ID# 9, 19, 136, and 127) along with another representative from California and a spokesperson for the U.S. Forest Service. In addition, representatives of two environmental groups (ID# 40 and 135) are found in two widely separated mini-clusters in the middle of the dendrogram.

Figure 9.4 dealing with the 1967–1972 period shows slightly more coherent coalitions. At the top is a mixed bag of six testimonies, three from environmental groups and one from a Nevada legislator outside the basin; but this "coalition" also includes representatives from Washoe County and a local chamber of commerce. Then comes a group of thirteen testimonies that are quite close together and that represent primarily environmental groups, California and Nevada agency officials, a couple of federal officials, and one TRPA representative; but it also includes three local government representatives, including two from Douglas County, the most conservative place in the basin. At the bottom are four testimonies, including two local government representatives, a California water official, and an outlier legislator from Douglas County.

Figure 9.5 presents the results for the 1973–1980 period. At the top are thirteen fairly close testimonies from environmental groups, some state officials, a couple of researchers, and a couple of California legislators. They are joined at a moderate distance by eight closely packed testimonies from the same groups, plus a representative from the city of South Lake Tahoe. Then comes another group of primarily local government officials at a moderate distance. Finally, at the bottom of the dendrogram and separated by a very considerable distance come ten representatives from local governments and property rights groups as well as Douglas County legislators.

Figure 9.6, dealing with the 1981–1984 period, indicates two clearly demarcated coalitions. At the top is a set of six closely grouped testimonies, followed at a moderate distance by another set of eight testimonies. These sets include representatives of environmental groups, California and Nevada executive agencies, the TRPA, and a nonbasin legislator from California; the only moderately unexpected testimony here is one from Placer County. At the bottom, separated by a great distance from the first clusters, are nine testimonies from developers, property rights groups, a Douglas County official, and Nevada legislators from the basin (especially Douglas County); the only unexpected case is a Nevada legislator from outside the basin testifying on the 1985 pullout bill.

The analysis thus far has used both intergovernmental scales and environmental protection scales to identify coalitions. If one separates the two topical areas, a few clarifications emerge.[11] First, using only the environ-

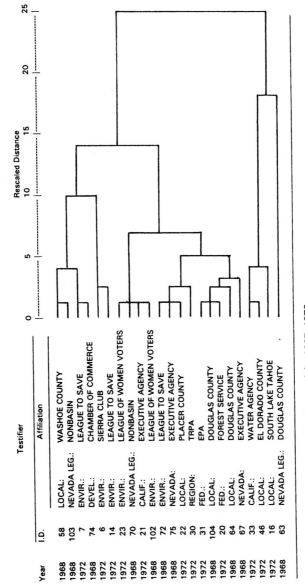

| Year | I.D. | Testifier | |
|------|------|-----------|--|
| | | | Affiliation |
| 1968 | 58 | LOCAL: | WASHOE COUNTY |
| 1968 | 103 | NEVADA LEG.: | NONBASIN |
| 1972 | 7 | ENVIR.: | LEAGUE TO SAVE |
| 1968 | 74 | DEVEL.: | CHAMBER OF COMMERCE |
| 1972 | 6 | ENVIR.: | SIERRA CLUB |
| 1972 | 14 | ENVIR.: | LEAGUE TO SAVE |
| 1972 | 23 | ENVIR.: | LEAGUE OF WOMEN VOTERS |
| 1968 | 70 | NEVADA LEG.: | NONBASIN |
| 1972 | 21 | CALIF.: | EXECUTIVE AGENCY |
| 1968 | 102 | ENVIR.: | LEAGUE OF WOMEN VOTERS |
| 1968 | 72 | ENVIR.: | LEAGUE TO SAVE |
| 1968 | 75 | NEVADA: | EXECUTIVE AGENCY |
| 1972 | 22 | LOCAL: | PLACER COUNTY |
| 1972 | 30 | REGION: | TRPA |
| 1972 | 31 | FED.: | EPA |
| 1968 | 104 | LOCAL: | DOUGLAS COUNTY |
| 1972 | 20 | FED.: | FOREST SERVICE |
| 1968 | 64 | LOCAL: | DOUGLAS COUNTY |
| 1968 | 67 | NEVADA: | EXECUTIVE AGENCY |
| 1972 | 33 | CALIF.: | WATER AGENCY |
| 1972 | 46 | LOCAL: | EL DORADO COUNTY |
| 1972 | 16 | LOCAL: | SOUTH LAKE TAHOE |
| 1968 | 63 | NEVADA LEG.: | DOUGLAS COUNTY |

FIGURE 9.4  Cluster analysis (dendrogram) for 1967–1972

| Year | I.D. | Testifier | Affiliation |
|---|---|---|---|
| 1980 | 112 | CALIF: | CTRPA |
| 1973 | 141 | REGION: | LAKE TAHOE AREA COUNCIL |
| 1978 | 139 | NEVADA: | EXECUTIVE AGENCY |
| 1973 | 151 | CALIF LEG: | BASIN |
| 1977 | 53 | RESEARCH: | OTHER |
| 1973 | 140 | CALIF LEG: | NONBASIN |
| 1977 | 182 | REGION: | TRPA |
| 1977 | 54 | ENVIR: | LEAGUE OF WOMEN VOTERS |
| 1980 | 100 | RESEARCH: | GOLDMAN TRG |
| 1973 | 152 | ENVIR: | LEAGUE TO SAVE |
| 1980 | 89 | ENVIR: | LEAGUE TO SAVE |
| 1980 | 93 | ENVIR: | LEAGUE TO SAVE |
| 1980 | 90 | ENVIR: | SIERRA CLUB |
| 1980 | 98 | ENVIR: | LEAGUE TO SAVE |
| 1973 | 148 | ENVIR: | LEAGUE OF WOMEN VOTERS |
| 1980 | 98 | ENVIR: | LEAGUE TO SAVE |
| 1980 | 110 | CALIF: | CTRPA |
| 1973 | 155 | ENVIR: | SIERRA CLUB |
| 1973 | 190 | LOCAL: | SOUTH LAKE TAHOE |
| 1980 | 161 | NEVADA: | EXECUTIVE AGENCY |
| 1978 | 150 | REGION: | LAKE TAHOE AREA COUNCIL |
| 1980 | 79 | LOCAL: | PLACER COUNTY |
| 1980 | 86 | CAIF: | EXECUTIVE AGENCY |
| 1973 | 121 | LOCAL: | SOUTH LAKE TAHOE |
| 1980 | 159 | NEVADA LEG: | DOUGLAS COUNTY |
| 1977 | 60 | LOCAL: | SOUTH LAKE TAHOE |
| 1980 | 160 | DEVEL: | PROPERTY RIGHTS |
| 1980 | 94 | LOCAL: | PLACER COUNTY |
| 1977 | 61 | LOCAL: | DOUGLAS COUNTY |
| 1977 | 189 | LOCAL: | DOUGLAS COUNTY |
| 1977 | 185 | DEVEL: | PROPERTY RIGHTS |
| 1977 | 49 | LOCAL: | DOUGLAS COUNTY |
| 1977 | 52 | DEVEL: | PROPERTY RIGHTS |
| 1973 | 153 | DEVEL: | PROPERTY RIGHTS |
| 1980 | 156 | NEVADA LEG: | DOUGLAS COUNTY |
| 1977 | 184 | NEVADA LEG: | DOUGLAS COUNTY |
| 1980 | 97 | DEVEL: | DEVELOPER |
| 1980 | 134 | DEVEL: | PROPERTY RIGHTS |

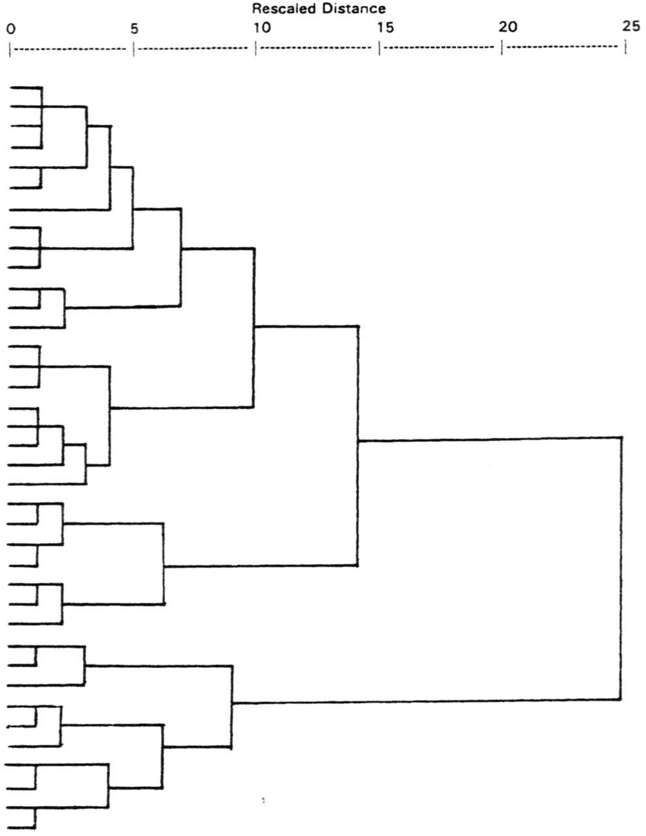


FIGURE 9.5 Cluster analysis (dendrogram) for 1973–1980

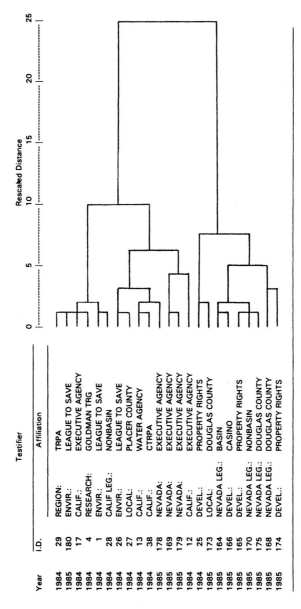

FIGURE 9.6   Cluster analysis (dendrogram) for 1981–1985

mental protection scales during the 1973–1985 periods produces two very distinct coalitions, but local government officials are split between the two: Those from Placer County and South Lake Tahoe tend to fall into the Environmental Coalition, while their colleagues from Douglas County are consistently in the Economic Growth/Property Rights Coalition. Second, using only the intergovernmental scales during the 1973–1980 period produces three coalitions, with representatives of environmental groups in all three; that is hardly surprising given their very mixed views of the TRPA during that period. By 1981–1985, however, the League to Save was back with its traditional allies in state agencies.

## IV. CONCLUSION

In sum, several different methods have shown how the intial years of the Tahoe land-use and water-quality subsystem in the early 1960s were marked by a preliminary consensus in favor of some form of environmental controls (especially sewering the basin) and some form of regional planning. This consensus began to dissipate in the 1968–1972 period as environmental controls increasingly came to mean restrictions on development, which, in turn, were perceived by some as adversely affecting economic growth and property rights.

By the mid-1970s there were two distinct coalitions at Tahoe. One included environmental groups and their allies in state governments, the TRPA, and the research community. This Environmental Coalition gave a high priority to environmental protection, was willing to support stringent restrictions on development and other forms of market activity, increasingly perceived housing construction as adversely affecting water quality, and sought the intervention of nonlocal governments to address these problems. The other coalition was composed of local business-people, property rights groups, local legislators (especially from Douglas County), and spokespersons for many local governments (except for Placer County and South Lake Tahoe on some environmental issues). This Economic Growth/Property Rights Coalition highly valued property rights and economic development, opposed stringent regulation of development in favor of more moderate mitigation measures and buyout programs, was reluctant to acknowledge declines in water quality or the role of land disturbance from construction in that process, and was increasingly hostile to the intervention of nonlocal agencies in the basin. These two coalitions became even more distinct during the early 1980s.

Thus the Tahoe case provides fairly strong support for Hypothesis 1, which expects to find stable coalitions on issues that span a decade or more. At Tahoe, this stability lasted from the mid-1970s until the end of our data base in 1985. At least as interesting, however, was the evidence of change within the subsystem as it went from a vague initial consensus to very distinct coalitions over the period of a decade (1964–1973). Had the data base for the OCS case discussed in the previous chapter begun not in 1969 but when the subsystem was formed in the mid-1950s, it might have seen a similar process of increasing polarization over the initial decade, marked by very distinct coalitions thereafter for at least ten to fifteen years.[12]

There is also preliminary support for Hypothesis 3, that actors will alter secondary aspects of their belief systems before they change policy core values. This principle was seen most clearly in the reaction of different groups to the evidence, first emerging in the late 1960s and early 1970s, of declines in water quality and the contribution of erosion from housing to that decline. Environmental groups and most state officials (many from natural resource agencies) readily incorporated these findings into their belief systems. In contrast, local businesspeople, property rights groups, and their allies in local governments and the Nevada Legislature were very reluctant to acknowledge these findings because of their adverse implications for policy core values of property rights and economic growth.

Finally, this chapter has illustrated the advantage of using systematic coding of hearing testimony to supplement more qualitative historical overviews. Previous histories of Tahoe (Strong, 1984; Ingram and Sabatier, 1987) were ambiguous about when the distinct coalitions seen in the late 1970s actually emerged. Our content analysis of hearing testimonies dating back to the early 1960s gives us a much clearer understanding of that process. Similarly, in the previous chapter Jenkins-Smith and St. Clair improved upon Heintz's (1988) analysis of the OCS subsystem, which had portrayed two monolithic coalitions highly resistant to change. They demonstrated that, although it was true that the interest groups in that subsystem were resistant, the administrative agencies (particularly the Department of Interior) moved back and forth depending upon the administration in power and economic conditions. In sum, the more precisely one views a situation, the more likely one is to see variations in the general pattern of events. The role of theory is to separate the *critical* variations from the merely curious.

### APPENDIX A: HEARINGS

Following is the list of public hearings utilized in the analysis of Lake Tahoe environmental policy presented in this chapter:

1. California Legislature, Assembly Committee on Natural Resources, *Regional Planning in the Lake Tahoe Basin*, Brockway Springs, CA., Sept. 10–11, 1964.
2. U.S. Department of the Interior, Federal Water Pollution Control Administration, *Conference in the Matter of Pollution of Lake Tahoe*, Proceedings, Stateline, NV, July 18–20, 1966.
3. Nevada Legislature, *Special Session on TRPA Compact (SB 9)*, Carson City, NV, Feb. 12 and 19, 1968.
4. California Legislature, Assembly Committee on Natural Resources, *Regional Planning in the Lake Tahoe Basin, Hearing*, Stateline, NV, Dec. 18–19, 1972.

5. U.S. Environmental Protection Agency, *Adequacy and Need for Extending Federal Oversight and Control in Order to Preserve the Fragile Ecology of Lake Tahoe, Hearing,* South Lake Tahoe, CA, Sept. 21–22, 1973.
6. Nevada Legislature, Senate Environment, Public Resources, and Agriculture Committee, *Hearings on the TRPA Compact,* Carson City, 1977.
7. Nevada Legislature, Assembly Environment and Public Resources Committee and Senate Environment, Public Resources, and Agriculture Committee, *Hearings on SB 266, AB 740, and SB 267 [Gaming],* Carson City, NV, March 14 and April 26, 1977.
8. Nevada Legislature, Senate, *Special Session on the TRPA Compact,* Carson City, NV, September 13, 1980.
9. California State Water Resources Control Board, *Lake Tahoe 208 Water Quality Control Plan,* Sacramento, CA, March 7, 8, 10, 26, April 21, and Oct. 25, 1980.
10. California Legislature, Senate Select Committee on Tahoe, *Land Acquisition and Land Use in the Lake Tahoe Basin, Hearing Transcript,* Sacramento, CA, March 6, 1984.
11. Nevada Legislature, Assembly and Senate Resources Committees, *Hearings on Bills to Withdraw Nevada from the TRPA Compact,* Carson City, Spring 1985.

We have no hearings from the California Legislature concerning revision of the compact during the 1977–1980 period because no transcripts were ever published. Several relevant hearings of the Nevada Legislature were not coded because only brief summaries of testimony were recorded. Three sets of congressional hearings were excluded because of time and resource constraints: The 1966 hearings of the House Committee on Public Works on water pollution were excluded because they overlapped considerably with the FWQCA Hearings held the same year, which we did code; the December 1972 hearings organized by Senator John Tunney were excluded because they overlapped considerably, and were less extensive than, the hearings of the California Legislature held the same month, which we had already coded; and the 1980 hearings of the Senate Energy and Natural Resources Committee on the Lake Tahoe Scenic Area Bill were left out because by that time we were, quite frankly, tired of coding. Testimony from TRPA and CTRPA hearings were excluded because, although summaries of testimony were available, we could not obtain verbatim transcripts (except at prohibitive expense).

## APPENDIX B: SCALES

Using the methods indicated in the text, we obtained seven scales: two at the policy core level, one that is a mixture of policy core and secondary aspects, and four that dealt with secondary aspects:

A. Policy Core Scales:
   1. Nonlocal Scale (n = 107 valid testimonies). This scale consists of four items, one dealing with the preferred level of government to deal with Tahoe problems, the other three dealing with the person's preference for more (or less) authority for local governments, bistate regional agencies like the TRPA, or the federal government. A score of 5 indicates a strong preference for supralocal control, while 1 indicates a strong preference for local government control.
   2. Environmental Priority Scale (n = 144). This scale has eight items dealing with normative orientations at Tahoe. Two deal with a preference for environmental quality over economic development and property rights. Two deal with the salience (from 1, not at all important, to 5, extremely important) of environmental/aesthetic quality and property rights (reversed). Three deal with the perceived seriousness of threats (from 1 to 5) to environmental quality, property rights (reversed), and economic/fiscal viability (reversed). And the last deals with the value of Tahoe as a natural resource (from 1, just another lake, to 5, unique, irreplaceable, should be preserved). A score of 5 on this scale indicates a strong preference for environmental quality and the perception that it is threatened, while a 1 indicates a strong preference for economic development and/or property rights.
B. Mixed Policy Core and Secondary Aspects:
   3. Environmental Regulation as a Policy Instrument (n = 148). This scale consists of three items that were originally included under secondary aspects but that are more general than most in that section and, given their strong intercorrelations, suggest a general preference for stringent environmental regulation (including reductions in the rate of development) over less burdensome regulations and purchase of property as a general strategy or policy instrument. The three items dealt with (1) orientation toward environmental protection measures being discussed at the hearing (where 1 indicates a perception that measures are unwarranted and 5 indicates the view that measures are insufficient to protect the environment); (2) development controls in the basin (from 1, undesirable, and 3, regulate location and quality, to 5, reduce rate of development); and (3) position on buyouts/inverse condemnation (where 1 signifies the view that buyouts not needed, 3 signifies the view that they are not legally required but politically desirable, and 5 signifies the view that they are legally required by the 14th Amendment at full market value); the last item was reversed when creating the scale.
C. Secondary Aspects of Belief Systems:
   4. Water-Quality Problems and Regulation Scale (n = 105). This scale consists of five items in three categories, which dealt with the perceived seriousness of water-quality problems, the identification of

erosion from housing development as a significant source, and the choice of methods to deal with that erosion (from 1, regulation undesirable, to 5, prohibit virtually all building in the basin). A score of 5 on this scale indicates that water quality at Tahoe is perceived as a serious problem and that stringent measures to regulate housing development are the appropriate means of dealing with it; a score of 1 indicates that water quality is not perceived as a problem and that development controls are undesirable. The perceived negative effect of sewage on water quality was not included in this scale because it loaded weakly, and in a rather confusing manner, with the other items.

5. Urbanization Problems Scale (n = 82). This scale consists of three items. Two deal with the perceived seriousness (from 1 to 5) of urbanization/population growth and air quality. The third concerns the regulation of casino development (from 1, no regulation, to 5, no new casinos and no expansion of existing casinos). A score of 5 on this scale indicates the view that urbanization and air quality are serious problems and that stringent controls on casino development are needed to address them; a score of 1 indicates the opposite view.

6. Proregional Planning Scale (n = 143). This scale consists of eight items. Four address the perceived ability of land use planning and regulation to deal with problems of water quality and urban sprawl; one deals with the ability of regional agencies to represent all affected interests; one concerns the person's evaluation of the TRPA; and two deal with expanding (versus reducing) the TRPA's legal authority. A score of 5 on this scale indicates a perception that regional agencies can efficaciously deal with the basin's problems and ought to be strengthened; a score of 1 indicates the opposite view.

7. Local Government Deficiences Scale (n = 139). This scale consists of seven items. Three deal with judgments that the basin is of importance beyond the local level and that nonlocal financial resources and regulation are needed; three deal with evaluations of local governments, the CTRPA, and the state of California; and one deals with the seriousness of transportation as a problem.[13] A score of 1 on this scale indicates great faith in local government while a score of 5 indicates a preference for the intervention of nonlocal (primarily state of California) authorities.

## NOTES

The authors would like to thank the National Science Foundation (SES 84–11032) and the dean of the College of Agricultural and Environmental Sciences at the University of California at Davis for providing the funds that made this research possible. We would also like to thank Wesley Ingram for spending untold hours assisting us in developing and applying the coding form and Neil Pelkey for assisting with portions of the data analysis. Finally, we would like to express our appreciation to Hank C. Jenkins-Smith for his advice throughout this project and for his helpful comments on an earlier version of this paper presented at the 1986 American Political Science Association Meetings in Washington, D.C.

1. Article VI(k) of the 1969 TRPA Compact stipulated that any permit application not acted upon by the TRPA Governing Board within 60 days would be "deemed approved," while Article III(g) required a majority vote of the members from *each* state for the board to take action with respect to any matter. Thus a development application would be "deemed approved" unless a majority from each of the two states voted to deny it or to impose conditions. Several large casinos were approved by the TRPA in the summers of 1972 and 1973 even though seven out of ten TRPA Board members voted to deny them. This vote did not, however, meet the dual majority requirement, because three of the five Nevada representatives voted to approve the projects (Ingram and Sabatier, 1987).

2. Such votes are consistent with the hypothesis in Gormley (1986): In issue areas characterized by high conflict and high technical expertise, the dominant actors will be high-level agency officials.

3. Jenkins-Smith and St. Clair have coded testimonies from a more diverse set of organizations—including state governments and other groups that testified only a relatively few times—but chose not to include them in the analysis for Chapter 8.

4. This is hardly surprising, as there was close communication between our two reseach groups.

5. Correlation coefficients cannot, of course, determine causality or direction. It might be that secondary aspects constrain policy core items. But if secondary aspects within a topical area were constraining, one would expect to see higher correlation coefficients between them. At any rate, the data here can only suggest that an interpretation of hierarchical constraint is reasonable.

6. The urbanization problems scale was not included because the total number of testimonies (eighty-two) was too small to allow meaningful numbers in the group categories except during the 1973–1980 period. In general, there was less variation across groups on this scale than on the others, as well as less change over time.

7. Recall that the water-quality regulation scale does not deal with sewage issues but rather with perceptions about declines in water quality and erosion from housing development as a source of the problem. Perceptions regarding sewage were only very weakly correlated with these other water-quality issues by people testifying.

8. Part of the increase in statistical significance can simply be attributed to an increase in the number of testimonies, from about forty in each of the first two periods to about eighty in 1973–1980. This increase is not pivotal, however. Note that in Table 9.3 the differences on two of the three scales are more significant in 1981–1985 than in 1973–1980, despite the low number (thirty) of testimonies for that period.

9. In Euclidean distance, the distance between two cases is the square root of the sum of the squared differences in values on each variable. Ward's method of hierarchical agglomeration optimizes the minimum variance within clusters. Ward's method provided slightly clearer results than the alternative, the average-distancing method, used by Jenkins-Smith and St. Clair in Chapter 8; the SPSS-PC manual advises using the squared euclidean distance along with Ward's (Norusis, 1986:B85).

10. The SPSS cluster program uses listwise deletion, which means that a testimony that did not present valid data on all four scales during that time would be omitted from the analysis for that period. During the 1964–1966 period, we eliminated the regional planning scale to increase the number of cases from ten to thirteen; during 1967–1972, omitting the environmental priority scale increased the number of testimonies from fifteen to twenty-three; and during the 1981–1985 period, deleting the local deficiencies scale increased the testimonies from fourteen to twenty-three.

11. The dendrograms from these "subset" analyses are available from the authors upon request.

12. According to Jenkins-Smith (private communication), the OCS hearings prior to the 1969 Santa Barbara oil spill included very little testimony dealing with the speed and breadth of leasing and virtually no participation from environmental groups. Instead, the focus was almost entirely on the distribution of authority between state and federal governments.

13. Transportation looks strange here, but it correlates well with the other items, was mentioned in a large number ($n = 59$) of testimonies, and has traditionally been a major preoccupation of local government officials in the basin.

# PART IV

## *Conclusion*

# 10

## The Advocacy Coalition Framework: Assessment, Revisions, and Implications for Scholars and Practitioners

### PAUL A. SABATIER AND HANK C. JENKINS-SMITH

This book began by critiquing the current state of theory in public policy, particularly the heavy reliance on the stages heuristic developed by Jones (1977). The next two chapters presented an alternative theory, the advocacy coalition framework (ACF): Chapter 2 dealt with policy change over several decades, and Chapter 3 focused more specifically on the role of policy-oriented learning over shorter periods of time within that broader process. The remaining chapters have involved the critical application of the ACF to cases of policy change over several decades in Canadian education, the regulation and deregulation of commercial airlines in the United States, the controversy over additional water projects in California, the development of television design standards by the Federal Communications Commission, the regulation of petroleum leasing on the outer continental shelf (OCS), and the regulation of land use and water quality in the Lake Tahoe Basin.

What have we learned? The first part of this chapter assesses the strengths and weaknesses of the advocacy coalition framework in light of the case studies and other events since its publication several years ago. As a result, we revise two hypotheses, add several new ones, and make several other changes. The second part adds a discussion of strategies and guidance instruments to the ACF. The final section discusses the implications for scholars—chiefly in terms of a list of major topics in need of further research—and for policy practitioners.

## I. THE ACF: AN ASSESSMENT

The major arguments of the ACF generally seem to be supported by the cases. Nevertheless, the cases suggest several modifications and additions to the ACF.

### The Importance of Advocacy Coalitions

First, and probably foremost, the cases confirm the utility of focusing on advocacy coalitions as a critical means of simplifying the hundreds of actors involved in policy change over a decade or more. An advocacy coalition consists of actors from a variety of governmental and private organizations at different levels of government who share a set of policy beliefs and seek to realize them by influencing the behavior of multiple governmental institutions over time. This approach departs substantially from that employed by most political scientists, who are still wedded to aggregating actors by specific type of institution—whether it be legislatures, administrative agencies, or interest groups—and who usually focus on only a single institution or single level of government. The emphasis on advocacy coalitions also represents a major departure from the stages heuristic, which either has no explicit means of aggregating actors or else uses traditional institutional categories (Jones, 1977; Anderson, 1979). The ACF also differs from Heclo's (1978) concept of issue networks. While both concepts can accommodate policy actors who change jobs or other institutional affiliations over time, the concept of advocacy coalitions aggregates most actors within a subsystem into a manageable number of belief-based coalitions, whereas Heclo views individuals as largely autonomous and thus risks overwhelming both himself and the reader with an impossibly complex set of actors.

The data are probably clearest in the Tahoe case, where Sabatier and Brasher used cluster analysis of several hundred testimonies at a dozen hearings over twenty years to demonstrate that actors from a wide variety of institutions tended to coalesce over time into two major coalitions: an Economic Growth/Property Rights Coalition composed of most elected officials and staff from local governments and public utility districts in the Lake Tahoe Basin, most local businesspeople, leaders of property rights groups, and several Nevada legislators from the basin. The opposing Environmental Coalition was composed of local and statewide environmental groups, officials from several California and Nevada resource agencies, several researchers, several California legislators from outside the basin, and even some representatives from two local governments in the basin. This case also demonstrated how the Tahoe subsystem evolved over time from a vague initial consensus in favor of *some* form of regional environmental planning to two coalitions espousing quite different belief systems.

The Mawhinney analysis of educational conflict in Ontario revealed a rather cohesive Francophone Rights Coalition composed of national francophone interest groups, their local affiliates, local school officials from francophone schools, and elected officials and political parties from Québec. In Mawhinney's view, the long-dominant Loyalist Coalition was less cohesive than the Francophone Rights Coalition and may in fact have been an alliance of traditional anglophone conservatives, Scots, and English-speaking Catholics. Perhaps minority coalitions have a greater incentive to remain cohesive in order to have any chance of gaining power, while those in a long-dominant coalition will become less cohesive over several decades.[1]

The Brown and Stewart analysis of airline regulation revealed three coalitions that remained remarkably stable over time: (1) a Proregulation Coalition composed of the major airlines, most airline unions, many smaller airports, and their congressional allies; (2) an Antiregulation Coalition composed of the smaller airlines, larger airports, most consumer groups, some economists, and their congressional allies; and (3) a Deregulation Coalition, which probably did not emerge until the late 1960s and was composed largely of academic economists, Alfred Kahn (an economist who became Civil Aeronautics Board (CAB) chair in the mid-1970s), some consumer groups, and a few critical members of Senator Ted Kennedy's staff in the mid-1970s (most notably, Stephen Breyer). The CAB was usually in the Proregulation Coalition, although it shifted around for a few years depending upon presidential appointments. In fact, Kahn moved it into the Deregulation Coalition in the late 1970s.

A final note regarding coalitions flows from Chapter 2 and is reinforced by the Tahoe case: Advocacy coalitons with clearly articulated and relatively stable belief systems take time to develop and may well do so only in the presence of sustained policy conflict. The OCS case suggests that, in addition to disputes marked by sustained conflict, disputes that are subject to periodic reopening during the annual budgetary cycle are likely to develop stable and coherent coalitions.

## Differences Among Interest Groups, Agencies, and Researchers Within Coalitions

The precision provided by the systematic analysis of testimonies at OCS leasing hearings (1969–1987) by Jenkins-Smith and St. Clair suggests an important amendment to our understanding of changes in the composition of advocacy coalitions over time. The companies and industry trade groups most directly involved in OCS development were always in the Proleasing Coalition, while environmental groups were always in the Environmental (antileasing) Coalition. The involved federal agencies—DOE, DOI, EPA and NOAA—were sandwiched between the competing interest groups. Over the course of the policy debate, the federal agencies—at least in their official pronouncements before congressional committees—shifted toward one coalition or the other in response to exogenous political and economic events. DOI and DOE were consistently closer to the proleasing side, however, while NOAA and EPA tended to be closer to the environmental side. The OCS case thus suggests a new hypothesis:

*Hypothesis 11:* Within a coalition, administrative agencies will usually advocate more centrist positions than their interest-group allies.

This argument merits a little elaboration. The ACF assumes that most administrative agencies—whether agriculture departments, environmental protection agencies, or social welfare departments—have missions that usually make them part of a specific coalition. That mission is generally grounded in a statutory mandate and reinforced by the professional affiliation of agency personnel and the agency's need to provide benefits to the dominant coalition in their subsystem (Meier, 1985; Knott and Miller, 1987). The OCS leasing case, and the recognition that most agencies have multiple sovereigns (sources of money and legal authority) with somewhat different policy views suggests, however, that agencies will generally take less extreme positions than their interest-group allies. In fact, the OCS case indicates that agencies that are usually sympathetic to a given coalition can be moved to a neutral position or even to switch sides—at least in their official pronouncements—by major exogenous events such as the election of a chief executive (president or governor) favorably inclined to the opposing coalition.

Administrative agencies must not, however, be viewed as monolithic. First, different sections of the same agency may be allied with different coalitions. In the long-standing debate over the use of economic incentives in environmental policy, for example, the U.S. Environmental Protection Agency (EPA) has been deeply split, with the Office of Policy Analysis generally favoring the expanded use of incentives such as tradeable emission rights while the Offices of Air and Water Programs have been very skeptical (Liroff, 1986; Cook, 1988). Second, the official agency position espoused by political appointees may not be followed by subordinates within the agency. To again use the EPA as an example, Wood's (1988) research clearly demonstrates that, although President Reagan was able to influence the behavior of the agency's political appointees—including their testimony before congressional committees—he was largely unable to alter agency outputs involving monitoring and enforcement decisions in air pollution control. It is quite likely that, in many administrative agencies, most program units are allied with specific coalitions, including strong ties to interest groups and legislators. Political appointees generally have only a limited ability to alter their subordinates' behavior—absent major changes in law (Heclo, 1977).

The evidence presented in the cases involving airline deregulation, California water policy, OCS leasing, and Lake Tahoe indicates that administrative agencies and university researchers are often not neutral or apolitical but instead are active members of specific coalitions. This should not be news (Friedson, 1971; Primack and von Hippel, 1974; Mazur, 1981; Knott and Miller, 1987; Jenkins-Smith, 1990; McGann, 1992), but we are continually surprised by the number of people who still subscribe to the textbook portrait of neutral civil servants and researchers. Of course, bureaucratic role orientations vary somewhat by country (Aberbach et al., 1981:97). But even in European countries with a strong tradition of elitist—and supposedly neutral—civil servants, bureaucratic role orientation varies with political ideology (Ibid:140) and professional training often guides agency behavior and creates de facto alliances with external groups (Sharpe, 1984; Laffin, 1986; Rhodes, 1988). Moreover, the corporatist style of policy making in many European countries encourages an administrative agency to arrange compromises among its constituency groups and to mobilize "its" groups in conflicts with other agencies (Jordan and Richardson, 1983). Finally, those same European countries have a very long tradition of politicized university faculty, especially on the Left.

In the United States, as economists and economically trained policy analysts become more and more active in public policy, an increasing number of policy subsystems will include an Economic Efficiency Coalition composed of academic and agency economists, the U.S. Office of Management and Budget, and finance departments and legislative analysts' offices in many states. Economists have certainly articulated a coherent and relatively comprehensive belief system (Rhoads, 1985; Nelson, 1987). Furthermore, leading economists such as Charles Schultze have long argued that public policy analysts must assume the role of "partisan efficiency advocates" to champion the cause of efficiency in policy domains typically dominated by more traditional political interests (Schultze, 1968). Our case studies suggest that Schultze's call has fallen on receptive ears. Economists were the principal members of the Deregulation Coalition discussed by Brown and Stewart. And, in our view, the California water policy subsystem has included an increasingly important Economic Efficiency Coalition since the early 1960s, although Munro chose to subsume it within the Protectionist Coalition.

### Intergovernmental Relations

The ACF explicitly argues that most policy subsystems, and the coalitions within them, include actors from multiple levels of government. This principle is based upon the recognition that: (1) almost all federal domestic programs rely heavily upon state and/or local governments for actual implementation (Van Horn, 1979; Mazmanian and Sabatier, 1989; Scholtz et al., 1991); (2) that intergovernmental transfers constitute a significant percentage of most state and local government budgets (Wright, 1988; Anton, 1989); and (3) that state and local agencies form a substantial percentage of the groups lobbying Congress and federal agencies (Salisbury, 1984). The same can be said for local governments at the state level.

This notion was certainly confirmed by the case studies in this book. All except the FCC's development of television design standards involved a significant intergovernmental dimension. In airline deregulation, local airports—depending on their size—were important members of either the Proregulation or the Antiregulation Coalitions. On OCS leasing, one of the major issues has been the distribution of authority between federal versus state and local governments, and state agencies have been important participants in congressional hearings.[2] California water policy is an intergovernmental thicket involving hundreds of local water and irrigation districts, three federal agencies (the Bureau of Reclamation, the Fish and Wildlife Service, and EPA), and three major state agencies (the State Water Resources Control Board, or SWRCB, the Department of Water Resources, and the Department of Fish and Game). Land-use and water-quality planning in the Lake Tahoe Basin involves six local governments, several state agencies from Nevada and California, two federal agencies (the Forest Service and EPA), and a bistate regional agency (the Tahoe Regional Planning Agency, or TRPA). Finally, the Mawhinney analysis of francophone education in Ontario indicated that this issue has been linked to both francophone rights in other provinces and, more important, to the pivotal constitutional issue of Québec separatism at the federal level.

There is also evidence that, as predicted by the ACF, members of a specific coalition will use a variety of agencies at different levels of government in order to achieve their policy objectives. The case is probably clearest at Lake Tahoe. The principal environmental group (the League to Save Lake Tahoe) and its allies supported the use of federal and state funds to help sewer the basin in the 1960s. When land-use issues became critical, they supported the creation of the bistate TRPA in 1967–1970. When the TRPA approved several major casinos, the League to Save first sued in both federal and state courts and then promoted the intervention of several California state agencies, especially the SWRCB and the CTRPA, in the basin. Finally, in order to put pressure on Nevada to renegotiate the TRPA Compact in the late 1970s, it pushed for the designation of a national scenic area in the basin, and it has supported buyout programs by both federal and state agencies (Sabatier and Pelkey, 1990). One could cite an equally varied set of counterstrategies used by members of the opposing Economic Growth/Property Rights Coalition. But the basic rationale for conceptualizing policy subsystems along an intergovernmental dimension should now be clear.

In contrast, Mawhinney's analysis of educational policy in Ontario indicates that conceptualizing subsystems in intergovernmental terms does *not* mean that everyone should be thrown into an undifferentiated, multilevel, subsystem. Different levels of government are semiautonomous, and coalitions spend a great deal of time and effort trying to restrict authority to the level at which they have a competitive advantage (Schattschneider, 1960). In the francophone case, for example, the Loyalist Coalition tried to keep education a purely provincial matter while the Francophone Rights Coalition sought to expand the scope of the conflict by linking it to Québec separatism. Ultimately, the Canadian government under Pierre Trudeau decided that keeping Québec in the country would require a new Charter of Rights and Freedoms providing educational rights for linguistic minorities in Ontario and the other provinces. This issue was, of course, very similar to the history of school desegregation in the United States, where racial minorities expanded the scope of the conflict from the states to the federal government and were eventually rewarded when the U.S. Supreme Court ruled, in *Brown v. Board of*

*Education*, that state-supported segregated schools violated the U.S. Constitution.

In the case of OCS leasing, the Proleasing Coalition sought to restrict the states' role in OCS regulation via a narrow interpretation of the Federal Coastal Zone Management Act (CZMA), while the Environmental Coalition sought to expand the states' role via an alternative interpretation of the same statute. In this case, Congress and the courts had to arbitrate the dispute. This struggle involved enormous stakes, since an expansion of the states' role under the CZMA would have given them a virtual veto over the *onshore* activities necessary to support OCS petroleum exploration and development.

In sum, conceptualizing a subsystem in intergovernmental terms means both (1) that the subsystem will include actors from multiple levels of government and (2) that the subsystem will be divided into different levels of government and, at each level, into different jurisdictions. The strength of those dividing lines is essentially an *empirical* question. In cases of federal preemption, such as the regulation of television and radio broadcasts, there is basically a single national subsystem. In cases of traditional local autonomy, such as the regulation of private land use, subsystems tend to be organized around local governments. Minority coalitions at the local level always have the option, however, of trying to involve state and/or federal officials, as environmentalists did successfully at Lake Tahoe and in many other areas of the country (Bosselman and Callies, 1971; Rosenbaum, 1976). In most domestic policy areas, subsystems will be demarcated into all three levels of government.

This finding means, however, that some revision is required in Hypothesis 4, which states that the policy core of a governmental program will not be significantly revised as long as the subsystem advocacy coalition that instituted the program remains in power. In the Ontario case, for example, the core attributes of education in the province were changed by the Canadian government even though the Loyalist Coalition remained in power in the province. We thus suggest the following:

> *Hypothesis 4 (Revised):* The policy core (basic attributes) of a governmental program in a specific jurisdiction will not be significantly revised as long as the subsystem advocacy coalition that initiated the program remains in power within that jurisdiction—except when the change is imposed by a hierarchically superior jurisdiction.

In such cases, according to the literature on the implementation of school desegregation and other reforms, the ability of hierarchically superior jurisdictions to alter not just the letter of the law but the behavior of governmental officals within the subsystem—in the absence of a change in the dominant coalition within the subsystem—is exceedingly difficult but not impossible (Rodgers and Bullock, 1976; Mazmanian and Sabatier, 1989).

## The Role of Policy-Oriented Learning
## in Policy Change

The ACF outlines a general argument and several hypotheses concerning the role that technical information and formal policy analysis play in policy-oriented learning and, in turn, in policy change. This approach contrasts with those of traditional political science—which has tended to ignore the topic altogether—and with the stages heuristic, which has generally confined policy analysis to the evaluation stage (Sabatier, 1991b).

Several of the cases support the ACF's argument that technical information and formal policy analysis are generally used in an advocacy fashion, that is, to buttress and support a predetermined position. They also seem to support Hypothesis 5, which states that policy analysis and the policy-oriented learning it engenders will not by itself lead to changes in the policy core of a coalition or public policy. Finally, the cases provide some support for Hypotheses 6 through 9, which state that learning across coalitions is more likely when an intermediate level of conflict is involved, when the issues are analytically tractable, and when a professional forum is utilized.[3]

According to Barke, technical information played a critical role in the ability of the Federal Communications Commission (FCC) to develop a uniform design standard for color television sets in the decade following World War II. Standard setting was facilitated by the analytical tractability of the topic (Hypotheses 7 and 8), by the presence of a classic professional forum, the technical advisory committee (Hypothesis 9), and by an intermediate level of conflict (Hypothesis 6). With respect to the last, the stakes were sufficiently high—involving millions of dollars invested in competing technologies—to encourage the various companies to spend substantial sums doing the technical studies. However, this was not a conflict involving the policy core: Everyone acknowledged financial self-interest as a legitimate goal and wanted the industry to come up with a uniform standard that would be sanctioned by the FCC; there was no alternative coalition arguing that color television represented a threat to consumer safety or to the moral fiber of the nation.

Likewise, the Brown and Stewart analysis of airline deregulation clearly stressed the importance of the evidence developed by economists in the 1950–1970 period concerning the inefficiencies of entry and fare restrictions set by the Civil Aeronautics Board (CAB). These findings were prominently publicized at the Kennedy committee hearings, which provided a forum for the Proregulation Coalition but were hardly the model of a professional forum. In Brown and Stewart's view, however, the economists' evidence was not *sufficient* to produce a change in the policy core from entry/fare regulation to deregulation. Consistent with Hypothesis 5, major policy revision also required several changes exogenous to the subsystem, including public concern with inflation and the inefficiencies of regulation in general. These inefficiencies were trumpeted by presidents Ford and Carter, who appointed proponents of deregulation—notably Alfred Kahn—to the CAB. Kahn then used ambiguities in the CAB's existing statutory mandate to push deregulation wherever possible, particularly in secondary airports such as Chicago Midway and Dallas Love Field. This change so destabilized major carriers like United Airlines that they agreed to changes in the law. Passage of the Airline Deregulation Act of 1978 was also facilitated by political compromises mitigating adverse impacts on employee unions.

The Tahoe case likewise provides evidence of the use of technical information consistent with Hypothesis 3 of the ACF. The accumulation of scientific evidence indicating that erosion from development adversely affected water quality was readily accepted by environmental groups and both state and federal resources agencies but not by most business owners, property rights advocates, and local government officials. The most plausible interpretation is that these findings were consistent with the policy core values of the former group but threatened the latter's adherence to economic development and property rights (and thus were rejected). In a high conflict situation such as Tahoe, combatants tend to assume a siege mentality in which all evidence put forth by opponents is highly suspect (Sabatier et al., 1987; Jenkins-Smith, 1990; Ingram, 1992).

Nevertheless, the CAB and OCS cases suggest a new hypothesis concerning policy-oriented learning:

> *Hypothesis 12:* Even when the accumulation of technical information does not change the views of the opposing coalition, it can have important impacts on policy—at least in the short term—by altering the views of policy brokers or other important governmental officials.

The influence of economists' arguments on Alfred Kahn, for example, and his impact on CAB policy has already been discussed. In the case of OCS leasing, millions of dollars spent on environmental impact studies during the 1970s had little effect on the beliefs of either oil companies or environmental groups (similar conclusions were reached by Heintz, 1988). But these studies apparently helped convince Cecil Andrus, secretary of the interior under the Carter administration, that improvements in drilling techniques meant that drilling posed far fewer environmental risks than he had previously believed. Combined with the exogenous shock from the 1979 oil crisis, this information led him to propose a greatly accelerated OCS leasing program in 1980.

When the policy dispute is characterized by high technical complexity and intense political conflict, senior agency officials (and probably legislative committee staff) play a critical role because they are the actors most likely to understand both the technical and the political aspects (Gormley, 1986). Any learning they do may well have a significant impact on public policy within the subsystem, even if the same information is rejected by most members of the dominant coalition. However, learning by such critical individuals will have a lasting impact on policy *only if* they are able to implement their views over time.

Finally, our own research and the arguments of several colleagues have convinced us that the analysis of policy-oriented learning will be facilitated if the structure of elite belief systems provided in Chapter 2 is modified somewhat.[4] Specifically, we propose that the policy core be subdivided into two components:

A. Fundamental Normative Precepts:
   1. Orientation on basic value priorities;
   2. Identification of social groups or other entities whose welfare is of greatest concern.
B. Precepts with a Substantial Empirical Component:
   3. Overall seriousness of the problem;
   4. Proper distribution of authority between government and market;
   5. Proper distribution of authority among levels of government;
   6. Priority accorded various policy instruments (e.g., regulation, insurance, education, direct payments, tax credits);
   7. Ability of society to solve the problem (e.g. zero-sum competition versus potential for mutual accommodation; technological optomism versus pessimism).

The fundamental normative precepts will be extremely difficult to change unless experience shows that actors or coalitions are holding incompatible values. The precepts with a substantial empirical content, although still very difficult to change, can be altered over time through the accumulation of compelling evidence from a variety of sources—the "enlightenment function" at its most profound level (Weiss, 1977a). The revised structure of elite belief systems is summarized in Table 10.1.

*Changes Exogenous to the Policy Subsystem*

Hypothesis 5 of the ACF argues that changes in the policy core of public policy within a subsystem will *not* come about solely because of activities internal to the subsystem. Instead, changes of that magnitude require some exogenous shock that alters the resources and opportunities of various coalitions.

The evidence presented in the cases generally supports this hypothesis. The clearest example was the influence of Québec separatism on francophone education in Ontario via its contribution to passage of the Federal Bill of Rights and Constitution Act. In the example of the Airline Deregulation Act of 1978, one could cite the role of inflation and the 1974 and 1976 changes in presidential administration in bringing about the radical change the act represented. On a somewhat lesser scale, California water policy changed from a clearly dominant Development Coalition in the 1960s and early 1970s to essentially a stalemate by the end of that decade, in large part because of the 1974 election of Jerry Brown as governor and the rise in oil prices (and thus pumping costs) following

TABLE 10.1  Revised Structure of Belief Systems of Policy Elites*

| | Deep Core | Policy Core | Secondary Aspects |
|---|---|---|---|
| Defining characteristics | Fundamental normative and ontological axioms | Fundamental policy positions concerning the basic strategies for achieving core values within the subsystem. | Instrumental decisions and information searches necessary to implement policy core. |
| Scope | Across all policy subsystems. | Specific to a subsystem. | Specific to a subsystem. |
| Susceptibility to change | Very difficult; akin to a religious conversion. | Difficult, but can occur if experience reveals serious anomalies. | Moderately easy; this is the topic of most administrative and even legislative policymaking. |
| Illustrative components | 1. The nature of man:<br>  i. Inherently evil vs. socially redeemable.<br>  ii. Part of nature vs. dominion over nature<br>  iii. Narrow egoists vs. contractarians.<br>2. Relative priority of various ultimate values: freedom, security, power, knowledge, health, love, beauty, etc.<br>3. Basic criteria of distributive justice: Whose welfare counts? Relative weights of self, primary groups, all people, future generations, nonhuman beings, etc. | Fundamental Normative Precepts:<br>1. Orientation on basic value priorities;<br>2. Identification of groups or other entities whose welfare is of greatest concern;<br><br>Precepts with a Substantial Empirical Component<br>3. Overall seriousness of the problem;<br>4. Proper distribution of authority between government and market;<br>5. Proper distribution of authority among levels of government;<br>6. Priority accorded various policy instruments, (e.g., regulation, insurance, education, direct payments, tax credits);<br>7. Ability of society to solve the problem (e.g. zero-sum competition vs. potential for mutual accommodation; technological optimism vs. pessimism). | 1. Seriousness of specific aspects of the problem in specific locales.<br>2. Importance of various causal linkages in different locales and over time.<br>3. Most decisions concerning administrative rules; budgetary allocations, disposition of cases, statutory interpretation, and even statutory revision.<br>4. Information regarding performance of specific programs or institutions. |

*The Policy Core and Secondary Aspects also apply to governmental programs.

the 1973–1974 and 1979–1980 oil crises. Finally, in the OCS leasing issue, the 1979 Iranian Revolution and subsequent oil crisis provided substantial impetus to changes in the Carter administration's policy.

Nevertheless, the cases suggest three modifications concerning the types and process by which exogenous events affect policy change. First, both Brown/Stewart and Mawhinney argue that exogenous events *by themselves* do not directly and unambiguously alter the resources and opportunities of subsystem actors (as implied by Figure 2.1 in Chapter 2). Instead, such events are *interpreted* by subsystem actors and then exploited with greater or lesser skill. Representatives of francophone school interests, for example, were particularly adept at exploiting—and even fanning—the flames of Québec separatism in order to achieve their policy objective. Thus, Hypothesis 5 needs to be revised:

*Hypothesis 5 (Revised):* Changing the policy core attributes of a government action program requires both (1) significant perturbations external to the subsystem (e.g., changes in socioeconomic conditions, system-wide governing coalitions, or policy outputs from other subsystems) and (2) skillful exploitation of those opportunities by the (previously) minority coalition within the subsystem.

Hopefully, the revised hypothesis makes it clear that, while external events provide opportunities to make changes in the policy core, those opportunities must be interpreted and exploited by the minority coalition if change is to be realized. Conversely, the majority coalition will seek to dampen the effects of such opportunities by, for example, suggesting the need for further research, confining change to small experimental projects, or diverting attention to other issues.

Second, the ACF presented in Chapter 2 gave relatively little attention to elections—except to note that a change in the *system-wide* governing coalition is one of a set of exogenous forces necessary for changes in the policy core within a subsystem. This is essentially what voting scholars have termed a "realigning election" (Asher, 1976): Members of the former minority coalition on the system-wide level now control both houses of a legislature and the chief executive's office within a particular political system. The basic argument concerning the need for system-wide changes in a governing coalition as one of a set of necessary conditions for substantial change in the policy core within a subsystem is probably still valid. In U.S. air pollution policy, for example, even the 1980 election that produced changes in the chief executive (the replacement of proenvironmental Carter with antiregulation Reagan in the White House) and the U.S. Senate (the first Republican majority since the 1950s) was *not* sufficient to produce changes in the policy core of federal air pollution policy. Members of the environmental coalition still controlled the House floor and the Senate Environment and Public Works Committee; they were able to block Reagan's attempts to amend the Clean Air Act in 1981–1982 and then negated his attempt to use political appointees and budgetary cuts to accomplish his objectives by giving widespread publicity to the Burford-Lavelle scandals (Cook and Wood, 1989; Cohen, 1992).

Nevertheless, elections that change critical actors—but not an entire system-wide governing coalition—can still inaugurate important changes in subsystem policies and, if combined with other factors, even changes in the policy core. This is particularly true of elections involving the chief executive because of their appointment powers (see also Wood and Waterman, 1991). Although most political appointees probably raise barely a ripple within a subsystem (Heclo, 1977), those who combine extensive knowledge of a subsystem with technical and political skill can produce waves of some magnitude. Obvious examples from the cases in this book include President Carter's appointments of Alfred Kahn as CAB chair and Cecil Andrus as secretary of interior, as well as Governor Brown's appointment of Ron Robie as director of the California Department of Water Resources. Kahn clearly helped facilitate a change in the policy core of airline regulation, while Andrus and Robie helped make less important, but still very significant, changes within their respective subsystems. Similarly, legislative elections that lead to changes in the chairs of critical committees can have very important impacts on a subsystem even if there is no realigning election. For example, the series of legislative elections in the early 1960s that resulted in the appointment of Senator Edmund Muskie as chair of the U.S. Senate Subcommittee on Air and Water Pollution—in conjunction with the general growth of the environmental movement—led over the next decade to changes in the policy cores of both federal air and water pollution control policy (Davies, 1970; Ingram, 1978). In sum, while realigning elections in general are one of a set of exogenous changes necessary for substantial changes in the policy core within a subsystem, elections that produce changes in chief executives and key legislators may be more important than was acknowledged in Chapter 2.

Third, the ACF as presented in Chapter 2 made no specific mention of public opinion on topics involving the policy subsystem. This factor was simply subsumed under "changes in socioeconomic conditions and technology," one of a number of external events. We continue to maintain that the general public has neither the expertise, nor the time, nor the inclination to be active participants in a policy subsystem; that role is reserved for policy elites.[5] Public opinion can, however, constitute a substantial constraint on the range of feasible strategies available to subsystem participants if it persists for some time and demonstrates some recognition of value tradeoffs. Examples would include Americans' relatively strong support for environmental protection (even when it involves some economic costs) since the early 1970s, strong and stable divisions on abortion, and Canadians' strong hostility to user fees in health care for several decades.[6] When public opinion changes, it is of sufficient importance to warrant inclusion as a separate category of external events (see Figure 10.1).[7]

### Beliefs Versus Interests: Does Importance Vary by Type of Coalition?

In Chapter 2 we took the position that common beliefs, rather than common interests, constitute the fundamental "glue" holding coalitions together. The two tend to covary, however, and disentangling them raises difficult methodological and theoretical issues on which the two of us sometimes disagree.

Nevertheless, systematic analysis of the OCS case provides some support for the argument that the relative importance of abstract beliefs versus "bottom-line" self-interest may vary across types of subsystem actors. Chapter 2 argued that more general and abstract core beliefs are more resistant to change than policy core or secondary beliefs. The premise of hierarchically structured beliefs led to Hypothesis 3, which stated that secondary beliefs would tend to be adjusted to protect the more general elements of the core. However, Jenkins-Smith and St. Clair showed that the relative propensity of group representatives to change

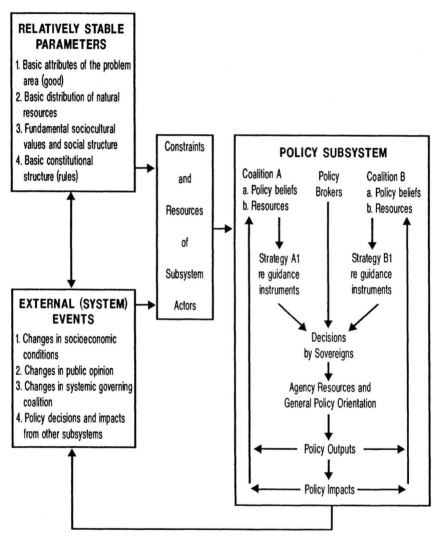

FIGURE 10.1    Revised diagram of the advocacy coalition framework

stated beliefs varied systematically by type of group. Purposive groups (e.g., environmental groups) showed relatively little tendency to change stated positions regarding *any* of the beliefs measured. Material groups (including trade associations and businesses involved in OCS development), however, were just as resistant as purposive groups to changing their positions on the bottom-line issue of the speed and breadth of OCS leasing but much *more* likely to change regarding the issues of the extent and severity of OCS regulations and the level of involvement of state and local governments in shaping OCS policy.

There are at least two interpretations of these findings. On the one hand, Jenkins-Smith is inclined to argue that the hierarchical structure of beliefs described in Chapter 2 may adequately describe representatives of purposive organizations but not of material groups. Instead, material groups may be operating on the basis of an "inverted hierarchy" in which commitment to material self-interest (profit) is primordial, with more abstract policy core beliefs (for instance, commitment to local versus national control) adjusted as necessary. As explained in Chapter 8, the rationale for this distinction comes from the application of exchange theory and principal-agent concepts to interest groups (Salisbury, 1969; Moe, 1980, 1984). Because purposive groups rely on members' commitment to a broad "platform" of policy positions—typically based on a specific ideology—they are very reluctant to change *any* part of that belief system. In contrast, members of material groups are preoccupied with bottom-line material benefits and willing to allow group leaders to say almost anything to obtain them.[8] Thus Jenkins-Smith would expect the stated beliefs of representatives of material groups to be more fluid than those of purposive groups and more conducive to the formation of "coalitions of convenience" containing members with very different beliefs (see Chapter 2).

An alternative interpretation, favored by Sabatier, is simply that profit (or market share or return to shareholders) is the principal, publicly acknowledged goal of petroleum companies and other material groups and thus part of their policy core. In OCS policy, profit is intimately tied to extent of leasing. By this interpretation, the fundamental value priorities in the policy core are still the most stable aspect of a group's belief system. It's just that the basic goals of material groups may be less abstract and have narrower scope than the fundamental goals of purposive groups. Belief systems are still hierarchically organized. Instead of abstract beliefs constraining more specific ones, it is fundamental goals that constrain implementing devices and perceptions of system states and causal relationships. Thus the hierarchical structure of belief systems outlined in Figure 2.1 and the basic argument of Hypothesis 3 can be maintained; all that is jettisoned is the assumption borrowed from Converse (1964) and Peffley and Hurwitz (1985) that *asbstract* beliefs constrain specific ones.[9]

Since the two of us obviously cannot decide on the "correct" interpretation, we'll leave it to individual readers.

### Generalizability of the ACF

The ACF is intended to apply to all policy areas in at least modern industrial polyarchies (Dahl, 1971). In our view and those of the case authors, it has proven relatively easy to apply to specific cases, although the case applications have also suggested several revisions.

Stewart (1991) has argued, however, that the ACF is less useful than another approach—institutional rational choice—in understanding subsystems with a clearly dominant coalition and virtually no minority coalitions. That may be true. Nevertheless, we would argue that the ACF is helpful in understanding even single-coalition subsystems because it forces the researcher to articulate and analyze the belief system of the dominant coalition—a belief system whose policy core value premises and causal assumptions generally remain implicit because they are never challenged. This process has two advantages.

First, it enables the researcher to understand the "true" magnitude of current policy disputes. In the FCC case discussed by Barke, for example, the conflict among telecommunications companies over the choice of a specific television technology was intense because millions of dollars were at stake. Nevertheless, it only involved a secondary aspect, the choice of a particular technology to implement policy core precepts that everyone agreed on. Imagine what the conflict would have looked like had an alternative coalition been urging governmental ownership of all television manufacturing or the distribution of 50% of the profits from television sales to publicly owned television stations.

Second, analysis of the belief systems of the dominant coalition may reveal causal assumptions that are subject to disproof over time through the activities of various researchers, whether neutral or members of a nascent minority coalition. As disconfirming evidence accumulates, it may eventually help undermine the dominant policy. In the case discussed by Stewart (1991), school segregation before 1950, an analysis of the segregation coalition's belief system would have revealed the premise that segregated schools were not inherently bad for racial minorities. It was that assumption that Kenneth Clark challenged in his research on the effects of segregation on black children's self-esteem—findings that provided one of the bases for the the Supreme Court's decision in *Brown v. Board of Education* (Cushman, 1963:256).

In short, we suspect that there is almost always one or more minority coalitions—however powerless at a given point in time. The ACF encourages researchers to examine the belief systems of these coalitions as well as their strategies for overturning the dominant coalition. That may take a while—just as it took the NAACP several decades to overcome segregated southern schools (Vose, 1959)—but any theory of long-term policy change needs to deal explicitly with the manner in which minority coalitions can transform a subsystem.

A related issue concerns the development of coherent coalitions over time. When a new subsystem emerges out of an existing one—as housing did out of the broader urban policy subsystem in the early 1960s—one can expect relatively distinct coalitions from the beginning. In contrast, when a subsystem emerges *de novo*, the initial years may see very diffuse coalitions with rather amorphous belief systems (Wildavsky, 1962). As the Tahoe case demonstrated, however, coherent and quite distinct coalitions can emerge from such fluid situations over time. In its present form, the ACF is best suited to examining established subsystems with distinct coalitions, but the Tahoe case suggests that it can be expanded to deal with new subsystems as well.

In the final analysis, of course, the generalizability and relative utility of the ACF will not be known until it is applied in many more cases by a variety of scholars.

## II. ELABORATING ON GUIDANCE INSTRUMENTS IN THE FRAMEWORK

One of the fundamental propositions of the ACF is that coalitions seek to alter the behavior of governmental institutions in order to achieve the policy objectives in their respective policy cores. The means of doing so involves the use of "guidance instruments." Unfortunately, Chapters 2 and 3 said very little about the nature of those instruments and the strategies for using them. They thus provided very little guidance about *how* coalition members might seek to alter policy in specific situations.[10] In rectifying this critical omission, we shall borrow heavily from a previous discussion by Sabatier and Pelkey (1987).

We start by assuming that administrative agencies have the most *direct* impact on a coalition's ability to achieve its policy objectives because agencies are the institutions that actually deliver services or regulate target group behavior. Thus a coalition can seek either to directly affect an agency's decisions or to indirectly affect them by appealing to the legislative, executive, judicial, or intergovernmental sovereigns who control the agency's budget and legal authority.[11]

Following is a tentative list of the guidance instruments available to coalitions:

A. Direct Effects on Agency Rulemaking, Case Specific, or Budgetary Decisions:
   1. Persuade agency officials through testimony;
   2. Change the personnel making decisions via transfer or reorganization;
   3. Change the professional background of agency staff by encouraging the hiring of staff with a different background or by changing professional education;
   4. Publicize agency performance gaps in the media;
   5. Provide research reports;
   6. Offer inducements (e.g., bribes or offers of future employment).
B. Indirect Effects via Sovereigns:
   1. Conduct systematic review of agency rules (e.g., by OMB);
   2. Alter political appointees;
   3. Pursue litigation;
   4. Pursue changes in legislation;
   5. Pursue changes in the agency's budget;
   6. Change the policy preferences of sovereigns by participating in elections (electoral strategy);
   7. Influence public opinion and, hence, sovereigns.

Note that the range of guidance instruments is much broader than simply changing the legal rules affecting the agency—which has been almost the sole focus of institutional choice theorists (Ostrom, 1990; Gregg et al., 1991).

In deciding which of these instruments to use in a specific situation, let's assume that coalitions attempt to be rational actors and thus that their choice will be a function of:

1. The cost to the coalition of pursuing the use of the instrument. Assume that costs are basically a function of (1) the number of major veto points involved and (2) whether the actors occupying those veto points are sympathetic to the coalition, opposed to the coalition, or relatively neutral. For simplicity's sake, let's assume that getting an agency to make a decision involves a single veto point and that a district court decision involves a single veto point, but that changes in law or an agency's budget involve five veto points when done at a single level of government (such as the California legislature and governor amending the California Clean Air Act), but often only one when there is an intergovernmental sovereign (such as the U.S. EPA requiring a change in California emissions regulations).[12]
2. The coalition's resources. These include money, members outside government, and, probably most important, agency officials and sovereigns who are coalition members or sympathetic to the coalition.[13]
3. The efficacy of a guidance instrument, including both (1) its scope and duration and (2) the lag time until it becomes effective. For example, testifying at a hearing can only change the agency's decision, which is likely to be fairly narrow in scope and perhaps of relatively short duration. Changes in law, in contrast, tend to be much broader in scope and much longer in duration. Lag times are critical for guidance instruments; producing research reports or altering public opinion, for example, usually takes several years to have any effect.
4. The coalition's extent of dissatisfaction with present policy outputs. The greater the dissatisfaction, the greater the willingness to expend resources to reduce the performance gap.
5. The probability of success of the instrument. Attempts to use a particular instrument are always uncertain, in large part because one can count on the opposing coalition(s) to mount counter-strategies.

Table 10.2 contains our very rough estimates of the costs and efficacy of various guidance instruments. At least two conclusions emerge. First, the cost of successfully employing any instrument varies tremendously according to the receptivity of the person(s) whom the coalition is seeking to influence. If they are sympathetic, the costs tend to be low to moderate; if they are opposed, the costs are high to impossible. Second, the

TABLE 10.2 Tentative Estimates of Costs and Efficacy of Different Guidance Instruments

| GUIDANCE INSTRUMENT | Probable Costs When Government Decisonmakers Are | | | Probable Efficacy | | |
|---|---|---|---|---|---|---|
| | Supportive | Neutral/Mixed | Opposed | Scope | Duration | Lag Time |
| **Seeks to Directly Affect Agency Decisions** | | | | | | |
| 1. Persuade through testimony | low | low | moderate | low | low | short |
| 2. Change personnel making decision via transfer or reorganization | low | moderate | high | low to high | low | short |
| 3. Change professional background of agency staff | low | moderate | high | high | high | long |
| 4. Obtain media publicity | -- | low | low | low to mod. | low | short |
| 5. Provide research reports | low | moderate | high | varies | varies | long (enlightenment) |
| 6. Offer inducements (e.g. bribes) | low | high | high | low | low | short |
| **Seeks to Indirectly Affect Agency Via Sovereigns** | | | | | | |
| 1. Conduct systematic review of agency rules | low | moderate | high | low to mod. | low to mod. | short |
| 2. Alter political appointees | low | low | high | low to mod. | low | low |
| 3. Pursue litigation | moderate for district court; high for appeals | | | usually low | varies | short to mod. |
| 4. Pursue major changes in legislation/legal authority | | | | | | |
| a. Sovereigns at same level | moderate | high | impossible | high | high | short to mod. |
| b. Intergovt. agency* | low | moderate | high | moderate | low to mod. | short |
| 5. Pursue major changes in agency's budget | | | | | | |
| a. Sovereigns at same level | moderate | high | impossible | mod. to high | low | short |
| b. Intergovt. agency* | low | moderate | high | low to mod. | low | short |
| 6. Pursue electoral strategy | -- | high | very high | ? | high | long |
| 7. Change public opinion | moderate | high | very high | varies | varies | long |

*Assumes hierarchically superior agency making a case-specific decision.

efficacy of most instruments is roughly proportional to the costs. It is relatively easy to alter an agency decision through direct testimony if the agency officials are sympathetic or neutral, but the scope of most agency decisions is quite narrow and the duration fairly short. At the other extreme, obtaining a major change in law is usually moderately difficult to impossible, but the scope is broad and lasts a long time. The major exception involves obtaining a change in budget and sometimes even legal authority from an agency's intergovernmental sovereign (assuming that the sovereign is itself an agency making a case-specific decision). These changes tend to be much easier to obtain than getting a comparable change through the five veto points at one's own level of government, while the scope and duration are often only slightly lower than for a change in state legislation. This suggests that agencies should work hard at cultivating their intergovernmental superiors.

It must be remembered, however, that the choice of guidance instruments is a dynamic process that may change rapidly over time because of crises or because of elections that alter the receptivity of personnel in critical governmental positions to a coalition's views. We would expect subsystem participants to monitor each of the variables affecting the use of guidance instruments—particularly the receptivity of officials in various governmental positions—in an effort to maximize the use of these instruments. In Kingdon's (1984) terms, such elections and crises provide "windows of opportunity" to a coalition.

Assuming that these conjectures concerning the costs and efficacy of various guidance instruments are roughly correct, they have some very important implications for the general strategies pursued by specific coalitions. First and foremost, they suggest that the members of a coalition will concentrate their efforts on agencies and sovereigns that are relatively sympathetic to their point of view (or at least neutral). This strategy is facilitated by the fact that most policy subsystems are intergovernmental in character and, in any governmental jurisdiction, there are usually several agencies involved. Thus, coalitions in a specific jurisdiction "shop around" among agencies and sovereigns for receptive people to influence. Of course, there is usually a focal agency that one must attempt to influence, even if it is hostile. But this analysis suggests that such attempts will largely be *pro forma* and will be supplemented by numerous other initiatives directed at more sympathetic governmental officials. At Tahoe, for example, environmentalists had to deal with the TRPA during the 1970s even when they perceived it to be quite unsympathetic. But they focused most of their energies on trying to get other state and federal agencies involved in the basin, in addition to the herculean task of convincing the two state legislatures to revise the TRPA Compact.

Second, coalitions will work hard to confine authority to agencies and levels of government where they have a competitive advantage while also seeking to minimize the authority of governmental units unsympathetic to their point of view. This strategy is simply an illustration of what Schattschneider (1960) termed "controlling the scope of the conflict." It is rendered quite difficult, however, by the intergovernmental nature of most subsystems. Most federal agencies rely on state and/or local officials to implement their programs. Conversely, most state and local agencies obtain their revenues and legal authority from institutions at several levels of government; if they cannot get what they want from one level, they search for a more sympathetic audience at another level and usually find it. In short, while coalitions work hard at controlling the scope of the conflict, this is a very difficult task—particularly in federal systems like the United States.

## III. IMPLICATIONS FOR SCHOLARS
## AND PRACTITIONERS

We conclude with brief discussions of some of the implications of the ACF, as seen through the cases, for both scholars and policy practitioners.

### Scholars

Scholars are interested in understanding the world. In order to accomplish that, they must use conceptual frameworks to help tell them what is probably important and what can be ignored.

The cases presented in this book and those previously published in Sabatier and Jenkins-Smith (1988) suggest that the ACF is a promising addition to the set of existing theories on the policy process. In our view, it is clearly superior to the stages metaphor of Jones (1977) because it meets all the requirements of a causal theory (Lave and March, 1975):

1. It has two *primary forces of causal change*: (1) the values of coalition members and (2) exogenous shocks to the subsystem.
2. It is *testable/falsifiable*. In fact, several of the hypotheses proposed in Chapters 2 and 3 have had to be revised as a result of the cases.
3. It is *relatively parsimonious and fertile*, that is, it produces a relatively large number of interesting predictions per assumption.
4. It may produce some *surprising results*, although this is not something we have focused on.
5. It has the potential for *contributing to a better world* by helping policy activists understand the policy process, by indicating the variety of guidance instruments available to them, and perhaps most of all, by showing how individuals with solid information can make a difference over time.

In fact, it is our hope that the ACF will join institutional rational choice as one of the two most useful theories of the policy process (Sabatier, 1991).

In order to do so, however, it will have to be applied in a great many more empirical settings and its utility examined by a variety of scholars. Following are simply a few of the aspects most in need of additional empirical and theoretical work:

1. How much information exchange and coordination of strategies goes on among members of a coalition? This is a surprisingly neglected topic in the literature on coalitions (Hinckley, 1981).
2. What are the different roles within a coalition and who is likely to fill them? Would it be useful to distinguish between members and sympathizers? If so, how would membership be determined? Who tend to be the leaders?
3. Under what circumstances are successful policy brokers likely to

emerge? What are the institutional affiliations of such brokers and
what skills do they tend to possess?

4. Do subsystem dynamics tend to vary by policy type (Ripley and
   Franklin, 1982; Meier, 1987)? For example, one might expect regulatory and redistributive policy areas to be characterized by several
   strong coalitions, while distributive policy areas may be more often
   characterized by a single dominant coalition with different cost
   bearers being in much weaker coalitions.
5. Do professional fora really promote learning across coalitions?
   What is the range of institutional arrangements meeting the definition of professional fora?
6. What are the conditions under which research reports can have an
   important impact on major policy decisions? Or, put differently, under what conditions can research have a major policy impact that
   does not involve a long-term "enlightenment function"?
7. Does the relationship among interest groups, sympathetic agency
   officials, and sympathetic researchers vary across countries? Are
   agency officials in the United States really more likely than their
   colleagues in other countries to be active members or sympathizers
   of coalitions, e.g., by obstructing undesirable programs, leaking information, and pushing professional values against the wishes of
   the administration in power?

### Practitioners

What are the implications of the ACF for practitioners of policy analysis? Some of the critics of analysis have held that policy analysts will be
mere handmaidens to the politically powerful, legitimizers of predetermined choices (Horowitz, 1970). Others more sympathetic with the aims
of policy analysis have worried that analysis is ineffectual, more often
ignored than abused in the political process (Nisbit, 1981).

The ACF suggests that the validity of these concerns depends in large
part on the characteristics of the subsystem in which the analysis is applied (Jenkins-Smith, 1990). Analysis is most likely to serve primarily as a
political resource when the issue under review is subject to high levels of
conflict. In such instances, the application of analysis bears directly on
beliefs and values of core concern to subsystem participants. For that reason, these participants will be loathe to consider the findings of analysis
unless those findings corroborate their previously held beliefs and
values. From the perspective of the individual analyst, a context of this
kind is one in which the analyst's client is likely to be committed to a
predetermined policy option and to demand analysis that serves as ammunition in the political debate.

Focus of debate on highly intractable policy issues will increase
the likelihood of advocacy analysis. The more intractable the issue, the
greater latitude the individual analyst has in "shading" analysis one way
or another without moving beyond the pale of analytical plausibility.
For an example, see the oil export debates described in Jenkins-Smith
(1990:Chapter 5).

The forum in which the issue is debated will also affect the propensity to employ analysis as a political resource. When contentious issues are reviewed in an open forum, the wide array of participants, with varying professional training and levels of analytical sophistication, reduces the likelihood of finding shared bases for verification of analytical claims. The cases dealing with California water policy and airline deregulation illustrate how open fora enable committed partisans to dismiss uncongenial analyses as "cooked" and to champion ones more supportive of their policy positions.

Thus it is in analytical debates characterized by high levels of conflict, over analytically intractable issues, and in open fora that analysis is most likely to be employed primarily as a political resource. Practitioners who expect their analysis to have an independent and influential role in shaping policy in contexts of this sort are likely to be met with disappointment.

Not all policy contexts are of this kind. Under some circumstances, analysis can significantly modify the policy-relevant beliefs of policy elites, and the content of analysis can be narrowly constrained by prevailing theory and data within professional circles. Of particular importance is that the issue be subject to moderate levels of conflict sufficient to encourage the mobilization of the necessary analytical resources yet not sufficient to lead policy elites to refuse to consider analytical findings that depart from their preconceptions.

Also of importance is the notion that the more analytically tractable issues restrict the range of plausible analytical claims. Barke's discussion of technical standard setting is illustrative of such conditions; in this case, the highly tractable issue permitted widespread adjustment of beliefs to accommodate the new findings *in spite of* very high monetary stakes for the participants.

Professional fora, in which participants to the debate are screened by virtue of professional training or technical competence, also contribute to restriction of the use of analysis as a political resource. The Barke chapter suggests that, in combination with an analytically tractable issue, the professional forum may be able to obtain consensual adjustment of policy-relevant beliefs even in the face of significant conflict.

In sum, in a policy context of moderate conflict, on analytically tractable issues, and in fora approximating the professionalized forum, policy analysis can be expected to make a substantial contribution to the ways that members of the policy elite perceive policy issues and options. Of course, most policy contexts are neither completely hospitable to the serious consideration of technical analysis nor wholly conducive to the use of analysis as a political resource but rather fall somewhere between these extremes.

How would these implications affect the analytical strategies of policy-analysis practitioners? First and formost, it is a mistake to view analysis as a discrete act in which a problem is analyzed, options reviewed, and advice given. Viewed in abstraction from the *process* of policy analysis within subsystems, "success" or "failure" of analysis is too often seen as wholly contingent on the technical perfection of its content and whether clients accept or reject the conclusions of the analysis. Such a view will fail to recognize that a particular analysis is more often one part of a many-sided, ongoing exchange about the way issues should be perceived, what values are affected and how, and what policy options merit consideration by policy elites. If fundamental values or causal perceptions are at stake, this exchange of views is likely to last at least a decade. Economic critiques of the inefficiencies of airline regulation, for example, took fifteen to twenty years to bear fruit. Such a view may also fail to recognize that what counts as the success of a particular analysis must be at least partly contingent on the policy context; to expect a scrupulously objective, technically precise analysis to make a substantive dent in a highly conflictual, intractable policy debate is to ask for disappointment and frustration.

A further implication of this view of the process of analysis within subsystems is that practitioners can learn under what circumstances to expect more from analytical effort. Analysts frequently have considerable discretion in how they address the issues and in how they allocate their efforts over the subelements of a given issue. If the objective is to change perceptions on policy issues or to generate consensus, the analysts would do well to avoid expending resources directly on problems mired in fixed, highly conflictual, and intractable issues. A better strategy would be to pick an aspect of the issue that, being out of the direct line of fire of clashing interests, may permit some consensual learning. Thus, attention to the context of analysis would not only forewarn the analyst of when analytical effort is unlikely to be successful but can also provide a guide to more effective allocation of that effort.

## NOTES

The authors would like to thank Joseph Stewart, Jr., and Hanne B. Mawhinney for their helpful comments on a previous version of this chapter.

1. Riker (1962) argued that dominant coalitions have another reason to remain as small as possible: In minimum winning coalitions, each member maximizes his share of the spoils.

2. For example, California and Massachusetts have often been members of the Environmental Coalition, while Louisiana has generally favored leasing. They were not discussed in Chapter 9 because they have not been active over the entire twenty-year period.

3. Several scholars—including Ted Marmor and Jonathan Lomas—have argued that Hypotheses 6 through 9 contain a *normative* assumption that policy-oriented learning consistent with scientific norms is good. They argue that, as a *positive* theory, the ACF should also deal with belief change brought about by charlatans and hucksters. In our view, however, charlatans are not likely to change the minds of policy elites from the opposing coalition—who will recognize them as charlatans. While they may change public opinion, the public is not knowledgeable enough to be part of the subsystem. Instead, as indicated in the section of this chapter entitled "Changes Exogenous to the Policy Subsystem," changes in public opinion are part of what the ACF terms "exogenous events."

Moreover, who is a charlatan depends very much on one's beliefs. To many monetarist economists, for example, *any* Keynesian is a huckster.

4. The most forceful proponents of this revision have been Tracy Gustilo and Jonathan Lomas. See also Sabatier et al. (1990).

5. Occupying an intermediate status between "the general public" and "policy elites" (most of whose jobs require susbystem participation) are what might be termed "the interested/attentive public." This group would include members of interest groups and other people who try to stay reasonably informed on an issue and are available for occasional mobilization by interest-group leaders. In our view, however, only interest-group leaders are sufficiently informed and willing to devote the time to be policy elites.

6. The Canadian example was provided by Jonathan Lomas, Ted Marmor, and other members of the Health Policy Group of the Canadian Institute of Advanced Research. The best data on Americans' support for environmental protection is in Dunlap and Mertig (1992:Chapter 10).

7. We recognize that public opinion is more subject to manipulation by advocacy coalition elites than are other types of external events, but we continue to insist that it is more like other external events—that is, largely beyond the control of subsystem participants—than it is like anything within the subsystem.

8. The data from the Tahoe studies is mixed on this topic. On the one hand, an analysis of surveys of policy elites in 1972 and 1984 provides some support for the Jenkins-Smith interpretation (Sabatier et al., 1990). On the other hand, the analysis in Chapter 9 of this book and an analysis of interest-group elites from 1972 and 1984 (Sabatier, 1992) tends to support the alternative view.

9. Sabatier is, of course, doing precisely what Lakatos (1971)—and the ACF, for that matter—would expect: When confronted with a challenge to the ACF's core proposition of hierarchically structured belief systems, he is jettisoning a relatively minor part (abstract beliefs constrain specific ones) in favor of an alternative interpretation that keeps the hierarchical structure intact.

10. We are indebted to Frank Gregg of the University of Arizona for making us aware of this omission.

11. The concept of "sovereigns" is taken from Downs (1966), while the focus on budgets and legal authority borrows heavily from resource dependency theory (Pfeffer and Salancik, 1978). An intergovernmental sovereign is an institution at another level of government that controls part of an agency's budget or legal authority. For example, the legal and financial resources of the California Air Resources Board are affected not only by the California governor, legislature, and courts, but also by the U.S. Environmental Protection Agency and, in turn, its sovereigns (the president, Congress, and federal courts).

12. The five veto points include four legislative decisions (the committee vote and floor vote of each house) and the chief executive. For intergovernmental sovereigns, there's only one veto point if it involves a case-specific funding decision or rule application by the intergovernmentally superior agency. Anything involving a change in that agency's legal or budgetary authoring involves five veto points. The concept of "veto point" is borrowed from Pressman and Wildavsky (1973).

13. This resource principle is analogous to the budget constraint used in economic models.

# Methodological Appendix: Measuring Longitudinal Change in Elite Beliefs Using Content Analysis of Public Documents

HANK C. JENKINS-SMITH AND PAUL A. SABATIER

Most models of political decision making assume a fairly close relationship between the beliefs of interested political elites and their policy decisions (Putnam, 1976; Azjen and Fishbein, 1980). The nature and content of elite beliefs has been examined with respect to legislators (Montjoy, Schaffer, and Weber, 1980; Jackman, 1972), the presidency and administrative officers (Holsti, 1970; Etheredge, 1985), bureaucrats (Aberbach, Putnam, and Rockman, 1981) and the Supreme Court (Gibson, 1978). The assumption of consistency between salient elite beliefs and political behavior has been reasonably well corroborated (Mazmanian and Sabatier, 1980; Krosnick, 1987; Walker, 1977).

Nevertheless, studies of elite beliefs *over time* are quite rare. Even more scarce are longitudinal studies of elite belief systems that use intersubjectively reliable data. Two notable exceptions are the two-wave panel of Italian elites over a six-year period by Putnam et al. (1979) and the two-wave panel of French elites over a two-year period by Converse and Pierce (1986). This lack is particularly distressing because it makes the empirical test of theories regarding systematic change in elite beliefs—and resultant changes in public policy—quite problematic.

This appendix presents a method for developing such data by coding the content of public documents. After discussing the current literature on the change of elite policy beliefs, we describe a coding frame and technique that can be used to generate reliable data on elite beliefs. The technique is then applied to two long-term policy debates: the debate over development of the Lake Tahoe region and the debate over the breadth and speed of oil and gas leasing on the U.S. outer continental shelf (OCS). The data are derived from a series of legislative and administrative hearings conducted regarding these issues over periods of more than a decade. We conclude by illustrating and discussing the kinds of research for which this method is most appropriate.

## I. EXISTING RESEARCH ON ELITE BELIEFS

Among scholars who are committed to intersubjectively reliable methods of data acquisition and analysis, studies of elite beliefs have tended to cluster along the following lines:

1. Cross-sectional and longitudinal studies of legislative voting behavior in which beliefs are usually operationalized through partisan affiliation, interest-group scorecards, or, in cross-sectional studies, attitudinal surveys (Entman, 1983; Poole and Daniels, 1985).
2. Longitudinal and cross-sectional studies of the ability of legislative and/or executive sovereigns to affect the decisions of administrative agencies. In this research, partisan orientation is generally used as the indicator of sovereigns' preferences, although survey data are occasionally employed (Gormley, 1979; Moe, 1982, 1985; Weingast and Moran, 1983; Cohen, 1985; Aberbach, Putnam, and Rockman, 1981).
3. Studies focusing on changes in elite beliefs over time, using attitudinal surveys in either a panel or a repeated cross-section design (Putnam et al., 1979; Greenberger et al., 1983; Converse and Pierce, 1986).
4. Cross-sectional studies of elite beliefs in a specific policy area based on attitudinal surveys (Pierce and Lovrich, 1980; Sabatier and McLaughlin, 1988; McClosky and Brill, 1983).

While the range and sophistication of such studies have increased substantially in the past ten years, some notable shortcomings remain.

First, the longitudinal studies have tended to use rather crude indicators of elite beliefs—primarily either partisan orientation or some sort of interest-group scorecard. Neither provides the researcher with much insight into the reasoning behind elite policy preferences. For example, neither can relate those preferences back to more abstract values via a set of causal assumptions or hierarchically ordered beliefs. Given the modest ideological orientation of U.S. political parties, partisan affiliation provides only the most general indicator of the reasons behind elite preferences. Interest-group scorecards provide virtually none, as they are simply compilations of votes.

This inability to trace reasoning processes makes elites appear less rational than they probably are and, more important, makes it very difficult for the researcher to explain (or predict) change over time. Explaining changes in preferences requires an understanding of elite reasoning processes so that predictor variables that are more subject to change than partisan affiliation can be correlated with changes in policy preferences. For example, do policy positions on specific issues flow from more general and strongly held normative and ontological beliefs (Peffley and Hurwitz, 1985)? Or do beliefs hinge more directly on matters of economic or political interests (Weiss, 1983)? Still another alternative explanation holds that policy positions derive from ideological bases for *some* kinds of elites, while economic interests dominate for others (Moe, 1980). In short, understanding changes in elite preferences requires a knowledge of the structure of their belief systems, including the multitude of causal assumptions and perceptions of important variables through which elites presumably view the world (Axelrod, 1976; Putnam, 1976; Greenberger et al., 1983; Sabatier and Hunter, 1989).

The second major limitation of the existing literature is that it is based heavily on attitudinal surveys. While such surveys provide a relatively sophisticated tool for assessing the complexity of elite beliefs and their relation to policy positions, they are heavily time- and culture-bound. The vast majority have been done in the United States and developed Western nations over the past twenty years (see, e.g., Aberbach, Putnam, and Rockman, 1981). That is a *very* small subset of elite behavior. In addition, the elite surveys that have been done are overwhelmingly cross-sectional in design. Longitudinal elite surveys—involving either repeated cross-sectional or panel designs—are extremely rare, presumably for a variety of practical reasons: the difficulties of replicating another scholar's survey done five to ten years earlier; the relatively short time spans of most scholars' interest in a particular topic, which makes it unlikely that they will replicate their own work a decade later; and the enormous difficulties in locating respondents in order to do panel surveys five to fifteen years apart. In fact, we know of only three such surveys; they involve time intervals of two years (Converse and Pierce, 1986), six years (Putnam et al., 1979), and fourteen years (Sabatier et al., 1990).

A third limitation is that the vast majority of studies of elite beliefs have used either legislators or administrative agency officials as their target population. What we are interested in, with the focus on long-term policy change, are belief changes in the range of policy elites populating what Heclo (1978) and Kingdon (1984) called policy subsystems or subcommunities. Included are representatives of interest groups, economic and trade groups, and private firms; scholars and media reporters specializing in the area; and executive, legislative, and judicial officials. Studies of the beliefs of interest-group elites are surprisingly rare (Kobylka, 1983), and those of the researchers and other intellectuals who play important roles in policy subsystems are virtually nonexistent.

The end result is that the scholarly community has only the vaguest understanding of how the beliefs of policy elites *change over time*, let alone the effects that those changes have on public policy. Moreover, although some very interesting theorizing has been done on the matter (e.g., Sabatier, 1987; Weiss, 1983), we have very little hard evidence about the relationships among interest, knowledge, and beliefs. Our ignorance is particularly acute with respect to changes in the beliefs of nongovernmental elites.

We argue that scholars have largely neglected a potential gold mine for examining changes in elite beliefs over time: the content analysis of public hearings, other government documents, and interest-group publications. Such an approach has numerous advantages:

1. It permits a much more detailed analysis of beliefs than can be captured by partisan affiliation or interest-group scorecards.
2. Content analysis of public documents is better suited than attitudinal surveys to the examination of changes in elite beliefs over time. It does not automatically limit analysis to replication of previous work, nor does it require scholars to maintain an interest in a topic for an extended period of time. Public documents spanning an enormous range of topics, cultures, and time periods are relatively easy to obtain, and coding several decades' worth of records can be done within a year or so.
3. The researcher is not limited to studying elites from legislatures or any other particular institution. In fact, most public hearings contain testimony from individuals representing a wide variety of interest groups, administrative agencies, legislative districts, research organizations, and so on. Content analysis is particularly suited to monitoring changes over time in the beliefs of actors in most policy subsystems (Heclo, 1978; Kingdon, 1984; Sabatier, 1987).

In short, the content analysis of public documents would seem to offer considerable promise. It also, as discussed below, has limitations.

## II. CONTENT ANALYSIS OF ELITE BELIEFS

Content analysis as a technique is not new (Hofstetter, 1981). In fact, it has been rather extensively used by political scientists interested in communications research, judicial politics, and international relations (Holsti, 1969; Krippendorff, 1980; Webber, 1985; Gates, 1986). In international relations, it has often been used to gather data on specific individuals, with Holsti's (1967) study of John Foster Dulles being a classic example.

Our interest, however, is in using content analysis of governmental and interest-group documents to explore the beliefs, interests, and policy positions of relatively large numbers of elites over periods of a decade or more. This task requires (1) the identification of the target population and a sample of that population to be coded; (2) the development of a coding frame consisting of the relevant elements in the belief systems of the target population; and (3) attention to reliability and validity problems in inferring beliefs from documentary sources.

## Selecting a Sample from the Target Population

In measures of long-term change in policy beliefs, the relevant population includes individuals, or group representatives, who make up what have variously been called issue networks, policy subcommunities, or policy subsystems. Subsystem members include those policy elites who, with relative regularity, follow and attempt to influence policy developments in a given issue area.

Identifying subsystem participants can be accomplished in several ways. One method, originally employed to identify elites in community power studies, involved the use of "reputational" sampling techniques whereby identified elites were asked to list other elites, who in turn were asked to identify still others, until no additional names were obtained (Hunter, 1963). Kingdon (1984:220–225) used a snowballing technique, much like the reputational approach, to collect a sample of subcommunity members in transportation and health at the federal level. While these techniques are appropriate for identifying current elites, our interest is in measuring beliefs of current *and* former elites over time.

A more appropriate method is to rely on records of participation in arenas in which subsystem members (or their representatives) regularly participate. The most useful source we have found consists of the set of public hearings conducted over time on the relevant policy issue area. Such series of hearings are available over a very wide range of issues and (for the United States) can be readily identified by use of the federal *Congressional Information Service* index of congressional hearings or comparable state references. On the Tahoe project, for example, state-level hearings and hearing transcripts were available covering the period from 1964 to 1984, and on the OCS project, transcripts were available for hearings from 1969 through 1987.

Once a set of hearing transcripts is obtained, one must decide which participants to code. Because we were interested in measuring change in beliefs over time, we included only participants (either as individuals or representatives of organizations) who participated in the hearings over periods of at least two years (i.e., one-shot participants were excluded). With the OCS project, this step was accomplished by taking the names, dates, and affiliations (and secondary affiliations) of those who testified from the indexes of a subset of hearings over time and entering them into a data base. The records were then sorted by name and affiliation over time to identify those participants or representatives that were regular, long-term participants. The testimony of these participants was then coded whenever it appeared over the entire set of hearings. For the Tahoe project, a less stringent test was applied because no one testified at every hearing. Instead, analysis was limited to organizations that testified at several hearings; these were then grouped into larger categories, such as "local governments" or "California executive agencies." For lists of participants in these two studies, see Tables 8.1 and 9.1.

### Developing a Coding Frame

Having selected the subject of research—that is, the substantive topic, time period, and target population(s)—the researcher needs to develop a coding frame indicating the set of items to be applied to the testimonies. In order to adequately measure elite beliefs in a specific policy area over a fairly long period of time, this coding frame will probably be quite extensive, as it will presumably contain a number of quite abstract beliefs as well as items dealing with the specific policy disputes that arose during the decade or so under investigation.

In general, the structure of the coding frame must be derived from the nature of the theoretical questions to be addressed in the analysis (Krippendorff, 1980). As discussed above, the coding frame must generate data capable of testing a range of hypotheses concerning the structure of elite beliefs, interests, and policy positions. For our studies, the code forms were designed to capture a range of "levels" of beliefs, ranging from quite fundamental values and ontological assumptions (deep core beliefs), to general policy beliefs that serve to translate the deep core into political practice (the policy core), and finally to very specific perceptions of causal relationships and perceived states of the world regarding the policy issue (the secondary aspect of beliefs). Once captured, data on such levels of belief would permit testing of a variety of propositions, such as Hypothesis 3: More abstract and fundamental core beliefs are relatively stable over long periods of time and serve to constrain variation in more specific secondary beliefs.

Whenever possible, the belief variables were designed as scales bounded by the "extreme" positions (e.g., the most hardline prodevelopment and proenvironmental positions) taken by participants in the debate. Also where possible, two kinds of scales were used to capture positions on a variable: (1) "absolute" scales, or concrete standards, to measure specific beliefs and policy positions over time, and (2) "relative" scales to measure beliefs and positions that are *relative to the status quo*. As in survey questionnaires, such scale construction allows the variables to be analyzed *as if* the data were interval level (Torgerson, 1958; Nunnally, 1978).

An abbreviated version of the coding frame for the Tahoe project is included in Figure A.1 (see end of Methodological Appendix). The deep core variables are identified in Section A, the policy core variables in Section B, and the secondary aspects in Section C. Section C is further divided into subsections designed to capture beliefs pertaining to: (1) perceptions regarding specific policy areas (e.g., water quality, land-use planning, property rights), (2) the evaluation of governmental institutions and interest groups, and (3) selected recurring issues regarding the TRPA. The coding frame for the OCS project had a very similar structure.

In addition to variables pertaining to beliefs, a variety of supplemental data was collected in the coding frame, including the date (year and month) of the hearings, the name and affiliation of the person testifying, and the identity of the coder. Finally, a "type" value was included to indicate whether the subject represented a private firm, trade (or economic) group or association, other interest group, or federal, state, or local government agency.

The OCS project required a coding frame of about 113 items; for the Tahoe project more than 200 items were included. In both codeforms a large majority of the items (70% in the Tahoe form, 66% in the OCS form) regarded the more specific secondary aspects of the belief system. In other words, the vast majority of the topics discussed in these policy areas would have been completely neglected in political scientists' typical models of elite belief systems, which consist of a few basic values, partisan affiliation, and then specific policy preferences (Sabatier and Hunter, 1989).

Developing a coding frame is an arduous task because it requires the researcher to have a thorough understanding of the issues that arose and the major positions taken throughout the period under study. Needless to say, coding frames typically go through several iterations as their preliminary applications to the material under investigation repeatedly uncover new items or positions that merit inclusion or refinement. The codeforms developed for the OCS and Tahoe projects took approximately a year to develop and suffered numerous revisions in the process of being fleshed out and refined.

### Validity

One of the major concerns with content analysis of this kind is the validity of the coded results: How does the researcher know if the speakers are expressing their "true" opinions? Some elements of this topic—such as the extent to which speakers "tailor" their arguments to fit a specific audience—have been investigated (Miller and Siegelman, 1978; Goggin, 1984). Several aspects of the use of public documents serve to mitigate the effects of such contextual positioning, however. First, as Goggin (1984:377–379) has shown, the propensity to alter beliefs to fit an audience diminishes as one moves from the general public to narrower sets of elites. The scope of the audience to whom the typical public document is addressed—particularly in the case of testimony before legislative committees—would seem to be restricted almost entirely to members of the policy subsystem. In addition, in the context of the policy subsystems, there is a reasonable incentive for representatives to adopt and maintain consistent beliefs because inconsistency may result in lost credibility and support (Moe, 1980). Subsystem members who plan to remain active within the subsystem for any reasonable period of time would presumably seek to avoid inconsistencies that would damage their credibility.

Even if such tailoring takes place, the problems with content analysis of public documents are probably no more serious than in survey questionnaires. At least the content analyst *knows* the (official) source of the statements coded—which is certainly more than can be said for mail or telephone surveys, where anyone at the respondent's address may be the actual source. In addition, hearings (like personal interviews) afford the opportunity for someone to question or probe suspect responses— which again is more than can be said for mailed questionnaires. Finally, content analysis certainly allows subjects to provide their own frame of reference which is not true of closed-ended questionnaires. Part of the difficulty of developing a coding frame, in fact, can be attributed to the need to continually revise its content to incorporate new frames of reference until the researcher decides that "enough is enough." Even after a "final" frame has been developed, revisions can still be made (and were in our studies) if coders report anomalies serious enough to warrant going back and redoing previously coded testimonies; here again, content analysis is probably superior to mailed questionnaires.

A final virtue of content analysis of the kind proposed here is that the data generated permit at least a partial test of the hypothesis that the content of public documents will vary according to the perceived audience. First, because the data represent expression of beliefs over time, it is possible to assess the degree to which expressed beliefs vary according to changes in the audience. In the OCS project, for example, the hearings spanned a period of time in which the incumbent president changed from Republican to Democrat and back again. As was seen in Chapter 8, while policy beliefs of representatives of government agencies *did* evidence significant swings over that period, the relative position of beliefs of representatives of major interest groups remained remarkably stable. Second, it is possible to track the positions of specific individuals who switch affiliations—that is, who leave one group to act as representative for another—in order to assess how their expressed beliefs change. Our experience suggests that such representatives are more likely to suppress statement of some beliefs (resulting in a "missing" code for that category) than they are to change the content of their expressed beliefs.

In sum, while there is cause for some caution regarding the validity of beliefs expressed in public documents, there is also cause for confidence that expressed beliefs reasonably depict true beliefs. Recent research suggests that these problems are not overwhelming for documents of the kind coded here and may well be less severe than those that plague telephone and mail surveys. Moreover, the data certainly allow for tests of problems regarding the effect of contextual tailoring on the content of expressed beliefs.

### Intercoder Reliability

The length and complexity of the coding frames can lead to some serious intercoder reliability problems. Standard reliability tests (Holsti, 1969; Tinsley and Weiss, 1975; Mitchell, 1979; Krippendorff, 1980) are inappropriate for data that include a high percentage of "absent" value codes, because to include them may inflate the coefficient of reliability. However, to omit the "absent" values fails to acknowledge that to agree not to code an item is also an important part of reliability.

Our approach has been to distinguish between (1) the decision to code an item as having been discussed in a testimony and (2) the numeric value given to an item. This procedure permits us to use the most straightforward measures of reliability—the percentage of intercoder agreement—while distinguishing between error that stems from decisions to code and from differences in imputed code values.

The overall intercoder reliability levels, measured as the percentage agreement on decisions to code *and* on the numeric value given, were 84% for the OCS project and 88% for the Tahoe project.

*The Decision to Code.* Our experience indicates that the greatest problem with the coding process lies with the decision to code an item. Coders must determine whether a portion of the subject's testimony relates to one of the 100 to 200 items in the coding frame. Obtaining and maintaining intercoder reliability has proved difficult because coders may differ greatly in their willingness to make inferences—that is, to "translate" the subject's testimony into the language of the coding frame.

Initial intercoder reliability tests highlighted the problem of agreement over decisions to code. In response, we initiated a process involving all the coders in periodic reliability tests, discussion of coding discrepancies, redesign (where necessary) of coding elements, and retest. In order to further reduce discrepancies in the decision to code, coders were enjoined to make only conservative inferences and required to document all codes with page and line numbers. Finally, it has proved valuable to have periodic "recalibrations" among coders in which several testimonies are coded by all coders and the discrepancies identified and discussed. Not only does recalibration provide an ongoing assessment of intercoder reliability, but it refreshes the coders on appropriate procedures for deciding when and how to code. Our rule of thumb is to reassess reliability on every twentieth testimony.

The results of these efforts have proved encouraging. For the OCS project, an intercoder reliability check of two coders on three testimonies, involving 339 items in all, resulted in agreement to code 85% of the time. Had code values been assigned randomly, "agreements to code" would have been expected only 72% of the time. For the Tahoe project, which used three coders and involved about 420 items, a still more impressive agreement to code of 89% was achieved in a set of two testimonies. Had code values been randomly assigned, "agreements to code" would have been expected only 59% of the time.

*Numeric Code Values.* Once a decision has been made by all coders to code a portion of testimony, the coding frame has proved highly reliable. When all coders agreed to code, agreement on the numeric value $(+/- 1)$ was over 97% for the OCS project and 80% on the Tahoe project. If all *pairs* of coders are counted, the Tahoe project obtained agreement $(+/- 1)$ 91% of the time. These high levels of reliability give us confidence that, once a decision is made to code, appropriately trained coders are highly likely to produce replicable results.

Summary results of the intercoder reliability tests and, for comparison, the results to be expected if code values were to be randomly assigned are shown in Table A.1.

TABLE A.1  Results of Intercoder Reliability Tests:  Actual Versus Expected-Random Results

|  | OCS Project | | Tahoe Project | |
|---|---|---|---|---|
| Number of codable elements | 339 | | 417 | |
| Number of coders | 2 | | 3 | |
|  | Actual | Random | Actual | Random |
| 3 coders agree to code |  |  |  |  |
| 3 codes similar ( + /-1) | NA | NA | 17 | (56) |
| 2 codes similar | NA | NA | 4 | (174) |
| 3 codes differ (> 1) | NA | NA | 0 | (12) |
| 2 coders agree to code |  |  |  |  |
| 2 codes similar | 83 | (122) | 24 | (75) |
| 2 codes differ | 2 | (113) | 1 | (69) |
| Only one coder codes | 51 | (94) | 21 | (29) |
| All coders agree not to code | 203 | (10) | 350 | (2) |
| TOTAL | 339 | (339) | 417 | (417) |

## III. CONCLUSION

The application of the content analysis technique to the Tahoe and OCS projects presented in Chapters 8 and 9 illustrates some of the types of research that can be facilitated by the coding of public documents. Included are: (1) the tracking of policy beliefs of groups and individuals across time; (2) testing for the existence of coalitions and coalition stability over time within policy subsystems; (3) changes in the level of advocacy coalition polarization over time; and (4) assessment of the relative stability of beliefs of different kinds of groups within the subsystem. Overall, these results demonstrate that the content analysis approach developed here has a great deal to offer students of long-term policy change.

FIGURE A.1   Coding Guidelines (11-7-86)

CODING GUIDELINES (11-7-86)

Theoretical Context
    The basic purpose of this study is to examine the content and the stability
of elite belief systems over time, and to test the proposition that people who
agree on specific policy positions of considerable importance will be members of
the same advocacy coalition--rather than simply members of a "coalition of
convenience."

Code Form Organization
    The code form is organized around the three levels of belief system
structure: A.Core Beliefs B.Policy Core and C.Secondary/Instrumental Beliefs.
(Refer to Sabatier Table 3, Structure of Belief Systems of Policy Elites).   The
ultimate values and ontological assumptions are found in the Core Beliefs (Deep
Core), these are viewed as logically prior to governmental intervention.   The
Policy Beliefs (Policy Core) consist of the fundamental normative conflicts,
causal assumptions and perceived performance gaps which are the subject of
policy disputes and can relate only to specific issues.   Secondary/Instrumental
Beliefs include perceived causal relationships instrumental to policy core,
perceived states of world (values of important variables at a particular point
in time), general policy positions (especially on matters instrumental to the
policy core), specific policy positions related to the policy matter (e.g. a
bill) under discussion at the hearing.

People to Be Coded
    Code only representatives of important organizations and individuals who
appear in several  hearings (i.e. those from the "political elite" list).
Remember that we are interested in important policy elites, not every Tom, Dick,
and Harry who shows up at hearings.  With respect to unaffiliated individuals:
when in doubt: do NOT code.

Spokesman
    If the person claims to be an official spokesman, code as YES.  If the
person claims NOT to be an official spokesman, code as NO. Otherwise code as DK
for don't know.

Affiliation
    Code stated affiliation. Note: for TRPA board members, list their non-TRPA
affiliation if any as well.

Coding Logistics
        Read all introductory materials for each hearing.
        Choose appropriate number on the scale of one to five for each category.
        Missing data/no information is coded as 0.
        Every blank must be filled in; using lines through a row (i.e. for 0's) is not
            acceptable--each blank must be coded separately.
        Refer to the original long codeform for elaboration of categories on the
            short codeform version.
        Along the margin, list page number and line each time a given
            category is mentioned with codable information.  For example, if decline
            in water quality was mentioned on page 20, line 28, in the left-hand
            margin by category C1 Water Quality at Lake Tahoe, code 20.28. If there
            are no line numbers, use paragraph numbers instead.

1

Don't code statements that appear to be typos or are in any other way incoherent. This includes "misinformation statements" (for example, calling runoff water "ground water").

Hearings occasionally have pages missing; simply code what is available and make a note on the codeform sheet as to what page is missing.

All coders must be familiar with Tahoe history. Coders should read and refer to the Tahoe History by Wes Ingram.

## General Coding Rules

BE CONSERVATIVE.

If you can't refer to a specific statement do NOT code it. You must give a specific citation (page and line number) for every non-zero code you choose.

As a general rule, "1" and "5" are coded only with EXPLICIT mention. Endpoints 1 and 5 are always extremes. In your mind preface the given statement on the short form with a VERY or EXTREMELY or GREATLY etc. Again, for further clarification of the numerical scale of a given category refer to the long form where the options are spelled out in more detail.

Under certain categories, it is possible to choose a code of "8". This code means that the author has expressed uncertainty about an outcome. The speaker must expressly acknowledge ignorance, or say there is a need for more research or demonstration projects. This category should NOT be used when you are uncertain or when the speaker is vague; it is reserved for specific mention of uncertainty.

When determining if and where to code a particular statement remember the statement must be close to verbatim; it should contain wording similar to the category. Always choose the more specific category. For example BMP's are coded under choice of erosion control methods where BMP's are listed as a choice and not under a more general category of technology. Another example is a general statement about being an environmentalist, which should be coded under categories specifically referring to the environment, such as magnitude of threat, and not under the general category of humans and nature where an appropriate statement to code would contain words about the RELATIONSHIP between humans and nature, such as humans should be stewards. However, if a speaker mentions two or more specific aspects of a general category, code the statement in the general category as well.

The section on Policy Core ...B...is for GENERAL statements only. If the statement would fit in a specific category, code in the section on Secondary Beliefs...C...which is for SPECIFIC statements. (General statements may be specific to Tahoe, but not about a specific policy). General statements may be subsystem specific (i.e. refer only to Tahoe), but not limited to a specific policy.

Don't code things from a "laundry list"; to code a specific item there must be further elaboration on it than in a passing mention in a long list.

Local statements concerning EITHER local governments or local communities or local businesses all can be coded where ever the opportunity to code local occurs (even if the codeform category specifies local government). Local governments include PUDs except in category C5De.

2

Specific Guidelines

Categories Denoted with *retro,pro,dk.
    Determine whether the statement is retrospective (code as R), prospective
(code as P), or don't know (code as DK). Place this letter code to the right of
the number code you have given to that particular category. For example if
future impacts of casinos on the economy was mentioned, choose the appropriate
code, e.g. 3, and next to it put a P for prospective: 3 P. Note: retrospective
refers to "has been and still is". RETRO/PRO/DK two situations: 1)a person makes
a statement referring to both the past and the future, code it as retro 2)a
person makes a statement referring to both the past and the future but with
opposite opinions (i.e. one negative, one positive), code it as retro and code
the opinion attached to the retro statement.

        Under Performance Evaluation (C5D):
code under the PAST option always (and leave the other blank), unless there is a
significant difference in the evaluation of the past and expectations for the future.
When past or present evaluations are made, code under the PAST category. When BOTH
the past and future are mentioned AND the evaluation is significantly DIFFERENT,
then code under both past and future.

Core Beliefs
    Categories under the heading of Core Beliefs generally refer to positions
pertaining to more than one policy area.

Absolute and Relative Scales
    Absolute scales should be used when a statement is not situation specific.
For example, "all government should be local government." Relative scales on
the other hand are comparative, referring to the status quo as the baseline.
For example, "we need more local control (than at present)." This may be an
implicit comparison.

If They Say It, Code It
    This refers to two situations specifically: 1)in opening statements when a
person characterizes themselves. For example, "I am an environmentalist" and
2)when an issue is mentioned. For example, a reference to traffic congestion.
In both of these instances a code of 3 for "mentions" would be appropriate. If
the speaker further elaborates, code accordingly.

Salience and Magnitude of Threat to Values
    Salience of the value refers to the importance accorded it by the speaker.
Salience refers to the speaker's personal attachment to a value--not merely
mentioning it in conjunction with others' statements. Repeated mention of a
given value in specific contexts is sufficient for a "3" code (repeated mention
means about 3 times per 5 pages). Also; mentioning at least two different
specific issues is sufficient for it to be coded in B9 core values. For
example, mentioning visual pollution and water pollution would be sufficient to
code under environmental quality here. Magnitude of threat refers to the
perceived magnitude of threat TO the value. Magnitude is the perceived threat to
the value regardless of whether it is held by the speaker. Coding magnitude is
NOT dependent upon coding salience. One can code one without coding the other.

Magnitude and Evaluation of Impact (C3 e-g)
    As above, coding either magnitude or evaluation is not dependent upon
coding the other.

3

**Basic Mechanism for Government Intervention (B3)**
The code "5" is used when the speaker chooses more than one mechanism for intervention. For example, coercion and government purchase could both be mentioned as intervention methods. When coding a "5", be sure to UNDERLINE the specific mechanisms that the speaker chose.

**Proper Distribution of Authority (B4)**
This can include conditional grants as a form of authority. However, if money (grants) but no involvement is sugggested, it should NOT be coded under B4.

**Core Values (B9)**
Requires explicit mention of a general proposition or major premise, NOT a specific policy or issue.

**Orientation on Substantive Policy Conflicts (B10)**
Must state a "tradeoff". If no tradeoff, the statement should be coded under "core values: salience and magnitude of threat" (B9).

**Negative Effect on Water Quality (C1B).**
When erosion or siltation is mentioned without specifying either development or roadways as the cause, code BOTH.

**Problems at Tahoe (C3A).** These are NOT limited to land use planning.

**job/business problems (C3Ac)**
If it mentions destruction of the economy, code as job/business problems.

**recreation areas (C3Af)**
Must mention outdoor, public recreation, beach, type recreation (as opposed to casinos).

**Impacts of Land Use Planning and Regulation (C3F)**
Require GENERAL statements about planning and regulation. Specific statements should be coded elsewhere. Secondly they must state "it will happen" or "it has happened" as opposed to "it would be nice if it happens". These categories are intended to deal with perceived causal relationships, not "wish" statements. LAND USE PLANNING includes traditional controls such as zoning regulations for type and quality of development. It also includes BMPs for housing, regulating construction, and public works remedial erosion control.

**Impacts of Planning and Regulation(C3G)**
Does not include sewage issues, this is specific to land use planning.

**General Orientation Towards Environmental Protection Measures(C3H)**
Includes any and all measures intended to protect the environment (including sewage export for example).

**Bailey Land Classification (C3K)**
Can be mentioned as land capability coverage, fragile lands and erosion (as long as you know they're talking about Bailey).

**Regional Agencies (C5C)**
Domination of TRPA by California or Nevada; do NOT include statements referring to the dual majority vote rule.

4

<u>Performance</u> <u>Evaluation</u> (C5D)
    1) Can't just <u>mention</u> a government agency or interest group.
    2) When a speaker suggests giving more authority to an agency this is
sufficient for a 4 code    (mention of just <u>cooperation</u> however is not).

TRPA ADDENDUM

(must be filled out for ALL speakers at a hearing about the TRPA)

See the appropriate hearing for explanations and text of specific bills.

Any testimony in a hearing concerned with the TRPA must be coded in
    the addendum, even if all of the codes would be zero.

In the space available for comments, please mention specific revisions
    suggested and/or specific complaints, observations etc.

Just use your judgement concerning the magnitude of support or opposition
    to a given bill.  Referral to anything mentioned under position on
    specific issues in the addendum, for example, may be considered as
    "major" revisions.

5

```
              HEARINGS CODEFORM (short version 11/11/86) coder_____
speaker_____affiliation_____
hearing_____ date of hearing_____ spokesman_____
```

### A.CORE BELIEFS

**A1.RELATIONSHIP BETWEEN HUMANS AND NATURE**
1.humans complete dominion 3.wise steward 5.humans as part of nature    _____

**A2.PRIORITY OF VALUES** (rank each value separately)
[1.not at all important 3.moderately important 5.extremely important]

| | |
|---|---|
| a.individual liberty _____ | e.economic well-being |
| b.sanctity of contracts _____ | f.knowledge _____ |
| c.beauty _____ | g.preserve natural environment _____ |
| d.security _____ | |

**A3.BASIC CRITERIA FOR DISTRIBUTIVE JUSTICE**
Absolute Scale     1.pure egoist 3.only certain groups 5.greatest good   _____
Relative Scale     1.egoist 3.status quo 5.general welfare   _____

======================================================================================

### B.POLICY BELIEFS/POLICY CORE

**B1.ABILITY OF TECHNOLOGY TO HELP SOCIETY TO SOLVE PROBLEMS**
Absolute Scale   1.techno optimism 3.can solve some 5.techno pessimism   8.UNC _____
Relative Scale   1.techno solutions 3.status quo 5.alternatives to tech  8.UNC _____

**B2.SCOPE OF GOVERNMENTAL VERSUS PRIVATE ACTIVITY**
Absolute Scale        1.exclusively market 3.balance 5.exclusively government _____
Relative Scale        1.much more market 3.status quo 5.much more government _____

**B3.BASIC POLICY MECHANISM FOR GOVERNMENTAL INTERVENTION**
Abs.   1.information 2.incentives/grants 3.coercion 4.gov purchase 5.more than one_____
Rel.   1.more voluntary 3.status quo 5.more coercion _____

**B4.PROPER DISTRIBUTION OF AUTHORITY AMONG VARIOUS LEVELS**
Absolute Scale             Primary locus of government authority _____
[1.local 2.within state regional 3.state 4.bistate regions 5.federal]
Relative Scale [1.much less authority 3.status quo 5. much more authority]

| | |
|---|---|
| a.local _____ | d.bistate regions _____ |
| b.regional within a state _____ | e.federal _____ |
| c.state _____ | |

**B5.DEMOCRATIC ACCOUNTABILITY VERSUS IMPARTIAL EXPERTISE OR APPOINTED OFFICIALS**
Absolute 1.only demo accountable 3.balance  5.only experts/appointed   _____
Relative 1.much more demo accountable 3.status quo 5.much more experts/appointed_____

**B6.CRITICAL DISTRIBUTIONAL ISSUE: WHOSE WELFARE SHOULD COUNT?**
Absolute 1.only directly and materially affected 5.future generations   _____
Relative 1.directly and materially affected 3.status quo 5.future generations  _____

**B7.DESIRED LEVEL OF POPULAR PARTICIPATION**
Absolute  1.only selected  3.all interested 5.gov encourage participation   _____
Relative  1.much less participation 3.status quo 5.much more participation   _____

**B8.UNIQUENESS OF TAHOE**
1.just a lake 3.doesn't justify extraordinary control 5.unique irreplaceable
so should be preserved                                      _____

**B9.CORE VALUES: SALIENCE AND MAGNITUDE OF THREAT**
Salience of Value     1.not at all important 3.average 5.extremely important
Magnitude of Threat   1.no problem 3.fairly important/mentions 5.extremely serious

| | | | |
|---|---|---|---|
| a.property rights _____ _____ | | c.economic/fiscal viability _____ _____ |
| b.environmental/aesthetic quality _____ _____ | | |

**B10.ORIENTATION ON SUBSTANTIVE POLICY CONFLICTS/TRADEOFFS**
    1.property rights   3.equally important 5.environmental quality    \_\_\_\_\_
    1.economic development 3.equally important 5.environmental quality   \_\_\_\_\_

==================================================================================

C.SECONDARY/INSTRUMENTAL BELIEFS

## C1.WATER QUALITY AT LAKE TAHOE

    **C1A.WATER QUALITY AT LAKE TAHOE**   *retro,pro,dk
        1.rapidly declining   3.remains the same   5.improving   8.UNCERTAIN   \_\_\_\_\_

    **C1B.PERCEIVED NEGATIVE EFFECT ON WATER QUALITY**   *retro,pro,dk
        [1.not at all important 3.fairly important/mentions 5.very important  8.UNC]

| | |
|---|---|
| a.erosion and siltation from development  \_\_\_\_\_ | f.natural processes  \_\_\_\_\_ |
| b.erosion and siltation from roadways  \_\_\_\_\_ | g.ground water  \_\_\_\_\_ |
| c.atmospheric deposition  \_\_\_\_\_ | h.fertilizer  \_\_\_\_\_ |
| d.changes in lake level  \_\_\_\_\_ | i.other  \_\_\_\_\_ |
| e.sewage  \_\_\_\_\_ | |

    **C1C.EFFECTIVENESS OF REMEDIAL EROSION MEASURES** (housing)   *retro,pro,dk
        1.will not work at all 3.can solve fairly sig amount 5.can solve all  8.UNC  \_\_\_\_\_

    **C1D.EFFECTS OF SEWERING THE BASIN** Retrospective
        1.reduced the nutrient load 3.no effect 5.increased nutrient load   8.UNC  \_\_\_\_\_

    **C1E.PRESCRIBED STRATEGY FOR WATER QUALITY AGENCIES**
        1.not needed 3.education and solve problems 5.enforce regulations  \_\_\_\_\_

    **C1F.SEWAGE EXPORT** Prospective
        1.negative impacts  2.unnecessary  4.necessary  5.essential  8.UNC  \_\_\_\_\_

    **C1G.EVALUATION OF 208 PLAN**  \_\_\_\_\_
        1.don't need a plan
        2.support 1978 TRPA board proposals
        3.support 1977 JB Gilbert proposals for TRPA
        4.1981 TRPA compromise, Nevada case by case
        5.support 1980 SWRCB Basin plan
        6.1980 plan is still not strong enough

## C2.PROPERTY RIGHTS AT LAKE TAHOE

    **C2A.COMPARATIVE MAGNITUDE OF THREAT TO PROPERTY RIGHTS AT TAHOE**   *retro,pro,dk
        1.much less than elsewhere 3.same as elsewhere 5.much more than elsewhere  \_\_\_\_\_

    **C2B.TRENDS IN PROPERTY RIGHTS AT TAHOE**   1.much better 3.the same  5.much worse \_\_\_\_\_

    **C2C.POSITION ON BUYOUTS/INVERSE CONDEMNATION**  \_\_\_\_\_
        1.buyouts not needed to compensate for land use restrictions
        2.undermines regulation
        3.not legally required but politically desirable
        4.highly desirable or legally required
        5.legally required by the 14th amendment at full market

    **C2D.POSITION ON SPECIFIC BUYOUT PROGRAMS**
        [1.strongly opposed 3.mixed/no clear position 5.strongly in favor]

| | |
|---|---|
| a.Burton-Santini federal program  \_\_\_\_\_ | d.Scenic Area Bill  \_\_\_\_\_ |
| b.California's 1982 Tahoe Bond Act  \_\_\_\_\_ | e.other  \_\_\_\_\_ |
| c.1980 208 buyout plan  \_\_\_\_\_ | |

    **C2E.POSITION ON SPECIFIC PURCHASES**
        [1.strongly opposed 3.mixed/no clear position 5.strongly in favor]

| | |
|---|---|
| a.Jennings Casino  \_\_\_\_\_ | c.The Nevada State Park  \_\_\_\_\_ |
| b.Kahle Casino  \_\_\_\_\_ | d.California State Parks  \_\_\_\_\_ |

C3.LAND USE PLANNING
   C3A.  **PROBLEMS AT TAHOE**      *retro,pro,dk
      [1.not a problem at all  3.fairly important/mentions  5.extremely serious problem]
        a.visual pollution            _____    d.housing shortage      _____
        b.urbanization/population      _____    e.sewage                _____
        c.job/business opportunities   _____    f.recreation areas      _____
                                         g.air quality           _____

   C3B.  **ECONOMIC IMPACTS OF EFFORTS TO CONTROL EROSION BY REGULATING CONSTRUCTION** _____
      *retro,pro,dk    1.net negative impacts
                 3.no impacts or balanced impacts
                 5.net positive impacts (water quality promotes tourism)
                 8.UNCERTAIN

   C3C.  **EFFECTS OF ENVIRONMENTAL REGULATION ON BASIN ECONOMY**   *retro.pro,dk
      [1.very great (negative)  3.balanced  5.very great (positive)   8.UNC]
        a.construction industry      _____    d.property values   _____
        b.tourist industry/casinos    _____    e.in general        _____
        c.tax revenues               _____

   C3D.  **IMPACTS OF CASINOS**    *retro,pro,dk
      magnitude of impact 1.nonexistent 3.fairly important/mentions 5.very great 8.UNC
      evaluation of impact  1.very negative 3.mixed 5.very positive
    a.economic impacts (private economy)
    b.fiscal impacts (tax base and services)  _____        _____
    c.social and cultural impacts              _____        _____
    d.environmental impacts                    _____        _____
    e.overall impacts                          _____        _____

   C3E.  **POSSIBLE PERVERSE EFFECTS OF LAND USE CONTROL**      *retro,pro,dk
        [1.strongly disagree  5.strongly agree   8.UNCERTAIN]
        a.accelerated development        _____    d.depressed land values _____
        b.displace development           _____    e.rich person's haven   _____
        c.created unsightly foundations  _____

   C3F.  **IMPACTS OF LAND USE PLANNING AND REGULATION**     *retro,pro,dk
      magnitude of impact 1.nonexistent 3.fairly important/mentions 5.very great 8.UNC
      evaluation of impact   1.very negative 3.mixed 5.very positive
    a.air quality        _____    _____    f.transportation    _____    _____
    b.water quality      _____    _____    g.recreation        _____    _____
    c.scenic beauty      _____    _____    h.reducing sprawl   _____    _____
    d.economic viability _____    _____    i.population growth  _____    _____
    e.housing            _____    _____

   C3G.  **ORIENTATION TOWARDS ENVIRONMENTAL PROTECTION MEASURES**       _____
        1.measures are unnecessary and unwarranted
        2.certain measures necessary but existing ones are too extreme/irrational
        4.existing/proposed measures are fair and reasonable
        5.existing/proposed measures are insufficient to protect the environment

   C3H.  **DEVELOPMENT CONTROLS IN TAHOE BASIN** (prescriptive)       _____
        1.undesirable  3.location and quality  5.reduce rate of development

   C3I.  **CHOICE OF METHODS TO PREVENT SILTATION**       _____
        1.regulation undesirable
        2.building okay using BMPs (plus regulating lake level and revegetation)
        3.some regulation necessary
        4.stringent regulation of construction
        5.prohibit virtually all building in basin

**C3J. BAILEY LAND CLASSIFICATION SYSTEM** _____
    1.incompetent/undesirable 3.principle okay 4.case by case 5.apply parcel by parcel

**C3K. EVALUATION OF IMPORTANT DOCUMENTS** [1.very negative 3.mixed 5.very positive]

| | | | |
|---|---|---|---|
| a.1963 McGaughy (sewage) report | _____ | e.1978 TRPA 208 Plan | _____ |
| b.1971 TRPA Plan | | f.1980 SWRCB 208 Plan | _____ |
| c.1975 CTRPA Plan | _____ | g.1982 Thresholds TRPA | _____ |
| d.Proposed 1976 TRPA Plan | _____ | h.Scenic Area/Lake Shore | _____ |

## C4.TRANSPORTATION

**C4A. TRANSPORTATION**    *retro,pro,dk
    1.not a problem 3.fairly important/mentions 5.very serious problem  _____

**C4B. FACTORS AFFECTING TAHOE AIR QUALITY**    *retro,pro,dk
    [1.no effect 3.contributor 5.major contributor 8.UNCERTAIN]
      a.in basin autos  _____     c.out of basin  _____
      b.in basin other  _____

**C4C. SOURCES OF TRANSPORTATION PROBLEMS**    *retro,pro,dk
    [1.not a source 3.fairly important/mentions 5.sole source 8.UNCERTAIN]
      a.casinos  _____     c.recreational tourists  _____
      b.agency restrictions  _____     d.in basin residents  _____

**C4D. EFFECTS OF INCREASING HIGHWAY CAPACITY ON HIGHWAY CONGESTION**
    1.very negative effect 3.no effect 5.very positive effect   8.UNC  _____

**C4E. EXPANSION OF PUBLIC TRANSPORTATION SYSTEM**
    1.greatly reduce 3.present system adequate 5.greatly expand  _____

**C4F. FINANCING A PUBLIC TRANSPORTATION SYSTEM**
    [1.strongly oppose 3.mixed/no clear position 5.strongly support]
    a.property taxes _____    b.sales tax _____    c.user fee _____

**C4G. EXPANSION OF HIGHWAY SYSTEM**
    1.greatly reduce 3.present system adequate 5.greatly expand  _____

**C4H. POSITION ON SPECIFIC TRANSPORTATION PROPOSALS**
    [1.strongly oppose 3.mixed/no clear position 5.strongly support]
    a.parkway system with Emerald Bay bridge
    b.highway 50 bypass in SLT
    c.loop road around casinos
    d.Gianturco mass transit proposals
    e.Tahoe City bypass
    f.auto use fee or road toll for all visitors to the basin

## C5.EVALUATION OF GOVERNMENT BODIES AND INTEREST GROUPS

**C5A. LOCAL GOVERNMENT**    *retro,pro,dk
    [1.strongly disagree 3.mixed 5.strongly agree]
    a.Local government tax bases dependent upon land development     a_____
    b.Local governments have difficulty resisting political
      pressures for development     b_____
    c.Don't have the resources to deal with basin problems     c_____
    d.Local governments are too fragmented and/or distrustful of
      each other     d_____
    e.Local governments are democratically accountable     e_____
    f.Members are knowledgable because they are close to the situation     f_____
    g.Local governments good problem solvers     g_____

C5B. **STATE AND FEDERAL GOVERNMENT**    *retro,pro,dk
              [1.strongly disagree  3.mixed  5.strongly agree]
       a.State and federal governments are not democratically accountable    a____
       b.Only using Tahoe to run for higher office; responding
         to out-of-basin constituencies                                       b____
       c.Outsiders are unable to effectively implement policy                 c____
       d.State and federal officials are not really interested
         in solving the problem (just arguing about regulation)               d____
       e.Basin is a resource of importance to people beyond the local
         level and thus fed/state govs should be involved in a
         nonregulatory manner (including financial assistance)                e____
       f.Basin is a resource of importance to people beyond the
         local level so should be subjected to nonlocal control               f____
       g.State and federal officials do not have personal stakes
         and are therefore better able to take a long-term view               g____
       h.Tahoe is in two states so should have state and federal
         involvement                                                          h____
       i.Federal gov has substantial financial and property interests so
         should be involved                                                   i____

C5C. **REGIONAL AGENCIES (TRPA)**    *retro,pro,dk
              [1.strongly disagree  3.mixed  5.strongly agree]
       a.Regional agencies are not democratically accountable                 a____
       b.Regional agencies are too dominated by locals                        b____
       c.Regional agencies are too dominated by nonlocals                     c____
       d.Regional agencies are able to view the basin as a
         whole (consistent with the magnitude of the problem)                 d____
       e.Regional agencies include representatives of all
         affected/interested parties                                          e____
       f.Regional agencies can apply rules consistently throughout
         the basin                                                            f____
       g.TRPA too dominated by California                                     g____
       h.TRPA too dominated by Nevada                                         h____

C5D. **PERFORMANCE EVALUATION**   rank each based on past performance
              [1.very poor  3.mixed  5.excellent]                  PAST        FUTURE
       a.TRPA                                                      a____       a____
       b.CTRPA                                                     b____       b____
       c.SWRCB                                                     c____       c____
       d.EPA/federal pollution control agencies                   d____       d____
       e.local governments                                        e____       e____
       f.PUDs                                                      f____       f____
       g.Lahontan                                                  g____       g____
       h.forest service                                           h____       h____
       i.Nevada pollution control agencies                        i____       i____
       j.federal government                                       j____       j____
       k.State of Nevada                                          k____       k____
       l.State of California                                      l____       l____
       m.California Attorney General                              m____       m____
       n.League to Save Lake Tahoe                                n____       n____
       o.other environmental groups                               o____       o____
       p.Lake Tahoe Area Council                                  p____       p____
       q.property rights groups                                   q____       q____

# References

Aaron, Henry (1978). *Politics and the Professors.* Washington, D.C.: Brookings.
Abelson, Robert, et al. (1968). *Theories of Cognitive Consistency.* Chicago: Rand McNally.
Aberbach, J., Putnam, R., and Rockman, B. (1981). *Bureaucrats and Politicians in Western Democracies.* Cambridge, MA: Harvard Univ. Press.
Ackerman, Bruce, and Hassler, William (1981). *Clean Coal Dirty Air.* New Haven: Yale Univ. Press.
Adams, Walter, and Brock, James W. (1982). "Integrated Monopoly and Market Power: System Selling, Compatibility Standards, and Market Control," *Quarterly Review of Economics and Business* 22 (Winter 1982): 29–42.
Ajzen, Icek, and Fishbein, Martin (1980). *Understanding Attitudes and Predicting Social Behavior.* Englewood Cliffs: Prentice-Hall.
Aldenderfer, Mark, and Blashfield, Roger (1984). *Cluster Analysis.* Beverly Hills: Sage.
Almond, Gabriel, and Powell, G. Bingham (1978). *Comparative Politics,* 2d ed. Boston: Little, Brown.
Anderson, Douglas (1981). *Regulatory Politics and Electric Utilities.* Boston: Auburn.
Anderson, James (1979). *Public Policy Making,* 2d ed. New York: Holt, Rinehart, and Winston.
Angell, L., and Buseck, C. (1976). "An Exploratory Study of Vehicle Type in Alcohol Related Crashes," in Leonard Evans and Richard C. Schwing, eds., *Human Behavior and Traffic Safety.* New York: Plenum.
Anton, Thomas (1980). *Administered Politics.* Boston: Martinus Nijhoff.
————— (1989). *American Federalism and Public Policy: How the System Works.* New York: Random House.
Argyris, Chris, and Schon, Donald (1978). *Organizational Learning.* New York: Wiley.
Arrandale, Tom (1992). "The Mid-1ife Crisis of the Environmental Lobby," *Governing* (April): 32–36.
Artle, R., and Averous, C. (1975). "The Telephone System as a Public Good: Static and Dynamic Aspects," *Bell Journal of Economics* 4 (Spring 1975): 89–100.
Asher, Herbert (1976). *Presidential Elections and American Politics.* Homewood, IL: Dorsey Press.
Ashford, Douglas (1981a). *British Dogmatism and French Pragmatism.* London: George Allen & Unwin.
————— (1981b). *Policy and Politics in Britain.* Philadelphia: Temple Univ. Press.
Asmerom, H. K., Hoppe, R., and Jain, R. B. (1992). *Bureaucracy and Developmental Policies in the Third World.* Amsterdam: VU Univ. Press.
Axelrod, Robert, ed. (1976). *Structure of Decision.* Princeton: Princeton Univ. Press.

Bacharach, S. B. (1990). *Education Reform: Making Sense of It All*. Boston: Allyn & Bacon.

Bailey, Elizabeth (1979). "Reform from Within: Civil Aeronautics Board Policy, 1977–78," in Michael A. Crew, ed., *Problems in Public Utility Economics*, pp. 19–40. Lexington, MA: D.C. Heath.

Balbus, Isaac (1971). "The Concept of Interest in Pluralist and Marxian Analysis," *Politics and Society* 1 (February): 151–177.

Balz, Daniel (1974). "Economic Report: Summer Inflation Meetings Highlight More Questions than Answers," *National Journal Reports* 6 (October 5, 1974): 1503–1505.

Banfield, Edward (1980). "Policy Science as Metaphysical Madness," in *Policy Analysis, Bureaucrats, and Statesmen*. Washington, DC: American Enterprise Institute.

Bardach, Eugene (1977). *The Implementation Game: What Happens After a Bill Becomes a Law?* Cambridge, MA: MIT Press.

Barnes, Barry (1982). *T. S. Kuhn and Social Science*. New York: Columbia Univ. Press.

Barrett, Susan, and Fudge, Colin, eds. (1981). *Policy and Action*. London: Methuen.

Beck, Nathaniel (1982). "Presidential Influence on the Federal Reserve in the 1970s," *American Journal of Political Science* 26: 415–445.

Behrman, Bradley (1980). "Civil Aeronautics Board," in James Q. Wilson, ed., *The Politics of Regulation*. New York: Basic.

Belcourt, N. A. (1910). *Whitney Papers: Copy of Resolutions*. Toronto: Ontario Archives.

Bell, D. V. (1984). *Political Culture in Canada*, in M. S. Whittington and G. Williams, eds., *Canadian Politics in the 1980s*, 2d ed. Toronto: Methuen.

Bell, Daniel (1960). *The End of Ideology*. New York: Free Press.

Bentley, Arthur (1908). *The Process of Government*. Chicago: Univ. of Chicago Press.

Berger, C. (1970). *The Sense of Power*. Toronto: Univ. of Toronto Press.

Berman, Paul (1978). "Macro- and Micro-Implementation," *Public Policy* 26 (Spring): 165–179.

Bernstein, Marver (1955). *Regulating Business by Independent Commission*. Princeton: Princeton Univ. Press.

Berry, Jeffrey (1977). *Lobbying for the People*. Princeton: Princeton Univ. Press.

Beyer, Janice, and Trice, Harrison (1982). "The Utilization Process: A Conceptual Framework and Synthesis of Empirical Findings," *Administrative Science Quarterly* 27 (December): 591–622.

Boffey, Philip (1975). The Brain Bank of America. New York: McGraw-Hill.

Bosselman, Fred, and Callies, David (1971). *The Quiet Revolution in Land Use Control*. Washington, DC: Council on Environmental Quality.

Bradfield, Stephanie A. (1984). *Press Release on Imperial Irrigation District Decision*. Sacramento: California State Water Resources Control Board.

Brecht, Arnold (1959). *The Foundations of Twentieth Century Political Thought*. Princeton, NJ: Princeton Univ. Press.

Brewer, Garry (1973). *Politicians, Bureaucrats, and the Consultant*. New York: Basic Books.

———— (1974). "The Policy Sciences Emerge," *Policy Sciences* 15 (September): 239–244.

Brewer, Garry, and de Leon, Peter (1983). *Foundations of Policy Analysis*. Homewood: Dorsey.

Breyer, Stephen (1979). "Analyzing Regulatory Failure: Mismatches, Less Restrictive Alternatives and Reform," *Harvard Law Review* 92 (January): 547–609.

Bromley, Daniel (1989). *Economic Interests and Institutions: The Conceptual Foundations of Public Policy.* New York: Basil Blackwell.

Brown, Anthony E. (1985). "The Regulatory Policy Cycle and the Airline Deregulation Movement," *Social Science Quarterly* 66 (September): 552–563.

————— (1987). *The Politics of Airline Deregulation.* Knoxville: Univ. of Tennessee Press.

Browne, Eric (1970). *Coalition Theories.* Beverly Hills: Sage.

Browne, Eric, and Dreijamis, John, eds. (1982). *Government Coalitions in Western Democracies.* London: Longmans.

Bulmer, Martin (1980). *Social Research and Royal Commissions.* London: Allen and Unwin.

————— (1983). Symposium issue on "Social Science and Policy Making: The Use of Research by Government Commission," *American Behavioral Scientists* 26 (May/June): 555–600.

Burnham, Walter Dean (1970). *Critical Elections and the Mainsprings of American Politics.* New York: Norton.

Buttel, Frederick, and Flinn, William (1978). "The Politics of Environmental Concern," *Environment and Behavior* 10 (March): 17–36.

California Department of Water Resources (1976). *Water Conservation in California.* Bulletin #198. Sacramento: DWR.

————— (1977). *Key Elements—SB 346.* Sacramento: DWR.

————— (1978). *Delta Water Facilities: Bulletin #76.* Sacramento: California Department of Water Resources, July.

————— (1982a). *Department of Water Resources Position on Proposition 9 (SB 200).* Sacramento: DWR, April.

————— (1982b). *Policies and Goals for the Next Twenty Years.* Bulletin #4. Sacramento: DWR.

————— (1987). *California Water: Looking to the Future.* Sacramento: California Department of Water Resources.

California Legislature, Assembly Committee on Natural Resources (1964). *Regional Planning in the Lake Tahoe Basin, Hearing,* Brockway Springs, CA, September, 10–11, 1964.

————— (1972). *Regional Planning in the Lake Tahoe Basin, Hearing,* Stateline, NV, December 18–19, 1972.

California Legislature, Senate Select Committee on Tahoe (1984). *Land Acquisition and Land Use in the Lake Tahoe Basin, Hearing Transcript,* Sacramento, March 6, 1984.

California State Water Resources Control Board (1980). *Lake Tahoe 208 Water Quality Control Plan Hearings,* Sacramento, March 7, 8, 10, 26, April 21, and October 25, 1980.

Cameron, James (1978). "Ideology and Policy Termination: Restructuring California's Mental Health System," in Judith May and Aaron Wildavsky, eds. *The Policy Cycle,* pp. 301–328. Beverly Hills: Sage.

Campbell, Donald (1977). "Reforms as Experiments," in Francis Caro, ed., *Readings in Evaluation Research,* pp. 172–204. New York: Russell Sage.

Caplan, Nathan et al. (1975). *The Use of Social Science Knowledge in Policy Decisions at the National Level.* Ann Arbor: Institute for Social Research.

Cardozo, Michael H. (1981). "The Federal Advisory Committee Act in Operation," *Administrative Law Review* 33 (Winter 1981): 1–62.

Caves, Richard E. (1962). *Air Transport and Its Regulators: An Industry Study.* Cambridge: Harvard Univ. Press.

Chubb, John E., and Moe, Terry M. (1990). *Politics, Markets, and America's Schools.* Washington, DC: Brookings.

Cibulka, J. G., Mawhinney, H. B., and Paquette, J. (1991). *Rationality and Progress in North American Education, 1967–1991: Problems of Administration and Governance.* Paper presented at the 1991 Annual Meeting of the American Educational Research Association, Chicago, IL.

Cobb, Roger (1973). "The Belief Systems Perspective," *Journal of Politics* 35 (February): 121–153.

Cobb, Roger, et al. (1976). "Agenda Building as a Comparative Process," *American Political Science Review* 70 (March): 126–138.

Cochrane, W., and Orcutt, G. H. (1949). "Application of Least Squares Regression to Relationships Containing Autocorrelated Error Terms," *Journal of the American Statistical Association* 44: 32–61.

Cohen, J. (1985). "Presidential Control of Independent Regulatory Commissions Through Appointment: The Case of ICC," *Administration and Society* 17 (May): 61–70.

Cohen, Richard (1977a). "Regulatory Focus: Making a Point on Appointment," *National Journal Reports* (February 19, 1977): 291.

———— (1977b). "Regulatory Report: Airline Deregulation Is Not Yet Cleared for Take-Off," *National Journal Reports* 9 (July 30, 1977): 1193–1195.

———— (1992). *Washington at Work: Back Rooms and Clean Air.* New York: Macmillan.

Congrès d'éducation des Canadiens-français d'Ontario (1910). *Rapport officiel.* Hawkesbury, ON: Congrès d'éducation.

Conover, Pamela J., and Feldman, Stanley (1984). "How People Organize the Political World: A Schematic Model," *American Journal of Political Science* 28 (February): 95–126.

Converse, Phillip (1964). "The Nature of Belief Systems in Mass Publics," in David Apter, ed., *Ideology and Discontent*, pp. 206–261. New York: Free Press.

Converse, Philip, and Pierce, Roy (1986). *Political Representation in France.* Cambridge, MA: Harvard Univ. Press.

Cook, Brian (1986). "Characteristics of Administrative Decisions About Regulatory Form," *American Politics Quarterly* 14 (October): 294–316.

———— (1988). *Bureaucratic Politics and Regulatory Reform: The EPA and Emissions Trading.* Westport, CT: Greenwood Press.

Cook, Brian, and Wood, B. Dan (1989). "Principal-Agent Models of Political Controls of Bureaucracy," *American Political Science Review* 83 (September): 965–978.

Costantini, Edmond, and Hanf, Kenneth (1973). *The Environmental Impulse and Its Competitors.* Davis, CA: Institute of Ecology.

Cushman, Robert (1963). *Leading Constitutional Decisions*, 12th ed. New York: Appleton-Century-Crofts.

Dahl, Robert (1971). *Polyarchy.* New Haven: Yale Univ. Press.

Davies, J. Clarence (1970). *The Politics of Pollution.* New York: Pegasus.

Davis, Charles, and Davis, Sandra (1988). "Analyzing Change in Public Lands Policymaking: From Subsystems to Advocacy Coalitions," *Policy Studies Journal* 17 (Fall): 3–24.

de Haven-Smith, Lance, and Van Horn, Carl (1984). "Subgovernment Conflict in Public Policy," *Policy Studies Journal* 12 (June): 627–642.

de Leon, Peter (1988). *Advice and Consent: The Development of the Policy Sciences.* New York: Russell Sage.

de Swann, Abram (1973). *Coalition Theories and Cabinet Formations.* Amsterdam: Elsevier.

Derthick, Martha (1979). *Policymaking for Social Security.* Washington, DC: Brookings.

Derthick, Martha, and Quirk, Paul (1985). *The Politics of Deregulation.* Washington, DC: Brookings.
Dewey, John (1938). *Logic: The Theory of Inquiry.* New York: Holt, Rinehart and Winston.
Dodd, Lawrence (1976). *Coalitions in Parliamentary Governments.* Princeton: Princeton Univ. Press.
Dodd, Lawrence, and Schott, Richard (1979). *Congress and the Administrative State.* New York: John Wiley.
Doggan, Mattei (1975). *The Mandarins of Western Europe.* New York: Wiley.
Dominion Bureau of Statistics (1935). *The Canada Yearbook, 1934–35.* Ottawa: King's Printer.
Douglas, J. (1976). *Investigative Social Research.* Beverly Hills: Sage.
Douglas, Mary, and Wildavsky, Aaron (1982). *Risk and Culture: An Essay on the Selection of Technical and Environmental Dangers.* Berkeley: Univ. of California Press.
Downing, Paul (1984). *Environmental Economics and Policy.* Boston: Little, Brown.
Downs, Anthony (1966). *Inside Bureaucracy.* Boston: Little, Brown.
——— (1972). "Up and Down With Ecology—The Issue Attention Cycle," *The Public Interest* 28 (Summer): 38–50.
Dunbar, Robert C. (1983). *Forging New Rights in Western Waters.* Lincoln: University of Nebraska Press.
Dunlap, Riley, and Mertig, Angela (1992). *American Environmentalism.* Philadelphia: Taylor and Francis.
Dunleavy, Michael (1981). *The Politics of Mass Housing in Britain, 1945–75.* Oxford: Clarendon Press.
Dunn, William (1980). "The Two-Communities Metaphor and Models of Knowledge Use," *Knowledge* 1 (June): 515–536.
——— (1982). "The Theory of Exceptional Clinicians." Paper presented at the Conference on the Production of Useful Knowledge, Univ. of Pittsburgh, October 28–30, 1982.
Easton, David (1965). *A Systems Analysis of Political Life.* New York: John Wiley.
"Education in Canada and the Charter of Rights and Freedoms" (1986) [Special issue]. *Canadian Journal of Education* 11, no. 3 (Summer).
Elmore, Richard (1979). "Backward Mapping," *Political Science Quarterly* 94 (Winter): 601–616.
Elmore, Richard F., and McLaughlin, Milbrey W. (1988). *Steady Work: Policy Practice, and the Reform of American Education* (Rand Publication Series No. R-3574-NIE/RC). Santa Monica, CA: National Institute of Education and The RAND Corporation.
Engelbert, Ernest A., ed. (1982). *Competition for California Water: Alternative Resolutions.* Berkeley: Univ. of California Press.
Entman, R. (1983). "The Impact of Ideology on Legislative Behavior and Public Policy in the States," *Journal of Politics* 45 (February): 163–182.
Environmental Defense Fund (March 1983). *Trading Conservation Investments for Water.* Berkeley: Environmental Defense Fund.
Etheredge, Lloyd (1981). "Political Learning," in S. Long, ed., *Handbook of Political Psychology.* New York: Plenum.
——— (1985). *Can Governments Learn? American Foreign Policy and Central American Relations.* New York: Pergamon Press.
Farkas, Suzanne (1971). *Urban Lobbying.* New York: New York Univ. Press.
Fenno, Richard (1973). *Congressmen in Committees.* Boston: Little, Brown.
Festinger, Leon (1957). *A Theory of Cognitive Dissonance.* Evanston: Row, Peterson.

Fink, Donald G. (1976). "The Role Played by the Two NTSC's in Preparing Television Service for the American Public," *Proceedings of the IEEE* 64 (September 1976): 1322–1331.

Fiske, Susan, and Taylor, Shelley (1984). *Social Cognition.* Reading, MA: Addison-Wesley.

Foley, Henry (1975). *Community Mental Health Legislation.* Lexington, MA: D.C. Heath.

Franklin, Mark, and Mackie, Thomas (1984). "Reassessing the Importance of Size and Ideology for the Formation of Governing Coalitions in Parliamentary Democracies," *American Journal of Political Science* 28 (November): 671–692.

Freedman, P. E., and Freedman, Anne (1981). "Political Learning," in Samuel Long, ed., *The Handbook of Political Behavior*, pp. 255–304. New York: Plenum.

Friedlaender, Anne, ed. (1978). *Approaches to Controlling Air Pollution.* Cambridge, MA: MIT Press.

Friedson, Eliot (1971). *The Professions and Their Prospects.* Beverly Hills: Sage.

Fritschler, A. Lee (1983). *Smoking and Politics*, 3d ed. Englewood Cliffs: Prentice-Hall.

Fullan, M., and Stiegelbauer, S. (1991). *The New Meaning of Educational Change.* New York: Teachers College Press.

Gates, John (1986). "Content Analysis and Judicial Research: A Pathway to Reliable Data?" Paper presented at the meetings of the Southern Political Science Association, Atlanta, GA, November.

George, Alexander (1969). "The Operational Code," *International Studies Quarterly* 13 (June): 110–222.

Gibson, James (1978). "'Judges' Role Orientations, Attitudes, and Decision: An Interactive Model," *American Political Science Review* 72: 911–924.

*Globe and Mail* (1979). February 15, p. 19; October 9, p. 5.

———— (1980). February 6, p. 1; March 7, p. 1; May 21, p. 1; May 26, p. 2; July 4, p. 2.

———— (1981). April 10, p. 6.

———— (1982). April 23, p. 4; June 1, p. 7.

———— (1983). March 25, p. 5; August 18, p. 4.

Goggin, Malcolm (1984). "The Ideological Content of Presidential Communications: The Message Tailoring Hypothesis Revisited," *American Politics Quarterly* 12 (July): 361–384.

Goldberg, B. Abbott (1966). "The State Water Project—Transition from Conflict to Accomplishment." Speech presented before the 34th Annual Conference of the California Utilities Association in Long Beach, CA, March.

Goldman, Charles (1973). "Will Baikal and Tahoe Be Saved?" *Cry California* 9: 19–25.

———— (1974). *Eutrophication of Lake Tahoe Emphasizing Water Quality.* EPA-660/3-74-034. Washington, DC: Government Printing Office.

———— (1981). "Lake Tahoe: Two Decades of Change in a Nitrogen Deficient Oligotrophic Lake," *Verh. Internat. Verein. Limnol* 21: 45–70.

Goldman, Charles, and Armstrong, Richard (1969). "Primary Productivity Studies of Lake Tahoe, CA," *Verh. Internat. Verein. Limnol* 17: 49–71.

Goodwin, Leonard, and Moen, Phyllis (1981). "The Evolution and Implementation of Federal Welfare Policy," in D. Mazmanian and P. Sabatier, eds., *Effective Policy Implementation*, pp. 147–168. Lexington, MA: D.C. Heath.

Gormley, William (1979). "A Test of the Revolving Door Hypothesis at the FCC," *American Journal of Political Science* 23 (November): 665–683.

————— (1986). "Regulatory Issue Networks in a Federal System," *Polity* (Summer): 595–620.

Governor's Commission to Review Water Rights Law (1978). *Final Report*. Sacramento: Governor's Commission to Review Water Rights Law.

Greenberger, Martin et al. (1983). *Caught Unawares*. Cambridge, MA: Ballinger.

Greenwald, Anthony, and Ronis, David (1978). "Twenty Years of Cognitive Dissonance: Case Study of the Evolution of a Theory," *Psychological Review* 85 (no. 1): 53–57.

Gregg, Frank, Born, Stephen, Lord, William, and Waterstone, Marvin (1991). *Institutional Response to a Changing Water Policy Environment*, Final Report for USGS Grant #14-08-0001-G1639. Tucson, AZ: Water Resources Research Center, Univ. of Arizona.

Grey, Brian (1989). "A Primer on California Water Transfer Law," *Arizona Law Review* 31: 745–781.

Griffith, Ernest (1961). *Congress: Its Contemporary Role*, 3d ed. New York: New York Univ. Press.

Grody, H. P. (1971). "The California Legislature and Comprehensive Water Resource Development." Ph.D Dissertation, Univ. of California, Los Angeles.

Guidon, H. (1990). "Quebec and the Canada Question," in J. Curtis and L. Tepperman, eds., *Images of Canada: The Sociological Tradition*, pp. 30–41. Scarborough, ON: Prentice-Hall.

Hagevik, George (1970). *Decision-Making in Air Pollution Control*. New York: Praeger.

Hahn, Robert W., and Hester, Gordon L. (1989). "Where Did All the Markets Go? An Analysis of EPA's Emissions Trading Program," *Yale Journal on Regulation* 6: 109–152.

Hamm, Keith (1983). "Patterns of Influence Among Committees, Agencies and Interest Groups," *Legislative Studies Quarterly* 8 (August): 379–426.

Hanson, Norwood (1969). *Patterns of Discovery*. Cambridge: Cambridge Univ. Press.

Hanushek, Eric, and Jackson, John (1977). *Statistical Methods for Social Scientists*. New York: Academic Press.

Hart, Jeffrey (1976). "Comparative Cognition: Politics of International Control of the Oceans," in R. Axelrod, ed., *Structures of Decision*, Chap. 8. Princeton: Princeton Univ. Press.

Harter, Philip J. (1982). "Negotiating Regulation," *Georgetown Law Journal* 71 (October 1982): 1–118.

Hartz, L. (1964). *The Founding of New Societies*. New York: Harcourt Brace.

Hasan, Nancy, and Simmons, James (1989). "The Issue-Attention Recycle: More Ups than Downs Anticipated." Paper presented at the Annual Meeting of the Western Political Science Association, Salt Lake City, UT.

Heclo, Hugh (1974). *Social Policy in Britain and Sweden*. New Haven: Yale Univ. Press.

————— (1977). *A Government of Strangers: Executive Politics in Washington*. Washington, DC: Brookings.

————— (1978). "Issue Networks and the Executive Establishment," in A. King, ed., *The New American Political System*, Washington, DC: American Enterprise Institute.

Heintz, H. Theodore (1985). "Core-to-Core Conflict in the OCS Debate: A Case Study in Policy Evolution." Paper presented at the meetings of the Western Political Science Association, Las Vegas, NV, March.

————— (1988). "Advocacy Coalitions and the OCS Leasing Debate: A Case Study in Policy Evolution," *Policy Sciences* 21: 213–238.

Heintz, H. Theodore, and Jenkins-Smith, Hank C. (1988). "Advocacy Coalitions and the Practice of Policy Analysis." *Policy Sciences* 21: 263–277.

Hibbs, Douglas, and Fassbender, H., eds. (1981). *Contemporary Political Economy*. Amsterdam: North Holland.

Hinckley, Barbara (1981). *Coalitions and Politics*. New York: Harcourt, Brace, Jovanovich.

Hjern, Benny, and Hull, Chris (1982). "Implementation Research as Empirical Constitutionalism," *European Journal of Political Research* 10 (June): 105–116.

Hjern, Benny, and Porter, David (1981). "Implementation Structures," *Organization Studies* 2: 211–227.

Hofferbert, Richard (1974). *The Study of Public Policy*. Indianapolis: Bobbs-Merrill.

Hofstetter, C. (1981). "Content Analysis," in D. Nimo and K. Sanders, eds., *Handbook of Political Communication*. Beverly Hills: Sage.

Hogwood, Brian, and Peters, B. Guy (1983). *Policy Dynamics*. New York: St. Martin's.

Holsti, Oli (1967). "Cognitive Dynamics and Images of the Enemy," *Journal of International Affairs* 21: 16–39.

————— (1969). *Content Analysis for the Social Sciences and Humanities*. Reading, MA: Addison-Wesley.

————— (1970). "The Operational Code Approach to the Study of Political Leaders: John Foster Dulles' Philosophical and Instrumental Beliefs," *Canadian Journal of Political Science* 3: 123–157.

Hope Commission (1950). *Royal Commission on Education*. Toronto: Ontario Archives.

Horowitz, Irving (1970). "Social Science Mandarins: Policy Making as Political Formula," *Policy Sciences* 1: 339–360.

Hunter, Floyd (1963). *Community Power Structure: A Study of Decision-Makers*. Garden City, NY: Anchor.

Hurwitz, Jon, and Peffley, Mark (1987). "How Are Foreign Policy Attitudes Structured? A Hierarchical Model," *American Political Science Review* 81 (December): 1099–1120.

Inan, Michele (1979). "Savior of the Cities—Would You Believe, Howard Jarvis?" *California Journal* 10 (April): 138–139.

Ingram, Helen (1977). "Policy Implementation Through Bargaining: Federal Grants in Aid," *Public Policy* 25 (Fall): 449–526.

————— (1978). "The Political Rationality of Innovation: The Clean Air Act Amendments of 1970," in Ann Friedlaender, ed., *Approaches to Controlling Air Pollution*, pp. 12–67. Cambridge: MIT Press.

Ingram, Wesley (1992). *The Influence of Scientific Information on the Evolution of Environmental Policy at Lake Tahoe*. Unpublished Ph.D. Dissertation, Univ. of California, Davis.

Ingram, Wesley, and Sabatier, Paul (1987). *A Descriptive History of Land Use and Water Quality Planning in the Lake Tahoe Basin*. Davis, CA: Institute of Ecology.

Innis, J. M. (1978). "Selective Exposure as a Function of Dogmatism and Incentive," *Journal of Social Psychology* 106: 261–265.

Jackman, Robert (1972). "Political Elites, Mass Publics, and Support for Democratic Principles," *Journal of Politics* 34 (August): 753–773.

Jackson, R. J., Jackson, D., and Baxter-Moore, N. (1986). *Politics in Canada: Culture, Institutions, Behaviour, and Public Policy*. Scarborough, ON: Prentice-Hall.

Jacobson, Gary (1985). "Congress: Politics After a Landslide Without Coattails," in M. Nelson, ed., *The Elections of 1984,* Washington DC: Congressional Quarterly Press.

Jakes, H. E., and Mawhinney, H. B. (1990). *A Historical Overview of Franco-Ontarian Educational Governance.* Ottawa: Faculty of Education, Univ. of Ottawa.

Janis, Irving (1983). *Groupthink,* 2d ed. Boston: Houghton Mifflin.

Jenkins-Smith, Hank (1982). "Professional Roles for Policy Analysts: A Critical Analysis," *Journal of Policy Analysis and Management* 2 (Fall): 88–100.

————— (1985). "Adversarial Analysis in the Bureaucratic Context," in Peter Brown, ed., *Advocacy Analysis.* Baltimore: Univ. of Maryland Press.

————— (1988). "Analytical Debates and Policy Learning: Analysis and Change in the Federal Bureaucracy," *Policy Sciences,* 21: 169–211.

————— (1990). *Democratic Politics and Policy Analysis.* Pacific Grove, CA: Brooks/Cole.

————— (1991). "Alternative Theories of the Policy Process: Reflections on Research Strategy for the Study of Nuclear Waste Policy," *PS: Political Science & Politics* (June): 157–166.

Jenkins-Smith, Hank, and Weimer, David (1985). "Analysis as Retrograde Action," *Public Administration Review* 45 (July): 485–494.

Jenkins-Smith, Hank, St. Clair, Gilbert, and Woods, Brian (1991). "Explaining Change in Policy Subsystems: Analysis of Coalition Stability and Defection over Time," *American Journal of Political Science* 35 (November): 851–880.

Jervis, Robert (1976). *Perception and Misperception in International Politics.* Princeton: Princeton Univ. Press.

Jones, Charles (1975). *Clean Air.* Pittsburgh: Univ. of Pittsburgh Press.

————— (1977). *An Introduction to the Study of Public Policy,* 3d ed. Belmont, CA: Wadsworth.

Jones, G. K. (1987). "The Development of Outer Continental Shelf Oil and Gas Reserves," in Ender and Kim, eds., *Energy Resources Development: Policies and Politics.* New York: Quorum.

Jordan, A. G., and Richardson, J. J. (1983). "Policy Communities: The British and European Style," *Policy Studies Journal* 11 (June): 603–615.

Jordan, William A. (1970). *Airline Regulation in America: Effects and Imperfections.* Baltimore: Johns Hopkins Univ. Press.

Kahn, Alfred. (1983). "Deregulation and Vested Interests: The Case of Airlines," in Roger G. Noll and Bruce Owen, eds., *The Political Economy of Deregulation,* pp. 132–151. Washington, DC: American Enterprise Institute.

Kahneman, Daniel, Slovic, Paul, and Tversky, Amos (1982). *Judgment Under Uncertainty.* Cambridge: Cambridge Univ. Press.

Katzenbach, Edward (1958). "The Horse Calvary in the Twentieth Century," *Public Policy* 8: 120–149.

Kaufman, Herbert (1960). *The Forest Ranger.* Baltimore: Johns Hopkins Univ. Press.

————— (1971). *The Limits of Organizational Change.* Univ., AL: Univ. of Alabama Press.

————— (1981). *The Administrative Behavior of Federal Bureau Chiefs.* Washington, DC: Brookings.

Kelleher, Herbert D. (1978). "Deregulation and the Practicing Attorney," *Journal of Air Law and Commerce* 44 (Summer): 261–296.

Keyes, Lucille. (1951). *Federal Control of Entry into Air Transportation.* Cambridge: Harvard Univ. Press.

————— (1980). *Regulatory Reform in Air Cargo Transportation.* Washington, DC: American Enterprise Institute.

Kindleberger, Charles P. (1983). "Standards as Public, Collective, and Private Goods," *Kyklos* 36: 377–396.

King, David (1989). "Representation Through Participation in Committee Hearings: House Ways and Means Committee Members and the 1978 Revenue Reform Act." Paper presented at the Annual Meeting of the Midwest Political Science Association, Chicago, IL.

Kingdon, John (1973). *Congressmen's Voting Decisions.* New York: Harper and Row.

———— (1984). Agendas, *Alternatives, and Public Policies.* Boston: Little, Brown.

———— (1988). "Ideas, Politics and Public Policies." Paper presented at the 1988 Annual Meeting of the American Political Science Association, Washington, DC.

Kirshner, Charles (1951). "The Color Television Controversy," *University of Pittsburgh Law Review* 13 (Fall): 65–84.

Kirst, Michael, and Jung, Richard (1982). "The Utility of a Longitudinal Approach in Assessing Implementation: Title I, ESEA," in Walter Williams, ed., *Studying Implementation*, pp. 119–148. Chatham, NJ: Chatham House.

Kiser, Larry, and Ostrom, Elinor (1982). "The Three Worlds of Action," in E. Ostrom, ed., *Strategies of Political Inquiry*, pp. 179–222. Beverly Hills: Sage.

Kneese, Allen, and Bower, Blair (1968). *Water Quality Management.* Baltimore: Johns Hopkins Univ. Press.

Knoepfel, Peter, and Wiedner, Helmut (1982). "A Conceptual Framework for Studying Implementation," in Paul Downing and Kenneth Hanf, eds., *The Implementation of Pollution Control Programs.* Tallahassee: Policy Sciences Program.

Knott, Jack, and Miller, Gary (1987). *Reforming Bureaucracy: The Politics of Institutional Choice.* Englewood Cliffs: Prentice-Hall.

Kobylka, J. (1983). "Organizational Response to a Changing Litigation Environment: The Effect of *Miller v. California* (1973) on the Litigation Patterns of Libertarian Organizations." Paper presented at the meetings of the Midwest Political Science Association, Chicago.

Kohlmeier, Louis (1974a). "Regulatory Focus: Some Evidence of Disenchantment," *National Journal Reports* 6 (June 22, 1974): 933.

———— (1974b). "Inflation Boosts Chance for Policy Change," *National Journal Reports* 6 (September 14, 1974): 1394.

Krasnow, Erwin G., Longley, Lawrence D., and Terry, Herbert A. (1982). *The Politics of Broadcast Regulation*, 3rd ed. New York: St. Martin's Press.

Krier, James, and Ursin, Edmund (1977). *Pollution and Policy.* Berkeley: Univ. of California Press.

Krippendorff, K. (1980). *Content Analysis: An Introduction to Its Methodology.* Beverly Hills: Sage.

Krosnick, J. (1987). "The Role of Attitude Importance in Social Evaluation: A Study of Policy Preferences and Voting Behavior," unpublished manuscript, Ohio State Univ., Department of Psychology, April.

Kuhn, Thomas S. (1970). *The Structure of Scientific Revolutions*, 2d ed. Chicago: Univ. of Chicago Press.

Laffin, Martin (1986). *Professionalism and Policy: The Role of Professions in the Central-local Government Relationship.* Aldershot, UK: Gower.

Lakatos, Imre (1971). "History of Science and Its Rational Reconstruction," *Boston Studies in the Philosophy of Science* 8: 42–134.

Landau, Martin (1977). "The Proper Domain of Policy Analysis," *American Journal of Political Science* 21 (May): 423–427.

Larsen, Judith K., and Rogers, Everett M. (1984). "Consensus Development Conference: A Cross-Cultural Study," *Knowledge* 5 (June): 537–548.

Lasswell, Harold (1951). "The Policy Orientation," in D. Lerner and H. Lasswell, eds., *The Policy Sciences*. Stanford: Stanford Univ. Press.

Lave, Charles, and March, James (1975). *An Introduction to Models in the Social Sciences*. New York: Harper and Row.

Lave, Lester, and Seskin, Eugene (1977). *Air Pollution and Human Health*. Baltimore: Johns Hopkins Univ. Press.

Lawton, S. (1989). "Political Values in Educational Finance in Canada and the United States," in S. B. Lawton and R. Wignall, eds., *Scrimping or Squandering? Financing Canadian Schools*. Toronto: OISE Press.

Lawton, S. B. (1991). "Issues of Choice: Canadian and American Perspectives." Paper presented to the conference, Schools of Choice: Canadian and American Perspectives Colloquium, State Univ. of New York at Buffalo.

Leege, David, and Francis, Wayne (1974). *Political Research*. New York: Basic Books.

Lester, James, and Hamilton, Michael (1987). "Intergovernmental Relations and Marine Policy Change," in Maynard Silva, ed., *Ocean Resources and U.S. Intergovernmental Relations in the 1980s*, pp. 197–220. Boulder: Westview Press.

Levine, Michael E. (1965). "Is Regulation Necessary: California Air Transportation and National Regulatory Policy," *Yale Law Journal* 75 (July):1416–1447.

——— (1981). "Revisionism Revised? Airline Deregulation and the Public Interest," *Journal of Law and Contemporary Problems* 44 (Winter): 179–195.

Lewis-Beck, Michael. (1986). "Interrupted Time Series," in *New-Tools for Social Scientists*. Beverly Hills: Sage.

Lindblom, Charles E. (1971). *The Policy-making Process*. Engelwood Cliffs: Prentice-Hall.

Lindblom, Charles E., and Cohen, David (1979). *Usable Knowledge*. New Haven: Yale Univ. Press.

Lipset, S. M. (1970). *Revolution and Counterrevolution*. New York: Anchor Books.

Liroff, Richard (1986). *Reforming Air Pollution Regulation: The Toil and Trouble of EPA's Bubble*. Washington, DC: Conservation Foundation.

Loreto, R., and White, G. (1990). "The Premier and the Cabinet," in G. White, ed., *The Government and Politics of Ontario*. Scarborough, ON: Nelson Canada.

Lowi, Theodore (1964). "American Business, Public Policy, Case Studies, and Political Theory," *World Politics* 16 (June): 677–715.

——— (1969). *The End of Liberalism*. New York: Norton.

——— (1972). "Four Systems of Policy, Politics, and Choice," *Public Administration Review* 32 (July/August): 298–310.

——— (1976). "Public Policy and Bureaucracy in the United States and France." Paper presented at the meetings of the International Political Science Association, Edinburgh, August.

Lynch, P. (1979). "Public Policy and Competency Testing," *Education and Urban Society* 12 (no. 1): 65–80.

MacRae, Duncan (1975). "Policy Analysis as an Applied Social Science Discipline," *Administration and Society* 6 (February): 363–388.

Majone, Giandomenico (1980). "Policies as Theories," *Omega* 8: 151–162.

——— (1989). *Evidence, Argument, and Persuasion in the Policy Process*. New Haven: Yale Univ. Press.

Majone, Giandomenico, and Wildavsky, Aaron (1978). "Implementation as Evolution," in Howard Freeman, ed., *Policy Studies Review Annual: 1978*. Beverly Hills: Sage.

Mandel, M. (1989). *The Charter of Rights and the Legalization of Politics in Canada.* Toronto: Wall & Thompson.

Mann, Jim (1978). "Hard Times for the ACLU," *The New Republic* (April 15): 12–15.

March, James, and Simon, Herbert (1958). *Organizations.* New York: Wiley.

Margolis, Howard (1974). *Technical Advice on Policy Issues.* Beverly Hills: Sage.

Marmor, Theodore (1970). *The Politics of Medicare.* Chicago: Aldine.

Marshall, C., Mitchell, D., and Wirt, F. (1989). *Culture and Education Policy in the American States.* New York: Falmer.

Mawhinney, Hanne B. (1991). *Policy Change in Education: An Assessment of Sabatier's Advocacy Coalition Framework.* Paper presented to the conference Theory into Practice: Policy Research and Development in Canada, Calgary, AB: Univ. of Calgary, May.

Mazmanian, Daniel, and Nienaber, Jeanne (1979). *Can Organizations Change?* Washington, DC: Brookings.

Mazmanian, Daniel, and Sabatier, Paul (1980). "A Multivariate Model of Public Policy-Making," in *American Journal of Political Science* 24 (August): 439–468.

————— eds. (1981). *Effective Policy Implementation.* Lexington, MA: D.C. Heath.

————— (1989). *Implementation and Public Policy.* Lanham, MD: Univ. Press of America.

Mazur, Allan (1981). *The Dynamics of Technical Controversy.* Washington, DC: Communications Press.

McClosky, H., and Brill, A. (1983). *Dimensions of Tolerance.* New York: Russell Sage Foundation.

McDonnell, L. M., and Elmore, R. F. (1987). *Alternative Policy Instruments,* No. JNE-03. Center for Education Research in Education, RAND Corp.

McGann, James G. (1992). "Academics to Ideologues: A Brief History of the Public Policy Research Industry, " *PS: Political Science & Politics* 25 (December): 733–739.

McGuire, William (1968). "Theory of the Structure of Human Thought," in R. Abelson et al., *Theories of Cognitive Consistency,* pp. 148–162. Chicago: Rand McNally.

McLaughlin, Milbrey (1990). "The Rand Change Agent Study Revisited: Macro Perspectives and Micro Realities," *Educational Researcher* 19 (no. 9): 11–16.

McPhee, John (1971). *Encounters with the Archdruid.* New York: Farrar, Straus, and Giroux.

Meier, Kenneth J. (1985). *Regulation: Politics, Bureaucracy, and Economics.* New York: St. Martin's.

————— (1987). *Politics and the Bureaucracy,* 2d ed. Monterey, CA: Brooks/Cole.

Meltsner, Arnold (1976). *Policy Analysts in the Bureaucracy.* Berkeley: Univ. of California Press.

Merchant, F. W. (1909). *Report on English-French Schools in the Ottawa Valley.* Toronto: King's Printer.

Metropolitan Water District of Southern California (1989). *Focus,* no. 1. Los Angeles: Metropolitan Water District of Southern California.

Miles, M. B., and Huberman, A. M. (1984). *Qualitative Data Analysis: A Sourcebook of New Methods.* Newbury Park, CA: Sage Publications.

Miller, L., and Siegelman, L. (1978). "Is the Audience the Message? A Note on LBJ's Vietnam Statements," *Public Opinion Quarterly* 42 (Spring): 71–80.

Milward, H. Brinton, and Wamsley, Gary (1984). "Policy Subsystems, Networks, and the Tools of Public Management," in Robert Eyestone, ed., *Public Policy Formation and Implementation,* Chap. 1. New York: JAI Press.

Mitchell, D. E. (1988). "Educational Politics and Policy: The State Level," in N. J.

Boyan, ed., *Handbook of Research on Educational Administration*, pp. 453–466. New York: Longman.

Mitchell, S. (1979). "Interobserver Agreement and Reliability," *Psychological Bulletin* 86 (no. 2): 376–390.

Moe, Terry M. (1980). *The Organization of Interests*. Chicago: Univ. of Chicago Press.

——— (1981). "Toward a Broader View of Interest Groups," *Journal of Politics* 43: 531–543.

——— (1982). "Regulatory Performance and Presidential Administration," *American Journal of Political Science* 26: 197–224.

——— (1984). "The New Economics of Organization," *American Journal of Political Science* 28 (November): 739–777.

——— (1985). "Control and Feedback in Economic Regulation," *American Political Science Review* 79 (December): 1094–1116.

Montjoy, R., Schaffer, W., and Weber, R. (1980). "Policy Preferences of Party Elites and Masses: Conflict or Consensus?" *American Politics Quarterly* 8 (July): 319–330.

Morton, D. (1990). "Sic Permanet: Ontario People and Their Politics, " in G. White, ed., *The Government and Politics of Ontario*. Scarborough, ON: Nelson Canada.

Mosco, Vincent. (1976). *Reforming Regulation: The FCC and Innovations in the Broadcasting Market*. Cambridge, MA: Harvard Univ. Program on Information Technologies and Public Policy.

Munro, John F. (1988) "Paradigms, Politics, and Long Term Policy Change Within the California Water Policy-making System." Ph.D Dissertation, Univ. of California, Los Angeles.

Murphy, Jerome (1990). "The Educational Reform Movement of the 1980s: A Comprehensive Analysis, " in J. Murphy, ed., *The Educational Reform Movement of the 1980s: Perspectives and Cases*. Berkeley, CA: McCutchan.

Nachmias, David (1979). *Public Policy Evaluation*. New York: St. Martin's.

Nadel, Mark (1971). *The Politics of Consumer Protection*. Indianapolis: Bobbs-Merrill.

Nakamura, Robert (1987). "The Textbook Policy Process and Implementation Research," *Policy Studies Review* (no. 1): 142–154.

Nakamura, Robert, and Smallwood, Frank (1980). *The Politics of Policy Implementation*. New York: St. Martin's.

National Acid Precipitation Assessment Program (1990). *Acidic Deposition: State of Science and Technology*. Washington, DC: Government Printing Office.

National Commission on Excellence in Education (1983). *A Nation at Risk*. Washington, DC: Government Printing Office.

Needham, Douglas (1983). *The Economics and Politics of Regulation: A Behavioral Approach*. Boston: Little, Brown.

Nelkin, Dorothy (1979). *Controversy: Politics of Technical Decisions*. Beverly Hills: Sage.

Nelson, Barbara (1984). *Making an Issue of Child Abuse*. Chicago: Univ. of Chicago Press.

Nelson, Robert (1987). "The Economics Profession and the Making of Public Policy," *Journal of Economic Literature* 25 (March): 42–84. Nevada Gaming Commission, Economic Research Division (1970). *Direct Levies on Gaming in Nevada, FY 1969–70*. Carson City, NV, November.

Nevada Legislature (1968). *Special Session on TRPA Compact (SB 9), Hearing Transcript*, Carson City, NV, February 12 and 19, 1968.

Nevada Legislature, Assembly and Senate Resources Committees (1985). *Hearings Withdrawing Nevada from the TRPA Compact*, Carson City, NV.

Nevada Legislature, Assembly Environment and Public Resources Committee and Senate Environment, Public Resources, and Agriculture Committee (1977). *Hearings on SB 266, AB 740, and SB 267 [Gaming]*, March 14 and April 26, 1977. Carson City, NV.

Nevada Legislature, Senate (1980). *Special Session on the TRPA Compact, Hearing Transcript*, Carson City, NV, September 13, 1980.

Nevada Legislature, Senate Committee on Environment, Public Resources, and Agriculture (1977). *Hearings on TRPA Compact*, Carson City, NV.

Newell, Allen, and Simon, Herbert (1972). *Human Problem Solving*. Englewood Cliffs: Prentice-Hall.

Nisbet, Robert (1981). "Defending Cost-Benefit Analysis," *Regulation* 5 (March/April): 42–43.

Nisbit, Richard, and Ross, Lee (1980). *Human Inference: Strategies and Shortcomings of Social Judgment*. Englewood Cliffs: Prentice-Hall.

Niskanen, William (1971). *Bureaucracy and Representative Government*. Chicago: Rand McNally.

——— (1975). "Bureaucrats and Politicians," *Journal of Law and Economics* 18: 617–643.

Norusis, Marija (1986). *SPSS PC+: Advanced Statistics*. Chicago: SPSS.

Nunnally, J. (1978). *Psychometric Theory*, 2d, ed., Chap. 12. New York: McGraw-Hill.

Okun, Arthur (1975). *Equality and Efficiency: The Big Tradeoff*. Washington, DC: Brookings.

O'Leary, Jack (1979). *Testimony Before the Subcommittee on Energy Regulations, Committee on Energy and Natural Resources, U.S. Senate, September 11, 1979*. Washington, DC: Government Printing Office.

Ostrom, Elinor (1982). "Institutional Arrangements and Learning." Paper presented at the ZIF, Univ. of Bielefeld, July 20.

——— (1986). "Institutional Arrangements for Managing the Commons Dilemma," in Bonnie McCay and Janis Acheson, eds., *Capturing the Commons*. Tucson: Univ. of Arizona Press.

——— (1990). *Governing the Commons*. Cambridge, UK: Cambridge Univ. Press.

Ostrom, Vincent (1982). "European Public Administration." Paper presented at the European Institute of Public Administration, Maastricht, the Netherlands.

Ostrom, Vincent, Tiebout, Charles, and Warren, Robert (1961). "The Organization of Government in Metropolitan Areas," *American Political Science Review* 55 (December): 831–842.

O'Toole, Randal (1988). *Reforming the Forest Service*. Washington, DC: Island Press.

Palumbo, Dennis (1988). *Public Policy in America*. New York: Harcourt, Brace, Jovanovich.

Peffley, Mark, and Hurwitz, Jon (1985). "A Hierarchical Model of Attitude Constraint," *American Journal of Political Science* 29 (November): 871–890.

Peltzman, Sam. (1976). "Toward a More General Theory of Regulation," *Journal of Law and Economics* 19: 211–248.

Peters, Guy (1986). *American Public Policy: Promise and Performance*, 2d ed. Chatham, NJ: Chatham House.

Petracca, Mark P. (1983). "The National Executive and Private Interests—Federal Advisory Committees: The 'Steel Bridge' to Corporatism." Paper presented at the 1983 Annual Meeting of the American Political Science Association, Chicago.

Petty, Richard, and Cacioppo, John (1981). *Attitudes and Persuasion.* Dubuque: Wm. C. Brown.

Pfeffer, Jeffrey, and Salancik, Gerald (1978). *The External Control of Organizations.* New York: Harper and Row.

Phillips, D. C. (1977). "When Evaluators Disagree: Perplexities and Perspectives," *Policy Sciences* 8: 147–159.

Pierce, John, and Lovrich, Nicholas (1980). "Belief Systems Concerning the Environment: The General Public, Attentive Publics, and State Legislators," *Political Behavior* 2 (no. 3): 259–286.

Pierce, Roy, and Rochon, Thomas (1984). "Attitudinal Change and Elite Conversion: French Socialist Candidates in 1967 and 1978," *American Journal of Political Science* 28 (May): 379–398.

Pisani, Donald J. (1984). *From Family Farm to Agribusiness: The Irrigation Crusade in California and the West.* Berkeley: Univ. of California Press.

Poole, Keith, and Daniels, R. Steven (1985). "Ideology, Party, and Voting in the U.S. Congress, 1959–1980," *American Political Science Review* 79 (June): 373–399.

Popper, Karl (1959). *The Logic of Scientific Discovery.* London: Hutchinson.

Posner, Richard. (1974). "Theories of Economic Regulation," *Bell Journal of Economics and Management Science* 2 (Autumn): 335–358.

Prang, M. (1969). "Clerics, Politicians, and the Bilingual Schools Issue in Ontario, 1910–1917," in R. Cook, C. Brown, and C. Berger, eds., *Minorities, Schools and Politics.* Toronto: Univ. of Toronto Press.

Premfors, Rune (1983). "Governmental Commissions in Sweden," *American Behavioral Scientist* 26 (May/June): 623–642.

Pressman, Jeffery, and Wildavsky, Aaron (1973). *Implementation.* Berkeley, CA: Univ. of California Press.

Primack, Joel, and von Hippel, Frank (1974). *Advice and Dissent: Scientists in the Political Arena.* New York: Basic Books.

Putnam, Robert (1971). "Studying Elite Political Culture: The Case of Ideology," *American Political Science Review* 65: 651–681.

———— (1973). *The Beliefs of Politicians.* New Haven: Yale Univ. Press.

———— (1976). *The Comparative Study of Political Elites.* Englewood Cliffs: Prentice-Hall.

Putnam, Robert, Leonardi, R., and Nanetti, R. (1979). "Attitude Stability Among Italian Elites," *American Journal of Political Science* 23 (August): 463–494.

Quirk, Paul. (1981). *Industry Influence in the Federal Regulatory Agencies.* Princeton, NJ: Princeton Univ. Press.

Rajecki, D. W. (1982). *Attitudes: Themes and Advances.* Sunderland, MA: Sinauer.

Rein, Martin, and White, Sheldon (1977). "Policy Research: Belief and Doubt," *Policy Analysis* 3 (Spring): 239–271.

Rhoads, Steven (1985). *The Economist's View of the World.* Cambridge, UK: Cambridge Univ. Press.

Rhodes, R.A.W. (1988). *Beyond Westminister and Whitehall.* London: Unwin and Hyman.

Rice, David M. (1980). "Regulation of Direct Broadcast Satellites: International Constraints and Domestic Options," *New York Law School Law Review* 25: 813–862.

Rich, Robert, ed. (1981). *The Knowledge Cycle.* Beverly Hills: Sage.

Riker, William (1962). *The Theory of Political Coalitions.* New Haven: Yale Univ. Press.

Ripley, Randall (1985). *Policy Analysis in Political Science.* Chicago: Nelson Hall.

Ripley, Randall, and Franklin, Grace (1982). *Bureaucracy and Policy Implementation.* Homewood, IL: Dorsey Press.

Robie, Ronald B. (1975). "Of Dinosaurs and Edsels." Speech presented at the spring conference of the Association of California Water Agencies in Sacramento. Sacramento: Department of Water Resources.

Robinson, John B. (1982). "Apples and Horned Toads: On the Framework-Determined Nature of the Energy Debate," *Policy Sciences* 15: 23–45.

Rodgers, Harrell, and Bullock, Charles (1976). *Coercion to Compliance.* Lexington, MA: D.C. Heath.

Rokeach, Milton (1973). *The Nature of Human Values.* New York: MacMillan.

Rokkan, Stein (1970). *Citizens, Elections, and Parties.* Oslo: Universitaetsforlaget.

Romesburg, H. (1984). *Cluster Analysis for Researchers.* Belmont, CA: Lifetime Learning Publications.

Rosenbaum, Nelson (1976). *Land Use and the Legislatures.* Washington, DC: Urban Institute.

Rourke, Francis. (1984). *Bureaucracy, Politics, and Public Policy,* 3d ed. Boston: Little, Brown.

Royal Commission on Bilingualism and Biculturalism (1968). *Report on Education, Book I.* Ottawa: Government of Canada.

Rushefsky, Mark (1990). *Public Policy in the U.S.* Monterey: Brooks/Cole.

——— (1984). "The Misuse of Science in Governmental Decision-making," *Science, Technology, and Human Values* 9 (Summer): 47–59.

Sabatier, Paul A. (1975). "Social Movements and Regulatory Agencies," *Political Science* 6 (September): 301–342.

——— (1978). "The Acquisition and Utilization of Technical Information by Administrative Agencies," *Administrative Science Quarterly* 23 (September): 386–411.

——— (1984). "Faculty Interest in Policy-Oriented Advising and Research," *Knowledge* 5 (June): 469–502.

——— (1986). "Top-Down and Bottom-Up Models of Policy Implementation: A Critical Analysis and Suggested Synthesis," *Journal of Public Policy* 6 (January): 21–48.

——— (1987). "Knowledge, Policy-Oriented Learning, and Policy Change," *Knowledge: Creation, Diffusion, Utilization* 8 (June): 649–692.

——— (1988). "An Advocacy Coalition Framework of Policy Change and the Role of Policy-Oriented Learning Therein," *Policy Sciences* 21: 129–168.

——— (1990). "Coastal Land Use Planning in Britain and France: Lessons from Implementation Research." Paper presented at the Annual Meeting of the Western Political Science Association, Newport Beach, CA.

——— (1991a). "Toward Better Theories of the Policy Process," *PS: Political Science & Politics* 24 (June): 147–156.

——— (1991b). "Political Science and Public Policy," *PS: Political Science & Politics* 24 (June): 144–156.

——— (1992). "Interest Group Membership and Organization," in Mark Petracca, ed., *The Politics of Interests,* pp. 99–129. Boulder, CO: Westview Press.

Sabatier, Paul A., and Hunter, Susan (1989). "The Incorporation of Causal Perceptions into Models of Elite Belief Systems," *Western Political Quarterly* 42 (September): 229–261.

Sabatier, Paul A., and Jenkins-Smith, Hank (1988). Symposium Volume, "Policy Change and Policy-Oriented Learning," *Policy Sciences* 21 (Summer and Fall): 123–277.

Sabatier, Paul A., and McLaughlin, Susan (1988). "Belief Congruence of Governmental and Interest Group Elites with Their Constituencies," *American Politics Quarterly* 16 (January): 61–98.

Sabatier, Paul A., and Pelkey, Neil (1987). "Incorporating Multiple Actors and Guidance Instruments into Models of Regulatory Policy-Making: An Advocacy Coalition Framework," *Administration and Society* 19 (September): 236–263.

———— (1990). *Land Development at Lake Tahoe: The Effects of Environmental Controls and Economic Conditions on Housing Construction.* Davis, CA: Institute of Ecology.

Sabatier, Paul A., and Whiteman, David (1985). "Legislative Decision-Making and Substantive Policy Information: Models of Information Flow," *Legislative Studies Quarterly* 10 (August): 395–422.

Sabatier, Paul A., Hunter, Susan, and McLaughlin, Susan (1987). "The Devil Shift: Perceptions and Misperceptions of Opponents," *Western Political Quarterly* 41 (September): 449–476.

Sabatier, Paul A., Pelkey, Neil, and Mclaughlin, Susan (1990). "Structure and Change in Elite Belief Systems." Paper presented at the 1990 Annual Meeting of the American Political Science Association, San Francisco, September 2.

Salisbury, Robert (1969). "An Exchange Theory of Interest Groups," *Midwest Journal of Political Science* 13: 1–32.

———— (1984). "Interest Representation: The Dominance of Institutions," *American Political Science Review* 78 (March): 64–76.

Salisbury, Robert, Heinz, John, Laumann, Edward, and Nelson, Robert (1987). "Who Works with Whom? Interest Group Alliances and Opposition," *American Political Science Review* 81: 1217–1234.

Samuelson, Paul A. (1954). "The Pure Theory of Public Expenditure," *The Review of Economics and Statistics* 36: 387–389.

Scharpf, Fritz (1982). "The Political Economy of Inflation and Unemployment in Western Europe: An Outline," Discussion Paper 81–21. Berlin: International Institute of Management.

Schattschneider, E. E. (1960). *The Semi-Sovereign People.* New York: Holt, Rinehart and Winston.

Schiff, Ashley (1962). *Fire and Water: Scientific Heresy in the Forest Service.* Cambridge: Harvard Univ. Press.

Scholtz, John, and Wei, Feng-heng (1986). "Regulatory Enforcement in a Federalist System," *American Political Science Review* 80: 765–800.

Scholtz, John T., Twombly, Jim, and Headrick, Barbara (1991). "Street-level Political Controls over Federal Bureaucracy," *American Political Science Review* 85 (September): 829–850.

Schultze, Charles (1968). *The Politics and Economics of Public Spending.* Washington, DC: Brookings.

———— (1977). *The Public Use of Private Interest.* Washington, DC: Brookings.

Seidman, David (1977). "The Politics of Policy Analysis," *Regulation* 1 (July/August): 22–37.

Sharpe, L. J. (1984). "National and Subnational Government and Coordination," in F. X. Kaufmann, V. Ostrom, and G. Majone, eds., *Guidance, Control and Evaluation in the Public Sector.* Berlin: de Gruyter.

Shooshan, Harry M., III, and Krasnow, Erwin G. (1985). "New Checks, Balances Affect FCC Policymaking," *Legal Times* (April 8).

Simon, Herbert (1955). "A Behavioral Model of Rational Choice," *Quarterly Journal of Economics* 69: 99–118.

———— (1979). *Models of Thought.* New Haven: Yale Univ. Press.

Skocpol, Theda (1979). *States and Social Revolution.* Cambridge, UK: Cambridge Univ. Press.

Skowronek, Stephen (1982). *Building a New American State.* Cambridge, UK: Cambridge Univ. Press.

Smith, Don (1968). "Cognitive Consistency and the Perception of Others' Opinions," *Public Opinion Quarterly* 32: 1–15.

SPSSX, Inc. (1986). *SPSSX User's Guide.* Chicago, IL: SPSS, Inc.

Stammer, Larry (1977). "Peripheral Canal Ok'd By Senate," *Los Angeles Times,* June 24, .

Statistics Canada (1974). *Canada Year Book 1974.* Ottawa: Information Canada.

Steinbruner, John D. (1974). *The Cybernetic Theory of Decision.* Princeton: Princeton Univ. Press.

Stewart, Joseph J. (1991). "Policy Models and Equal Educational Opportunity," *PS: Political Science and Politics* 24 (June): 167–173.

Stokey, Edith, and Zeckhauser, Richard (1979). *A Primer for Policy Analysis.* New York: Norton.

Strong, Douglas (1984). *Tahoe: An Environmental History.* Lincoln, NE: Univ. of Nebraska Press.

Sundquist, James (1983). *Dynamics of the Party System.* Washington, DC: Brookings.

Taylor, Michael, and Laver, Michael (1973). "Government Coalitions in Western Europe," *European Journal of Political Research* 1 (September): 205–248.

Taylor, Serge (1984). *Making Bureaucracies Think.* Stanford: Stanford Univ. Press.

Television Digest (1977). *Television Factbook, 1977 Edition.* Washington, DC: Television Digest.

Tesser, Abraham (1978). "Self-Generated Attitude Change," *Advances in Experimental Social-Psychology* 11: 289–338.

Tetlock, Phillip (1984). "Content and Structure in Political Belief Systems," in D. Sylvan and B. Chuns, eds., *Foreign Policy Decision-Making.* New York: Praeger.

Tinsley, H., and Weiss, D. (1975). "Interrater Reliability and Agreement of Subjective Judgments," *Journal of Counseling Psychology* 22 (no. 4): 358–376.

Torgerson, W. (1958). *Theory and Methods of Scaling.* New York: Wiley.

Townsend, R. G. (1988). *They Politick for Schools.* Toronto: OISE Press.

Truman, David (1951). *The Governmental Process.* New York: Alfred Knopf.

Udelson, Joseph H. (1982). *The Great Television Race.* University, AL: Univ. of Alabama Press.

U.S. Civil Aeronautics Board (1977). *Annual Report to Congress, Fiscal Y 1977.* Washington, DC: Civil Aeronautics Board.

U.S. Congress, House of Representatives (1978). *Conference Report on the Airline Deregulation Act of 1978.* H. Rept. 95-1779, 95th Cong., 2nd Sess.

——— (1981). "Satellite Communications/Direct Broadcast Satellites," Hearing of Committee on Energy and Commerce, December 15.

U.S. Department of the Interior, Federal Water Pollution Control Administration (1966). *Conference in the Matter of Pollution of Lake Tahoe, Proceedings,* Stateline, NV, July 18–20.

U.S. Environmental Protection Agency (1973). *Adequacy and Need for Extending Federal Oversight and Control in Order to Preserve the Fragile Ecology of Lake Tahoe, Hearing,* South Lake Tahoe, CA, September 21–22, 1973.

U.S. Soil Conservation Service (1971). *Soils of the Tahoe Basin: Report and General Soil Maps.* South Lake Tahoe, CA: Tahoe Regional Planning Agency, September.

Van Horn, Carl (1979). *Policy Implementation in the Federal System.* Lexington, MA: D.C. Heath.
Vig, Norman, and Kraft, Michael, eds. (1984). *Environmental Policy in the 1980s.* Washington, DC: Congressional Quarterly Press.
Vose, Clement (1959). *Caucasians Only.* Berkeley: Univ. of California Press.
Walker, Richard, and Storper, Michael. (1982). *The Expanding California Water System.* San Francisco: American Association for the Advancement of Science.
Walker, S. (1977). "The Interface Between Belief and Behavior: Henry Kissinger's Operational Code and the Vietnam War," *Journal of Conflict Resolution* 21: 129–168.
Wamsley, Gary (1983). "Policy Subsystems as a Unit of Analysis in Implementation Studies." Paper presented at Erasmus Univ., Rotterdam, June.
Warwick, Paul (1979). "The Durability of Coalition Governments in Parliamentary Democracies," *Comparative Political Studies* 11 (January): 465–498.
Waterman, Richard (1989). *Presidential Influence and the Administrative State.* Knoxville: Univ. of Tennessee Press.
Webber, David (1983). "Obstacles to the Utilization of Systematic Policy Analysis," *Knowledge* 4 (June): 534–560.
——— (1986). "Explaining Policymakers' Use of Policy Information," *Knowledge* 7 (March): 249–290.
Webber, P. (1985). *Basic Content Analysis.* Beverly Hills: Sage.
Weekly Compilation of Presidential Documents. (1974). Oct. 8.
——— (1978). Oct. 24.
Weinberg, Alvin (1972). "Science and Trans-Science," *Minerva* 10 (April): 209–222.
Weingast, B., and Moran, M. (1983). "Bureaucratic Discretion or Congressional Control: Regulatory Policymaking by the Federal Trade Commission," *Journal of Political Economy* 91 (October): 765–800.
Weiss, Carol (1972). *Evaluation Research.* Englewood Cliffs: Prentice-Hall.
——— (1977a). *Using Social Research in Public Policy Making.* Lexington: D.C. Heath.
——— (1977b). "Research for Policy's Sake: The Enlightenment Function of Social Research," *Policy Analysis* 3 (Fall): 531–545.
——— (1983). "Ideology, Interests and Information: The Basis of Policy Decisions," in D. Callahan and B. Jennings, eds., *Ethics, the Social Sciences, and Policy Analysis.* New York: Plenum.
Wenner, Lettie (1982). *The Environmental Decade in the Courts.* Bloomington, IN: Indiana Univ. Press.
Western Federal Regional Council (1979). *Lake Tahoe Environmental Assessment.* El Paso, TX: Energy Policy Studies.
Weyant, John P. (1988). "Is There Policy-Oriented Learning in the Analysis of Natural Gas Policy Issues?" *Policy Sciences* 21: 239–261.
White, Lawrence J. (1982). *The Regulation of Air Pollutant Emissions from Motor Vehicles.* Washington, DC: American Enterprise Institute.
Wicklund, Robert, and Brehm, Jack (1976). *Perspectives on Cognitive Dissonance.* Hillsdale, NJ: Lawrence Erlbaum Assoc.
Wildavsky, Aaron (1962). "The Analysis of Issue Contexts in the Study of Decision-Making," *Journal of Politics* 24: 717–732.
——— (1979). *Speaking Truth to Power.* Boston: Little, Brown.
——— (1982). "The Three Cultures: Explaining Anomalies in the American Welfare State," *The Public Interest* 69: 45–58.

———— (1987). "Choosing Preferences by Constructing Institutions: A Cultural Theory of Preference Formation," *American Political Science Review*, 81: 3–22.

Wildavsky, Aaron, and Tenenbaum, Ellen (1981). *The Politics of Mistrust*. Beverly Hills: Sage.

Wilker, Harry, and Milbrath, Lester (1972). "Political Belief Systems and Political Behavior," in D. Nimmo and C. Bonjean, *Political Attitudes and Public Opinion*, pp. 41–57. New York: David McKay.

Wilson, James Q. (1973). *Political Organizations*. New York: Basic Books.

————, ed. (1980). *The Politics of Regulation*. New York: Basic.

Wilson, J. (1980). "The Red Tory Province: Reflections on the Character of the Ontario Political Culture," in D. C. MacDonald, ed., *The Government and Politics of Ontario*, 2d ed. Toronto: Van Nostrand Reinhold.

Wise, S. F. (1990). "The Ontario Political Culture: A Study in Complexities," in G. White, ed., *The Government and Politics of Ontario*. Scarborough: Nelson Canada.

Wittrock, Bjorn (1983). "Planning, Pluralism, and Policy Intellectuals," in T. Husen and M. Kogan, eds., *Researchers and Policy-Makers in Education*. Oxford: Pergamon.

Wood, B. Dan (1988). "Principals, Bureaucrats, and Responsiveness in Clean Air Enforcements," *American Political Science Review* 82 (March): 213–234.

———— (1991). "Federalism and Policy Responsiveness: The Clean Air Case," *Journal of Politics* 53 (August): 851–859.

Wood, B. Dan, and Waterman, Richard (1991). "The Dynamics of Political Control of Bureaucracy," *American Political Science Review* 85 (September): 801–828.

Wright, Neil (1988). *Understanding Intergovernmental Relations*, 3d ed. Pacific Grove, CA: Brooks/Cole.

Zariski, Raphael (1984). "Coalition Formation in the Italian Regions," *Comparative Politics* 16 (July): 403–420.

# About the Book

The field of public policy analysis is undergoing major change and development in the theories its practitioners employ and the way those theories are tested. In this book, the contributors clearly lay out the advocacy coalition approach to public policy analysis and apply it to a variety of public policy problems and arenas. In the process of looking at case studies in education, airline deregulation, communications, energy, and the environment, Sabatier and Jenkins-Smith offer the fullest exposition and application of the advocacy coalition framework to date, revising the approach in significant ways for future research and analysis.

Students are treated to a textbook example of how theory illuminates the policy world, while scholars and policy makers are brought up-to-date on developments in the advocacy coalition framework and its potential to account for many factors that elude the classic stages model of agenda setting, formulation, and implementation. Tables, figures, and a methodological appendix enhance the teaching value of the text.

# About the Editors
# and Contributors

*Richard P. Barke* is associate professor of public policy at the Georgia Institute of Technology. His research interests include science and technology policy, risk perception and public policy, and the impacts of evolving technology on regulatory policies. His work has involved science and technology issues at the state level and with Congress as well as in China and Belgium.

*Anne M. Brasher* is a doctoral student in the Graduate Group in Ecology at the University of California–Davis. After finishing her work on the Tahoe project, she decided to switch from environmental policy to aquatic ecology—presumably to get as far away from Paul Sabatier as possible. She is presently completing her dissertation on the ecology of freshwater fish populations in Hawaii.

*Anthony E. Brown* is an associate professor in the Department of Political Science at Oklahoma State University. He also serves as director of academic programs at the University Center in Tulsa. His publications include *The Politics of Airline Deregulation* (1987).

*Hank C. Jenkins-Smith* is associate professor of political science at the University of New Mexico. His current research interests include environmental policy, the politics of risk, and the roles of experts in policy controversies.

*Hanne B. Mawhinney* is an assistant professor in the Faculty of Education at the University of Ottawa, Canada. Her recent research on the politics of educational policy change is supported by a Canadian Social Sciences and Humanities Research Council Doctoral Fellowship.

*John F. Munro* received his Ph.D. in political science from the University of California–Los Angeles. He currently manages an environmental policy group for BDM, International, Inc., based in Washington, D.C. This group provides environmental policy and planning support to the Department of Energy's Office of Environmental Restoration and Waste Management.

*Paul A. Sabatier* is a political scientist and professor of environmental studies at the University of California–Davis. His research has focused on policy implementation, long-term policy change, and figuring out a way to outlast Joe Stewart in the consumption of anything stronger than water. On the last, he has failed miserably.

*Gilbert K. St. Clair* is director of the Institute for Public Policy at the University of New Mexico. He is especially interested in economic development policy and intergovernmental relations.

*Joseph Stewart, Jr.,* is professor of government and politics at the University of Texas–Dallas. His research and teaching interests span civil rights policy, particularly in education, minority politics, and regulatory politics. He enjoys thinking about how (not if) one can improve upon the ideas advanced by Paul Sabatier.

# Index

Printed in the United Kingdom
by Lightning Source UK Ltd.
107337UKS00002B/176